THE
WILSON
PLOT

Also by David Leigh

*The Frontiers of Secrecy: Closed
Government in Britain*

The Thorpe Committal
(with Peter Chippindale)

Michael Foot – A Portrait
(with Simon Hoggart)

High Time – The Life and Times of Howard Marks

Not With Honour – The Westland Affair
(with Magnus Linklater)

The Worst Accident in the World – Chernobyl
(with an *Observer* team)

THE WILSON PLOT

HOW THE SPYCATCHERS AND THEIR
AMERICAN ALLIES TRIED TO
OVERTHROW THE BRITISH GOVERNMENT

DAVID LEIGH

PANTHEON BOOKS · NEW YORK

**Library of Congress
Cataloging-in-Publication Data**
Leigh, David.
The Wilson Plot.
1. Wilson, Harold, Sir, 1916–   .
2. Great Britain
—Politics and government—1945–   .
3. Intelligence service—Great Britain—
History—20th century.   I. Title.
DA591.W5L45   1988   941.085'6'0924
88-43027
ISBN 0-394-57241-6

ACKNOWLEDGEMENTS

There are few authors in this field who have not been led into mistakes, even those most academically scrupulous. This is because of the universal concealment or destruction of British Intelligence documents, and the notorious inability of Intelligence officers to tell the unvarnished truth. I shall be lucky if I have been an exception to the prevailing rule. Nevertheless, there are some pioneers in Intelligence writing to whom every Intelligence author owes debts. They appear in the bibliography, but special mention should be made of Bruce Page and Philip Knightley (for Philby); Andrew Boyle (for Blunt); Anthony Verrier; and Jonathan Bloch and Pat Fitzgerald (for, in very different ways, demystifying the British secret service).

There are a number of Intelligence officers who it is impossible to acknowledge here for their contribution, because of the determination of the British government to penalise such disclosures. Under proposed British censorship laws, it may soon be illegal for books such as this to be published at all. Then authors and sources alike will be in danger of imprisonment.

Until that day, I would however like to thank, for assistance and advice: Robin Arbuthnot; Ludmila Benvenuto; Jeffrey Care of the *Observer* library; Anthony Cavendish; The Rt. Hon. Barbara Castle; Sally Chippindale; Leo Cooper; Stephen Dorril; Penny Fishlock; Jean Floud; Professor Roderick Floud; Shiela Grant Duff; Jenifer Hart; Mark Hollingsworth; Chris Horrie; Anthony Howard; Lord Kagan; John Lenkowicz; Rita Marshall; William Massie; Niall MacDermot; Tony McGrath; Bart Milner; Brian Perman; John Pilger; Andrew Roth; Martin Tomkinson; Lord Weidenfeld; Francis Wheen; and Anne Wollheim. I owe a special debt to John Ware, formerly of *World in Action*, for his journalistic dedication to truth in this affair: he was a model.

My thanks are due to Donald Trelford, editor of the *Observer*, for once again fighting a long legal battle to protect free speech, and for making it possible for me to write this book. I should also like to thank Paul Greengrass in particular, and Malcolm Turnbull, who both performed a public service by helping Peter Wright get his MI5 memoirs on the record.

Jeannie Mackie has, as always, helped me greatly.

It should be made absolutely clear that the author does not regard Harold Wilson, or any other individual targets of MI5 and CIA activity mentioned in this book, as in any way disloyal to their country or deserving of suspicion on those grounds. Nor are the patriotic motives put in question of any past or present CIA, MI5 or MI6 officer or agents identified herein, merely because their methods and activities are criticised.

D.L.
London, 1988

The author and the publisher are grateful to the following for permission to reprint previously published material: Curtis Brown Group Ltd.: Excerpt from *Out of the Wilderness* by Tony Benn. Copyright © 1988 by Tony Benn. Reproduced by kind permission of Curtis Brown, London. David Higham Associates Ltd.: Excerpts from *The Making of a Prime Minister* by Harold Wilson. Rights throughout the open market administered by Michael Joseph Ltd. Holmes & Meier Publishers, Inc.: Excerpts from *The Castle Diaries, 1964-1970* by Barbara Castle. Copyright © 1980 by Barbara Castle. First published in the United States of America in 1981 by Holmes & Meier Publishers, Inc. Reprinted by permission of Holmes & Meier Publishers, Inc., New York. Rights throughout the open market administered by David Higham Associates Ltd. Sidgwick & Jackson Ltd., Publishers: Excerpts from *Inside Story, Too Secret Too Long, Secret Offensive,* and *Web of Deception* by Chapman Pincher. Reprinted by permission. George Weidenfeld & Nicolson Ltd.: Excerpt from *The Labour Government 1964-70* by Harold Wilson. Reprinted by permission.

Thanks also to the following for permission to reproduce photographs: Associated Press, p. ii (below), p. vi (below right); BBC Hulton Picture Library, p. i (above and below), p. iv (above), p. v (above and below right), p. vi (above & below left), p. vii (all four photographs), p. viii (above right, below left, & below right); *Observer,* p. ii (above); Jane Bown/*Observer,* p. iv (below right), p. viii (above left); David Fowler/*Observer,* p. iv (below left); John Wildgoose/*Observer,* p. iii (below); *Sunday Express,* p. v (below left); Tim Anderson/*Today,* p. iii (above left).

GOD SAVE THE QUEEN

O Lord our God Arise
Scatter Her Enemies
And make them Fall.
Confound their Politicks
Frustrate their Knavish Tricks
On Thee our Hopes we Fix
God Save Us All

(Second verse of the British national anthem, never
normally sung in polite society. Its origin is obscure; it
was first printed in the *Gentleman's Magazine*, 1745.)

PREFACE

On March 16, 1976, Harold Wilson, the Labour Prime Minister of Britain, suddenly announced his resignation. It came as a surprise. Wilson had only recently celebrated his sixtieth birthday, and was youthful in political terms. His Cabinet colleague and old friend Barbara Castle, listening to him tell the rest of the Cabinet the news, puzzled over his 'abrupt and unnecessary' decision.[1] His colleague who took over the premiership, the Foreign Secretary James Callaghan, was several years older. It emerged later that Wilson had been dropping careful hints among his intimates for several months that he might soon retire; even so, most of the public and the newspapers were completely taken aback. His sudden retirement followed the departures from office – in unusual circumstances – of two other western left-of-centre leaders – Willi Brandt of West Germany and Gough Whitlam, Prime Minister of Australia. Both had fallen foul of the secret Intelligence agencies of the West, although the true facts were to take many years to emerge.

Wilson was, despite his relative youth, a veteran professional politician. His experience as a Cabinet minister went back twenty-nine years. He had won four General Elections for the Labour Party, in 1964, 1966, March 1974 and October 1974. The son of a Yorkshire dyestuffs manager, Wilson had grown up very modestly in Huddersfield and Merseyside. He had gone to state schools and won a scholarship to Jesus College, Oxford, where he spent an even more penurious three years and won a first-class degree. He spent the war in the civil service, rapidly shouldering responsibilities in wartime Whitehall. In 1945 he became an MP representing the working-class constituency of Ormskirk in Lancashire; was immediately made a junior minister, and was in the Cabinet by 1947 as President of the Board of Trade in Attlee's Labour government. It was perhaps adequate explanation to say that he had had enough of politics by 1976: his wife Mary certainly seemed pleased at the announcement.

But rumours started at once that a secret reason lay behind Wilson's decision. Shortly afterwards, the Liberal leader Jeremy Thorpe also resigned, over a homosexual scandal. Wilson, as he had done whilst in office, leapt to his defence, hinting that Thorpe had been the victim of South African 'smears'. This prompted the editor of one Conservative British newspaper, the *Sunday Express*, to write:

What is old Gravel Voice rabbitting on about? I have asked the question before, and I will ask it again. Is his purpose really to defend Jeremy Thorpe? Or is there some sensational revelation still to come concerning himself which dear Harold plans to blame on either Johannesburg, or failing that, on Fleet Street?[2]

What the editor, John Junor, did not mention, was that his defence correspondent, William Massie, was in regular touch with MI5, the British 'security service': his contacts there repeatedly alleged that Wilson had covered up Soviet bloc connections among his friends and ministers. Furthermore, they said, the CIA regarded Wilson as a 'security risk'.[3]

Others in the Intelligence services were circulating this kind of subterranean rumour as well. A right-wing journalist on Massie's companion paper, the *Daily Express*, was Harry 'Chapman' Pincher. He said later:

Only one person ever said he knew why Wilson resigned. He refused to enlighten me for what he called 'international reasons' – and if he knew what it was, the secret died with him.[4]

This person who claimed to know was a man called Bruce Mackenzie. (Pincher later admitted it was 'probably' Mackenzie who told him.)[5] Mackenzie was a white liberal politician in Kenya who had long worked for MI5's sister organisation, MI6, which specialises in espionage overseas. Pincher recalls:

Bruce had hinted at odd things about Wilson . . . I used to go round to his house: Maurice Oldfield, the head of MI6 would be there, and George Young, the former Vice-Chief of MI6, with three or four other people – people from MI6, SAVAK [the Shah of Iran's secret police], South African intelligence . . . – Bruce knew everybody – he set up the Kenyan intelligence service with Maurice's help . . . I used to go fishing in Norway with him.[6]

Bruce Mackenzie eventually 'planted' on Pincher the story that Harold Wilson himself had been bugged by the Intelligence services.[7] The implication was, of course, that Wilson had been under surveillance because he had been detected doing something wrong.

Pincher received considerable prodding on this subject from MI6. He recollects in his memoirs:

. . . the message I received from a very senior member of MI6 was that I would not be wasting my time trying to find out why Wilson resigned because there was 'something of a mystery there.[8]

Maurice Oldfield, the head of MI6, confided something rather similar to his former MI6 colleague Anthony Cavendish. Cavendish now recalls:

If something came into Maurice's hands concerning the Prime Minister of the day, his duty would be clear. He would show it to one of three people – the Prime Minister himself, the Cabinet Secretary, or his immediate boss the Foreign Secretary. I believe from things Maurice said that something did come into his hands and that he showed it to the Foreign Secretary, James Callaghan.[9]

While these hints were being put about, fragmentary evidence pointed to something strange within the recesses of MI5 itself. In 1976, Sir Michael Hanley, the organisation's head, wrote a private letter to one of his retired assistant directors, Peter Wright, who had gone to live in Australia. 'You will be pleased to hear,' he wrote, 'that the service has passed its recent exams.' But Wright's other colleagues seemed to shun him. He complained that both Hal Doyne-Ditmass and Peter Marychurch of GCHQ seemed to have been instructed to avoid him on visits to Australia.[10]

While Labour MPs were preparing to elect Wilson's successor as Prime Minister, Sir Michael Hanley held one of his regular seminars for MI5 officers in the country outside London, at Ware, in Hertfordshire. One of the candidates for premier was Michael Foot, regarded, just as Wilson had been when he originally gained the Labour leadership, as a radical left-winger. A junior officer stood up and asked: 'Sir, what would be the implications for the service if Michael Foot won?'

Hanley said soothingly that he liked to think the democratic system had more checks and balances in it than those provided by MI5. But, if Foot became Prime Minister, 'I and every other officer in the service will have to consider our position.'[11]

These were bizarre rumours, and bizarre remarks. Both Wilson and his left-leaning colleague Foot were in fact loyal and patriotic men. What on earth was going on?

The answer to this question has turned out to involve a considerable search. The false rumours from within the Intelligence services about the reasons for Wilson's resignation proved to be the final act of an extraordinary and entirely unjustified effort to discredit him and his ministers, a campaign that had been waged for thirty years. That campaign by members of the British and US Intelligence services has come to be known as the 'Wilson plot'. Its history is the theme of this book.

Behind Wilson's resignation announcement of March 1976 lay a firm decision to hand over the premiership which had actually been taken eight months earlier in the summer of 1975. It coincided with a dramatic confrontation on August 7 of that year, between the Prime Minister and the head of MI5. Harold Wilson angrily told 'Jumbo' Hanley, the florid-faced security chief, that a secret campaign was being waged against their own Prime Minister by 'unreliable' elements of MI5 and MI6. He knew all about it, Wilson said.

What Wilson did *not* know was that behind his explosive confrontation with Hanley that hot summer afternoon lay the scheming of two extraordinary men from the closed world of the Western Intelligence community. One was the drawn and cadaverous figure of James Jesus Angleton, long-serving head of CIA counter-intelligence.

The second was Angleton's protegé, the subsequently notorious British 'Spycatcher', Peter Wright.

Angleton, whose father was a businessman in Italy, had been educated at an English public school. On the advice of Edward VIII's chaplain, Angleton was sent to Malvern College, in Worcestershire, where he was a corporal in the Officers' Training Corps. After his Yale days as a devotee of that self-aggrandising poet of the obscure, Ezra Pound, Angleton spent the rest of his life in counter-intelligence.

He edited a little literary magazine at Yale – *Furioso* – until 1941. His last contribution to the magazine was in the summer of that year, when he commented on the poet Marianne Moore's discovery of 'Imaginary gardens with real toads in them'. Angleton was not a very successful academic, but this interesting phrase could serve as a motto for the rest of his professional career.

During the war Angleton served as an officer in the OSS – the Office of Strategic Services and the precursor of the CIA. He remained in Intelligence, first in Rome and then in Washington, until he was dismissed from his job at the beginning of 1975. The reasons for his dismissal were only partly a matter of bureaucratic politics – they were also to do with his contempt for civil liberties, his alcoholism, and his paranoid conviction that the hand of the Kremlin was everywhere. At the time of his dismissal, Angleton had been convinced for eleven years that Harold Wilson was a Soviet spy. He also believed – just as wrongly – that Whitlam of Australia and Brandt of West Germany were 'security risks' as far as US interests were concerned.

The second key figure in the Wilson affair later became notorious in Britain and the US as the best-selling author of a banned book, *Spycatcher*. Peter Wright was much less sophisticated than Angleton: he never went to university (but for a truncated war-time course), he liked farming and broad jokes – and he was eventually to appear on the world's TV screens outside an Australian courtroom wearing the kind of caricature hat which is generally depicted in cartoons with corks dangling from the brim. In his later life, Wright liked to act as something of a buffoon. But, like James Angleton, Wright had spent most of his life in counter-intelligence. He had been a Principal Scientific Officer and then an Assistant Director of MI5 – which in MI5 terms meant merely a section head under a department chief. He was not important, but he was very influential. Peter Wright, too, thought Harold Wilson was a Soviet agent. He had also been personally involved in the MI5/CIA gathering of secret 'evidence' against Brandt.

Wright's decision to write his unauthorised memoirs after his retirement to Tasmania was the first truly illuminating breach of the dam which the British government had built around itself after the flood of CIA memoirs in the mid-1970s, which began with Philip Agee's exposé, *Inside the Company*. Eventually, the CIA had been forced to allow Intelligence memoirs, provided they were first submitted to official vetting. The British – who had as much, and in some cases more to hide – were determined to prevent the British public finding out anything about the true workings of their own 'Secret Service'. Official files were ruthlessly locked out of the national archives: Intelligence officers, authors and journalists were all threatened with the archaic Official Secrets Act if they spoke out of turn.

Two Englishmen started Peter Wright on his career of 'exposures'. One was Sir Anthony Blunt, war-time MI5 officer, art-lover, Surveyor of the Queen's pictures, and Russian spy. The other was Blunt's old Cambridge undergraduate friend, Lord Rothschild, millionaire banker and Intelligence aficionado. In 1964, Blunt confessed his treachery to MI5. Because of the Royal connection and the danger to MI5's reputation if it became known they had harboured a spy, Blunt's treason was covered up for fifteen years. It was Peter Wright, for much of that time, who was his MI5 'controller'. Wright thus possessed a very dangerous secret. It was dangerous to MI5 and particularly dangerous to Rothschild. Rothschild was ambitious; but he seemed to fear that his intimate links with Blunt would cause him, Rothschild, to be wrongly implicated if the story ever came out. He kept close to Peter Wright, and assisted him by denouncing several others to him as suspect 'Communists'. In 1977, when speculation started about a 'Fourth Man' in the Cambridge spy ring, Rothschild wrote anxiously to Wright: 'Who planted the evidence, and why?'[12] Later, the idea arose that Wright might sign a testimonial for Rothschild, exonerating him from suspicion. Rothschild's wife Tess wrote off to Australia, passing on a message from her husband. He wanted Wright to put something down on paper, but was anxious not to have it put in the ordinary mail. Rothschild's wife explained that her husband would make direct contact himself. Tess Rothschild also mentioned, revealingly, how worried her old friend Blunt was becoming that journalists would ferret out his treachery: 'Anthony . . . is a bit nervous,' she wrote. He was particularly anxious about a planned book by writer Andrew Boyle, formerly of the BBC.

Boyle's 1979 book *The Climate of Treason*, written with information from the CIA, finally helped expose Blunt. The resultant uproar led to panic, both in MI5 and on the part of Rothschild. Barry Russell-Jones, a senior MI5 officer who headed 'S' computer branch, wrote to his old friend Peter Wright in December 1979 describing the publicity over Blunt. He and his colleagues were hopeful that: 'we are not going to have an inquiry'. But the 'severe storm' might whip up again any minute, if the press found any more details out, he confided to his old colleague.

Six months later Rothschild wrote to Wright in even more alarmed terms. He had already attempted – apparently without success – to persuade the new Prime Minister, Mrs Thatcher, to give him a post in which he would handle all 'sensitive' Intelligence matters: they had dined together at the instigation of Lady Avon, the widow of former Conservative Prime Minister, Anthony Eden. Rothschild said, 'Things are starting to get rough.' He begged the retired MI5 officer to write down every single point he could recall of the ways Rothschild had helped MI5. Rothschild tried to persuade him it would not break the British Official Secrets Act to do this, and to pass it on to Rothschild. He invited him to return, discreetly, to Britain.

The upshot was a visit which seemed to satisfy both the near-bankrupt Wright and the fearful millionaire. Rothschild got a three-page typed document signed by Wright, headed 'Victor Rothschild's help since 1951 to the Security Service', which concluded: 'I do not believe it is conceivable that either Victor Rothschild or Tess Rothschild have ever been Soviet agents . . . I am willing to testify to that effect in any way deemed suitable.'[13]

Wright, for his part, got an introduction from Rothschild to a ghostwriter for his memoirs – the journalist Harry Pincher. Rothschild also provided help in secretly channelling to Wright, via a Swiss bank, the proceeds from the sale and publication of the memoirs (which were to be written under Pincher's name). After the manuscript had been secretly passed to the then head of MI6, Sir Arthur 'Dickie' Franks, Franks passed back word that no obstacle would be put in their way. The book, *Their Trade is Treachery*, grossed £92,000 in royalties, of which Pincher gave Wright £30,000, via the secret Swiss bank and a dummy company in the Dutch Antilles. The book carefully omitted all mention both of Victor Rothschild and of Wright's remarkable personal campaign – which he shared with Angleton – to prove that Harold Wilson was a Soviet spy.

But once Wright started talking, there was no stopping him. He subsequently collaborated with another British journalist, Paul Greengrass, on a set of memoirs, *Spycatcher*, to be written under his own name. This time he made a few guarded admissions in the manuscript about a 'Wilson plot', and his role in it. The result was hysteria within both Whitehall and MI5. The British government embarked on a worldwide campaign to ban the book, claiming it contained 'breaches of confidence'.

But at each step, Wright and his publishers, Heinemann, outsmarted them in what turned into one of the greatest publishing coups of the decade. The manuscript was secretly completed in England by Greengrass and smuggled to Australia. The British Prime Minister, Mrs Thatcher, became personally obsessed by the issue and obtained court injunctions in Sydney suppressing all mention of the book's contents pending two years of diehard litigation.

In London, where the Australian court's writ did not run, the *Observer* newspaper revealed the nature of the book's key disclosures in an article written by the author of this book.[14] The British government hastily obtained injunctions against the *Observer*, and tried to gag the entire British press. Prolonged British litigation followed, all the way up to the House of Lords. I was censored under an unprecedented personal injunction for more than two years, preventing me from publishing what I knew until 1988. There followed a devastating cross-examination in a Sydney courtroom of the British cabinet secretary, Sir Robert Armstrong. The formidable young Australian lawyer Malcolm Turnbull, by combining theatrical panache with an incisive command of the evidence, reduced Whitehall's chief mandarin to stumbling admissions that the truth was not being told by the British about the Rothschild affair.

Meanwhile, the *Spycatcher* manuscript appeared to have been smuggled again – this time out of Australia and into the United States. There, an English company, Pearson Longman, published the entire book via their US subsidiary, Viking Penguin, under the protection of the free-speech guarantees of the US constitution. Discredited by their own chronic disingenuousness, all MI5's legal moves eventually collapsed – in Australia, Canada, Ireland, New Zealand, and finally in London itself. Peter Wright became a millionaire.

These were the circumstances in which the outlines of a 'Wilson plot' first began to emerge. Wright was still not telling the truth in his memoirs: for one of the two chief plotters against Harold Wilson was, in fact, Peter Wright himself. Mrs Thatcher, forced onto the defensive, made an official statement to Parliament on behalf of the British government. She decided to deny everything:

The director-general [of MI5; by this time, the diplomat Sir Anthony Duff] has advised me he has found no evidence of any truth in the allegations. He has given me his personal assurance that the stories are false. In particular, he has advised me that all the Security Service officers who have been interviewed have categorically denied that they were involved in, or were aware of, any activities or plans to undermine or discredit Lord Wilson and his government when he was Prime Minister. The then director-general [Sir Michael Hanley] has categorically denied that he confirmed the existence within the Security Service of a disaffected faction with extreme right-wing views. He has further stated that he had no reason to believe any such faction existed. No evidence or indication has been found of any plot or conspiracy against Lord Wilson by or within the Security Service. Further, the director-general has also advised that Lord Wilson has never been the subject of a Security Service investigation or of any form of electronic or other surveillance by the Security Service . . . It is time to stop raking over the embers of a period over ten years ago.[15]

This remarkable statement was coupled with renewed legal attempts to prevent the British press from investigating the facts, by claiming it was unlawful for anyone to talk to any British Intelligence officers. It was necessary to do this, because Mrs Thatcher's statement simply is not correct. One day, perhaps, the British Parliament will commission an investigation into how this statement came to be made.

This book will demonstrate what the facts of the 'Wilson plot' really were. They reveal the existence of a surprising network of contacts between MI5 officers, journalists, businessmen and Conservative MPs, which belies the claim that MI5 is a passive 'secret' organisation. The City Golf Club in Fleet Street, the Special Forces Club in Knightsbridge, and the Carlton Club in St James were the venues for this secret side of British life. This history also reveals the true calibre of some of the men from MI5 and the CIA – people whose training, background, and lifelong isolation within organisations which never had to explain themselves made them very bad judges of character. This is unfortunate, because it is what their job is supposedly all about.

CHAPTER 1

The story of the 'Wilson plot' begins, like so much else in this particular period of Western history, with the Second World War. The economic slump, widespread unemployment and the political collapse of the 1930s culminated in fighting in Europe. This led to some strange alliances. In 1939, Stalin's Russia concluded a cynical pact with Hitler's Germany. It gave Hitler a free hand to dismember much of Europe, and to set about exterminating the Jews. The British Empire briefly 'stood alone', under Winston Churchill, on the brink of invasion. It was her 'finest hour'. By 1941, however, both the US and the Soviet Union had been brought into the war. Stalin, his country invaded by Hitler, became an ally of Britain and America, and all the forces of Western propaganda swung round to depict 'Uncle Joe' as a heroic figure. The US, meanwhile, was persuaded to prop up Britain. In return for cash, ships and manpower, Britain trained the US Intelligence services, and shared her scientific secrets. She was to survive the war, but lose her dominant position in the world during the subsequent peace: in 1945, to the astonishment of many in the US and at home, the war-weary British celebrated their victory by throwing out Winston Churchill and fourteen years of right-wing political rule. They elected a Labour government, pledged to change everything.

It was out of this global turmoil that the attitudes of those involved in the post-war 'Wilson plot' were shaped.

The renewed development of secret organisations in the West began as soon as World War II ended. In the new contest between the super powers, the US had the atom bomb and Stalin had a network of agents already in place carrying out espionage, guerrilla warfare, propaganda and political subversion. Both sides quickly tried to remedy their shortcomings.

Britain lacked either capability, and tried to develop both. Hansard records that in May 1947 the Foreign Secretary Ernest Bevin told the House of Commons that 'His Majesty's Government do not accept the view that we have ceased to be a Great Power.' Work went ahead on developing a British bomb and, in concert with the Americans, a secret shadow state was erected, most of which was invisible to the general public, and, indeed, to many members of the British Labour government.

Enigmatic buildings went up under heavy guard in Britain and her colonies – tall chimneys at Windscale on the mountainous coast of

Cumbria; a wire compound with peculiar water outlets on an isolated Cornish cliff at Nancekuke; a set of pontoons with cages of monkeys moored off the remote island of Lewis in the Hebrides; clusters of huts at Eastcote near Ruislip and at more remote spots in Britain and her colonies – Wincombe, Flowerdown, Brora, Gilnahirk, Edzell, Mauritius, Ascension Island, Cyprus, Singapore, and Darwin in the remote northern territory of Australia; war-time airfields, re-populated this time with American planes, at Lakenheath and Mildenhall; trucks, uniforms and fresh barbed wire at the supposedly disused Fort Bin Jema in Malta; office blocks with the nameplates of hitherto unknown publishers and international news agencies; moorings for what appeared to be war-time German high-speed S-boats with, to all appearances, their original German crews . . .

What was not so visible was the constant shuttle across the Atlantic of unusually anonymous government officials; the posting of men who had thought their war-time adventures were over to carry guns in Germany and on the dusty streets of the Middle East for secret agencies whose initials were still unfamiliar; and – least visible of all – the division of British politicians, officials and scientists into those who were trusted by the United States and those who were not.

For the Cold War made Britain particularly dependent on the US. What was exceptionally embarrassing in the circumstances was the eventual realisation that while the North Americans supplied the cash, the weaponry and the bulk of the secret Intelligence for the new contest, Britain was unusually rich in one unwelcome commodity – Soviet sympathisers. As a result, most of the secret activities of the Anglo–US partnership between 1945 and 1951 were – insofar as they depended on secrecy – a waste of time. Bevin, although he came from a working-class background, was vigorously – even brutally – anti-Communist. It was not the case with his officials. Between them a considerable impact was made by the activities of the head of his American department, Donald Maclean; his Secret Service US liaison officer, Kim Philby; the personal assistant to his junior minister, Guy Burgess; and the former MI5 officer with royal connections and the closest links of all to senior security men, Anthony Blunt.

It is well-known by now, thanks mainly to the pioneering work of Andrew Boyle in his book *The Climate of Treason*, how the Soviet Union set out to capture Oxbridge in the 1930s. It was the cleverest piece of Intelligence work of the whole period. Faced with the narrow class-based society of Britain, in which a remarkably small network of families constituted the ruling group, the Comintern turned this very impenetrability into an unexpected weakness. Only two universities needed to be targeted, so tight were British channels of social movement. Idealistic and self-assured young men from male boarding schools, often clannishly homosexual, if they could be converted as undergraduates, would be 'insiders' already, and above

2

suspicion. The rise of Hitler, Franco and Mussolini, the visible un-employment, persecution and suffering in Europe: all this made British domestic politics seem ineffective and disgusting. Few of the quasi-religious converts realised quickly enough that Stalin's Russia was closer to an oriental despotism than a progressive Utopia.

Peter Wright and his MI5 colleagues later listed nearly forty 'spies' they said were recruited in this way. This was an exaggeration. Only a few seeds germinated. Of those who became secret members of the Communist Party in the 1930s, quite a few refused to do any spying in later life – Michael Straight, the rich American, for example, or the civil servants Bernard Floud and Jenifer Hart. There were too many cynical twists and turns by the Soviet Union during and after the war: it was one thing to hunger for world revolution, but it was another to realise that one was merely an instrument of Russian foreign policy. Many idealists declined to be recruited: Stuart Hampshire, the distinguished academic, for example; Flora Solomon, the Marks & Spencer executive; or Shiela Grant-Duff, the *Observer*'s corre-spondent in Prague during the Munich crisis. Many left-wingers like the rich banker Victor Rothschild, for instance; or Dennis Proctor, who rose to be Permanent Secretary at the Ministry of Fuel and Power, merely had the wrong friends when young. Others were open Communists all their lives but did not constitute 'spies' – James Klugmann, for example, who influenced many Cambridge fellow-students and worked for SOE in Cairo during the war; or Brian Simon, who became an academic at Leicester. The list of committed KGB servants who put themselves in a position where they could spy usefully for Russia and then went ahead and did so was really quite small.

But because they were so closely linked to the British Intelligence services, the few who did spy had a devastating psychological effect. It was not until 1964 that it became fully clear that Philby and Blunt, in particular, had made fools of James Angleton of the CIA, Sir Stewart Menzies (the aris-tocratic head of MI6), the British Royal Family, Victor Rothschild, Guy Liddell (the post-war deputy chief of MI5), MI5's counter-intelligence special-ist Dick White, and even the determinedly anti-Communist Labour right-winger, Hugh Gaitskell. All these had helped, or confided in, the spies. It was an impressive list. The real subversive rot was never in the British Labour Party – it was in the supposedly 'patriotic' secret organisations of the Cold War.

But it was the Labour government which re-launched these organisations on a scale comparable to war-time. All of the elements of the post-war secret 'special relationship' with the US were put in place during the term of office of Clement Attlee's government.

The first was the ABCA military agreement reached in Quebec in 1946.

This committed Britain to four-power military links with America, Australia and Canada (hence the acronym). When British Army officers and Intelligence men, thirty years later, spent as much time in joint meetings with the officers of a foreign power as in considering how best to serve their elected government, this agreement was at the root of the relationship. It pre-dated NATO and, in British eyes, still overrules it. Under the Quebec agreement, the four countries agreed to share top-secret military information. They were to be in 'Category A'. Other friendly states were to be in 'Category B', entitled to less secret material, and unfriendly states, including Russia, in group 'C', were to be entitled to no classified military information at all. It was the first unacknowledged alliance of the Cold War.

The British hoped that this agreement would enable them to continue the war-time co-operation that had led to America's atom bomb. They wanted a bomb of their own, although their partner Canada did not. While complaining bitterly and repeatedly at US attempts to renege on this co-operation, Britain on the other hand was determined to exclude France from atomic research. In later years, this was to lead to great French resentment, without preventing the French from eventually building their own weapons. In the US, the McMahon Act soon put a stop to the sharing of US nuclear secrets with Britain, and most of the 1940s were taken up with British recriminations. America's ostensible objections were that British personnel were 'insecure' (which was perfectly true), and that in a war with Russia, Britain and the secrets of the atom might be rapidly overrun and captured.[1] To defend Britain against Russia, the US proposed to station her own atomic-armed bombers on British airfields, thus beginning the process of military occupation of Britain which continues to this day. The ongoing use of British bases constitutes one of the fundamental US national interests in Britain, and the US is not willing to withdraw from them.

The same is not true of the British 'independent deterrent', which the US had no wish to see come into existence. Without involving the rest of the Labour cabinet, Attlee and Bevin decided in 1947 that Britain must develop her own atom bombs, in strict secrecy. While bread and shoes were rationed, the atomic piles were constructed at Windscale in Cumbria, and a primitive bomb eventually successfully tested in Australia in 1951. This enabled a nuclear relationship to be resumed with the US, and thanks to uranium-swapping and other technological deals, it has continued ever since.

While this was going on, Britain failed to stay in the technical race to develop her own delivery system of missiles, and thus lost real military independence: she has to buy them from the US. The Soviet code-clerk, Igor Gouzenko, when he defected in Canada in 1945, had said that Communist Party zealots were already looking forward to World War III. It is only fair to point out that throughout this period Attlee's Chiefs of Staff repeatedly tried to persuade ministers that all-out war with Russia, which had acquired atom bombs in 1949, might only be a matter of weeks away: their ambition was to obtain a stockpile of 200 A-bombs to sling under British bombers as fast as possible. This was only achieved in the mid 1950s, by which time manned bomber fleets had become obsolete.

The atomic dimension provided Britain with a vast new peacetime range of top-security military 'secrets'. There were equations and manufacturing techniques to be kept secret, plants to be protected from sabotage in Britain, and test-sites to be guarded in Australia. Political intentions, raw material agreements and military stockpiles had to be kept hidden; quantities of very dangerous substances kept safe; and intensely secret diplomatic exchanges enciphered back and forth across the Atlantic. A new 'requirements' section of MI6 had to be set up to carry out atomic espionage – 'R7' – whose designation used the old war-time code-name 'Tube Alloys liaison'. The Atomic Energy Authority had to have MI5's own deputy director, Guy Liddell, seconded to it to handle security.

The British military did better out of the other two secret forms of warfare which were being pursued. Both the US and the Canadians co-operated from the start in research on gas and germs. The cliff-top compound which was built at Nancekuke in Cornwall was a pilot production plant for 'V-agents' – the Nazi nerve-gas derivatives, a drop of which on the skin could kill. Pontoons moored out of sight off the Hebridean island of Lewis contained monkeys being experimentally sprayed by the Navy with plague bacilli, in the presence of US and Canadian observers – a development of British war-time work on the bacteriological 'anthrax bomb'. Both of these grisly programmes turned out to be blind alleys, although the British biological laboratories at Porton Down remained available to develop poisons for MI6, and chemical artillery shells are now in the arsenals of both the East and West.

The next secret war-time joint system to be re-activated was that which had produced ULTRA, to use the joint Anglo-American codeword fixed by the 1943 BRUSA ('Britain–USA') agreement for the most secret bits of paper produced. Huge worldwide code-breaking organisations were established by both sides in World War II. Military staff with headphones intercepted enemy radio transmissions from ships, tanks, planes, staff officers' caravans, embassies and command bunkers. They also captured the output from radar and pathfinder beams. Using direction-finding and 'traffic analysis', the first task was to find out who was transmitting where. The next was to re-transmit these enciphered fragments of Morse to headquarters such as the huts at Bletchley where some of Britain's foremost academic brains, using the occasional captured codebook or cipher machine, together with primitive precursors of the computer, attempted to crack the codes.

If they had any success, a second large organisation of people was then needed to analyse the Intelligence, re-cipher it, and distribute it in ways which strictly concealed the source in time for those to whom it mattered to get it – whether Winston Churchill in his War Office bunker, or a destroyer captain in the North Atlantic. The Allies were more successful than the Axis at this, although it is sometimes forgotten that the Germans had their victories and sank, for example, much merchant shipping after penetrating convoy codes.

One stimulus for re-building the system for the Cold War was a US discovery, code-named BRIDE, which enabled the Americans to crack Russian ciphers. A cryptanalyst with the American National Security Agency called Meredith Gardner found a laborious method of extracting fragmentary messages from secret Soviet cipher transmissions which used the hitherto uncrackable 'one-time pads'. Messages were encoded twice, first using a code-book and secondly using pads with random groups of four-figure numbers. With part of a code-book found on a Finnish battlefield, and with the discovery that the Russians had economised during the war by duplicating some pads, Gardner and the NSA started to penetrate some KGB messages. The British had a formidable reputation for code-breaking, and also possessed a further batch of Russian traffic collected from 1945 onwards, code-named DRUG (subsequently VENONA). Later it was discovered that the method could be used to break into KGB traffic in Australia.

BRIDE gave the clues which, patiently pursued, led to the prosecution of the atomic spy from Britain, Klaus Fuchs; the US official Alger Hiss; and ultimately Donald Maclean. Unfortunately, the method had a tantalising weakness: easiest to break out were long lists of 'cryptonyms' of live agents, but these provided no genuine clues as to who they really were. In Britain, for example, the 1945 'valuable agentura' listed as 'STANLEY, HICKS and JOHNSON' was, after many years, identified as Burgess, Philby and Blunt. But the pair listed as 'DAVID and ROSA' have never been found to this day.

In 1947, the highly classified UKUSA treaty arranged by Attlee and Bevin re-launched a worldwide signals Intelligence collection system. Britain and the US would pool everything between them, both the work and the Intelligence 'product'. Australia, Canada and later New Zealand would join in, but with less access. Britain was to cover Africa, the Soviet Union west of the Urals (largely from stations in Cyprus, Turkey and Germany), and the Far East from stations in Mauritius, Singapore and Hong Kong. British headquarters, which became known as GCHQ – 'Government Communications Headquarters' – were to be at Eastcote, near Ruislip (they later moved to Cheltenham); the US operated from Fort Meade, Maryland. In Britain, GCHQ was removed from the war-time control exercised by MI6 and set up as a separate secret government department under the Foreign Office. The pooling of 'communications intelligence' was supposed to be demonstrated in practical form by funnelling all the worldwide take through designated joint 'CCCCs' – Centralised Comint Communications

6

Centres. The Anglo-US CCCC was at the military base at Chicksands Priory in Bedfordshire.[2]

The BRIDE-DRUG counter-espionage programme never matured because it was rapidly betrayed to the Russians, who changed their cipher system in 1948. But, with the development first of computers and eventually of satellites, the lure of completely authentic 'live' military and political Intelligence was so great that SIGINT (Signals Intelligence) code-cracking continued to be a major growth industry. It was extremely expensive, both in machinery and in the thousands of military and civilian staff needed to man the headphones and teleprinters round the world. It changed emphasis, focusing on Third World eavesdropping, monitoring of arms, oil and gold deals, and, above all, Soviet missile telemetry. It is conventionally estimated that 80 per cent of the West's 'hard' Intelligence continues to come from interception of communications. Britain's ability to match US hardware has dwindled over the years since the advent of satellites, and as Britain steadily withdrew from her imperial bases, the GCHQ operation became very vulnerable to US pressure. The UKUSA treaty activated a vast new area of 'security' – code-cracking requires complacent opponents who do not grasp what is going on – and gave one of the biggest hostages of all to the Anglo-US 'special relationship'.

While this eavesdropping was a secret, there was also an Intelligence need to scoop up all the ordinary radio programmes that were being broadcast round the world and analyse them for 'Communist propaganda' or political significance. Another set of Anglo-US arrangements were made for this. Although not particularly secret, they forced the State-owned British Broadcasting Corporation into an Intelligence-gathering role which it has never been anxious to advertise. The world was again divided up – this time between the CIA and the British Foreign Office. The BBC monitors its share of international programmes for the CIA from its station at Caversham, near Reading, while the Foreign Broadcast Information Service does the same job in the United States. The CIA keeps a liaison officer at Caversham to dictate requirements, and the Foreign Office pays the BBC's bills.

The next of the secret British war-time organisations to be resurrected by Bevin was the propaganda department PWE – the Political Warfare Executive which had dripped pornography and pessimism into German ears with the help of the politician Richard Crossman and journalists like Sefton Delmer. The revival of an unacknowledged propaganda campaign – this time against Communism – was the idea of Intelligence 'insider' Christopher Mayhew, now a Labour junior minister, who had worked closely with Gaitskell and SOE during the war, and played golf with the young Roger Hollis. 'Keep it dark,' warned Attlee in 1948, anxious not to split the Labour Party. Mayhew says, 'It had to be secret because millions of

7

people including Labour parliamentarians were singing the praises of dear old Uncle Joe.'[3] Re-christened IRD – the Information Research Department – Mayhew's organisation recruited Soviet emigrés to compose anti-Communist literature.

In time, the CIA came to provide most of IRD's funding for this psychological warfare. The Committee for a Free Europe and Radio Free Europe set a regular American pattern by being nominally the work of private foundations, but in fact backed by US Intelligence. Clusters of British and US 'front' organisations – magazines, institutes, student and labour organisations – sprang up as the counterpart of Soviet-backed bodies. The BBC was once again dragooned into functioning as an arm of government: although it retained some journalistic independence, its broadcasts were directed and funded by the Foreign Office, and its programme-makers were required to accept batches of undercover IRD material.

Mayhew worked closely with MI6 and those who were far from being Labour sympathisers – the Albanian SOE veteran Alan Hare was later involved with IRD, and so was Conservative minister Maurice Macmillan. The last official head of IRD, nearly thirty years later, Ray Whitney, promptly re-surfaced after leaving the Foreign Office as a Conservative MP. Like so many of these would-be Labour enterprises, it turned out in the end to be a largely Tory performance, sabotaged by Communists. Guy Burgess became Mayhew's personal assistant and undoubtedly passed all IRD's secret launch plans to Moscow before getting himself rapidly sacked.

IRD planted anti-Communist tracts on journalists in Britain and abroad. It resurrected the Secret Service war-time news agency Britanova as the Arab News Agency (ANA), based in Cairo, and subsidised Reuters and the *Observer* Foreign News Service, in the hope of using these independent agencies as channels for its material. Publishers were given grants to bring out books on anti-Communist themes. Middle-Eastern newspaper editors were bribed to print IRD material. To reliable trade unionists, secret anti-Communist 'digests' of propaganda were circulated: in 1963, the veteran Labour right-winger Bessie Braddock could still boast of getting these publications, replete with warnings of 'Communist fronts' and subversive organisations.[4]

One of IRD's priorities was to inoculate the British colonies against nationalist agitators, who were to be regarded as, by definition, Communists. Among the more amusing fragments about IRD which have escaped the censor's pencil in the Foreign Office archives in the Public Record Office at Kew is an urgent plea sent in 1949 for propaganda with a better African 'angle':

Such material as is produced by IRD . . . very limited use has been made of this material in Central and East Africa simply because it is not 'angled'

8

... to an African audience ... During his recent visit to northern Rhodesia, the Secretary of State addressed a meeting of chiefs at which he gave as an example of the evils of Communism the case of the British men who had been unable to bring their Russian wives to England with them. After the meeting, the chiefs, much puzzled, said to the District Commissioner that they did not understand why Communism was a bad thing – after all, they strictly forbade any of the women of their tribes to marry outside the tribes.[5]

This Colonial Office memo went on to propose a specifically African-based 'underground' political warfare organisation instead:

to maintain close contact with the security authorities in regard to the activities of Communist agents in the region; to prepare suitable anti-Communist material in the form of pamphlets, press articles and broadcasts ... [and] to establish and maintain liaison with the French, Portuguese and Belgian authorities, and to supply them with copies of local anti-Communist material.[6]

The final secret organisation to be re-born in the Cold War was the SAS. Although it had a strong flavour of anti-Communism about it, the truth was that the Special Air Service was re-activated to suppress unrest in British territorial possessions. SAS-style techniques first emerged after the war in Palestine, to counter Jewish guerrillas, and it is in Palestine that we encounter another figure who was to become of importance in MI5. Harry Wharton, born in 1920, was short and stocky, a sandy-haired Army officer described by a colleague who worked with him immediately after the war as 'a highly intelligent, foxy character, intense in everything he set out to do – withdrawn, but with a highly-developed sense of humour.' As a Captain in the Sherwood Foresters Regiment, Wharton was sent to the London School of Oriental Studies with two other captains in June 1946, to learn Hebrew and Arabic. They were then posted undercover to Palestine in mid-1947, to work with special military groups.

Although the term 'Special Air Service' was not used until the Malayan anti-guerrilla campaign in 1950, the techniques used in Palestine were the same. Among those in Palestine was Captain Roy Farran, late of the wartime SAS, whose activities became an international *cause célèbre* when it was alleged that he and his men had abducted a Jewish activist because of a threat to 'execute' British soldiers taken hostage. He was charged with the torture and murder of the suspect named Alexander Rubowitz, and eventually acquitted at a court-martial after his alleged confession was ruled inadmissible. But the Zionists had their revenge: they killed his brother with a parcel bomb addressed to Farran and opened in error. Farran, who later became a Conservative parliamentary candidate and Attorney-General of a

9

Canadian province, has been a stalwart of the Special Forces Club in London for the rest of his life, and something of a cult figure. The special squads formed to fight against guerrillas had differing names – 'pseudo-gangs', 'ghost squads', 'counter-gangs' – but stretch in an unbroken line from Palestine, through the Rhodesian 'Selous Scouts' to modern squads in Northern Ireland. The Intelligence Service was to find the guerrillas; the propaganda department was to depict them as communists; and undercover military squads were to infiltrate and liquidate them.

Wharton's job was to get Intelligence on the Jewish guerrillas of the Irgun Zvai Leumi and the 'Stern Gang', who were fighting the British occupation and its unsuccessful attempt to crush Zionism. He and his colleagues could be seen sitting in plain clothes in the Café Vienna and in the main square in Jerusalem at Finks' restaurant, picking up gossip and information. Terrorists were raiding British bases, lobbing in hand-grenades and raiding the armories. Maurice Oldfield, later to head MI6, had been engaged in similar work in Palestine and Cairo: he was to recount in later years, with guffaws, how he would conduct interrogations by plunging suspects' heads into buckets of water. At the end of 1947, as Bevin's violently anti-Jewish policy failed, Wharton was posted to Egypt, to the headquarters at Fayid of Security Intelligence Middle East (SIME), run by MI6. He rose to the rank of Lieutenant-Colonel by 1951. Major Tommy Thomas of the Intelligence Corps recalls dining with him there and Wharton also met the MI6 officer George Young in the 1950s 'on committees to do with the Middle East'. Just as Ernest Bevin irrationally thought an independent Zionist Israel would be a Soviet puppet, to the point where Harold Wilson described him as 'anti-semitic', so George Young asserts baldly that the Zionist guerrilla campaign was a Communist plot:

> The last major terrorist effort directly mounted by the Soviets against a Western European state was the supply in 1946–7 of base facilities, arms and explosives for Jewish groups to operate against British targets – an operation carried out on Stalin's personal instructions by the Deputy Minister of Defence, Marshal Vasilevsky.[7]

Crucial, of course, to the establishment of the post-war 'secret state' was the reconstruction of the Intelligence agencies. They were not re-launched merely in order to gather Intelligence. In the US, an independent body was established to undertake 'covert action': known as the OPC (Office of Policy Co-ordination), it was founded in June 1948 from the ashes of the abruptly disbanded OSS (Office of Strategic Services). The OPC was later to be swallowed up by the Central Intelligence Agency, which was officially founded in 1947. In Britian, the re-launching had a different shape.

Sir Stewart Menzies, the head of MI6, told his brother Major Ian Menzies that he was 'depressed' when the Labour government won the general election in 1945. Because they did not support his wish to take a more aggressive line against Russia in Central Europe, his retirement in 1951 came as 'a great relief'. According to Ian Menzies:

> Stewart said he had got his hands on things ahead of the Russians moving in on areas. Instead of acting as Churchill would have done, the Government said: 'Let them be.'[8]

This was probably a reference to the Attlee government's refusal to let Menzies intervene in Hungary, which had been agreed as being part of the Soviet 'sphere of influence'.[9] But, otherwise, Menzies had an outrageously free hand to mount operations (all promptly betrayed to the Russians by his own appointee, Kim Philby). Not only did Menzies keep his war-time job, but under Attlee and Bevin the swashbucklers of SOE were given a new lease of life inside MI6. Most of them, ironically, were Buchanesque Tories – indeed some, like Billy McLean and Julian Amery, were active Conservative politicians of the Right (Amery's brother, John, was executed after the war for going over to the Nazis). Only in recent years has the story finally emerged of the series of militaristic undercover adventures authorised by Bevin. In Albania, the Black Sea, Latvia, the Caucasus and the Ukraine, bands of emigrés were parachuted in or landed on beaches at night 'to set the Soviet Union ablaze'.

The machinery was initially set up in Britain by the 'Russia Committee' chaired by Gladwyn Jebb of the Foreign Office. After strenuous lobbying by Julian Amery, and under the apocalyptic influence of Air Marshal Tedder, the 'Cold War sub-committee' of this secret group decided in November 1948 'to liberate the countries within the Soviet orbit by any means short of war.'[10] Tedder's aim was to win the Cold War, by which he appears to have meant the overthrow of the Soviet regime itself, within five years. The plan was to set about 'promoting civil discontent, internal confusion and possible strife in the satellite countries.' Stalin would then be worn out garrisoning his satellites, much as Nazi Germany had been forced to keep dozens of divisions in occupied Europe to cope with the various resistance movements.

This was 'setting Europe ablaze' all over again. Even had the plans for these secret adventures not been betrayed at birth by Philby and others, they were mindless schemes. Brute military force and good Intelligence had won World War II – the tying down of Hitler's divisions by resistance fighters and SOE operatives in occupied France had helped the vast Allied armies which won Stalingrad and eventually crossed the Rhine. Where were the new armies poised for D-Day? And had not everything changed strategically with the atom bomb? Perhaps the truth was, with Czechoslovakia and Poland swallowed up by the Soviet Union, Berlin under pressure, and Greece in a state of civil war, that the urge to hit back somehow was

11

irresistible to a certain type of mind. There was also a continuing fantasy that Britain could win by Secret Service trickery what she could not hold by force of arms.

A hint of cheeseparing was added to this mélange of incoherence and betrayal. Ivone Kirkpatrick of the Foreign Office told the committee on November 25 that 'partly for financial reasons' it might be best to start with a small and obscure target such as Albania. There is some evidence that Amery and his colleagues hoped to try Bulgaria after that. Even so, although Britain had the war-time SOE local expertise, the US would have to be persuaded to put up the bulk of the cash. Only the previous year, Britain had tried to hand over the burden of running the Greek civil war against the Communists to the US on grounds of expense. In March 1949, a wholesale programme of Intelligence co-operation was agreed at a three-day conference in Washington, attended by Frank Wisner of the OPC and Lord Jellicoe of the Foreign Office. The West's own 'subversive activities' (in the words of the Russia Committee) were to end up not only being bankrolled but also directed day to day in Washington, by an Anglo-US team. That it included Kim Philby of Menzies' MI6 was to turn out to be a regrettable mistake.

Some of the men later involved in the Harold Wilson affair were drawn into this romantic world of active anti-Bolshevism. Tony Brooks, for instance, SOE's war hero of the French Resistance under the code-name ALPHONSE, returned home with the Military Cross and the DSO. A fluent French-speaker who worked for a Swiss cement company before the war, Brooks was trained in sabotage for SOE by author Selwyn Jepson, who remembers an 'extrovert' youngster of barely twenty. In July 1942, he was parachuted in and organised resistance groups in the Lyons area for no less than three years, one step ahead of the Gestapo. He narrowly avoided serious injury when his parachute landed in a tree. Meanwhile, he was posted as a 'deserter', to the distress of his family. His saboteurs – French schoolgirls – put grit in the axle-boxes of railway tank-transporters and slowed down D-Day reinforcements.[11] Friends say he needed plastic surgery for the injuries he sustained in the final fighting in France. He was recruited back into MI6 in 1948, along with dozens of other SOE men, and sent to the Balkans. In the winter of 1949 there is a rare glimpse of him on the historical record. A 43-ton schooner, the *Stormie Seas*, rigged out at MI6's expense with a big 90-horsepower engine and a radio in a secret compartment, spent that winter under the command of two young ex-naval officers, Sam Barclay and John Leatham, travelling between Greece and the Black Sea. Having landed the first groups of emigré agents on the coast of Albania that autumn, they were now shipping agents and supplies into Bulgaria. The MI6 man in Sofia under diplomatic cover at the embassy was Brooks, identified in the Foreign Office list as a 'Third Secretary (local rank)' in the visa section.

Barclay and Leatham were returned to the MI6 school near Gosport to be trained for their last, US-sponsored, job in the Balkans – launching home-made hydrogen balloons filled with leaflets issued by the US 'Committee for a Free Europe' from off the Albanian three-mile limit. They were then paid off. The wisest of the group of Albanian emigré 'pixies' who had been trained in the disused Bin Jema fort in Malta turned out to be the one who attempted to swallow his British-issued cyanide pill in advance. His stomach was pumped out and he was hastily shipped off the island before he could demoralise the others.[12] His fellows, infiltrated into Albania, were rounded up within days. The whole adventure had been betrayed.

Shortly afterwards, the Bulgarian networks and their radio control were handed over, as part of the general US takeover, to a CIA base on the island of Panaghia disguised as a radar station in the Greek 'military zone'. Brooks was moved on to Tito's Yugoslavia where, before disappearing from the diplomatic lists for ever, he is briefly listed in the embassy at Belgrade. The importance of Yugoslavia in Amery's Balkan project was the hope that a million Albanians living in the Kosovo frontier region might be encouraged by British agents to attack Albania from the rear. The hope did not materialise. Brooks disappeared temporarily from sight, only to surface again in the guerrilla war against nationalists in Cyprus: he had become a secret agent for life.

George Kennedy Young, a red-haired Scots racial theorist who came into his own in war-time Italy, setting up MI6 stations in conjunction with the American OSS, was another man who became a career secret serviceman at this time. He, too, was an anti-Communist crusader who hankered for a re-birth of SOE and found an outlet for a while in the 'Special Operations Branch' and the later 'Special Political Action Group' of MI6. Young was chief of station at the crossroads of the Cold War – in Berlin and then in Vienna during the immediate post-war years when all the work of MI6 was vitiated by its innocent harbouring of Philby, the Soviet super-mole. Young strongly opposed the return to Stalin's mercies of the Cossack prisoners who had backed Hitler, one of the most controversial decisions of the immediate post-war period.

One of Young's greatest admirers in MI6, who was later to join him in the ultra-right 'Unison' organisation of the 1970s, was Anthony Cavendish. Cavendish had what was probably a typical MI6 pattern of activity in the Cold War. As a young army officer in the Control Commission for Germany, who had previously worked against dissident Jews and Arabs from Cairo, he was recruited in the major surge in MI6 numbers in 1948. Many of his seniors had connections with the Conservative Party – Dick Brooman-White, for example, who was a member of his interview board, had been station chief in Turkey and was to become a Tory MP. Another Tory MP-to-be was Commander Anthony Courtney, who handled the shipping of

13

'resistance' agents up the Baltic to Latvia – from whence they rarely re-emerged. (Courtney was later ruined in 1965 when the KGB circulated a compromising photograph of him – perhaps they regarded it as an overdue revenge.)

Cavendish was one of some fifty MI6 officers in Germany – each issued with a personal Volkswagen 'Beetle' – almost as many men as in the rest of MI6 put together. He would have served under Donald Prater, who was later to work for George Young in Beirut. Other MI6 men were sending emigrés into Byelorussia and the Ukraine under Colonel Harold Gibson; more agents went into Albania under the veteran anti-Jewish operative Colonel Harold Perkins from a base near Frankfurt, and into Latvia from Hamburg. Sometimes they were captured and their radios 'played back' by the Russians with false messages. Sometimes they merely disappeared, and sometimes they re-appeared in the dock at show trials, followed by execution.

Some MI6 officers were posted to the Cold War beach-head in Vienna. Much of their time appears to have been spent on contingency planning for a full-scale Russian invasion of Germany and Austria – burying radio sets, planning escape-routes, and trying to recruit 'stay-behind' agents. But many of their duties were more like those of the old SOE. Cavendish later marvelled at the amount of aggressive anti-Soviet activity that was allowed by a Labour government; almost the only political brake put on MI6 in this period was what George Young contemptuously calls 'the Attlee doctrine' – that no offensive espionage was to be carried out against the colonies newly given their independence. Even this became in time, Young says, 'a dead-letter'.

As director of the Middle East region after 1951, George Young was able to exercise his belief in an independent, British, covert group of intriguers who would propose and dispose, topple petty Arab governments at will, and demonstrate that, as he wrote later, 'The non-European world still looks on us as the master culture.'[13]

A Foreign Office directive to Menzies and MI6 dated as early as October 27, 1945 had summarised the active role envisaged for the Special Operations Branch in 'Persia, Iraq and the Levant states'.[14] After clearing up and disbanding the Malta operations against Albania, Young's triumph was the overthrow in 1953 of the nationalist Iranian leader Mossadeq. Young led an MI6 team that included Robin Zaehner, a veteran of the Albanian operation who had worked undercover in war-time Persia, Christopher 'Monty' Woodhouse (later to become a Conservative MP) and Arthur Franks, who later became a hawkish head of MI6 itself. Young's principal agent was an associate of the Shah, Shapor Reporter. He had the help of British oil company staff and two local businessmen, the Rashidian brothers. One of Young's principal weapons was bribery of the Iranian crowds and – as usual – the CIA had to be embroiled to take the lion's share of the expense. It later irritated Young and the British considerably that Kermit Roosevelt of the CIA wrote a vainglorious book taking much of the credit. Neither party chose to dwell over-much on one key event – the assassination of Mohammed Afshartus, the police chief loyal to the regime. There is no evidence this was done at the specific behest of MI6 or the CIA, but it greatly assisted their cause.

Young himself, who kept control of events by radio from Cyprus, implies he disobeyed the 'unreal' orders of MI6 chief Admiral 'Sinbad' Sinclair over 'setting the stage for the overthrow of Mossadeq,' but does not explain what he means. The coup in Iran was presented as an anti-Communist crusade; in fact it was closely connected to the question of British oil supplies. With Mossadeq deposed, the Shah of Iran returned from exile. Thereafter, he placed enormous orders for British military equipment, and Reporter became wealthy as an intermediary. He was eventually given a knighthood by Britain and the Shah became an MI6 protegé for the rest of his reign.

Young, who was awarded the CMG in 1955 as a reward for this coup, did not rest on his laurels. His next scheme was an attempt to embroil the CIA in a plan to mount a putsch in Syria – Operation STRAGGLE, which CIA representative Wilbur Eveland described as 'lunacy'.[15] Some friction developed with Mossad, Israeli Intelligence, during this period, as a result of intrigues with double-agents against Nasser – Young's attempts to topple Nasser as he had Mossadeq were not successful. At the urging of Anthony Eden, Britain's then Prime Minister, nerve-gas poison canisters were designed at Porton Down for an MI6 assassination attempt on the nationalist Egyptian premier.

Eventually, in 1956, Eden attempted a full-scale military invasion at Suez on a bogus peace-keeping pretext. The United States turned off the financial taps, and British pretensions took a sharp dive. Young says the Israelis, partners in the Suez invasion, were told (presumably by him or his MI6 colleagues), 'There is a complete failure of will here'. Certainly the 'activists' in the Intelligence agencies were deeply disappointed. Suez spelled the frustrating end of the fantasy that the spirit of the SOE could live again. But Young had risen to be Vice-Chief of the Secret Service (VCSS) on the strength of it – a position he was to cling on to until 1961 when he left, saying he was tired of waiting for the chief of MI6, Dick White, to retire.

We shall hear of Young again in this story, but it is worth noting here that it was he who helped to arrange that Kim Philby – under suspicion and already forced to resign from MI6 – should be sent to the Middle East in 1955, with a job as an *Observer* and *Economist* correspondent arranged by MI6 and – according to Philby – with various modest MI6 tasks to perform. Young conceded that he had been involved when Philby surfaced in

Moscow to say so in 1988. In 1975, Young had taken substantial libel damages off the *Guardian* newspaper for saying it was he 'who had inflicted Kim Philby on a gullible British intelligence.' He protested at the inaccurate suggestion in the paper that his lack of judgement had enabled Philby to join MI6 in the first place, and his lawyer boasted of his 'very distinguished career in MI6'.[16] Young certainly did not recruit Philby in the first place, but his action in later helping compromise both two distinguished newspapers and his own agency scarcely seems praiseworthy. Nor does his behaviour in later extracting damages and an apology from the *Guardian*, although he was entitled to them. If he was among the group who thought Philby deserved to be made further use of, then he was participating in an act of great folly.

And, of course, Philby was not the only Soviet agent in MI6. In 1947, the Dutch Jewish SOE veteran George Blake was recruited by MI6 and posted under diplomatic cover to South Korea. Interned by the North Koreans, he was released in 1953 and went on to betray all MI6 operations in Berlin and Poland. He was not arrested until 1960.

As we have seen, the fate of every one of these secret British Cold War institutions hinged on the attitude of the United States. Within the newborn CIA, James Jesus Angleton was one of those most interested in Britain, and the most obsessional about it. There were plenty of Anglophiles among the wealthy East-Coast families who staffed the upper reaches of the CIA. The job of London chief of station was considered a plum posting for social reasons, and those who held it over the post-war years included many of the most senior CIA names – Winston Scott, Chester Cooper, Frank Wisner, Archie Roosevelt, Cleveland Cram, Bronson Tweedy, Cord Meyer, Edward Proctor.

But Angleton's relationship with Britain was different. He had grown up and been educated in London. He had been posted there again during the war. And in his ambition to rise as a counter-intelligence officer in the secret crusade against Communism he, like others, leaned heavily on the most bright, thorough and companionable Englishman he knew: Kim Philby. This hideous mistake may have made Angleton neurotically suspicious thereafter. In later years, lost in a maze of conflicting 'mole' denunciations by defectors, Peter Wright claims to have heard Angleton mutter obsessionally, 'This is Kim's work.'

The end of the war found Angleton in Italy. When the OSS was disbanded Angleton was instructed, by Lt.-Col. William Quinn of the Pentagon, to stay in Italy and control 'long-term counter-intelligence' against the Russians. Quinn shared Angleton's view that it was a mistake for US forces to rush home just because Germany was defeated. So Angleton stayed: he too would be a secret agent for the rest of his life.

The components of the dismantled OSS passed through a bureauc
alphabet soup for the next three years. While the men with guns in t
hands re-formed as OPC before merging into the new CIA, Anglet
more devious anti-Communist departments went through the hands of
SSU (Strategic Services Unit), CIG (Central Intelligence Group), and O
(Office of Special Operations), before reaching the same destination.

Angleton haunted the streets of Rome, infiltrating political parties, hir
agents, drinking with officers of the Italian Secret Service, and sitting up
night in his Via Archimede office reading agents' reports. It would ha
been Angleton, for example, who encouraged the Italian Secret Service
file reports on the activities of Nikolai Gorshkov, apparently the mc
powerful man in the new Russian diplomatic mission in Rome, who
'cover' was an interest in distributing Russian cinema films. Omnivorous a
he was, Angleton would certainly have taken note even of the trivi
observation that Gorshkov appeared to be employing a young woman c
half-Russian extraction who had been noted by Mussolini's police on he
arrival from the Soviet Union in 1938, allegedly as a refugee. All the evi
dence pointed to strong NKVD (the KGB's precursor) activity. Inter
national 'Intelligence' files like those on Gorshkov and his assistant would
later reappear in the plot against Harold Wilson.

Angleton reported back to Washington that the Italian partisans were
largely controlled by the Kremlin and that the Soviets were bent on European domination. He also made links with Italian Jews, many of whom
were helping run the British blockades into Palestine. (MI6, meanwhile,
were blowing up their chartered ships in Italian harbours.) The American
academic Robin Winks, whom Angleton briefed privately in detail about
these years, says:

> The subject of Jewish emigration, especially from the Soviet Union, was
> tied to his main preoccupation. Over the long run, Jewish emigration
> from the Soviet Union would provide a valuable source of information
> on the Soviet system; it would also give the KGB an opportunity to put
> its agents into the Middle East and . . . into the US.[17]

Still under thirty, Angleton coughed incessantly from heavy smoking and
was called 'the cadaver' by men in his unit; he appears to have been obsessed
by an isolating ambition in this peculiar world of crusading 'insiders'. Over
the next three years Angleton and his men pursued US policy in Italy. In a
nutshell, this was to fund and dominate the re-launched Italian Intelligence
services; to undermine the British, who had plans to restore the Italian
monarchy; and to bribe or browbeat Italians into voting for 'centrist' parties
and against Communists.

Italian-Americans were organised to write identical letters to their relations begging them to vote the right way: it was made clear that no more

17

food parcels would arrive from the US otherwise. It was hinted to the Italian army that weapons would be available for a coup if necessary. When these tactics were disclosed in the 1970s, it was admitted that the CIA were still putting $10 million a year into Italian local elections, campaign expenses, disruptive splinter parties and anti-Communist propaganda. It was a relatively crude approach to 'Intelligence' work based on money – but cash was the major US resource in these lean post-war years.

In August 1946, Angleton's friend Kim Philby called on him in Rome. He was on his way back from a failed mission to Istanbul where Constantin Volkov, an NKVD officer, had offered to defect and identify a Soviet agent working in British counter-espionage. After the news reached MI6, Volkov had mysteriously disappeared. Angleton expressed sympathy that so promising a case had been lost, and put Philby on the London plane after a drinking session. Philby's purpose was, presumably, to deflect US speculation: he had, of course, rapidly arranged to have the dangerous Volkov liquidated by Moscow.[18] Later that year Angleton went on leave to London and looked up his colleague. Philby offered to take him to see an interesting spectacle – Philby's investiture with the order of Commander of the British Empire at Buckingham Palace, as a reward for his war-time service. Walking away from the Palace, Philby could not resist remarking to his American friend, 'What this country needs is a good stiff dose of socialism.' The remark was later to echo in Angleton's memory, although there is no proof whether what he later allegedly said to Allen Dulles – 'You know, he sounded like a Commie' – was uttered with foresight, or with hindsight.[19]

In November 1947, Angleton was back in Washington, combining his Italian work with the re-launch of a full-scale Soviet Division. His star rose when he was able – thanks to his Italian Intelligence service links – accurately to predict the outcome of the crucial 1948 elections there, which the Communists narrowly lost. In 1948, his empire-building took a dramatic step forward. Israeli affairs were being handled by the same Middle East Division of the CIA that dealt with Arab matters. As Arab and Jew were at each other's throats in Palestine, loyalties soon became strained. A State Department employee was found passing classified material to the Israeli embassy and a Jewish woman working for the Middle East Division caused a panic by asking for a transfer on grounds of divided loyalties. The head of division, she recalled, 'practically accused me of being a traitor.' In the ensuing uproar, Israeli affairs were transferred en bloc to Angleton. He clung on to the 'Mossad monopoly' for the rest of his career.[20]

Angleton's extreme right-wing political views made him hostile to OPC's Albanian schemes. They seemed to entail subterranean co-operation with the anti-Stalinist Tito, and in Angleton's book Tito was a Communist. He also took the classic Intelligence-gathering point of view – that 'covert operations' would disrupt his agents. To further his ambitions, Angleton prefer-

18

red, temperamentally, crab-like manoeuvre to Boy Scouting. In not backing Wisner, Angleton showed early on how, as Anthony Verrier notes in his study of the Albanian affair, his 'innate gifts as an intelligence officer were weakened by an almost morbid suspicion of those different from himself in temperament and background.'[21]

No doubt Philby encouraged Angleton's hostility towards the Albanian venture. From that September, when Philby arrived as MI6 link-man in Washington, the two were constantly in each other's company: they had no fewer than twenty-six lunches together in a period of a few months. Angleton kept no records, but CIA officer Clare Petty pieced this together many years later from office log-books. Angleton kept up his links with the Italian Secret Services: when the first Albanian boatload left the Italian port of Otranto on October 2, 1949, Angleton phoned Jim McCargar, OPC's operational commander, 'with great glee', in McCargar's words, to say that Italian agents had been watching through telescopes, and that the operation's security was blown. Afterwards, Angleton repeatedly tried to persuade those who would listen that there had been other sources of Albanian leaks than Philby. The memory of those lunches in Harvey's restaurant clearly appalled him. He also tried to persuade later authors that his dealings with Philby had been part of some subtle 'double' operation to mislead the Soviets, and that he had suspected him all along. This seems unlikely.

But in the burgeoning CIA bureaucracy, Angleton, with his air of secret omniscience, was soon seen as 'legendary'. As a public-relations officer for himself, he was brilliant. What was remembered about the Albanian fiasco was that Angleton had been against it. He continued to have manipulative triumphs in Italy. On December 20, 1954, Wisner announced the creation of a special counter-intelligence department within the CIA. At the age of thirty-seven Angleton was to be its chief. He was to hold the position for another twenty years, and during that time, he, more than any other individual, was to be responsible for the climate of deceitfulness, paranoia and mutual denunciation of which Harold Wilson became a victim in 1974.

CHAPTER 2

Although it was a Labour government that was responsible for the renaissance of the Secret Services, most MI5 ('Security Service') officers remained deeply suspicious of their ostensible masters. They already had a bad record not merely of suspiciousness towards Labour, but of active party political malice: members of MI5 had misbehaved towards both previous Labour governments.

In 1924 there had been the notorious 'Zinoviev letter'. During Ramsay MacDonald's election campaign, the *Daily Mail* published a letter intercepted by the Intelligence services from the head of the Comintern to the British Communist Party. It urged them to pressurise sympathisers in the Labour Party, increase 'agitation-propaganda work in the armed forces', and generally prepare for revolution. On publication in the *Mail*, the Conservatives, well-primed, accused the Labour government of having tried to hush up the affair. In fact, at the time, MacDonald had been busy drafting, in all innocence, what was intended to be a strong public protest to the Russians. The leak to the *Mail* was a set-up, and Labour believed it lost them the election. Subsequently there was considerable controversy over whether the Zinoviev letter had been forged. It may have been – but that is not the central point: evidence exists to show that its leaking was a calculated plot involving Intelligence service links to a group of former MI5 and MI6 officers, including Admiral 'Blinker' Hall, former director of Naval Intelligence and, by a strange coincidence, principal agent at Conservative Central Office in 1923. It was in character for him: during the war, Hall had leaked homosexual extracts from Sir Roger Casement's diary, in the hope of blackening his name.[1]

The electoral plot against the 1929 Labour government was just as sordid, though in a different way. It involved explicitly turning MI5 into a branch of Conservative Central Office (or possibly vice versa). In 1927, the head of MI5's 'Investigation Branch', Major Joseph Ball, was taken into the employ of the Conservative Party chairman, J. C. C. Davidson, to help him run 'a little Intelligence service of our own'. Ball employed his MI5 techniques (and no doubt his access to MI5 facilities) to infiltrate 'agents in certain key centres and we also had agents actually in the Labour Party headquarters, with the result that we got their reports on political feeling in the country as well as our own.'[2]

In 1930, on the strength of the fact that, in Davidson's words, he 'had as much experience as anyone I know in the seamy side of life and the handling of crooks,' Ball (later Sir Joseph) was rewarded by being appointed the first director of the Conservative Research Department. Among those he hired in that capacity was Graham Mitchell whom he then, in something of a merry-go-round, urged to join MI5 in 1939. By the time of the Attlee government, Mitchell, who had a limp through polio, was head of 'F' division, which investigated 'subversion' by the British Communist Party. Guy Burgess reportedly also ingratiated himself with Sir Joseph Ball to get himself an MI5 job in 1941, supposedly penetrating neutral embassies.[3]

The way this rather dowdy security department worked in practice during Attlee's term of office emerges in the experiences of a Labour politician in 1948. The politician was George Thomas, who in later life was to become Speaker of the House of Commons, one of the most dignified offices of the British parliamentary system.

As a young MP, Thomas went to Greece on behalf of the National Union of Students to inspect a situation in which the US and Britain were supporting what was virtually a puppet pro-West Greek administration against Communist guerrillas. Greece was a Cold War cockpit and the entire Balkans region, as we have seen, was seething with troops, spies and 'resistance' agents. George Thomas later wrote in his autobiography that he had been 'naive' and should have left foreign affairs to those with more experience.[4]

Thomas's hosts appear to have arranged his 'capture' by the guerrillas of General Markos, who waylaid him, took him to their leader, and asked him to give a letter to the United Nations explaining their political position. This was a propaganda stunt. On his return to London, Thomas was disconcerted to find that the Foreign Office already had a briefing on his movements in Greece and were even able to quote conversations he had had with Greek officials. He was yet more disconcerted to be contacted by an ex-MI5 employee who said he had resigned in protest at the organisation's methods. 'Now you are back in England again,' he told Thomas, 'an MI5 man has been sent to your home town to keep an eye on you.' Thomas protested to Attlee, who found his story hard to believe. But a few days later, the Prime Minister apologised to him. As Tony Bunyan partly outlined in his book, *The Political Police in Britain*:

> He explained that he had looked in the suspects' book and had found [Thomas's] name was there. He said that what had happened had been done by the Secret Service people and had not been authorised by him. He told the MP [Thomas] that he himself had torn the page out of the book and that he hoped he would forget about it.[5]

Apparently, not all MPs and Labour ministers were so hapless in their dealings with the military mind. Verrier writes:

Although many of the 259 new Labour MPs had been front-line soldiers and airmen, MI5 at once proceeded to probe and pry. Chuter Ede, the Home Secretary, did not find this investigation acceptable. He was an old-fashioned English radical and disliked MI5's conspiracy-ridden world. Ede had a word with Herbert Morrison who, having been Home Secretary during most of the War, knew the Whitehall ropes. The new intake – and the new Ministers – saw more of their files than MI5 realised.[6]

MI5 officers may have imagined they were riding high after the war, because of the successes of the 'Double-Cross' system and its complicated deception schemes against the Germans. These triumphs in fact had very little relevance to internal security in peace-time: Soviet agents were unlikely to land, dripping, on beaches in the black-out. Nor could they be offered the brutal war-time choice: 'Co-operate, or be executed.' In fact, MI5's hopes were soon dashed when Attlee refused to appoint the 'internal' candidate, Guy Liddell, as head of MI5 in succession to the retiring Sir David Petrie.

Instead, in November 1945, he acted on a relatively brief mention of MI5 in the report on Secret Service post-war structures from Sir Findlater Stewart, a former member of the 'XX Committee' which had supervised Double-Cross. (Stewart's nephew, Patrick Stewart, an old Rugbeian who ended the war in a wheelchair with a Military Cross, was taken on by MI5 itself and ended up – as we shall see – being involved in the affair which drove promising Labour ministers out of office on 'security' grounds.'[7]) Findlater Stewart thought MI5 should be kept separate from MI6, although there were plans, never carried out, to house them in a joint Whitehall building in Horseferry Road. He saw MI5 as essentially a military operation, which should be only lightly controlled by the Minister of Defence or the Prime Minister: 'Having got the right man, there is no alternative to giving him the widest discretion.'

Attlee decided the right man was an outsider and a policeman – the Chief Constable of Kent, Percy Sillitoe. He wrote later: 'In a world where so many millions groan under the tyranny of the Police State . . . [Sillitoe] exhibits the qualities which have made the British policeman the protector, not the oppressor of society.'[8] Sillitoe himself said he did not want the ordinary citizen 'to go in constant helpless fear of a secret police against whose decrees he would have no redress . . . I myself would rather see two or three traitors slip through the net.'[9] He was a typical British policeman in that he had risen from the ranks and was suspicious of 'long-haired intellectuals' – at the age of twenty, he was not at an Oxford college, but

22

serving in the British South Africa police.

Partly, no doubt, Attlee intended Sillitoe's appointment to reassure the electorate who might have believed Churchill's election gibes about the 'Gestapo' that would be needed to enforce socialism. (Wilson, when he became Prime Minister, would feel the same nervousness.) Before the war, MI5 had been tiny – no more than twenty-five men. It was clear to Attlee, ever since the unpleasant revelations in Canada of the defector Igor Gouzenko, that in the world of the Cold War it was going to have to be a great deal bigger. But he also determined to strip away some of its secrecy and give it a less threatening image. The old guard in MI5 were mortified. Some took out their resentment on Sillitoe, who, because he did not hide his identity and attended trials, they called 'the publicity-loving policeman'.

Sillitoe's son says there was a campaign of hostility, led by Roger Hollis, and including Guy Liddell and Dick White, against his father. He recalls meeting him once during what the MI5 executives called the 'afternoon tea-club' in the canteen:

Suddenly, Hollis half-turned his back on my father and switched into Latin, a language he was well aware my father did not understand. I knew enough to know they were talking in epigrams. I thought it was some joke but they carried on and on and it was evident they were simply snubbing the man. My father called his chauffeur and stormed out of the building. When we got in the car, I said 'What was all that about?' He said, 'One word – Bastards!'[10]

The atmosphere of public-school spite speaks volumes. In Peter Wright's MI5 memoirs there is a plausible picture of the mores of these civil servants. He describes how they would take a day off during test matches to form a little MI5 encampment at Lords cricket ground; give new recruits Masonic handshakes; and phone each other up in the mornings with facetious coded queries about clues in the *Times* crossword – 'My left rump is giving me trouble'.[11]

Disdain came very ill from people such as Hollis, who was conducting a lengthy affair with his secretary, or Liddell who went to the homosexual Chelsea Palais on Friday evenings, sought advice from Anthony Blunt about his art collection, and attended Guy Burgess's farewell party to wave him goodbye en route to his final, doomed, US posting.

But it would be wrong to think that the relationship between MI5 and Labour ministers and their appointees was merely one of sulky tension. Christopher Mayhew, a junior minister at the Foreign Office, was an Intelligence 'insider' who had served with SOE as one of Hugh Dalton's assistants; so too was Hugh Gaitskell. He had even played golf with Roger Hollis at Worcester College, Oxford in the 1920s. And when he was appointed Minister of Fuel and Power, the anti-Communist Gaitskell set out to use his MI5 links.

23

Whitehall was pre-occupied, then as now, with Communist influence among the miners. Arthur Horner, General Secretary of the Miners' Union was a prominent Communist Party member. As soon as he was appointed, Gaitskell scribbled in the agenda of things to find out in his private notebook, 'Robin, MI5 and the Party Line'. 'Robin' was almost certainly Sir Robin Brook, a banker who, like Gaitskell and Mayhew had worked with SOE during the war. After the war he worked for MI6. Gaitskell remained friendly with him and was a frequent visitor to his Kent house throughout the 1950s. The Communist coal miners in Britain, unlike those in France, never tried to exploit massive industrial action during the Cold War, although they showed no enthusiasm for government 'productivity drives'. Gaitskell clearly got himself briefings – in January 1948 he confided to his diary: 'The mining industry has been given a sort of exemption by Pollitt [the CPGB general secretary] from the general attack the Communist Party is going to make.'[12]

At least one left-wing Labour MP – Tom Driberg – was being run throughout the Attlee government as an agent by Maxwell Knight, the bizarre figure from 'F' Division ('Political Parties') who became popular with a generation of children as 'Uncle Max' the radio naturalist. It was a peculiarly personal relationship based on their common homosexuality – Knight's colleague Joan Miller later said sourly that Knight was 'besotted' with the MP. Opinions differ about Driberg, who was a person with a number of sides to his character.

Perhaps the most sensible thing to say is that his career showed the futility of trying to cram individuals into Cold War categories. A brilliant journalist and temperamentally a left-winger, Driberg was persuaded by Knight before the war to report on the British Communist Party, which he had joined. Anthony Blunt, spotting one of Driberg's war-time reports inside MI5, tipped off the Russians. Driberg, to his chagrin, was expelled from the CP without explanation. He became an MP and continued to be 'run' by Knight, reporting on the Labour Party and the Bevanites. He was also allowed by the CP to re-join in secret and – according to Peter Wright and others – was paid cash by the KGB for information. Driberg went to Korea for three months in November 1950, neglecting his parliamentary duties. Ostensibly a war correspondent, he was reporting back to MI5 on leftist groups.

When Knight left MI5, Driberg was dropped, but successfully exploited his connections with all parties to visit Guy Burgess in Moscow and write a lucrative book about him. He was delighted, too, in the 1960s, to be recruited by the Czechs, who also paid him for Labour Party tittle-tattle. When Peter Wright discovered this, he pressurised Driberg into resuming work for MI5, demanding to know if there was any scandal about Harold Wilson.

People in MI5 tried to spread stories about Driberg on the strength of this career, to the effect that he was part of the Communist conspiracy in the Labour Party. Nothing could have been more absurd. There is no evidence that Driberg ever passed anyone any secret information of consequence about anything. The only piece of concrete information he is known to have given MI5 was a deliberate red herring. The reality was that, as a homosexual, he needed protection from arrest and disgrace: the MI5 connection gave him that. As a homosexual, it is reasonable to say, he adored a further excuse for having secret lives. And the ability to score off various Intelligence agencies by separating them from their money must have given him acute personal pleasure. It was some compensation for the fact that Driberg's florid sexual tastes barred him, for ever, from ministerial office, on 'security' grounds.

There was also a smaller number of Labour politicians who had, in fact, been full members of the Intelligence agencies, either before or during the war. If MI5 believed that no one really ever 'left' the Communist Party, it was certainly true that no one ever 'left' the Intelligence services. The ritual of signing copies of the Official Secrets Act constituted a kind of perpetual masonic handshake. Kenneth Younger, for example, elected in 1945 as Labour MP for Rutherglen, had been a war-time director of MI5's 'E' Division, responsible for the supervision of all aliens.[13] On the strength of these insider qualifications, he was later put on the 1962 Radcliffe Tribunal into security shortcomings in the Vassall case. Richard Crossman, later to become one of Wilson's cabinet ministers, had worked on the black propaganda schemes of PWE and regarded himself in consequence as a great expert on both psychological warfare and 'security'. He later told his ministerial colleague Tony Benn (who was appalled) that he was all for fierce security measures:

[He] said that, as a Minister, he would think it right that his phones should be tapped and all his letters opened. This is quite mad.[14]

The most unusual Intelligence officer in the Labour parliament was probably Attlee's minister for civil aviation, Rex Fletcher, created Lord Winster. He appears to have been involved in handling a sex scandal which casts an odd light on the behaviour of Ramsay MacDonald around 1931. MacDonald was, of course, the Labour Prime Minister who by staying in office during the slump and forming the so-called 'National Government' split and wrecked his party in 1931; his behaviour pushed a whole generation of disillusioned undergraduates towards the Comintern.

Fletcher, a former naval officer with a ruddy, weatherbeaten air, joined the Labour Party in 1929. He also, covertly, joined MI6, under Menzies and his then chief, Admiral Sinclair. He had been interested in politics since officially retiring from naval Intelligence in 1924, standing unsuccessfully as a Liberal. Fletcher's secret job was a senior one – as one of the group of 'G officers' at Broadway headquarters in St James's who organised the foreign operations conducted by station chiefs and field agents. Fletcher's division was Europe and the Near East.

According to Sir Walford Selby, who was Principal Private Secretary to the Foreign Secretary at the time, and would have handled Secret Service links, Fletcher and MI6 used their facilities to purchase and retrieve on the Prime Minister's behalf a series of compromising letters. They had been written some years earlier to a 'continental cocotte' who was threatening to reveal them. MacDonald – who would have been ruined by such a scandal – was thus propped up by the Intelligence agencies. Christopher Andrew, the historian who unearthed some named sources for this event, describes MI6's role as 'probable, but not certain'. Fletcher, who complained in 1933 that MacDonald was 'notoriously ungrateful to his friends,' won a Labour seat in 1935 and was a minister in the war-time coalition government. One will look in vain in reference books for mention of his Secret Service activities, but the most constructive thing he probably did was to urge the Secret Service to think more about Nazi re-armament in the 1930s, and less about its perennial Russian bogey.[15]

The relations between Intelligence officers and the 1945 Labour government were thus more intricate than one might think. What began to alter the power relationship, however, were the Cold War growths of excessive secrecy, blacklisting and bugging.

In these immediate post-war years, Attlee made an attempt to de-mystify MI5 (although the cluster of Foreign Office 'funny' departments were always swathed in deep secrecy). Sillitoe's appointment was openly announced and he gave press conferences. This led to some embarrassments at airports, when he was badgered and photographed whilst en route to Washington, for example, on a trip to explain the defections of Burgess and Maclean to a scowling J. Edgar Hoover of the FBI. Any embarrassment was probably well-deserved. Sillitoe himself said, 'Such routine interrogations by the Press did not really annoy me,' although he was irritated at having his holidays disturbed. The publicity did no harm. Sillitoe was not assassinated by the KGB as a result of his relaxed attitudes. But internal pressure about his 'love of publicity' led to newspapers being ordered, for reasons of 'national security', under the newly revived D-Notice system (another Cold War product), not to name Dick White, his successor. The idea that even the identity of the head of MI5 was a State secret took hold again.

Sillitoe also wrote his memoirs. This might seem surprising, in view of the extravagant claims by the British government thirty-five years later that Intelligence service memoirs had never been permitted in British history. Published under the title *Cloak Without Dagger* by Cassell in 1955, Sillitoe's book had an approving foreword by Attlee himself. But the memoirs – which were entirely harmless – were published against strenuous internal opposition, and only after long extracts had been excised at MI5's behest. Alec MacDonald, one of Sillitoe's staff at that time, revealed before his death that one of the episodes had been censored because MacDonald himself was singled out for praise in it:

[it] mentioned me in fairly full terms and showered a lot of praise on me, and to his chagrin, they deleted that because they thought it was bad for the rest of the service.[16]

Similarly, the identities of staff MI5 officers were not always shrouded in secrecy. The counter-espionage officer Arthur Martin travelled on the Stratocruiser to Washington with Sillitoe in 1951, was listed on the passenger manifest, and was named in the *Daily Express*. MacDonald, too, was identified in the early 1950s, when he was sent to Kenya:

For a policy reason purely, and government policy, not MI5 policy. They wanted to assure Parliament and the public and the very influential white settlers in Kenya that they were getting somebody from MI5 who had previous experience in Malaya and in India and so on, and that they were being looked after. And the next day, there it was . . . me leaving for Kenya, photographs all over the place.[17]

Attlee also supported the publication in 1947 of Sir John Masterman's history of the disinformation practised on the Germans by the XX Committee – at least in some form. It was argued that it would boost MI5 and cheer up the British public to know what had been achieved in the war. Tedder and the Chiefs of Staff vetoed this. They gave two reasons: one, that the Germans might identify and retaliate against the families of some of the agents, however well-disguised; and secondly that such disinformation might be useful in the future, by which they meant the Cold War. The second reason is most likely to have been the real one: fourteen years later, Hollis, as Director-General of MI5, was still attempting to suppress the book whilst Peter Wright discloses in his memoirs that throughout the 1950s, Graham Mitchell, Hollis's deputy, repeatedly employed Double-Cross methods against the Russians by trying to 'turn' agents. He was never successful. (Masterman's account, *The Double-Cross System*, was eventually published in the US in 1967.)[18]

While secrecy slowly returned to war-time levels, war-time internment was replaced by a somewhat milder tactic – blacklisting. As early as March 1947, Attlee had set up a working party on subversive activities in response to the disclosures made by Gouzenko in 1945 about Stalinist attitudes, and the complaints of the Chiefs of Staff that both British Communists and visiting Russians were getting access to military secrets. The result, in 1948, was a relatively limited decision to blacklist Communists off secret work. Over the decades, however, it turned out to be the thin end of a wedge. Communists, predictably, complained. But there were also some prescient civil libertarians who remembered the scandals of war-time internment and knew just how mischievous or incompetent MI5 could be. Maxwell Knight – although no one knew at the time who was to blame – had seriously over-reached himself by having an innocent pacifist from a well-known family, Benjamin Greene, locked up on the word of a venal informer, Harald Kurtz. The family, by good luck, had managed to identify and trap Kurtz into a confession, and Greene was released. But he never recovered from the experience. It was a reminder that MI5, if it was given powers to interfere in people's lives, was bound to abuse them, if only out of stupidity.[19]

Lord Chorley, a Labour lawyer, gave another example in a later debate from his experiences in the war-time Ministry of Home Security. A man had been locked up for several months for having made a concrete pit, allegedly to flash signals to enemy aircraft. It had taken Sir Norman Birkett, chairman of a review committee, to discover that the man had merely been improving his garden; the allegation had never been put to him by MI5. Chorley understood MI5's particular stupidities:

> The quality of the [MI5] report is extraordinarily uneven in character . . . the people who are employed . . . are a very heterogeneous group of people. Moreover, these very people often become emotionally involved in a quite extraordinary way in the cases on which they are reporting. They begin to regard it as a personal affront if anybody disagrees with them . . . it makes the estimate which the security officer forms of a man's reliability very unreliable.[20]

The parliamentary debate on Attlee's 'purge' of the civil service came less than a fortnight after Masaryk, the non-Communist Czech foreign minister, had been pushed to his death out of a window. Under the circumstances, the Prime Minister had a relatively easy time. One of the two Communist MPs in the House, Phil Piratin, demanded to know whether Attlee supported 'a policy of inciting the bourgeoisie of other countries in Europe to rise up in civil war against working-class governments.' Attlee replied bitingly, 'I was not dealing with *working-class governments* at all.' To a tirade from Willie Gallacher of Fife about American millionaires planning aggression against the USSR, he spoke dryly of the 'usual cloud of dust' kicked up by the Communists. He deplored, he said, the rise of 'these subversive parties', and he did not want to 'damnify the man' by naming any civil servant who was moved off secret work. In a measured and sensible statement he said the present situation was 'a very difficult problem of government'. Attlee also defused complaints by accepting a call for an

28

advisory tribunal which, in MP Bill Brown's words 'might qualify the police character of the [MI5] report by reference to political horse sense'. There was an interesting speech from the Conservative benches, when Nigel Birch pointed out:

> There are many devoted people in the Security Services, but I have noticed ... when one is trying to carry out a purge, some isolated incident in a man's past is seized hold of ... he is regarded as being something quite other to what he really is.'[21]

Clearly, the mood in Britain was far from McCarthyite. A number of civil servants' careers were subsequently spoiled – one of them was Bernard Floud, a principal in Harold Wilson's Board of Trade, and by now an open member of the 'Civil Servants Communist Group'. Informed that he would never rise above his present rank, Floud abandoned the civil service and attempted to take up farming. MI5 and the Chiefs of Staff were right that people like him had come under earlier pressure to spy; they were scarcely right in thinking that one day such political idealists would rise up in the Board of Trade and throw Harold Wilson out of a window Masaryk-style, in the interests of the Soviet Union.

The practical effect of the 'purge' was very limited. It merely gave MI5 the opportunity to increase the number of 'personal files' they held on individuals. Dedicated Communist Party members were forced to go underground. Espionage continued to take place by those who, as Attlee privately predicted, were not open Communist Party members. And so, inexorably, the pressure for blacklisting spread.

In summer 1950, for example, at the height of the Korean War, it was suggested that MI5 ought also to remove from their jobs Communist workers at power stations. These men were not, of course, doing 'secret' work. Walter Citrine, the veteran trade union leader who had been placed at the head of the state-owned British Electricity Authority, approached the Fuel minister, Philip Noel-Baker, and told him he was convinced the Russian saw power stations as the nerve centre of British industry. There were perhaps twenty or thirty men working at London power stations who were active and dangerous Communists who 'would not stop at sabotage'. Citrine wanted to invite MI5 in. Attlee was duly approached on August 3 and called in Sillitoe, who gave the job to Roger Hollis, by now head of 'C' Division, which handled private firms and sabotage. Hollis and a junior colleague, P. A. Osborne, put the 'dangerous Communists' under investigation. They did not find much and the Home Secretary, Chuter Ede, later told the Cabinet, 'There is no reason to believe any organised outbreak of sabotage is imminent.' But Hollis and Osborne's report was considered so important that they were invited to attend in person the August 15 meeting of the Cabinet's Emergencies Committee, when it was considered.

Documents disclosing these events escaped – probably by mistake – into the Cabinet papers released to the public archives thirty years later.[22]

Following hard on the US exposure, with MI5 help, of the 'atom spy' Klaus Fuchs, came the immense trauma of the defection in 1951 of Burgess and Maclean. The defections in turn came on the heels of another British working-party report, chaired by General Templer and Gladwyn Jebb, predicting further Communist infiltration of the trade unions and the media.[23] American pressure increased: the upshot was a tri-partite agreement by the US, Britain and France to introduce 'positive vetting' in order to detect not open Communists, but closet 'security risks'. Suddenly, the field in which MI5 could poke and pry was widened to include the private lives and backgrounds of thousands of people. The measure was directed not only at civil servants and soldiers doing classified work – of whom, of course, in the Cold War, there were thousands. It also covered defence contractors, and employees of the BBC and the Post Office. The use of 'security procedures' in large companies, and the close links between those companies and MI5, spread the sharing of files on 'security risks'. In practice, positive vetting was introduced in such a lukewarm way that, at first, it had very little impact. It was certainly easy for spies to beat. But, in time, it was to broaden MI5's scope for mischief.

The widening of MI5's remit from spy-catching to blacklisting went hand in hand with the development of new techniques of intrusion. It was in 1949, in the wake of the Berlin blockade, that Sillitoe haltingly tried to put MI5 on a more modern footing. He called in Sir Frederick Brundrett, the Defence Ministry's chief scientist, a small energetic man who was one of the war-time 'boffins' on whom Britain had relied. From his office in Storey's Gate, Whitehall, Brundrett was presiding over attempts to improve naval submarine detection. What, he was asked, could research scientists do to overcome Britain's Intelligence blindness? It seemed virtually impossible to run agents behind the Iron Curtain – the NKVD was always in wait for them. The Russians tightly controlled the movements of foreigners and British diplomats, while their own outposts seemed invulnerable.

Brundrett commissioned a round-table seminar in his office of scientists from the various military research laboratories, with Colonel Malcolm Cumming and Hugh Winterborn from MI5 and John Henry from MI6. Among those whose brains they attempted to pick were the Wrights, father and son. Maurice Wright, chief engineer of the Marconi electronics firm, was a reformed alcoholic who had lost his job during the slump in the 1930s, after spying on German naval radio transmissions in Norway for MI6 during World War I.

His son Peter, then working for the Services Electronic Research Laboratory, had an odd, troubled background. As a boy he had rickets and a stammer, but considerable intelligence. He took a keen amateur interest in

30

his father's ambitions to develop worldwide radio communications. In 1931, at the age of fifteen, his hopes of going to university were abruptly ended when his father was sacked from Marconi at the height of the Depression, following a merger with a cable company. Wright was taken out of his small private school. His stammer worsened dramatically, and, to add to his troubles, his father took to drink. His hopes dashed, the teenage Wright worked as a farmhand in Scotland and Cornwall, until, in 1938, he eventually raised enough money to get a place at the Oxford School of Rural Economy with a view to becoming an agricultural scientist. When war broke out the school was shut down, and Brundrett, a longstanding friend of his father's, got both men scientific work with the Admiralty – Maurice processing secret naval signals intercepts, and Wright wrapping giant electrical coils round navy ships to 'degauss' them against magnetic mines.

Wright topped the entrance exams for the Scientific Civil Service at the end of the war: this bright, but hardly well-rounded young man was now about to be recruited for a long secret career in the anti-Communist underworld.

Wright was scarcely suitable material to be a secret policeman, but then, it might be asked, who was? Sir Martin Furnival Jones, after he retired as head of MI5, remarked approvingly, 'Somebody once said to me that four or five years in counter-espionage is too long, and causes insanity.'[24] He might have pointed to the case of Admiral Sir Barry Domville, Director of British Naval Intelligence from 1927 to 1930, who became unhinged even faster than that. He found Hitler 'absolutely terrific; absolutely A1,' and attempted to expose 'what Masons, Jews and other secret forces in our society were up to.' In 1940, he had to be interned.[25] Furnival Jones might also have mentioned Frank Wisner, head of CIA covert operations against Albania, and CIA station chief in London in 1961, who eventually had to be carried out of the CIA building by force and placed in a mental institution.[26]

It was also work which attracted more than its share of emotional cripples – although often boring, to some people it offered an addictive combination of government job security, a sense of secret power, and the vengeful satisfaction of disrupting other people's lives. Secret agents – whether Communist 'moles' or Western 'patriots' – tend to be busybodies by nature. Wright, furthermore, needed to prove himself. What is a little chilling is that, twenty-seven years later, when he emerged from MI5, it was to the warmth and plaudits of many senior secret policemen and their friends on both sides of the Atlantic. With hindsight, many of Wright's former Intelligence service colleagues later tried to characterise him as an aberration. The truth is that he fitted in rather too well.

After several years of unpaid consultancy, Wright managed to get into MI5 as a career scientific officer – MI5's first. He was anxious to join the secret world, and it may be that his job as a more orthodox government

31

scientist was not going too well. We have some unnerving testimony from one of his scientific colleagues at that time – Neville Robinson, who was Wright's immediate junior in the naval scientific service from 1947–1950 told friends:

He really knew damn all about what we were doing . . . He was frankly an ignorant shit and quite impossible to work for. He was the real reason why I left in 1950 for Oxford. I just couldn't stand working for him any more. Nothing Wright touched ever came to anything. People outside the lab – scientists or people from industry would come up and ask me if I was making progress on a project I'd never heard of but Wright had commissioned mainly for his own self-aggrandisement. I became very disenchanted although he had a great gift of the gab . . . He was more of a radio repair man, a kind of ham radio enthusiast, than a physicist with a good grounding in the subject. He could fix a radio and set up a receiver in Nigeria – that sort of thing . . . .[27]

Others would regard such a characterisation as unfair, or even snobbish.

At first Wright worked part-time with John Taylor, a former signals officer who ran an Intelligence gadgets laboratory at the Post Office 'Special Investigations Unit' at Dollis Hill, North London. Wright says, 'It was clear they urgently needed new techniques of eavesdropping which did not require entry to premises.' As an unpaid 'external scientific adviser', he wrote monthly reports to Brundrett's committee on his progress in developing a snooping microphone which could pick up sound waves from office furniture. The world of portable 'bugs' was the fundamental post-war development in the technology of eavesdropping. It went alongside the better known Post Office activities of 'telephone taps' and letter-opening using a piece of split bamboo or a steam kettle, which made entrusting one's messages to Her Majesty's Post Office such a hazardous business.

'Bugging' was not as easy a technology as might be imagined. The principle was straightforward: a miniature radio transmitter attached to a microphone could be hidden somewhere in a room and would relay every conversation within earshot 'live'. But there were serious practical problems. First, the 'bug' had to be introduced into the room. This meant either a burglary or a subterfuge. Second, it had to be small enough to remain hidden: a radio transmitter the size of a cigarette pack seemed an impressive achievement until one tried to decide where it could be hidden undiscovered for a long period. Third, the 'bug' needed a battery. When it ran out, it went dead. And fourth, any power supply small enough to be hidden was likely to be so weak that it would not just run out quickly, but would only transmit over a distance of a few yards. Finally, the continuous output of even a small radio transmitter could be 'swept' and discovered, if its existence was suspected.

32

This was a fair range of problems. Over the next thirty years, bugging was to develop to the point where no one in authority dared hold a secret conversation without either leaving their office to walk around outside – preferably near a waterfall – or else retiring to a 'strong-room' suspended in the centre of a building with double walls and loud music playing. No conversation held within range of an outside window is safe nowadays – microphones can pick up the vibrations of the window-pane (this is why modern MI5 buildings can be identified by the net curtains at the windows – like pot-plants, they tend to spoil radio reception). No conversation held anywhere near a telephone is safe – using what MI5 call 'SF' or 'Special Facilities', a telephone can easily be turned by remote control into a bug with its own built-in power supply. The massive growth in the use of computer terminals and word processors has made bugging easier still: unless electrically shielded, they will freely 'leak' their contents into the ether.

But in 1949 bugging was in its infancy. Wright was attempting to invent a microphone which would resonate under the effect of a radio beam, thus cutting out the need for a power supply. The Russians beat him to it. In 1951, just after the shock of the defection of Burgess and Maclean, the British also accidentally discovered that a bug was operating in their Moscow embassy, and shortly afterwards the US embassy there found a primitive cavity microphone installed in the Great Seal of the United States on the wall behind the Ambassador's desk. Wright's first triumph was to demonstrate how 'the Thing' worked, enabling Western Intelligence services to copy the design and put it into production for their own use under the codename SATYR.

In his memoirs Wright describes the amateur manner in which MI5 worked in those days. Brundrett provided for a secure hut to be set up as a laboratory at the Marconi plant at Great Baddow, Essex. Here Wright tinkered with the captured Russian object – an eight-inch-long device with an aerial feeding into a metal cavity. 'Inside the cavity was a metal mushroom with a flat top which could be adjusted to give it a variable capacity. Behind the mushroom was a thin gossamer diaphragm to receive the speech . . .' Wright's boss Cumming's reaction to the discovery was to lobby for the Admiralty to pay for the development of a production model, on the grounds that 'The Treasury will never agree to expand the Secret Vote [the annual sum voted by Parliament, without debate, supposedly to finance the Secret Services].'

Eventually, the work of six navy scientists produced a prototype which Wright personally demonstrated to Hollis, by now deputy chief of MI5, on the fifth floor of Leconfield House. The remote-controlled transmitter and receiver dishes were disguised as umbrellas. According to Wright, Hollis said, 'Wonderful, Peter: it's black magic.' SATYR sets were later sold to the

Americans, Australians and Canadians, the other members of the WASP secret partnership.

If Wright is to be believed, the British Intelligence services spent much of this post-war period begging for technical funds from the increasingly reluctant armed services. It was not a need for secrecy which led to the use of outside defence contractors and British military procurement departments: it was a penny-pinching attempt by Intelligence bureaucrats to avoid pressure on their budgets. Hollis, as MI5 chief, later acquired a reputation for triumphantly under-spending his annual budgets – than which, in a British accounting system, there is no more absurd sin.

This attitude was combined with the military tradition, which lingered on anachronistically in the secret departments, that officers were gentlemen who did not require to live on their military pay. Men like Colonel Cumming of MI5 owned large estates in Sussex and played the squire at weekends; the chief of MI6, Stewart Menzies, was a monument to inherited privilege and wealth. Only with the advent of Sillitoe were MI5's staff salaries put on a properly audited civil service basis, instead of being scattered under War Office heads.

The bad effects of this tradition were that representatives of MI5, MI6, IRD and GCHQ, with their unaccountable, secretive ways, continually infected the rest of British public life. In the boardrooms of large companies, senior common rooms of ancient universities, the lobbies of the Commons, regimental messes, and the homes of individual wealthy tycoons, there were the men from the Intelligence services, apologetically asking favours, swearing those concerned to secrecy, offering favours in return . . . In addition, the extensive links with secret work of defence contractors and defence departments made their own budgets hard to control. Wright says revealingly of his initial meeting with MI5: 'It had been so gloriously unpredictable, in the way that Whitehall often was during the War.'

This sense of being engaged in patriotic undercover adventures, exciting exceptions to Whitehall's dull routines, may have enabled grown men to rediscover the excitement of the war. It was not a wholesome way to develop a secret police. CIA men were sometimes shocked by the number of privileged amateurs who were allowed to hang around the fringes of MI5 and MI6. Leonard McCoy, a senior counter-intelligence officer, says he was startled, reading Peter Wright's memoirs, to discover the access allowed by MI5 to supposedly retired officers like Blunt, and 'out-of-house' agent-runners like the rich businessman Victor Rothschild. Carter's CIA chief, Stansfield Turner, in his own memoirs, recounts with surprise how Maurice Oldfield, by then MI6 chief, lectured him on the virtues of using amateur businessmen for Secret Service work.[28]

Neither of these Americans understood the British predilection for saving money by projecting Intelligence activity as a romantic and rather socially exclusive hobby to be enjoyed by the denizens of gentlemen's clubs – often conducted, indeed, at the bars of the Special Forces Club, White's Club, the Carlton Club, or in Peter Wright's rather lowly case, the Oxford and Cambridge Club. The chief of the French Secret Services, the SDECE, the Comte de Marenches, observes rather more crisply:

> The French secret services have never attracted the intellectual or even social elite who in Britain have always considered it a great honour to serve in the shadows ... Our national temperament inclines us not to have much use for the people who do this sort of work ... In France it is not very fashionable to be in Intelligence.[29]

While MI6 engaged in fantastical military freebooting in the Mediterranean and the Middle East, MI5 spent – or misspent – much of its energies on trying to keep the Empire free of 'Communists'. MI5 employed more people in the Colonies than it did in London: the important men on its staff – Bill Magan, Arthur Martin, Tony Healey, Alec MacDonald, at times even the scientist Peter Wright – were to be found in Malaya, Singapore, Kenya, the Gulf, Cyprus. It is typical of priorities that when General Gerald Templer, the former head of Military Intelligence, was sent to Malaya in 1952 to mount a massive Intelligence and propaganda offensive against the guerrillas who threatened British rubber earnings, he attempted to appoint Dick White – MI5's only really gifted counter-intelligence specialist, who was about to take over the director-generalship – as the head of his Special Branch.[30] Meanwhile, in the real world, American influence was growing, and the Empire evaporating.

The result of the lack of realism in MI5 and MI6 was that, from 1961, when the first of a series of truly traumatic Intelligence events occurred in the West, the British Intelligence establishment went more than a little insane. It was, perhaps, Harold Wilson's bad luck that he should be on the way, at this point, to becoming Britain's next Labour Prime Minister. For Wilson it was the culmination of a political career that had begun with the triumphant sweep to power of the Labour Party in the 1945 General Election.

CHAPTER 3

Members of Britain's victorious 1945 Labour Parliament sang 'The Red Flag': some even flew real red flags from rooftops.[1] Of course, hardly any of them were actual Communists, despite their exuberance. Most were Methodists, if anything, or Oxbridge radicals like Harold Wilson and Michael Foot, who started their political life as adherents to the Liberal Party.[2] The real Communists were deep underground, in the Intelligence services, the Foreign Office and the scientific research laboratories, where nobody noticed them. They were often very upper-class people.

The whole issue of who was a Communist and who was not had gone into cold storage for the duration of the war, while Stalin, Roosevelt and Churchill were allies. In Britain, Churchill deliberately ordered Soviet Bloc radio traffic not to be intercepted. British Secret Service chief Stewart Menzies' attempts to keep private lines open to Germany with a view to a separate peace were treated with reservation.[3] Although Churchill drew the line at sharing 'ULTRA' German decrypts with Stalin, there were enough Soviet sympathisers to pass on even that information.

There were many British Labour idealists, like Sir Stafford Cripps, the war-time ambassador to Moscow, who thought this new climate could continue and be built on, enabling Britain to stay out of an East-West fight. People like him got it wrong. They underestimated the violence and paranoia of Stalin, the economic aggression of the US, and their intense mutual suspicion. Within three years from the end of the war, a large galaxy of interests had built up which regarded professional anti-Communism as a desirable way of British political life. It consisted of the right wing of the Labour Party, the British military and Intelligence establishment, the Conservative Party, and the United States.

It was Harold Wilson's misfortune to find himself – partly by accident – on the wrong side of the political blanket. This young minister was an Oxford-educated statistician from the unfashionable North of England, with what a contemporary called his 'smooth cherry-stone face', and a small moustache he had rather touchingly grown in an effort to make himself look older.[4] He was clever – even brilliantly clever – but did not belong in any of the inner circles of public school, club, regiment and 'Secret Service work' with which even the British Labour Party was enmeshed. Despite the 1945 red-flag-waving, British political society was still thoroughly secretive and snobbish by US standards. Britain's war had been very different from America's war or Russia's war. Her war was one in which a fundamentally weak power had survived only by using secret diplomatic and Intelligence tricks: victory had reinforced those clannish attitudes.

Many of Wilson's fellow ministers and parliamentarians were Intelligence 'insiders', both Labour and Tory. Those Labour ministers who had served in the war-time coalition Cabinet – Attlee, Bevin, Dalton, Strauss – were acutely aware of the central role secret Intelligence and secret projects had played in a war of strategic deception, ULTRA and the atom bomb. Wilson was not in this group of insiders. He had spent the war in Whitehall building up coal stocks. He was not involved in the 'black life' of propaganda and deception masterminded by Hugh Dalton; the code-breaking feats of the Bletchley academics; the derring-do behind enemy lines of the Special Operations Executive adventurers; or the atomic manoeuvrings of 'Tube Alloys'.

Now, in the uncertain years before the Cold War began, Wilson's first major political activity was to strike up trading relations with the Russians. This brought about his first political triumph, was eventually to enable him to earn a handsome personal income, and gave him a life-long enthusiasm for links and deals with the Soviet Union, an area in which Wilson came to believe he had special skills. Unfortunately, he almost immediately fell foul of MI5 and British military Intelligence, because one of the first items he was involved in trying to sell to the Soviet Union was advanced British fighter planes.

The Board of Trade files on the 1947 sales of British jets to Russia have been suppressed. Although they should have been released to the public archives in 1978 under the 'thirty-year-rule', introduced, ironically, by Harold Wilson himself in the 1960s to improve his administration's 'liberal image', they were closed for fifty years under the authority of a later Labour government. The key closed file, which contains the correspondence between the Board of Trade, the Foreign Office, the Air Ministry and the Intelligence departments, is labelled '1947-48 Sale of Jet Aircraft to Russia'.

One should not jump to the conclusion that the documents have been suppressed to spare Harold Wilson's reputation. It is just as likely that they contain references to Intelligence and MI5 views, automatically regarded as 'sensitive'. On the other hand, merely closing the documents for fifty years is an unusual procedure for Intelligence-related material. What normally happens is that it is 'retained' indefinitely in the original government department concerned, under a special power granted by the Lord Chancellor after lobbying in 1965 by the Intelligence services themselves, in an effort to preserve the fiction that they do not exist.

The later history of these papers proved even more remarkable because of what happened to them after the expiry of the first thirty years. The archives of the Public Record Office at Kew disclose that the whole batch of dusty files were in fact fetched up for routine review by officials at the Board of Trade several years before their formal 'release-by' date of 1977–78. The files were brought up from the basement in 1972, with a second review under the Labour government of 1974. The procedure would have been that any files with a bearing on the Soviet Union and military matters would have been referred to the Ministry of Defence for an opinion on whether they still had a 'security' aspect. The Air Intelligence staff, with their close links to MI5, would have eventually found these intriguing old dossiers on their desk.

It was at just this time – when the campaign against Wilson within MI5 was at its height – that a tendentious account of the content of these yellowing dossiers somehow found its way into the hands of first *The Times* and then the scurrilous magazine *Private Eye*. At a time when Wilson was Prime Minister, it was implied that he had controlled the key events in 1947, and used his political position to aid Russian espionage. As the secret files themselves were to be suppressed for twenty more years, there was little likelihood of a different view emerging.

It has only been possible to prove Wilson's innocence of this charge by painstaking research. The attempts at censorship broke down: the official 'weeders' missed certain key cables buried in the Board of Trade archives – some confidential annexes to Cabinet committee meetings – and they also failed to spot an obscure minute stamped 'Secret' in the 1950 files of the Foreign Office which rehearses the full details of what was termed 'the sad history of the Nenes and Derwents which went to Russia'. These documents turn out to tell the story of Wilson's own – rather hapless – involvement in the Russians' coup of developing their own formidable jet fighter, the Mig-15, on the back of British research.

But the documents place the responsibility for the fiasco firmly at the door of Cripps and Attlee, the senior ministers concerned. They exonerate Wilson from charges of anything graver than merely doing what he was told. When the main decisions were taken, Wilson did not head the department, although he did preside over the Board of Trade throughout the autumn of 1947 while the last seventeen of the batch of jet engines were physically shipped to Moscow, and he did negotiate personally with Mikoyan, the Soviet trade minister, with a view to selling him more.

At the end of the war, the jet engine had been invented and developed, largely by the British, but also independently by the Germans, who put a jet-propelled Messerschmitt into the air with technology later captured by the Russians. Jets came too late to make a big difference to the outcome of the war, and the first gas-turbine jet fighters were none too powerful whilst burning up fuel at an impossible rate. But they represented the future – not only for fighters, but for the passenger planes which were soon to become one of the world's biggest new industries. The Gloster Meteor IV twin-jet British fighter with a Rolls-Royce Derwent V engine set a world speed record of 606mph in 1945. The de Havilland Vampire also went into service, with the Rolls-Royce Nene I, a primitive centrifuge-type jet engine with a very modest 4,500lb thrust. Both engines rapidly became obsolete as new types were refined.

The question for war-shattered Britain was the central one which dogged all her post-war relationships with the US: was her powerful war-time ally to call all the economic and political shots in the future? The US had a strategic interest in throttling trade with Russia; it also had a commercial interest in stifling independent British trade generally. In these brief and now forgotten years before the Cold War froze in, many Labour ministers, including both Sir Stafford Cripps (who was chief trade minister as President of the Board of Trade) and Wilson himself, wanted to break out of anti-Soviet perspectives.

Wilson shared the sense of bitterness over the fact that the US, with its shrewd terms for war-time 'lend-lease', had not only colonised Britain's lucrative pre-war markets in Latin America, but had also stolen her scientific heritage by getting free manufacturing rights to British inventions in return for desperately needed supplies. Jet aircraft were one of the key technologies Wilson singled out in his later reminiscences, along with nuclear research, radar and antibiotics:

> Had Churchill been able to insist on adequate royalties for these inventions, both our war-time and our post-war balance of payments would have been very different. The Attlee government had to face the consequences of this surrender of our technological patrimony.[5]

In August 1946, the first moves towards negotiating a trade agreement with Russia were set in train. As the Board of Trade announced their plan, the head of English Electric, Sir George Nelson, took a delegation to Moscow for a fortnight, in the (unfulfilled) hope of getting a £1 million deal to sell plant to the Russians. What did not attract public attention was the simultaneous 'sweetener' offered by the British government for Rolls-Royce to supply Russia with twenty Air Force jet engines, followed that autumn by the issue of a special Board of Trade export licence to allow the deal to go ahead. Behind the scenes, in the highly secret Whitehall committees where British government business was transacted, Marshal of the Royal Air Force Lord Tedder was already fighting the deal tooth and nail on 'security' grounds.

British jet fighters and their Nene and Derwent engines had been taken off the secret list in December 1945. The Chiefs of Staff later claimed that they had agreed to items being released wholesale only after the Board of Trade had reassured them that it did not automatically follow that any

39

foreign government would be entitled to purchase such items. The engines had one key patent secret process – the heat-treatments used by the Mond Nickel Co. to make their 'Nimonic' alloys for the turbine blades, which had to withstand searingly high temperatures. Foreign governments were only getting early versions of the alloys: the British were keeping later ones for themselves.

The early versions of the engines and planes were already being sold to the US, Belgium, France, Holland, Sweden, China, Turkey, Switzerland and Argentina – some with manufacturing licences. Argentina wanted 400 Meteor IVs, for example, and Sweden was buying 70 Vampire IIIs. In March 1946, Russia had also asked to buy them, and they wanted to buy a manufacturing licence as well. On May 1, 1946 the deputy Chiefs of Staff committee had grudgingly agreed to the sale of ten sample jet engines of each type, although not the manufacturing rights. The Ministry of Supply said sales of the engine would only cut Britain's five-year technical lead over Russia by two years.[6]

The Air Staff did not like even this restricted decision. On June 25, at their insistence, the Vice-Chief of the Air Staff went to a second meeting to review it: he protested that even selling the engines as they stood would give the Russians technical information they did not yet possess. Rolls-Royce were asked 'to stall with the Russians as long as possible' while it was demanded of Cripps what information Britain would get back from Russia in return. Cripps at first appeared to cave in, agreeing 'that it was out of the question to bargain security information against goods', although he said he did not know what information was wanted in exchange from the Russians – this was up to the military. He agreed that 'Rolls-Royce . . . must make the best excuse they could to the Russians.'

In September, as the first exploratory government trade negotiations began in Moscow, Kotchourov, the head of the Russian trade delegation in London, delivered a protest to Cripps: 'He was at a loss to understand why we refused Rolls-Royce permission to export these engines to Russia when we apparently allowed them to go to other countries.' Cripps then went over the Air Chiefs' heads to Attlee, the Prime Minister, and got the sale reinstated. Attlee called in all the Chiefs of Staff and made plain his view that Russia was not to be discriminated against. The Chiefs of Staff seemed to capitulate, promising that 'they would raise no objections to the sale.'

Cripps gave the Soviet trade delegation the good news, and submitted a shopping list of urgently needed supplies Britain wanted from Russia. The most desperate shortages were of timber, to re-build Britain's blitzed housing, and of grain, for bread and cattle-feed.

The contract for the twenty engines also meant that Soviet engineers could come to England, in the normal way, to get technical instruction at the Rolls-Royce plants. The first six Russians were given visas, and duly arrived that December to spend four weeks going through the Rolls-Royce training course, as the first jet engines were crated up and put on Russian ships.

In the New Year of 1947, the Russians, further emboldened, now asked if they could apply to buy half a dozen examples of complete jet planes as well – the Meteor and Vampire fighters themselves. The Air Ministry was predictably appalled. They 'strongly opposed' such sales because it would give away tactical knowledge of 'the latest RAF front-line aircraft'. Furthermore, it would give the Russians 'fairly recent' examples of high-speed airframe construction. They were again overruled by the Cabinet Defence Committee under Attlee's chairmanship. 'No discrimination ought to be exercised against the USSR . . . once equipment has been removed from the secret list, its sale cannot be denied to the Russians.' Fortunately, the manufacturers could not offer delivery for fifteen months, so the government's moment of truth could be postponed. While Cripps told the Russians that 'favourable consideration would be given' to export licences when the planes were ready for delivery, the Ministry of Supply quietly gave the manufacturers to understand that 'they would not be displeased if delivery were delayed still further.'

In March 1947, as a prelude to the dispatch of, it was hoped, a full-scale British government trade mission to Moscow, the Russians demanded a further 'sweetener': twenty more Derwent and fifteen more Nene engines. The Cold Warriors made their counter-attack at once: they enlisted the help of MI5.

Attlee had already set up a working party of his Committee on Subversive Activities to organise a major Cold War development – wholesale anti-Communist vetting of civil servants. On March 26, 1947, the Chiefs of Staff wrote an aggressive protest about Russian spying in Britain. It was a short, four-paragraph document stamped 'Top Secret'. They made five recommendations:

1. Soviet officials should be prevented as far as possible from visiting British defence plants and the factories of defence contractors.
2. All Communist Party members should be blacklisted off secret work of any kind in Britain.
3. Soviet trade officials should be kept out of Britain by refusing them entry visas.
4. Many more items of hardware should be placed on the 'secret' list and embargoed for export.
5. The criteria for taking military equipment off the secret list in future should be made more stringent.

Clearly Tedder, who attended a cabinet committee to argue for the paper, was one of its prime movers; equally clearly, his main aim was to stop

41

Cripps' continuing sales of jet engines and planes to Russia to boost East-West trade. The Air Intelligence Staff, with help from MI5, appeared to be the authors of most of his paper. The fiercely anti-Russian Foreign Secretary Ernest Bevin, was away from London, busy banging the desk and unrolling maps before bemused US generals as he expounded the Russian threat to 'reach the Dardanelles'.[7]

In Bevin's absence, the Defence Secretary, A. V. Alexander and the Air Chief made the running against Stafford Cripps. Alexander attacked the whole notion of trade with Russia, maintaining that Britain was unlikely to get much benefit from it. However tight the 'security precautions', he said, Soviet representatives who got access to British factories were bound to pick up secret information or at least make contact with factory staff. The Russians should be kept out of British factories as much as possible. Furthermore, Russian Intelligence officers ought to be excluded by 'reducing the inflated staffs of the Soviet Embassy and the Soviet Trade Delegation in the UK.'

Undercover Soviet agents were everywhere: this had been shown by the exposure in Canada, as a result of the defection of Soviet code clerk Igor Gouzenko, of the British scientist Alan Nunn May and the High Commission secretary Kay Willsher as Soviet spies. These cases had also revealed 'how difficult it was for the Security Service [MI5] to detect and counter these activities,' argued Alexander. Communist employees would therefore have to be blacklisted out of government service from the start.

Tedder's argument was that whatever commercial gain Britain might achieve from sales to Russia of small quantities of hardware was 'negligible compared with the danger to our security':

An example of what was happening was the Russian proposal to purchase small numbers of Vampire and Meteor jet-propelled fighter aircraft. In our own interest we ought to prevent the sale to the Russians of these aircraft and licenses to manufacture them.

What the Russians clearly wanted to do, he said, was to get hold of samples of Britain's most up-to-date military hardware in order to mass-produce them themselves. There were far more Soviet military attachés at large in Britain than there were British attachés in the USSR, and British attachés were not allowed to visit Russian military and industrial plants.

Cripps fought back. Russia might shortly have a timber surplus for sale, 'which we badly need.' And there was another good reason to boost trade with Russia:

Visits by Soviet representatives to factories which are producing goods for export should be encouraged, for we will find in Russia a valuable market for our exports when the present world-wide demand for goods has passed.

It was on the issue of excluding Communists from government service that Cripps made his most revealing remark. He hinted that the priority was for Britain to make her own atom bomb, and that if this required the help of scientists with Communist sympathies it was a price worth paying. There was, indeed, some justification for MI5's later complaints that the Labour government was prepared to give disloyal nuclear scientists like Klaus Fuchs the benefit of the doubt because it needed their services so urgently.

Considering the determined scheme at the time by the US to freeze Britain out of nuclear technology, this attitude scarcely proved any 'red plot' by Labour ministers; it simply demonstrated once again a truth invisible to the Secret Service mind – that there were sometimes more things to fear in life than a little Russian espionage.

According to the minutes of the meeting, Chuter Ede, the Home Secretary, told the committee that it would in any case be very difficult to blacklist Communists on a large scale. Although . . .

> He was most concerned about the risks which arose from the employment of persons of Communist sympathies in the higher scientific posts where they were in a position to obtain and disclose to the Soviets secret information of special importance . . . it had to be remembered that many scientists had a strong and genuine belief that all scientific knowledge ought to be made freely available for the common benefit of mankind. He saw no practicable way of dealing with most of these persons except by prosecution after definite breaches of the Official Secrets Act had been proved.

Cripps made his point even more bluntly:

> A policy of removing all known Communists who were engaged on secret scientific work may seriously cripple scientific development in the United Kingdom.

He was supported by the Air Secretary and the Minister of Supply, George Strauss. The latter pointed out that most of the factories in question had a mixture of secret and non-secret contracts. This made bans on Russian visits hard to organise. Even in his own department, where he had dutifully called for a list of all known communists on the staff to be compiled, it was difficult to draw a line between the secret and non-secret jobs.

As Prime Minister, Clement Attlee had the last word. The Air Chiefs were rebuffed again on the jets: 'It is obvious that once an item has been removed from the secret list, its sale cannot be prevented.' Nor would the banning of known Communists from secret work counter the problem of undeclared Communists which would require thorough probing of would-be government officials. In what would later turn out to have been a major understatement, Attlee observed, 'Some of those who are or might become important Soviet agents are probably not open members of the Communist Party.'

For the rest, the Chiefs of Staff got some satisfaction. It was agreed that Soviet visits to government defence plants 'should be restricted so far as possible'.

Cripps had got a reasonably free hand to use the promised planes and engines as bargaining counters in his bid to secure a trade agreement. A few days later, on April 2, Cripps met Kotchourov, the Soviet trade representative in London. Delivery dates for the engines and planes, he said, 'could best be settled in Moscow in connection with other current factors'. The military hardware the Russians wanted so badly was being dangled as bait.

A little more than a fortnight later, on April 18, Harold Wilson, the new young Secretary for Overseas Trade, was bumping through the skies to Moscow via Berlin in what he called 'a tatty old aircraft hired from a private company'. The party was made up of four men and two women – Wilson's assistant, Eileen Lane, and Miss Montague, secretary to John Leckie, one of the Board of Trade officials. Wilson had an invitation to explore the ground for a comprehensive trade agreement with the USSR. Briefing him before the three-week trip, Cripps had told him he fully intended to give the Russians their export licence, for the engines at least, but Wilson could affect at first to take a tough line.

Wilson in fact took a tougher line than Cripps had expected. When the Soviet trade minister, Anastas Mikoyan, brought up Cripps' promise to settle delivery dates in Moscow, Wilson coolly replied that he was agreeable to discussing this question, but delivery dates were 'a problem'. The Board of Trade were meanwhile cabling that 'The President [Cripps] is anxious to fulfil the pledge he made to Kotchourov. We ought now to issue export licences both for the aircraft and the 35 engines.' Wilson cabled back that negotiations had stalled badly; Mikoyan was demanding easier terms for the £100 million war debts Russia already owed: 'Would you please ensure export licences are not (repeat not) issued for either engines or aircraft.' His sang-froid appeared to pay off: Wilson threatened to return home on the spot and on April 28 his delegation cabled back that negotiations had improved again – 'The Russians want to re-open credit agreements along with machine tools, jets and lumber machines.' The Russians were 'particularly anxious' to get their planes and engines. When could London actually offer delivery?

Cripps replied in a 'top secret' cypher that Rolls-Royce could hand over seven engines per month as already arranged, starting that July; the aircraft were a bigger problem. The number of planes the Russians wanted were 'negligible' compared to the total being built in 1947, 'but the Air Council, for security reasons, are not anxious to improve on delivery dates.' To date, the only foreigners to have got special deliveries were the Argentines; in an unsubtle bargaining hint Cripps said he was sure the Russians would understand that the Argentines had got favoured treatment because they had struck a parallel deal to sell food to the hungry British. Cripps told Wilson that if he thought concessions on delivery of the planes would 'make all the difference to our getting really large supplies from the Russians,' he would go and argue it out with his colleagues. The exploratory talks ended on a reasonable note. The groundwork had been laid.

The export licences for the second batch of engines were issued 'following, it is understood, personal consideration by the President of the Board of Trade.' The total price for the two transactions, totalling fifty-five engines, was approximately £277,000. Ernest Bevin later claimed the decision had been made behind his back.

At the end of June, Wilson returned to Moscow for a marathon five-week substantive negotiating session. This time he took a party of thirteen experts, including three women – Eileen Lane; a second personal assistant, Miss E. M. Goddard; and John Leckie's secretary, Miss Montague. They flew to Russia in a somewhat larger Skyways Consul plane.

Before the delegation's departure, the purpose of their mission was, it appears, deliberately leaked. A Tory MP, William Shepherd, put down a curiously oblique Parliamentary question. What arrangements had been made, he asked Stafford Cripps, 'whereby the Soviet Union receives industrial and scientific secrets in return for supplies of materials?' Cripps replied evasively, in writing, 'I am not aware of any arrangement of the kind.'

When the negotiations began, the Russians demanded as the price of their continued co-operation a promise of immediate delivery of three Vampires and three Meteors, as well as the balance of the fifty-five jet engines already ordered and supposedly on their way. The talks deadlocked, and on July 4 Wilson threatened to withdraw. 'It would certainly be worthwhile to indicate [to Kotchourov],' he cabled Cripps, 'that the jet aircraft on which they were counting will not be forthcoming, though how they are to be blocked is a matter for your consideration.'

According to Foreign Office records, 'the Chiefs of Staff had opposed the sale of the six aircraft, but the Prime Minister approved and the aircraft were promised orally, largely as a bargaining counter in the talks. The Russians were warned that delivery would not be for twelve or fifteen months after the date of firm order.' They were, however, permitted to receive the second batch of jet engines. Delivery started immediately.

These negotiating sessions must have been an extraordinary experience for Wilson's party, marooned in Moscow in the National Hotel. Wilson had a healthy respect for his chief adversary in the talks, Anastas Mikoyan: 'He was an Armenian, a race noted for their superb negotiating ability as carpet-traders.' They kept up friendly links for years afterwards. The Russians interspersed all-night negotiating sessions with compulsory drinking bouts conducted in Armenian brandy to the accompaniment of innumerable toasts to Anglo-Soviet friendship. Wilson enjoyed playing the professional Yorkshireman to Mikoyan's professional Armenian – he took up smoking a pipe in the hope that it would make him appear enigmatic.[8]

Wilson subsequently boasted that at a six-hour lunch given by Mikoyan he had become 'probably the only one of Her Majesty's ministers who had drunk a Soviet Minister under the table.' His young secretary – he did not specify whether this was Miss Lane or Miss Goddard – had been the heroine of the occasion, he said, staying the course and leading the company at the end in a rendering of 'Auld Lang Syne'.[9]

There was no doubt that all the party's hotel rooms were bugged and that the liquor-filled British delegates were spied on ceaselessly by the NKVD in the hope of compromising or out-guessing them. Their chief target was Wilson himself, and on one occasion when he was in the company of a young woman member of his staff the NKVD took a photograph of the pair, which they kept on file, presumably intending to use it to support any future blackmail attempt. (One MI5 officer insists that the photograph was of a Soviet woman.) The Russians certainly made no attempt to blackmail Wilson at the time, and there is no evidence to suggest that the photograph was anything other than innocent, misleading, or faked. It was not until almost thirty years later that it surfaced – passed into the hands of MI6, who probably got it from a Soviet agent. While it had never been of any use to the USSR, the photograph was grist to the mill of MI6 – they handed it over to the K6 secret registry section of MI5, from whence the news spread like wildfire among the 'Wilson coterie' there, just before Wilson resigned his premiership for good in 1976.

By July 14, 1947, Wilson had become more accommodating in his attitude over the jet planes. He made what is the nearest thing to a pro-Russian statement in the available records. Wilson clearly hoped Cripps could get him an attractive delivery data for the jet aircraft after all:

Please telegraph to me the President's views . . . about jet aircraft. It may be that in last resort if President is prepared to agree to an approach to his colleagues, this will be a valuable concession to throw into the pot, possibly saving us millions in finance.

Cripps replied three days later: 'Ministers decided to consult air ministry before authorising any concession on deliveries . . . We will telegraph further as soon as possible.'

But that was the end of it: the Air Ministry reacted with a predictable blast of rage, and Bevin's Foreign Office stiffened the terms for repayment of Russian war-time debts. Furthermore, and most significantly, the US began to attack Cripps and Wilson for being soft on Communism. The draft trade agreement abruptly stalled and Wilson returned home, temporarily cheated of his triumph.

Close to midnight, the delegation's small propeller-driven plane landed in London: its brakes failed and the plane ran off the end of the runway into a stream. Wilson cracked a rib, and Miss Goddard badly injured her head. Back in London, the atmosphere was sulphurous.

The Foreign Office minuted: 'Alarmed criticisms were being made in America that we were now giving our latest aircraft and information to a potential enemy. Reassurances were given by [Bevin] to the US Ambassador in August 1947 and later to Mr Marshall [the US Secretary of State], explaining that the only aircraft to be sold were on the open list.'

Bevin's tone among his own colleagues was much more violent than the reassuring phrases to the Americans might suggest: on August 8, at a Defence Committee meeting called to enable the Foreign Secretary to have his say about visas for Soviet trade visitors, Bevin laid about him vehemently. The Russians had now put in yet another request for forty more engines. In the Cabinet Office minute's decorous prose, he was 'profoundly disturbed at the situation revealed'.

He had not been a party to the original decision to let these engines go out of the country. The removal of an item such as these engines from the secret list should only be authorised by the Defence Committee.

His discovery was that no fewer than seventeen Russian engineers were now applying for entry to England for up to seven months to be trained on the engines, as well as three members of the trade delegation currently in residence at Rolls-Royce, representing 'a very difficult and quite unnecessary problem'.

Hearing that 'The Security authorities [MI5] would have preferred that these Russians be excluded altogether,' and that Britain might have already lost the monopoly over 'certain secret manufacturing processes,' Bevin angrily demanded a full report. The Chiefs of Staff, pouring petrol on the flames, said they 'were much disturbed at the advantage the Russians were gaining from the sales of these engines.' Unable to prevent their sale, the Air Staff wanted at least to stop any more engines being handed over, and to safeguard the secrets of steel treatments used in their manufacture – these, they hinted, might have been 'prejudiced' already.

The sudden introduction into the debate of the views of the US government was not a coincidence. Britain desperately needed the goodwill of America in the summer of 1947. When lend-lease had been abruptly cut off at the war's end, Britain had only averted bankruptcy by a huge US loan, the terms of which were rapidly crippling her. In June General George Marshall, the US Secretary of State, held out the prospect of a comprehensive aid programme (what was to become the Marshall Plan). This now took priority over all else. Selling jets to Russia was an irrelevant luxury compared to the urgent necessity of pleading with the owner of the US pawnshop to fetch out the keys to his safe.

At a full meeting with Cripps and Tedder on September 24, chaired by George Strauss, the Minister of Supply, the Air Chiefs' counter-attack finally triumphed. They produced a resolution passed by the Defence Committee at the end of 1945 which authorised the Chiefs of Staff to issue special directives about disclosure of information to Russia. Such a special directive had now been issued, they said, which demanded 'strict reciprocity' in any deals with the Russians. Tedder said: 'There is a very efficient aircraft industry in Russia . . . Thus there is something of value which we can obtain from the Soviet government.' The Air Staff 'strongly opposed' the latest Russian request to buy another forty engines:

> They take the line that when the original decision was taken to supply a total of 20 engines . . . their main concern was that the Russian would obtain additional technical information . . . But now that the Russians have asked for a total of 95 engines, the Air Staff strongly oppose the sale since the more of these engines the Russians obtain, the more they can install and operate them in front-line aircraft and the better is their chance of reducing the gap between the fighting efficiency of the Soviet Air Force and the RAF.

Furthermore, the Russians were now producing eleven different types of jet aircraft powered mainly by units of German design. Possession of numerous Rolls-Royce engines would help the Russians carry out performance trials to decide which types of unit to copy.

Tedder's trump card was that MI5 had changed their tune. Although they had previously professed themselves 'reasonably satisfied' with security precautions at the various aero plants, 'the Security Services . . . now point out that it would be possible for foreign engineers to contact during off-duty periods, factory personnel engaged on secret work.'

The MI5 officers involved in giving this new piece of advice in support of the RAF and against the Labour Ministers Wilson and Cripps will appear again in this story. Although the ex-policeman Sir Percy Sillitoe headed MI5, these reports would have come via the head of 'D' Division, which dealt with Air Force liaison, and of 'C' Division, which handled security precautions at commercial plants. 'C' Division was run by the stoop-shouldered and tubercular Roger Hollis, who, lacking a degree, had clawed his way into MI5 on the strength of social connections in the 1930s, stayed in for life, and rose to be its unimaginative head in 1956, when his boss, Dick Goldsmith White, was suddenly switched to lead MI6. The head of 'D' Division was Martin Furnival Jones, before the war a rather dull and dour solicitor with the City firm of Slaughter & May. He too stayed in MI5 all his life and succeeded Hollis as its head in 1966. When Wilson was Prime Minister, the two men repeatedly clashed, Furnival Jones accusing a number of Wilson's ministers of being 'security risks'. The historical record would suggest that Furnival Jones – if his memory was long and his files comprehensive – would have recalled doubts about Wilson's insufficient zealousness for 'security' stretching back over twenty years.

The jet planes were never delivered. Nor were any more engines. When Cripps and Wilson, with the country in difficult economic straits, planned to return in the winter of 1947 for a final attempt to tie up the Moscow trade agreement, they had to drop the jet aircraft as a potential inducement. Lord Inverchapel, British ambassador in Washington, was briefed to tell the Americans, in confidence, the position. The 'principle of reciprocity' was to be applied to all countries and all armaments, whether or not on the secret list. 'This would avoid any appearance of discrimination,' but, as the US was to be privately told, what it meant was that, as far as the Russians were concerned, 'We were to give them no more engines, equipment or information than they gave us.'

That same November, the British Commercial Counsellor and Air Attaché in Moscow were ordered by Bevin to go to the Kremlin and see Krutkov of the Ministry of Foreign Trade. The Russian was discount-enanced to be told that 'they were interested in buying some Soviet aircraft and in inspecting a range of Soviet air equipment as the Russians had been doing here. They implied orally that, if reciprocity was refused, it would have an adverse effect on outstanding and future Russian orders from the UK ... After this, neither HMG, the Embassy, nor Rolls-Royce heard anything more from the Russians on the subject.'

Nonetheless, Wilson set off for Moscow for the third time in December 1947. In the hard winter of 1947, Britain was in a pitiful state – knee-deep in snow, its citizens had no coal, and bread was rationed. The Foreign Office had been persuaded to relent on Russia's debt repayment terms; and the Russians had had a good harvest. On this visit, Wilson seems to have been more concerned about eavesdropping: he took with him as a political aide his Parliamentary Private Secretary, the Scottish MP Tom Cook.

> He was an agreeable companion, moderately to the left but not extremely so, and a strong critic of communism. More than that he was a highly qualified electrician. I had already made considerable use of the bugs which I knew would have been planted in my suite, though as I did not know their exact location I had to speak loud and clear. Tom was sent to find them and achieved considerable success. What shocked me was his discovery that there was one under the bath ...[10]

The affable Mikoyan did his best to curdle Wilson's blood by describing how he had witnessed a senior minister of Stalin's being executed by shooting at a 'Cabinet' meeting, but Wilson remained undaunted and, after an all-night bargaining session, came out with not only the prospect of annual timber shipments, but also with what even the Conservatives agreed was a major prize – in return for machine tools and railway equipment, the Russians would ship to Britain, at a reasonable price, 750,000 tons of desperately needed cattle feed over the winter. This averted mass slaughter of herds. Wilson gives a vivid – and boastful – picture in his memoirs of how he out-faced Mikoyan until 5a.m., refusing to accept stalling invitations of dinner with Stalin, while the NKVD unsuccessfully sought to find out the price Britain had paid Australia for comparable wheat purchases. When the breakthrough came, Wilson records:

Tom Williams [the Agriculture Minister], on hearing the details of the agreement, had burst into tears of sheer relief.

When the knowledge of the 1947 delivery of the fifty-five jet engines eventually became public, it became an intermittent Cold War football. The Foreign Office recorded: 'In April 1948, further American indignation had to be soothed with a categorical statement to the effect that no aircraft had been sold to Russia since the end of the war, and that no engines on the secret list had been or were going to be supplied.' In May 1948, the Conservative MP Peter Thorneycroft demanded and got from Harold Wilson details of the jet deliveries. In November 1948, following the Berlin blockade, Conservative MPs were briefed to ask about Soviet officials being allowed to inspect British jet production. There was a flurry in the newspapers about 'Russian espionage.'

While Wilson was still President of the Board of Trade, Finland also made an attempt in 1950 to order civil jet aircraft. The papers do not clearly show whether the Board of Trade backed this: it is a point of some interest because MI5 officers later claimed that Finland's trade relations were part of the pattern of Soviet espionage around Harold Wilson. Finland, a 'neutralist' country under Russia's shadow, was regarded as pro-Soviet.

It was also later alleged by a former Labour minister, Hartley Shawcross, who repeatedly called Wilson a Communist 'fellow-traveller', that an aircraft company paid large bribes to a senior Board of Trade civil servant unconnected with Wilson himself in the hope of getting export licences to sell planes in this period to an unidentified Communist country. What has come to light is a rather embarrassed Foreign Office telegram to the embassy in Washington – 'This telegram is of particular secrecy and should be retained by the authorised recipient and not passed on' – asking for the US attitude to be discreetly sounded out on whether their embargoes on jet plane sales to the Soviet bloc covered Yugoslavia, China and Finland:

50

The potential market in Finland is not negligible and in making this self-denying ordinance, we are sacrificing an export to security ... You will appreciate that we are not anxious to raise this matter directly with the Americans because of the sad history of the Nenes and Derwents which went to Russia.

In Washington, it soon passed into folklore among right-wing opponents of the Marshall Plan that the British Socialists were using America's money to arm Russia. The Republican Senator Malone from Nevada was not unusual in a 1950 debate when he alleged:

Jet planes which Russia is supposed to be turning out by mass production are copies of jet planes sold to Russia by England.[11]

When the Tories returned to power on October 25, 1951, at the height of the Korean War, military Intelligence men had their revenge on Labour. In January 1951, a Conservative candidate, J. Wentworth Day, had already claimed that 'one of the most distinguished men in the aircraft industry' had tipped him off that Russia had got hold of steel treatment specifications as well as the jet engines:

Armed with these secrets, they have put the Mig-15 turbo-jet into the air – a deadly weapon in the hands of our deadliest enemies. That is Socialist treachery. There is no other word for it. The Minister responsible should be impeached.[12]

Eleven months later the same William Sheperd MP who had been tipped off about the original 1947 jet negotiations fed a parliamentary question to the new Conservative Under-Secretary for Air, Nigel Birch. A Mig-15 had been recovered off the Korean coast: Birch was happy to tell the House that 'Examination of captured parts of Mig-15 fighters has shown they are powered by engines which are copies of the Nene.'[13] His answer was based on 'information supplied by the Intelligence experts of the Air Ministry,' he said. It enabled Shepherd to respond: 'Is it not clear from that reply that the sale of these engines was not merely an act of foolishness, but struck a real blow against the free world?' Less emphasis was given in the subsequent publicity to the fact that the British Meteors and Vampires which used those engines were by now thoroughly obsolete, and that the Russians had developed the Nene extensively by their own efforts, to give it extra thrust. The strongest claim, made later by Duncan Sandys, the Conservative Supply Minister, was that, as predicted by Labour ministers themselves back in 1946, the Russians might have saved two years development by the purchase. Wilson's 1947 role in the project to deliver entire jet planes to Moscow against Air Intelligence objections, remained a secret. Wilson himself chose

51

not to refer to the jet engines at all in his 1986 reminiscences of the Board of Trade years, *The Making of a Prime Minister*.

The saga of the jets for Russia had all the elements of the later smears which developed against Wilson as Prime Minister – he found himself on the opposite side of the political divide to an anti-Communist gallery comprising the Intelligence services, the Labour Right, the Conservative Party and the US administration. It was during this eposide that the false suggestion that Harold Wilson was secretly acting in the interests of the Soviet Union first emerged. It was to be made again and again in the years that followed.

This early period in Harold Wilson's life was later also quarried by his enemies for evidence of lechery. Two false stories were circulated subsequently by members of the Intelligence services – that Wilson got on badly with his wife, and that, while in Canada, he had slept with Barbara Castle, who was, twenty years later, to become his Cabinet colleague.

Barbara Castle, born Barbara Betts in Bradford, was abrasive, devastating, endlessly talkative – a pre-war Oxford disciple of Stafford Cripps, who had sat up late at night in her tiny Bloomsbury attic reading Marx with Labour activist Michael Foot, and writing columns with him in the left-wing newspaper *Tribune*. She was one of the most attractive and energetic of Labour's young left-wing MPs, and Cripps had taken her on in 1945 as a Parliamentary Private Secretary – an unpaid political aide. The thirty-one-year-old Wilson inherited her when he succeeded Cripps as President of the Board of Trade in 1947, and kept her on as his PPS. Her political energy and talent were enormous; she was also formidably sexually attractive. Marcia Williams, who became Wilson's political secretary, could record, even ten years later:

> She likes pretty clothes and has an eye for fashion. Her nails are always polished, her hair beautifully done . . . Barbara was always very much a woman. In those days she was an extremely attractive young woman with her petite figure, beautiful pink and white complexion and gorgeous auburn hair. She looked dainty and feminine but she had this razor-sharp mind and powerful personality – a colourful person thrown into sharp relief by Harold Wilson himself. In those days he was, by his own admission, 'a bit of a pudding' with his addiction to detail, facts, figures – a character whose greyish tones contrasted sharply with Barbara's brilliant hues.[14]

Wilson, the 'Yorkshire pudding', certainly had a wistful and schoolboyish eye for a pretty face. Those close to him at this time say he would occasionally make roguish remarks of the 'I dreamed about you last night, Barbara' variety. Similarly, in the Board of Trade, where Wilson busied himself, among other things, in promoting the native British film industry against the Hollywood megalith, there was mild departmental amusement at how bowled over he was by one film actress who came to listen to his parliamentary speeches on the subject. Wilson had a crush not so much on movie actresses in particular as on the movies in general, which lasted all his life. While President of the Board of Trade he launched the British Film Finance Corporation and poured much of its money into the productions of Hungarian-Jewish tycoon Alexander Korda, who made the cinematic flop, *Bonnie Prince Charlie* and the masterly *The Third Man*. It is unlikely that Wilson realised that Korda was also a major British Intelligence secret 'asset'. Much of the finance for his pre-war company, London Film Productions had also come via government intervention in the shape of Colonel Claude Dansey, vice-chief of MI6. Dansey used London Films as international cover for the agents of his 'Z' organisation, and Korda financed Jewish anti-Nazi refugees who supplied MI6 with Intelligence – much of it wrong.[15]

In April 1949 Wilson launched a new drive for dollar exports. Because of an economic recession in the US, fewer British goods were being bought, and 'Export or Die' was the slogan of the day. Firms which could sell to the US or Canada basked in ministerial favour, and Wilson threw himself into the role of Britain's chief commercial traveller. The following month he invited Barbara Castle to fly out to Canada with him on an extended sales tour.

It was scarcely a seduction ploy – the energetic young Castle had been badgering him for months not to be exluded from trips merely because she was a woman. His others PPS, Tom Cook, had accompanied him on the plum trip to Moscow to get the trade agreement. Wilson's sexuality – of an entirely blameless kind – was to prove of far less significance in his life than the fact that he liked talented women and he liked to give them political opportunities. He was not, despite his masculine-minded Yorkshire background, a male chauvinist pig. The same could not be said of many of those who spread false gossip about him later.

In the event, male chauvinism made the trip rather a fiasco from Barbara Castle's point of view. The Canadians had a strictly limited view of women. In each town at which the plane touched down, the routine was the same. First the young political aide had to listen to a repeat of Harold Wilson's basic speech in which he praised British goods. His audience of businessmen would then point out that British goods were too expensive (which they were until devaluation forced a new realism on Britain), and that British manufacturers insisted on exporting styles no one wanted to buy, such as, for example, white cotton towels when the market was for colour-coordinated ones. After these predictable exchanges, Wilson would retire to a stag dinner with the local male politicians, from which Barbara Castle was excluded.

When she finally protested at the last port of call, a dinner was duly arranged for her as well – with the politicians' wives in a separate anteroom. By all accounts, she ended the trip in a very bad temper. 'No, I did not go to bed with him,' she says, laughing at the thought forty years later, 'far from it.'

The other element in Wilson's early life which was later fastened on by MI5, was his relationship with his wife. Mary Baldwin, the shy, unshowy daughter of a Lancashire congregational minister, met Wilson when he was a schoolboy and married him in 1940, when he was a young don about to be directed into work in the war-time civil service. She thought she was marrying a university lecturer, and made it clear in subsequent years that she did not relish the hectic and aggressive scramble of life in international politics. Wilson himself says:

> What she would have preferred would have been to go through life as the wife of an Oxford don, a pleasure she was to enjoy for only a few brief months in 1945.[16]

In the early years of his career as a rising young minister, Wilson spent far too many days and even months away from home. At the end of 1946, for example, Attlee sent him to Washington for almost three months to negotiate the setting-up of FAO, the international Food and Agriculture Organisation. Mary remained alone in Oxford with their small son Robin. The foreign trips were frequent; Mary's hopes of continuing to live in the academic atmosphere of Oxford soon foundered while her husband camped in a London flat. As she said in 1947, 'He is supposed to visit us at weekends, but out of the last fifteen, he's had two free ones.'[17] The family eventually moved into a London house, but Mary still refused to have it turned into a political salon. This meant that Wilson did his socialising and political conspiring elsewhere, accidentally laying himself open to repeated attempts to associate his name with sexual scandal. When he because more firmly entrenched in power, his widely assorted enemies resorted to increasingly outrageous slanders: they suggested that his wife wanted to divorce him; that he had slept with not only Barbara Castle but later also his political secretary Marcia Williams; that he had fathered children on Mrs Williams; that he had exposed himself to blackmail by the KGB in Moscow by sexual misconduct. All these false stories were collected up by the Intelligence services of London and Washington, there to be circulated by officers or former officers of MI6, MI5, the CIA and the FBI.

The earliest of these stories dates back even before the Canadian trip with Barbara Castle in 1949. It was alleged that, in 1947, at the time of Wilson's prolonged Washington visit, the strain on his marriage became acute. As a result, his wife met a Polish academic in Oxford and they fell in love. In order to maintain his political career, the false story went, Wilson

54

patched his marriage up. A similar story, with different circumstances, was to surface thirteen years later, again in an attempt to discredit Wilson when he looked likely to win the Labour leadership. Wilson manifested understandable resentment when a version of the false 1947 story finally appeared in print in a 1977 biography, *Harold Wilson, Yorkshire Walter Mitty*, by a reputable Canadian political journalist, Andrew Roth. Roth said that Mary Wilson 'met another man' in 1947, and quoted one of Mary Wilson's own poems as rather unlikely evidence. Wilson issued a libel writ challenging a variety of points in the book – on the 1947 story, Roth was unable to mount any defence, and Wilson was awarded £10,000 damages. The book was withdrawn.

The sexual stories were untrue. It is, however, worth asking a question that will recur in the history of rumour and innuendo attached to Wilson. What if the stories had actually been accurate? What would it have mattered if – like most other people – the Wilsons had occasionally found their long marriage in difficulties and the occasional outside sexual relationship had occurred? After all, even if every one of the false rumours had been correct, they would scarcely have added up to a picture of depravity reminiscent of the Borgias. Far from it. They might have fluttered an eyebrow or two in Hampstead Garden Suburb.

What made the difference was the growing post-war world of 'security'. As evidence mounted that sexual blackmail was a regular Soviet Intelligence technique, the British and US Intelligence agencies found themselves increasingly licenced to pry into the possible sexual peccadilloes of an ever-widening range of officials and employees who had access to so-called 'secrets'. Once it was ruled that 'character defects' could turn the average adulterer, homosexual or drunkard into a 'security risk', it was open season on human frailty. Over a generation MI5 thus came to exercise a new and unpleasant power in the intimate lives not merely of prime ministers, but of many hundreds of thousands of people.

There was a third aspect of Wilson's early political career that made him vulnerable to MI5 rumour: his Jewish businessmen friends, many of them involved in East-West trade. For all its battery of rationing and controls, the 1945 Attlee government did not eschew capitalists. Indeed, it needed their skills, and was in a position to issue them with licences and permits worth a great deal of money. Wilson, first at the Ministry of Works and then at the Board of Trade, had a great deal to do with timber. He began a long relationship with the big London firm of timber importers, Montague Meyer. Wilson says:

The arrangement derived posthumously from Ernie Bevin, who had known old man Meyer before the war when he had had to negotiate with him on trade union matters and had developed a high regard for his straight dealing.[18]

Roth, Wilson's biographer, says that Wilson's boss, the Minister of Works George Tomlinson, was also a friend of the Meyers. He dates the beginning of the link to autumn 1946, when Wilson was in Washington and met Tom Meyer, Montague's son, who was touring the US looking for timber supplies. The Government's promise to re-build blitzed houses depended on getting timber, which had to be bought with scarce foreign currency. On his return to London, Wilson helped organise a Board of Trade purchasing mission which encountered Meyer in the US and did a deal with him for American timber. (Whitehall had insisted that no US timber was available and had briefed the mission accordingly.) More supplies were purchased from Finland and Sweden, and, as we have seen, timber was high on Wilson's negotiating agenda in Moscow. He recalls that 'Montague Meyer was one of the beneficiaries. They needed fresh supplies of timber and it was one of the few commodities the Soviet Union had for export.'[19]

There were many other entrepreneurs Wilson encountered at the Board of Trade. He met small businessmen through Labour peer Lord Piercy's Industrial and Commercial Finance Corporation – one such man was Harry Kissin, a Liberal commodity trader with a Russian-Jewish background. Another was Frank Schon, Austrian-Jewish this time – Wilson helped him to get state backing for a detergent plant in Cumberland, and later for a sulphuric acid plant in the same area.

The publisher George Weidenfeld was another friend, who brought out Wilson's first book, *New Deal for Coal* in 1945. Like Alexander Korda, he had, according to Wilson, a record as an Intelligence 'insider':

I was recommended to a new publisher named George Weidenfeld, who had come to Britain as a refugee before the war and had done valuable work in various secret departments. He has since published nearly all my books.[20]

There were to be other Jewish emigrés who were very much Intelligence 'outsiders'. MI5 tried to attack them in later years with hints or direct accusations that they were pro-Soviet Bloc. It was easy to do so when they came from Central Europe – where else would Jewish refugees come from? – and when they sometimes made a living by energetically exploiting trading and family links behind the Iron Curtain. For Wilson, of course, it made for a community of interest: he appreciated and could help people who, like him, sought to strike trade deals with the East. He also appreciated people who were, like him, outsiders in the power-structure of English society. One of Wilson's political objectives was to 'release the energies' of unfashionable, largely ignored British technicians and entrepreneurs. He eventually turned

this dream into a public-relations slogan about 'the white heat of technology', but any student of Wilson becomes aware that it was a genuine
political attitude. And just as he liked the vigorous outsiders who built
themselves up from nothing by sheer sweat and by giving people what they
wanted, they – because they were excluded by the British business establishment – tended to adhere to the Labour Party in return.

Among these outsiders were Joseph Kagan – a raincoat manufacturer
from Lithuania with a factory near Huddersfield in Yorkshire – and Rudy
Sternberg, a chemical engineer from Austria who opened a button factory
in Lancashire in 1948 and later traded in fertiliser with East Germany.
Another was Beattie Lapsker, who married Dick Plummer, a newspaper
executive involved in managing the Labour government's unsuccessful
groundnut-growing scheme in Africa – the firm of Meyer was also called in
to handle timber clearance there. Some were apparently anti-Soviet, such as
Kagan, whose family had owned factories in Lithuania before the Soviet
takeover. Some, like Sternberg, seemed to the anti-Communist mind to care
more about money than about the fate of Soviet satellites. Others, such as
Plummer, who later became a Labour MP, were more or less leftish in
sentiment. Tom Driberg recalls in his memoirs: 'Between the wars he had
been well to the left; but in August 1939, when the Nazi-Soviet pact hit us
staggeringly, he burst into my room and exclaimed: 'You can include me
out as a Friend of the Soviet Union!'[21]

Oddly, although all these people were made peers by Wilson, and many
later contributed towards his political expenses, he omits any mention of
them in his published reminiscences, even Beattie (later Lady) Plummer,
who was one of his closest personal friends. Perhaps he did not want to re-
open controversy.

Others who came into the unhappy category of Jewish Labour supporters
vilified behind their backs by members of the Intelligence services included
Sidney (later Lord) Bernstein, the founder of Granada; Solly Zuckerman,
the Wilson government's scientific adviser; and the Czech-born newspaper
tycoon Robert Maxwell. Needless to say, none of them were Soviet agents
or sympathisers in any shape or form whatsoever.

There was a deeply equivocal attitude towards Jews within the British
Intelligence services: George Kennedy Young, by this time rising steadily
towards the post of vice-chief of MI6, referred to Jews as 'snipcocks' and
later led an unashamedly racialist political group. Young thought of Jews
as 'cosmopolitan' and not truly loyal to Britain. The same kind of sentiment
was uttered privately by Peter Wright, although he protested later – and
correctly – that he had many Jewish personal friends. There was also a
more understandable pattern of anti-Zionism: many young Intelligence
officers learned hostility towards Jews from the bitter bloodshed of the
British mandate in Palestine. In the immediate post-war years, the policy of

the anti-Communist Labour Right was implacably hostile towards the Jews in Palestine – Bevin appears to believe that a Zionist Israel would become a Soviet puppet. Wilson himself says:

> It is not too strong a phrase to say that Ernie was anti-Semitic. In his policy for Palestine and the Middle East generally, he never accepted the conference decisions and election pledges of the Labour Party.[22]

There is one final aspect of Wilson's dealings with businessmen in the first post-war Labour administration which his enemies tried to use. This was corruption. In August 1948, Wilson's chief official, the Permanent Secretary, approached him about 'a very serious matter'. A firm was complaining they were being asked for bribes to escape prosecution for a breach of paper-rationing rules. Wilson authorised co-operation with the police and went to see Attlee that night.

Wilson's own junior minister, John Belcher, was implicated and disgraced in the one major corruption scandal which the Attlee government threw up. Wilson himself had to be cross-examined by the Lynskey Tribunal, set up with judicial powers to crucify those involved. Attlee required high moral standards in these matters. Wilson himself quotes the Prime Minister's private warning to ministers about what Wilson coyly terms 'industrial contacts':

> A Tory minister can sleep in ten different women's beds in a week. A Labour minister gets it in the neck if he looks at his neighbour's wife over the garden fence.[23]

For the last two months of 1948, Wilson's department was put under ruthless public scrutiny by Hartley Shawcross, the Attorney-General who was later to leave the Labour Party and become one of Wilson's most hostile critics. What emerged was a rather sordid story of petty corruption. A 'spiv', the Polish-Jewish fixer Sidney Stanley, plied Belcher with gifts of a down-market nature – a free holiday in Margate, a new suit and a gold cigarette case. He then introduced him to the Sherman brothers, who ran the firm facing prosecution, and Belcher decided to drop the case. After the tribunal's finding that favours had been exchanged, Belcher resigned his seat. Wilson was not implicated.

Harold Wilson continued as President of the Board of Trade until April 23, 1951, when, at the age of thirty-five, he made a dramatic decision to resign from the government. In doing so, he aligned himself irrevocably, and for the rest of his political life, with the wrong faction in the Cold War. The resignation was an anti-American act. It was therefore seen as a pro-Communist one. In a world apparently teetering on the brink of global war, Britain was under pressure to become a re-militarised society, full of

Intelligence 'secrets' and operating as an agent of US foreign policy on a short leash. Hugh Gaitskell, the Chancellor of the Exchequer and a former administrator in the SOE, was the chief cheer-leader for the United States and the 'anti-Communists'. Aneurin Bevan, and Harold Wilson, were on the other, losing, side.

Since the outbreak of hostilities in Korea in 1949, those who saw the war as the latest move in a Communist plan for world domination had possessed the loudest voices. Britain was already sending conscripts to fight alongside the US in Korea, but in December 1950 Attlee, alarmed by American belligerence, flew to Washington and pleaded with President Truman not to endorse General MacArthur's threats to drop atomic bombs on China, which was backing the North Koreans. His mission succeeded but the price was an agreement that committed both Britain and the United States 'to increase their military capabilities as rapidly as possible.' The US demanded that Britain launch a huge re-armament programme – £6 billion was at first suggested, later scaled down to £4.7 billion. Wilson protested that it would wreck Britain's economy, and certainly wreck Wilson's own ambitions to solve Britain's nagging balance of payments crisis. He argued that a huge, over-fast arms-building project would cause inflation and create stockpiles of rusting unassembled parts waiting for production bottlenecks to be solved elsewhere: 'All we would get would be a lot more Army officers with cars to ride around in.'[24]

Wilson's resignation was overshadowed by that of Aneurin Bevan, the brilliant Welsh left-winger who had created the National Health Service. He was the chief totem of the Labour Left, unlike Wilson, the colourless technocrat. Bevan had exploded in rage at Gaitskell's attempt to make people pay for false teeth and spectacles in order to help finance a re-armed anti-Communist Britain.

Their resignations, together with that of a third minister, John Freeman, split the Labour Party. Henceforth, Wilson was one of the stars of the group of left-wingers, known as the Bevanites, who harried the Labour leadership, dominated by Gaitskell, throughout the 1950s. It was a war, literally to the death – it was only to end with the death of Bevan, followed by the sudden death of Gaitskell in 1963, when Wilson stepped triumphantly into his shoes. There may have been an element of calculation in Wilson's melodramatic shift from bureaucrat to agitator: if the tired Attlee government was going to be discredited at the polls by price rises and economic problems because it had to toe the US line, then Wilson may have reasoned he was better out of it. There may have also been some pique – Gaitskell had just been made Chancellor of the Exchequer, a post Wilson may have hoped for for himself.

We do not have any direct evidence of the immediate reaction of the US and British Intelligence services to the resignation of Wilson and the other two to set themselves up as anti-American oppositionists. But there are some inferences it is reasonable to draw. The resignations occurred at a time of major Cold War crisis. Only one month later came the most traumatic espionage event in post-war Anglo-US relations. Guy Burgess and Donald Maclean ran away, presumably to Russia, leaving a senior secret serviceman – Kim Philby – under deep suspicion, and a former MI5 officer – Anthony Blunt – in a considerable panic. Soviet agents were revealing themselves in Britain at every turn. Wilson already had a reputation as one of the ministers whom a few US politicians went so far as to think should be impeached for traitorous sales of armaments to Russia. And the Labour Right, many of them with connections to the Intelligence services, were open in their accusations that the renegade ministers were pro-Communist.

Wilson's new-found political friends were the 'Keep Left' group of backbenchers, which included some significant names – Michael Foot, Ian Mikardo, Barbara Castle, George Wigg, Stephen Swingler and Tom Driberg. Other MPs referred to them as 'Communist lickspittles'.[25] The former MI6 officer, Lord Winster, was among the most hostile. When the 'Bevanites' published a pamplet explaining themselves, he announced: 'The sponsors of this pamphlet and the authors have put their heads in the sands, thus exposing their thinking parts.' Shawcross, fresh from prosecuting the Soviet agent, scientist Klaus Fuchs, saw Wilson as a Communist fellow-traveller: he dismissed him viciously in public as one of those 'highbrows educated beyond their capacity'.[26]

The right-wing Shawcross also took over the Board of Trade itself from the defecting Wilson for a few months. In later life he made it clear he regarded Wilson's 'industrial contacts' with disdain – particularly the commercial consultancy given to him after he left office by the firm of Montague Meyer, with whom Wilson had had official dealings. Wilson's grasp of government machinery, and his official standing with the Russians, were obviously commercially valuable to Meyer. Considering the inadequate salaries paid to MPs in those days, and the numerous Cabinet ministers of all parties – and their relations – who regularly go on the pay-roll of private firms who deal with the government, Shawcross's attitude seems rather puritanical.

One possible explanation may be his discovery of the sheer speed with which Wilson, who had been considering resigning for months, had attached himself as private consultant to Meyer. As Wilson himself tells the story:

Once I was in Opposition, the firm approached me through an intermediary to see if I could help them pick up the threads. I was to act as their diplomatic adviser.[27]

Wilson told his constituency party officers by May 14, 1951 that the deal with Meyer had been arranged. He got an office in the Strand, a large car, the services of a secretary, Mrs Elise Cannon, and £1,500 a year. This was barely three weeks after the announcement of his resignation. In a letter to *The Times* in 1974, Shawcross, careful to name no names, claimed that

> Knowledge which came to me when I was President of the Board of Trade caused me a great deal of anxiety in regard to one individual occupying a far more exalted position than the comparatively small fry [in the later Poulson corruption cases]. In the absence of a power of interrogation, I could do nothing.

The next day he explained that he had felt his case was one 'of anxiety only'. 'If there had been a legal power of interrogation at the time, the true facts might have been elicited, and might have shown innocence or naiveté.'[28] These veiled remarks were taken at the time – with no justification – to point towards Wilson.

Shawcross also got hold of much more concrete evidence of alleged bribery at Wilson's Board of Trade during this period, which he and the Lynskey Tribunal seemed to have missed. He says that a firm – understood to have been an aircraft company – came to consult him in 1952 as a barrister in private practice, asking how they could get their money back from a departmental head. They had bribed him to get an export licence for sales behind the Iron Curtain, but appeared to have been cheated. Shawcross says professional ethics stopped him notifying anyone: the 'evil-doer', whose name he says he no longer recalls, was eventually given a knighthood and died un-exposed (and presumably wealthy). Alleged bribes taken by his civil servants had, of course, nothing to do with Wilson, but it was in this poisoned atmosphere that Wilson's period of office in Britain's first post-war Labour government came to an end. Every single category of smears developed between 1945 and 1951 was to be resurrected a decade later when Wilson looked likely to become leader of the Labour Party – with some melodramatic new twists provided by MI5 and the CIA.

CHAPTER 4

At 10.30p.m. on St Valentine's Day – February 14, 1963 – a silver-haired, slightly portly figure arrived at the Pimlico home of left-wing Labour MP, Ben Parkin. Greeted by cheers, he was smoking a pipe to give the right PR effect, and wearing a Gannex coat, donated by Joe Kagan, the Lithuanian-Jewish rainwear manufacturer who was his friend and backer. Harold Wilson had just become leader of the British Labour Party: the previous leader, Hugh Gaitskell, had died in January 1963 of a sudden and mysterious illness and Wilson had come from the vote-counting in Committee Room 14 of the House of Commons where he had trounced his right-wing rivals for the succession by 144 votes to 103. Wilson would probably have been startled and frightened to know that, in Intelligence agencies on both sides of the Atlantic, he was about to be marked down as a suspected KGB spy.

During those twelve years of exile as a 'left-wing' rebel, Wilson had blossomed as Montague Meyer's commercial adviser, making frequent trips to Moscow on the timber firm's behalf, and becoming something of an influential intermediary for those interested in East-West trade. In the eyes of the more prejudiced members of the Intelligence agencies, he had flirted with 'Communists' at home, and with Russians abroad. Gaitskell, on the other hand, had been the very model of the kind of pro-American, anti-Communist centrist whom the CIA had backed with cash and propaganda all over the world. In 1960 Anthony Sampson painted a vivid picture of this Socialist intellectual from one of Britain's most famous boarding schools:

> At parties – which he loves – he can often be seen in a jaunty suit and a shiny tie, waltzing dreamily on the dance-floor. His friends, who call him 'Gaiters' or Hugh, treat him loyally but casually, and he never likes to be thought square ... he can be seen at Belgravia lunch-parties, at night-clubs, at the celebrations of café society or – more rarely – at trade union socials ... Gaitskell dinner parties can include tycoons, Tory peers and American intellectuals ... In his gaiety, his freedom and his apparent rootlessness, he seems more like an American egg-head; he loves America, and gets on with Kennedy's dons.[1]

No one had ever been tempted to call Harold Wilson 'Willers', or waltz round the dance-floors of Belgravia with *his* friends – button manufacturers, squat raincoat salesmen from the North of England, or Marxist hobble-dehoys from the Labour back benches. The only common social ground shared by the two men was the functions given by the glamorous US socialite Fleur Cowles: Gaitskell because he fitted naturally into café society, and Wilson because he worked for her husband, Tom Meyer.

Over the years Gaitskell and his circle had done their best to crush the 'Bevanites' who had resigned in 1951, and their successors in the Campaign for Nuclear Disarmament. That circle was also described by Anthony Sampson in 1960:

> Hovering round Gaitskell are the group of sociable intellectual Labour MPs known as the 'Hampstead set' – the most prominent of whom are Patrick Gordon-Walker, Douglas Jay, Anthony Crosland and Roy Jenkins. Their ambience is lively, cultured and wide-ranging, interested in music and art as well as politics, and more urban than their Tory equivalents, a world roughly represented by *Encounter*.[2]

Sampson was presumably unaware at the time of writing this passage that the magazine *Encounter* was being funded by the CIA. Gaitskell himself may have known. He certainly had friends who would have done. He was a friend of the US labour attaché, Joseph Godson, while his anti-Communist colleague, George Brown, was friendly with the CIA station chief in London Archie Roosevelt, according to Roosevelt's memoirs. When, in 1962, the former chief of station, Chester Cooper, and the CIA's director of national estimates, Sherman Kent, flew into a US airbase in Britain with a briefcase of photographs during the Cuban missile crisis, it was Archie Roosevelt who decided to invite Brown and Gaitskell to his London house so that they could inspect the pictures, while the ambassador David Bruce briefed Macmillan, the Prime Minister, and Cooper briefed Dick White, the head of MI6 separately.[3]

During his years in 'exile' Wilson was aware of the danger of being tarred with 'Communism':

> There were indeed undercurrents of which one had to be wary. Almost from the day of my resignation, I began to receive invitations from left-wing constituencies and local trade union branches to address meetings. These I treated with some reserve. While very few parties were under communist influence, one had to watch out carefully for those that were. The same caution had to be applied to approaches from local trade union branches and federations. There were some extremely active left-wing operators, whose influence tended to be a direct function of small local membership, and those of us who were supporting Nye Bevan had to be very careful not to become tainted by their company in the eyes of the right wing of the Party.[4]

He was tainted nonetheless. In October 1952, Gaitskell whipped up violent ill-feeling between the 'Social Democrats' and the leftists, by attributing Bevanite support to Communism. 'One sixth of the constituency party delegates appear to be communist or communist-inspired,' he warned. Since the 1950 election, Wilson had had to fight off accusations in his largely Catholic Liverpool constituency of taking 'the road to Moscow' with his repeated trade trips. His answer was a model of anti-Communism: 'Anyone who knows anything about communism knows that the best bulwark against communism in this country is social democracy . . . the communists have been fighting the Labour government . . . they . . . know that it is in the disease-spots of uncontrolled capitalism that communism can breed and spread.' It did him no good with the Roman Catholic bishop of Leeds, John Heenan. He told his flock that the Bevanites were 'crypto-Communists'.[5]

In later life Wilson conceded readily that a minority of Labour-held constituencies were controlled by 'the extreme left of the party', and that the 1945 election landslide had brought in some MPs with Communist leanings: 'The minuscule though articulate Communist Party was well placed to spread dissension in Labour's ranks,' he says, in the unhealthy atmosphere after the split in the Labour Party and its subsequent defeat.[6] But despite being aware of these dangers he remained true to the principles that had led to his resignation. In 1954, for example, he opposed the re-arming of Germany that was being urged by the US government, a view regarded by some Labour right-wingers as Communist-inspired. Wilson did not go out of his way to appear anti-Soviet. In 1956, for example, he declined to sign a letter sent to *Pravda* by five impeccably left-wing colleagues from the Bevanite group to protest about the Soviet crushing of the Hungarian uprising. And in 1961, as Labour's foreign spokesman on the Berlin Wall, we find him arguing that the West should make it 'clear by word and deed that we are prepared to renounce the use of West Berlin as an advance battle headquarters and centre of provocation in the cold war. The price we pay, in terms of suspicion and ill-will for insisting on keeping West Berlin for Radio Free Europe and similar organisations, and as a centre for spies and provocateurs, is out of all proportion to any value that may be thought to derive from these activities.'[7]

This was the kind of statement that was guaranteed to set the Intelligence agencies' teeth on edge. The 'value' derived from their major Intelligence activity in Berlin had been precisely zero. There had just been the hideously embarrassing public disclosure that the CIA and MI6 had built, at a cost of $25 million, a wire-tapping tunnel from West to East Berlin, which had been betrayed at the outset by the renegade MI6 officer George Blake.[8] ('What a good agent Blake is turning out to be,' Berlin MI6 station chief Peter Lunn confided to visiting British MP and former MI6 man Montgomery Hyde at the time.)[9]

Wilson was well aware that the Russians still distrusted and feared the Germans after what they had suffered in the war. His views tended to be sensitive to Russian feelings, although ultimately they were always fundamentally pro-West and pro-Nato. More cynically, one could explain his stance by saying that Wilson was keen to retain the sympathy of left-wing MPs in the Labour Party, men who constituted his political base. He also had a vested interest in not needlessly becoming *persona non grata* with Soviet officials: he was constantly doing business with them.

Hugh Gaitskell and George Brown, by contrast, got on badly with the Russians. On the occasion of Khrushchev's visit to London in April 1956, there had been some embarrassing scenes. Khrushchev's temper may not have been sweetened by his probable knowledge that MI5 were bugging his suite at Claridges (using a radio beam to 'activate' the phone) and that MI6 were sending an unauthorised frogman under the keel of the warship on which he arrived, in an attempt to measure its propeller. (Khrushchev studiously confined his remarks in his hotel room to discussions about the fit of his clothes; the frogman, Commander 'Buster' Crabb, was never heard from again – later, his headless body was washed enigmatically ashore.)

Meanwhile, a dinner was arranged for the Russian leader to meet the National Executive of the Labour Party. Gaitskell had already raised the case of some imprisoned Social Democrats in the Soviet Union, and told Khrushchev that good relations could not be achieved by the use of 'front organisations' and 'fellow-travellers' to peddle Soviet propaganda. The mercurial Khrushchev had reacted badly – he told Gaitskell that trade unionists were always visiting Russia and complaining about conditions. He found the Conservatives, he said, 'much more congenial'. At the dinner, Krushchev spoke defensively of the Nazi-Soviet pact at the beginning of World War II. George Brown, who had a reputation for drunkenness and rudeness, interrupted noisily: 'May God forgive him!' Gaitskell again raised the issue of the imprisoned Social Democrats. Khrushchev jumped up and said, 'If you want to help the enemies of the working class, find someone else!' He then stormed out of the room, refusing to shake hands with Brown.[10] A Czech defector, General Jan Sejna, later told the CIA that Khrushchev had remarked darkly in Moscow: 'If communism were to triumph tomorrow, Gaitskell would be the first to be shot outside the Houses of Parliament as a traitor to the working class.'[11]

Throughout the entire decade of the 1950s Wilson travelled to Moscow on business for Montague Meyer and other firms. His first trip was in May 1953. He had already gone to Canada and 'succeeded in arranging substantial shipments' of timber. Now, he says, as a Privy Counsellor – the honorific Royal office granted to senior ministers which requires a special oath of secrecy – he was obliged to ask the Prime Minister of the day for permission. 'Certainly you should go, my boy,' Churchill said, ordering him a drink in the Members' Bar, 'you'll meet some of the top leaders.'[12] Wilson threw his weight about in Red Square when he was arrested for taking photographs: 'I succeeded in conveying to [the arresting officer] that I was seeing Mikoyan the next day.' Mikoyan also obligingly arranged an hour-long interview with Molotov, the Foreign Minister, for Wilson and the British ambassador. Wilson released news of his coup to the press agencies, and flew on to Budapest to discuss Anglo-Hungarian trade, saying that an imprisoned British businessman, Edgar Sanders, must be released before progress could be made. On his return he spoke warmly of the 'industrial revolution' in the USSR.

In June 1954 he was back in Moscow: this time Mikoyan enabled him to be the first British politician to meet Stalin's temporary successor, Georgi Malenkov.[13] He was accompanied, according to Andrew Roth, by his secretary at Montague Meyer, Mrs Elise Cannon – 'a tall, dark girl, who was photographed with him when he visited the ancient monastery of Zagorsk.' Poor Mrs Cannon, too, was later subject to the stream of false sexual speculations about Wilson, merely because she was there, doing her job.

In 1958, Wilson assisted Frank Schon, the Austrian-Jewish businessman who had dealt with the Board of Trade in earlier days, to sell a detergent plant to the Russians. His personal influence with Mikoyan helped to clinch the deal, and Schon subsequently hired him as a consultant, paying him £1,000 a year as a retainer. Altogether, as Peter Wright of MI5 laboriously calculated, in his twelve years out of office in the 1950s, Wilson made no fewer than twelve trips to Moscow.

'So what?' anyone who was not in Intelligence might reply. But to the mind of a Peter Wright or a James Angleton, these visits were, if not compromising, at least dangerous: the KGB always tried to compromise Western visitors. Wilson had not only exposed himself by going to Moscow three times in 1947, he had returned there, again and again. It was inconceivable that a prominent Labour politician who was anxious to be on friendly terms with the Soviets would not be the victim of a blackmail attempt or a bribery offer in all this time. *And yet Wilson never reported such an approach.* Peter Wright was to boom at questioners many years later, 'No one should have been allowed to become Prime Minister who made twelve trips to Moscow!'[14] It was on the basis of such reasoning that both MI5 and the CIA were to open files on Wilson. All that remained for them to do, having decided that the Moscow visits constituted a suspicious circumstance, was to find some facts which could be made to fit into the theory. It is a methodology which perhaps explains why Wright never made much of a success of his career in orthodox science, and why neither Wright nor Angleton would have lasted long as detectives in a conventional police force; nor, indeed, as reporters on a newspaper. This mental activity is called '*a priori* reasoning'. Its conclusions may not be wrong – but there is no logical reason why they should be right. Wilson's friend Joe Kagan, a victim of the same process, says more harshly, 'Give me a name. That's what it comes down to. Give me a name and I'll make a case against them!'[15]

In 1956, Wilson acquired a new secretary – Marcia Field, a twenty-four-year old who was married to an engineer, Ed Williams. She was a politically talented history graduate who was already working for the Labour Party. 'She's a bit neurotic, but she's got a good political brain,' Wilson told his colleague Barbara Castle. Mrs Williams who, as a woman, was to be made the butt of unscrupulous gossip in years to come, was possessed of strong political interests. In the next twenty years – some of them tempestuous – she became less of a secretary and more of a *chef du cabinet* or chief of staff. Some said *eminence grise* would have been a more appropriate term, had she not been inclined to make her presence felt by raising her voice on occasions. But there was undoubtedly a strong flavour of sexism in the complaints from some of her male colleagues that she asserted herself too much. She says, and there is no reason to doubt it, that everyone in the Wilson 'kitchen cabinet' raised their voice from time to time. The professional relationship between Wilson and Williams was an interesting one. It was characterised by loyalty and occasional displays of temperament on Williams' part, and by a certain over-willingness to rely on Marcia Williams on Wilson's part, accompanied by forbearance and gratitude. Observers saw it as a sort of political partnership, filling the vacuum caused by the fact that Mrs Mary Wilson, probably with great good sense, had no wish to spend her days as a 'political wife'.

Marcia Williams worked long hours for Wilson, shared his political hopes and dreams, controlled access to him by his political colleagues, and travelled with him on Meyer business to Moscow. It was a political opportunity for her. In 1957, her husband was offered a highly paid job by Boeing in Seattle on a two-year contract. The couple hoped to raise money for a house by the enforced separation. In 1959, however, Ed Williams intimated that he wished to marry a woman he had met in Seattle. In January 1960, Wilson, on an eighteen-day lecture tour of American universities in New York, Chicago, Minnesota and Regina, Canada, took Marcia with him. Seattle was nearby, and she called on Ed Williams to discuss the problem. Marcia Williams was understandably anxious that a divorce, which could cause mischievous gossip, should not needlessly hamper Wilson's political career.

This seems an understandable attitude. It would have been not in the least reprehensible of Wilson to feel the same way. Ed Williams insisted that he wished to go ahead with the divorce: this too was understandable.

67

The divorce proceedings began on November 1, 1960, just as Wilson was entering his first, unsuccessful contest against Gaitskell for the party leadership, and were quietly finalised in King County, Washington State, on April 7, 1961. A Conservative MP who was also an MI6 agent later said he had heard that some of Wilson's political friends had later assisted in putting together a financial settlement on Ed Williams' behalf. Marcia Williams says this was not, in fact, correct. Had it been true, it is hard to see that it would have been discreditable in any event, knowing how prone unscrupulous politicians are to invent sexual scandal about their rivals, and the tendency of Conservative newspapers to offer huge payments for information they can then misuse.

For it was – as those involved perhaps realised – a situation ripe for misleading sexual gossip. This occurred very quickly. Like so many other scurrilous rumours, one can trace the earliest origins of it back to the Special Forces Club and the Conservative Party. By the autumn of 1960, Colonel Douglas Dodds-Parker, who was a member of both, had been wrongly informed that Harold Wilson had had sexual relations with his left-wing parliamentary colleague, Barbara Castle, when they were both on a visit to Canada. Dodds-Parker was also told that Wilson had had an affair with his secretary, Mrs Marcia Williams. It had taken place, so the story went, in Moscow, while they were travelling on behald of Montague Meyer.

Marcia Williams is quite amused about this notion. She said some years later:

Poor souls – obviously the only place they could actually go together to be quiet and on their own ... Well, you know, only a nutter would say that because only nutty people would do it. You'd have to be certifiable to actually *choose* the Soviet Union ...[16]

That these two stories – both false – had reached the ears of Dodds-Parker said much about the circles in which they were being generated. Dodds-Parker was at the fulcrum of the Secret Service-Conservative Party axis. He was a former Conservative minister in the Foreign Office – the department which was so closely connected to MI6. At the time he was temporarily without a parliamentary seat and was assisting at the headquarters of the party machine – Conservative Central Office. A former Grenadier Guardsman who was to become president of the Special Forces Club, he had had a high-level war-time career in the Special Operations Executive. By the end of the war, having served in Cairo, North Africa and Italy, he was the most important liaison officer between SOE and the fledgling US Intelligence agency OSS, from which so many CIA executives later came. It is no reflection on Dodds-Parker that such stories should have come to his ears, but it indicates nonetheless the areas in which they were being circulated.

It took a few years longer before these scandalous rumours reached the ears of US Intelligence. Charles Bates, the FBI legal attaché in London from 1958 to 1965, picked them up at the US embassy and 'on the cocktail party circuit,' he says, probably nearer 1963 than 1961. The FBI mission's work certainly included supplying Intelligence on British Labour politicians, in a monthly 'country report'. In Washington, Hoover was 'delighted', Bates recalls, to be able to place on file the fact that the leader of the British Labour Party was reputed to have a girlfriend. 'I think some of it was made available to President Johnson. Hoover said, "Give me more of this".'[17] One can safely assume that Archie Roosevelt's CIA London station had collected and transmitted the same rumours.

After Gaitskell's death in January 1961, the rumours multiplied. Wilson was tipped off that right-wing Labour MPs were spreading the story that he was never seen with his wife. The innuendo was obvious. At Gaitskell's memorial service Mary Wilson was conspicuous on his arm. It was a re-run of the public-relations manoeuvres that had been necessary three years earlier during the first leadership contest, when Wilson's campaign managers arranged a well-publicised tea for four at the Harcourt Room of the House of Commons. Round the table sat Harold, Mary, Marcia and a male companion who was generally presumed to be her husband (it was probably her brother, Tony).[18] The story about Wilson and Marcia Williams was to re-appear during the 1964 General Election, when, Wilson's biographer Roth records, dozens of men appeared simultaneously in pubs in different parts of Britain, falsely alleging to drinkers that the Labour leader was having an affair with his secretary.

From the point when Wilson first seemed to be a possible alternative party leader, MI5 were heavily involved in operations against the Labour Left generally. The founding of the Campaign for Nuclear Disarmament (CND) led to new accusations of a 'Moscow conspiracy' among Labour politicians. Some twenty years later, an MI5 desk officer, Cathy Massiter, disclosed that Hollis's MI5 had immediately listed the campaign as a 'subversive organisation' on the grounds that it was dominated by Communists. This automatically provided a justification for opening personal files – 'PFs' – on anyone who joined, and for instituting surveillance on CND members. There were many Bevanites who were prominent in CND: Wilson himself, although he took an equivocal attitude to unilateral nuclear disarmament, moved in these circles and was sympathetic to his friends' fears about a nuclear holocaust. He eventually made rather lukewarm promises that the British 'so-called independent deterrent' (the Polaris submarines being purchased from the US) might be abandoned. CND, led by the philosopher Bertrand Russell, campaigned for the dismantling of US nuclear bases in Britain as well as for getting rid of Britain's own nuclear weapons. It therefore constituted a movement hostile to US national interests.

Once again, certain logical fallacies were at work. Just because Moscow would have been pleased at a diminution of US weaponry, and even urged its followers to support the campaign, it did not follow that CND was an agency of the Kremlin. Such a proposition was no more logical than to say that because the Russians probably wanted to avoid a third world war, everyone who also wanted peace was a Communist. But knee-jerk reactions appear to have been common currency at Leconfield House, the headquarters of MI5. So, too, Gaitskell was determined to fight off CND. When unilateralist resolutions were passed at the Labour Party conference in 1960, Gaitskell launched a passionate campaign which certainly had US support:

> I know there are people who would like to see the Americans out. But they were glad enough to see them in 1942. There are some of us who will fight, fight and fight again to bring back sanity and honesty and dignity, so that our party – with its great past – may retain its glory and its greatness.

The previous year, Hollis had made a shameless attempt to add to his stable of agents within the ranks of Labour MPs, by approaching the right-wing former minister Christopher Mayhew, on the strength of their games of golf together and Mayhew's long involvement in what he calls 'anti-Bolshevism'. Mayhew had helped to found the underground government propaganda organisation IRD, which was still going strong, and he could look forward to high ministerial office in any forthcoming Gaitskell government.

> Two chaps were with Hollis. They gave me a very stiff gin. I thought he was going to ask me to spy on the Russians because I was active in the anti-Bolshevik movement, and had been invited to the Soviet embassy and made several trips to the Soviet Union. I was all ready to say yes.

Instead, the head of MI5 asked him to supply Intelligence on 'the Bolsheviks in the Labour Party'.

> Hollis quite surprised me by asking me to spy on Labour MPs. I just felt I couldn't. It would have taken too much time and I would have been uncomfortable.[19]

However, some of Mayhew's Gaitskellite colleagues were only too anxious to do business with MI5 as part of the process of 'fight, fight and fight again'. In August 1961 a small committee – Gaitskell, Brown, and Patrick Gordon-Walker – assembled a list of more than a dozen left-wing MPs whose activities they found most objectionable. Brown later told the journalist Harry Pincher ('Chapman' is a name adopted for his writing) that one of them was Tom Driberg.

70

According to Pincher's memoirs, he had lunch with Brown at the Ecu de France in Jermyn Street. Brown confided that the Gaitskellites wanted MI5 and MI6 to supply them with dossiers on their dozen suspects, so that they could be publicly drummed out of the Labour Party:

> Regrettably, George explained, the committee knew neither the names nor the telephone numbers of the heads of MI5 and MI6, so it had been decided to ask me to provide them. In return, if and when MPs were to be expelled, I would be given the information in advance for publication exclusively in the *Daily Express*.[20]

It is hard to believe this was so. It is true that the identities of Roger Hollis and Dick White of MI6 were regarded as a secret, but, as we have seen, Gaitskell's friend Christopher Mayhew played golf with Hollis, who had indeed tried to recruit him, and Brown himself was a personal friend of the CIA London station chief Archie Roosevelt. When Wilson became leader of the Opposition, Harold Macmillan, the Conservative Prime Minister, was perfectly prepared to introduce him to the head of MI6, Sir Dick White. In fact, Gaitskell had his own Intelligence connections. Nothing could have been easier than for the Labour Right to discover the relevant names and numbers on the clubland network. Come to that, nothing could have been easier than for Brown to get the names out of Pincher, who would have been ready to boast of his knowledge, without telling the journalist the whole story. It seems more likely that Brown wished to 'plant' the information on Pincher for PR reasons, a belief strengthened by the fact that Pincher also records that Brown was 'happy' for him to inform Lord Beaverbrook, proprietor of the *Daily Express* of the arrangement.

Peter Wright, then privy to much of 'D' Branch's counter-espionage gossip, takes up the story:

> George Brown: yes, I remember the request. Everybody was against meeting it because it would have blown all our sources in the [Communist] Party . . . the cryptos – we knew their identities mainly from our access to the Party's secret records. The fact that we had this access was a top secret.[21]

Wright is referring to operation PARTY PIECE in 1955, when the former Army officer Hugh Winterborn and his 'technical' department, 'A2', burgled a Mayfair flat containing all the membership records of the British Communist Party, and microfilmed them for MI5 before painstakingly replacing them. Among the 55,000 files were those of Labour Party members, trade unionists and civil servants who had been forced underground after 1948 by blacklisting. Presumably the sweep included both current CP members and lapsed ones – but the idea of political evolution was not well-developed inside MI5. How many 'secret Communists' among Labour MPs did it disclose? Pincher, who was the beneficiary of leaks from Wright before the veteran rumourmonger signed his name to his own memoirs, claims the number was thirty-one, quoting anonymous 'MI5 sources'.[22] Curiously, Peter Wright himself, who arrived in MI5 shortly after PARTY PIECE and claims he discussed it with Winterborn, does not give a figure of any kind in his subsequent memoirs.

All one can say with confidence is that George Brown was given the answer, 'None'. He was, according to Pincher, given only one titbit of imformation by Hollis – that the head of the press department at Labour Party HQ, Arthur Bax, had been taking money from the Czechs for four years, in return for trivial information about Labour. The hapless Bax, who claimed the cash was for journalistic articles, was sacked on the spot.

The information about Bax probably came MI5's way after the defection of a minor Czech spy. In around 1961, Antonin Buzwk, a 'correspondent' with the Czech Press Agency, defected in London. He also disclosed that a Czech agent, 'Lev', had penetrated the Free Czech Intelligence office in London. It was a small taste of the widespread and rather promiscuous espionage being carried out by the Czechs at the time – the chargé d'affaires at the British embassy in Prague, Edward Scott, was compromised with a housemaid in the same year; a young RAF man, Nicolas Prager, was handing over full details of the 'Blue Diver' air-jamming system quite unbeknownst to MI5; and the best-looking Intelligence officer at the Czech embassy in London, having contrived an acquaintance with the wife of Conservative minister Maurice Macmillan (another Tory MP with Intelligence connections), cabled Prague for permission to try to seduce her . . . It was refused, with ribald remarks about the officer's virility. When that information came out of Czechoslovakia ten years later, MI5 – always tender to their own – suppressed its publication. They were less tender towards Wilson's ministers.

Whilst 'exposing' Bax, MI5 continued to put agents of their own into the Labour Party's headquarters. A party official working for MI5 tried to recruit George Caunt, Wilson's campaign manager, as a 'sub-agent' in 1963, once Wilson gained the party leadership. According to Caunt, he reported this at once to Harold Wilson, who replied, 'I knew it!'[23]

Wilson may indeed have thought he knew about everything that was going on, and that he would deal with the Intelligence agencies when he achieved power. It was a vain hope, for Wilson's ignorance was profound. There were five critical facts about 'national security' that the new party leader did not know in February 1963. Exposure of any one of these five would have been enough on its own to cause the public scandal which the British Intelligence agencies deserved and dreaded. Together, had they been known, they added up to a strong case for disbanding MI5 entirely. There would also have been irresistible public pressure to mete out the same punishment to MI6. It was not to work out that way.

Firstly, Wilson did not know that the previous month Kim Philby, a senior officer of MI6, had finally confessed in Beirut to having been a Soviet spy since the 1930s. By July, the Conservative government was forced to make a brief and evasive statement that not only had Philby been guilty after all, but that he had been allowed to run away. Macmillan, the Prime Minister, was nettled by Wilson's point-scoring – 'You do not know the difference between invective and insolence,' he told him, rather desperately. Cornered, Macmillan now made a fool of Wilson by a master-stroke. He invited him to a confidential meeting and introduced him to the head of MI6 himself, the urbane Sir Dick White. Wilson was awestruck by being made, as he thought, an Intelligence 'insider'. He repeatedly referred to this meeting with his colleagues, and in his memoirs, and was still doing so thirteen years later:

> I asked to see Macmillan. He was accompanied by the head of MI6 whom the Prime Minister asked to tell me the whole facts. While what was public knowledge could not have justified the manifest failure of the Secret Service to keep Philby under control, one simple fact I was given made sense of the story. I was satisfied and felt it my duty to say so in the House without giving any reason, and to ask my Hon. Friends to let it go. (I was promptly criticised in the press for gagging my back-benchers.)[24]

There was no such 'simple fact'. No one knows what White told Wilson to put him off the scent, but Wilson thus failed to bring into the open the fact that Philby had not been a mere 'Foreign Office official' but a most important MI6 officer who had destroyed every significant Anglo-American 'covert operation' between 1946 and 1951. He failed to expose the fact that Philby had been put back into the Middle East as a 'journalist' by George Young, the vice-chief of MI6, despite being under suspicion. He failed to bring out that Philby had later been offered a disgraceful 'deal' to hush the matter up – immunity from prosecution in return for coming home and talking. He failed to show how Philby had been allowed to rat even on that, being left overnight by a trusting MI6 colleague after supplying a fake 'confession'. And he failed to bring out that Philby had probably had advance warning that Lord Rothschild and his old friend Flora Solomon had finally provided conclusive evidence against the super-mole back in London. It was left to journalists to dig out the story four years later, in the face of considerable obstacles erected by Wilson's own government.

The backbenchers Wilson was reining in included Niall MacDermot, a lawyer who knew very well that Philby had been a senior MI6 officer because he had met him in the war. MacDermot had been posted to MI5 and recalled embarrassingly clearly how Dick White, then a talented young counter-intelligence officer, had taken him to meet Philby:

Dick White was thrilled by Philby and thought he was wonderful. He introduced me to him. Philby was then head of section V1 in MI6. Dick White asked me to come along – he told me how brilliant he was and what a pity he wasn't the head of section, he was so able. Philby, I remember, had a very strong personality. He was intelligent, charming . . .[25]

Macmillan appealed for the Philby affair to be covered up, telling MPs, 'I hope the House will accept that it would not be in the national interest for Hon. Members to inquire any further into the past history of the case.' But MacDermot would not be diverted, alleging that 'The most serious aspect of the matter [is] the position then held by him [Philby].' Macmillan was forced onto the defensive, saying guardedly, 'I appreciate [MacDermot's] knowledge of these matters, in which I think he has some experience,' but he was also able to appeal to Wilson for support of his view 'that we should not discuss some of these aspects of our national functions.' On cue, Wilson said that, in his two meetings with Macmillan, he had been given 'a very full and frank account of this case which raises a number of issues which frankly cannot be discussed across the floor of this House . . . the matter should now be left where it is.'[26]

It may, of course, be entirely a coincidence that some years later, when the abscess of the Philby affair finally did burst, MI6 found themselves with an immediate opportunity to take an unpleasant revenge on Niall MacDermot. It was MI6 who took the initiative in a successful move to drive him out of office on bogus 'security' grounds, and thus ruin his ministerial career.

The Philby affair was the first Intelligence matter on which Wilson was naively ignorant. The second was that in Washington, US Intelligence were about to be informed that Anthony Blunt, a prominent member of the Establishment with connections with the Royal Family and an officer of the sister-service MI5, had been an undiscovered Soviet spy alongside, and for the same length of time as, Philby. Michael Straight, a rich American who had been at Cambridge in the 1930s and was the brother of Rolls-Royce's deputy chairman in Britain, after repeatedly threatening to turn in Burgess and his friends over the years, had finally come clean. (It had been Straight's encounter with Guy Burgess in a Washington street in 1951 that had frightened Burgess into defecting.) Offered a US government job in June 1963, Straight decided to make a clean breast to the FBI. It was several months before the FBI entrusted this shattering new information to Arthur Martin of MI5. Martin and Hollis dealt with the matter by offering Blunt complete legal immunity and a cover-up. Blunt 'confessed' with remarkable speed, and settled down to eight years of more or less untruthful conversations with Martin and Wright over bottles of gin. One of the few tangible consequences of this, years later, was to prove to be the hounding of another parliamentary colleague of Wilson's – Bernard Floud – into suicide.

It was perhaps not Wilson's fault that he was totally unaware of Blunt's treachery while Leader of the Opposition. As Peter Wright says:

We were very concerned that it would leak that Blunt had been a spy and that we had given him immunity . . . Remember that at the time of Philby, MI5 was purer than white! If it had leaked in 1964 that Blunt was a spy and we had let him off, the consequences could well have been disastrous for the Service. It was therefore emphasised *from the beginning* to Blunt, that it must not blow and any admissions he made to third parties must be under our control. We had strict orders from successive Director-Generals to do nothing that might provoke Blunt to go public. All DGs saw his reports of interview as indeed did successive 'Cs' [heads of MI6] who concurred in the secrecy.[27]

The truth about Blunt was to be concealed for fifteen years.

Another Intelligence secret that Wilson did not know was that both the deputy head and eventually the chief of MI5 itself, Graham Mitchell and Roger Hollis, were to be placed under successive secret internal investigations by an MI5 'gestapo' on suspicion that they, too, might be Soviet spies. That was a secret so dark and lunatic that Wilson was not to find out about it for twelve years. In 1964, before Wilson came to power, Hollis did his best to close the whole mole-hunt down prematurely before it increased its scope to focus on him as well. A bizarre 'investigation' of Mitchell had been going on in which microphones and a TV camera were rigged up behind a one-way mirror in his office – he was seen to pick his teeth and groan occasionally. A team of MI6 men were brought in from outside to follow Mitchell about, as far as the railway station where he caught his train home. (Stephen de Mowbray, who led the team, was described by Wright as 'hot-headed and overimpressionable' – a good case of the pot calling the kettle black.) Wright claims that in 1964 Hollis said:

An election is coming soon, and I feel it is much better for the Service if we can resolve this case now, so that I do not have to brief any incoming Prime Minister.[28]

The fourth Intelligence fact of which Wilson was ignorant in February 1963 was that the KGB were about to turn the tables on an MI5 entrapment attempt by fatally compromising the Conservative war minister, John Profumo, who was having sex with the girlfriend of a Soviet spy.

But this was the only one of the five scandals which surfaced at the time

– carefully wiped clean of some of the more embarrassing MI5 connections. Its consequences were drastic enough. MI5 and Roger Hollis were subjected to a judicial inquiry which Hollis managed to mislead. The Conservative government, headed by Harold Macmillan, was discredited, and within a year fell from office. It was a pot the KGB were delighted to stir and even Harold Wilson adroitly exploited what he knew of this one 'security' scandal for party-political purposes. He was helped to become Prime Minister the following year by it, manifesting a pompous but nicely calculated concern for sexual 'security risks'.

The bitter resentment of the Conservative Party and the unchecked paranoia of rabidly anti-Labour Intelligence officers were to guarantee that, in gaining office in this way, Wilson was riding a tiger. While one is bound to feel sympathy with someone who was later made the victim of monstrous smears, there is, nonetheless, a certain irony in the fact that Wilson, when it suited him, was to urge the British public more than once to peer under the bed looking for Reds.

The fifth and final Intelligence matter which the Leader of Her Majesty's Opposition did not know about when he assumed his new dignity in February 1963 was to have even more direct consequences for his own career. Harold Wilson did not know that a KGB defector, Anatoli Golitsin, was at that very moment en route from Washington for London where he was to accuse Harold Wilson, too, of being a Soviet spy . . .

It would be a mis-statement to describe the atmosphere inside parts of the CIA, MI5 and MI6 as paranoid in the first four months of 1963. It was madder than that. Defectors, false defectors, true confessions and wild suspicions were dominating the counter-intelligence departments to a degree where cooler heads than they possessed would have become feverish.

The false allegations against Harold Wilson were kept secret, and were secretly pursued for thirteen years, with the connivance of the CIA. For eight of those years, Wilson himself was Prime Minister and entitled – in theory at least – to the unqualified loyalty of his Security Service staff. He did not get it.

Golitsin arrived in England the month after Wilson took over the Opposition Leader's office, in March 1963. He had already been in the US for two years since defecting from Finland. As an officer of the KGB he was a rare catch. When the Soviet Division of the CIA had wearied of his cloudy, doom-filled pronouncements, James Angleton had taken him up and was using his control of Golitsin as a high card to increase his power and influence within the 'Company'. The way a counter-intelligence department prospered was by finding spies – or, in default of that, by at any rate making denunciations. Archie Roosevelt, at that time chief of the CIA London station, says:

While the [Soviet] division chief was generally responsible for handling defectors, Jim Angleton managed to get control of . . . Golitsin . . . It did affect us all in further poisoning the atmosphere.[29]

Defectors were, on the face of it, the Soviet Union's one great weakness in the Intelligence game. Few Westerners engaged in secret work wanted to go and live in the East, but those behind the Iron Curtain frequently did want to cross to the West. Beginning with Gouzenko's defection in 1945, the West had compensated for its stream of misguided undergraduates and blackmail victims with a flow in the opposite direction of those who 'chose freedom'.

However, defectors were dangerous. Contrary to anti-Communist propaganda, there was little obvious incentive for defectors from the KGB or the military Intelligence wing, the GRU, to make the trip into exile. They did not suffer from the Soviet system: on the contrary, they were privileged members of it. Only if they fell foul of the system – by failure or incompetence – were they likely to want to leave. The dangers of the KGB wanting to seek revenge were great, which made their new life in a foreign country permanently uncomfortable. Sometimes the bright lights of the West or a sexual entanglement could be used as lures – but those the West was able to catch by such means were not likely to be the most intelligent or scrupulous of men.

In many ways, the CIA and MI5 did not want defectors to 'choose freedom'. They were much more useful in place, providing 'live' information about an unwitting adversary. Help to escape, a new life, money – these were one side of the bargain. The other side was that, if the defector was going to come out, he had to snoop, memorise, sometimes guess, in order to collect enough secret material to give him a meal-ticket on the other side. And the KGB, just like the CIA, husbanded its secrets carefully. Defectors were also psychologically vulnerable: they needed to feel wanted and important. This often put them under pressure to tell their new interrogators things that they thought would please them, whether true or not.

What was more, secret agents tended to cheat, and this made the contents of headquarters files in Moscow, Warsaw or Prague deeply misleading. Nothing was easier than for a field officer to boost his expenses and justify his existence by claiming to have recruited all sorts of 'agents', especially in the fields of politics and diplomacy, who were merely people he had met over a drink. The defector might therefore expose, in good faith, completely bogus 'spies' to his new hosts.

There was a final factor which, in the course of the 1960s, operated against defectors. The KGB learned to turn an apparent weakness into a strength by manipulating defectors. Fake defectors could be sent over to feed disinformation to the other side, or to undermine true disclosures made by earlier defectors. Fake defectors could also provide true information – if there was something the Soviet Union wanted to convey, and wanted to be believed. And of course, fake defectors could be sent over with a mixture of true information which was worth having and false information which was actively misleading.

All in all, this meant that the average defector was liable, at best, to be a somewhat erratic informant. Frustratingly for the British, he also usually tended to be US or Canadian property. Gouzenko, whose clutch of undoubtedly authentic radio messages had some claim to have begun the Cold War, was, in the words of Conservative MP Rupert Allason (who writes spy histories under the name 'Nigel West'):

A classic egotist who had succumbed to 'defector syndrome', a combination of a paranoia, self-righteousness, persecution mania and an overwhelming desire constantly to be the centre of attention.[30]

Allason, who has an eye for the *modus operandi* of plausible rogues, established after Gouzenko's death that he had financed his spendthrift drinking by selling 'exclusive' interviews, having books ghost-written under his name, trading in film rights, borrowing extensively, and extracting large libel cheques from the media for real or imagined slights. He embroidered 'disclosures' which seemed likely to get him cash and attention. One such was a second-hand hint he picked up in Moscow about a spy called ELLI, which he passed to MI5 thereby helping to foment the destructive belief that Roger Hollis himself was a Soviet spy. As Allason has said:

Most agreed that Gouzenko was nothing more complicated than a typical Slav from a peasant background who was ruthlessly determined to avoid starvation and make a better life for his family in a land of comparative plenty.[31]

Michael Goloniewski – a renegade Polish Intelligence officer who gave himself the pseudonym SNIPER – was another problem character. He, too, was the cause of time-wasting and destructive behaviour by MI5. In later life he claimed to be the last of the Romanovs and campaigned to have himself recognised as the Czar. Wright says the CIA believed he was becoming clinically insane as early as 1963, two years after his defection. Nonetheless, in that bizarre year of Harold Wilson's rise to power, MI5 men travelled to Washington and picked his brains.

They returned with a story which was eventually to lead to the interrogation of Michael Hanley, the second Director-General of MI5 to be falsely accused of being a Soviet spy. It was later concluded that false information had been 'planted' on SNIPER before his defection. And yet, some of his revelations had been important and true: it was SNIPER who had already handed over on a plate both George Blake (who had taken up the task of rendering MI6 operations futile where Kim Philby had left off) and Harry Houghton, who had been selling extremely significant naval secrets. What was true and what was false?

Turning Anatoli Golitsin loose into this group of confused British secret policemen was like tipping a toad into a warm pond: he laid spawn everywhere.

Since his defection to the CIA in December 1961, this temperamental KGB major had helped to identify John Vassall, a homosexual Admiralty clerk who had been selling yet more naval secrets. He had also made more vague references to a 'Ring of Five' British spies. This had put Philby and Blunt under suspicion all over again. Golitsin spoke menacingly of continuing 'penetration' of both the CIA itself and of MI5 in Britain. The KGB, he warned, had developed deception schemes of unimaginable elaborateness and subtlety. After a long session with Golitsin in Washington in spring 1962, one of MI5's most aggressive counter-intelligence officers, Arthur Martin, had successfully encouraged Golitsin to leave Angleton's care and come to the UK. He was promised enormous sums of money. His wife could also see an excellent gynaecologist. Golitsin, pleased at the interest shown in him, told Angleton and his assistant Ray Rocca that he intended to live in England henceforth. One CIA officer involved says:

> The way that Golitsin went to the UK was very unusual. He suddenly said one day, 'I'm fed up with you guys. I want to go England and I'm going to go to England.' Golitsin was almost solely in Arthur Martin's custody ... He was always very difficult to handle ...

Angleton was upset: not only did Golitsin have sensational possibilities still, but the CIA had also spent time and money giving him a $40,000 Washington house and a new identity as 'John Stone'.

Still, there was nothing to be done: after some delaying tactics, Golitsin was allowed to board a liner for England, where his arrival was awaited with excitement. Martin's anxiety to get his hands on Golitsin at this point was understandable. He had at last got hard evidence against Philby in the shape of the woman Victor Rothschild had produced out of the blue, Flora Solomon, who said Philby had tried to recruit her to the Communist cause before the war. Philby had fled to Russia, leaving behind an artful 'confession' of a misleading nature. Martin, who must have been beside himself with frustration, was more than ever convinced that MI5 was penetrated from within.

Golitsin had already produced for the British no less than 153 'serials': numbered statements of items he remembered, documents he had caught glimpses of, old KGB training cases with doctored names which he thought might have originally been British. But there was a problem. As Wright puts it:

79

The vast majority of Golitsin's material was tantalisingly imprecise. It often appeared true as far as it went, but then faded into tantalising obscurity, and part of the problem was Golitsin's clear propensity for feeding the information out in dribs and drabs. He saw it as his livelihood. . .[32]

All the CIA sources who handled Golitsin before his departure for England are unanimous on one point. He had nothing to say about the new Leader of the British Labour Party before he got on the boat; and he had plenty to say when he came back.

There was a little group of British officers in 'D' branch – the counter-espionage section of MI5 at the time – who had dealings with Golitsin or his material. One was Martin, the 'D1' (Soviet Counter-espionage), a man whose convictions flared up over the years into strong quarrels with his superiors. Another was Patrick Stewart who, in his post as 'D3 (Research)' and later 'D1', had the task of turning Golitsin's vague leads into named individual suspects. Then there were investigation officers such as Charles Elwell, who had been the case officer who had searched Harry Houghton's premises during that recent successful case. Peter Wright, as the resident scientist, managed to involve himself repeatedly, with Martin's encouragement: Wright had been heavily under Angleton's influence since he had first visited him in Washington in 1957 to drum up CIA support for his radio and bugging projects. These men were to be joined later by another officer from MI6 – Stephen de Mowbray. As MI6 liaison in Washington after the Mitchell fiasco, he, too, was heavily influenced by Angleton's theories. CIA officers at the time recall that, in the words of one, 'He was never out of Angleton's office.' De Mowbray was to become convinced over the years of the rightness of Angleton and Golitsin's view of the world.

Peter Wright claims that Golitsin, during his English visit from March to July 1963, told some or all of these men that Harold Wilson was a Soviet spy. This is partly corroborated by officers in the CIA. One directly involved says:

Mr G did tell the British about Wilson while he was in the UK. When he returned, he told us, and said: 'Ya, I tell British.' And we thought: 'Wow, this is serious.'

And it is at least partly corroborated by Alec MacDonald, who organised the 'safe houses' where Golitsin could stay. It was Golitsin, he says, who volunteered the idea that Hugh Gaitskell had been assassinated by the KGB (presumably on the bad-tempered Khrushchev's orders) in order to have the right-wing Labour leader replaced by Wilson:

It was Golitsin who came out with the idea, yes ... It seemed to me a bit far-fetched ... Perhaps he wanted to save something for the Britons ... I think he wanted to increase his influence. I mean, he seriously expected that he would be able to interview the Cabinet, and I told him there wasn't a chance.[33]

The notion was taken seriously by Peter Wright, MacDonald says, and by 'one or two others who thought the same ... because they were all devout believers in Golitsin, as some of the CIA were.' It was not, on the other hand, greeted with any enthusiasm by either the overall head of 'D' branch at the time, Martin Furnival Jones or by Hollis and Mitchell at the head of the organisation.

In 1980–81, when Wright was leaking material to the journalist Chapman Pincher, he wrote to him:

Golitsin was convinced that [Gaitskell] was murdered by the KGB. He knew before he came out that 'a wet affair' had been planned to ensure in a Western country that their agent would become head of a political party which could come to power.[34]

Wright's version then was that it was the head of the KGB's Northern European Department from whom Golitsin had got the story. But Wright's 1987 version of what Golitsin said showed an improvement of memory:

During the last few years of his service he had had some contacts with Department 13, which was known as the department of Wet Affairs in the KGB. This department was responsible for organising assassinations. He said that just before he left he knew that the KGB were planning a high-level political assassination in Europe in order to get their own man into the top place.[35]

Golitsin therefore 'knew' little in reality. He claimed to have a piece of gossip about something that might have been intended for an unknown political leader in an unknown country, which had been mentioned in Moscow a year before Gaitskell's death. He had one other point, according to Wright: that Britain could well have been the country in question, because General Rodin, the new head of Department 13, had just returned from Britain to take up the job.

Although Golitsin's story was so vague as to be worthless, Peter Wright, according to MacDonald, 'was all for believing it.' When looked at a little more closely, one key aspect becomes even more dubious. Wright claims it was Golitsin who came out with the specific idea that Gaitskell's replacement – Harold Wilson – was a Soviet asset. But this claim is disputed by MacDonald, who is entitled to be regarded as a more impartial witness:

He didn't really suggest that. If I remember, he said: 'Your best leader on the socialist side ... Gaitskell – was eliminated.' He didn't suggest that he was to be replaced by anybody else.[36]

MacDonald also confirms that Golitsin did not claim any first-hand knowledge of this assassination plot, still less that it was directed specifically at Gaitskell: 'I think it was more a hunch.'

So, in plain English, Golitsin was guessing. Every month that Golitsin was in England continuing to provide interesting guesses, an MI5 officer paid £10,000 sterling into his bank account. But how had the recent death of Gaitskell and the elevation of the 'leftist' Wilson originally become a topic of conversation between the defector and his hosts?

Once again, accounts vary. Peter Wright claims that 'Gaitskell's doctor' had already contacted MI5 because he was puzzled by the circumstances of his death. *Lupus disseminata erythematosis*, the cause of death, was a tropical disease of which only two or three cases a year occurred in temperate climes. Gaitskell had not been to the tropics. Arthur Martin, as the head of Russian counter-espionage, therefore went to see the doctor, as requested. (In the version of events Wright gave to Pincher, he claimed that the police had also brought the circumstances of Gaitskell's death to MI5's attention.)

This account is contradicted by Walter Somerville, Gaitskell's consultant at the time of his death. He denies that either he or John Nicolson, the chief medical officer at the Manor House hospital where Gaitskell was treated, got in touch with the Security Service: 'I did not, as has been reported, inform MI5. Nor – I know – did Nicolson.'[37]

Furthermore, the post-mortem on Gaitskell carried out on January 18, 1963 had shown that he was not in fact suffering from Lupus. No Lupus cells had been found in his body: 'It was a condition like Lupus. What he actually had was what we call an immune complex deficiency. His immune system broke down as the cells degenerated.' Somerville has a possible explanation of what happened: 'Somebody close to Gaitskell told me they feared a pill may have been dropped in his coffee while on a visit to Poland. They hadn't seen this happen – they were speculating ... I don't know if somebody who had been with Gaitskell told MI5.'

In the various Wright-inspired manuscripts that later surfaced, the scenario was developed further to include the fact that Gaitskell had suddenly fallen ill in December 1962 after visiting the Russian consulate to apply for a visa; he had been kept waiting there for no good reason, and been supplied with coffee and biscuits.

In fact, the whole theory was exploded in 1979 by Gaitskell's biographer Philip Williams, who interviewed many of Gaitskell's colleagues, family and medical attendants. Williams also studied the literature on the disease, which had improved greatly in the intervening sixteen years. Gaitskell did not become ill after going to the Russian consulate in December 1962. Nor did he do so after visiting Poland in August 1962. The first symptoms developed in early 1962. 'Rheumatic pains' he had previously developed in his shoulder returned; it became hard for him to dig his garden. On June 13 1962 he was taken ill and briefly 'blacked out', to the alarm of his friends. He was noticeably fatigued all summer, was unable to drive his car because of his shoulder pains by autumn, and claimed to have 'picked something up in Paris' on December 7. At that point he had planned to go to Russia on January 1. On December 15 he went into Manor House hospital, left on December 23 and immediately had a relapse, with symptoms of full-scale immunological collapse. He died on January 18.

The whole notion of the assassination was conceived by Arthur Martin. There are impeccable MI5 sources for this. Martin was suspicious after Gaitskell's death. Golitsin, having heard talk about Gaitskell, said to Martin and Wright, 'Could Gaitskell have been assassinated?' He produced, for the first time, his story that the KGB had planned to assassinate someone. Intrigued, Martin said: 'Well, we do have a case. Can you tell us what you know about this person who was to be assassinated?' Between the three of them, they had soon convinced themselves that it could have been Gaitskell. Martin contacted the British Medical Association and asked to be put in touch with a virus specialist, who mentioned there had been Soviet work on the disease, but said it was impossible to imagine that a Lupus poison might have been developed.

This was enough for Martin. He then dropped the case. Peter Wright, however, was convinced he was on to something. Wright's ambitious imagination may well have had a special stimulus to work overtime. For he claims to have been a personal acquaintance of Gaitskell:

I knew him personally and admired him greatly. I had met him and his family at the Blackwater sailing club, and I recall that about a month before he died, he told me he was going to Russia.[38]

It is hard to say how many of the Arthur Martin circle shared his theories. But Angleton certainly did, for we know what happened next in Washington. On his return to the States in July, Golitsin excitedly retailed the story of Gaitskell's assassination and the rise to power of Wilson the 'Soviet agent'. It caused consternation in the Agency. For good measure, Golitsin added that he now realised that Oleg Penkovsky, the Soviet defector handled by the British the previous year, who had played an important role in supplying information during the Cuban missile crisis, was a KGB 'plant'. And Averell Harriman, the US war-time ambassador to Moscow, he said, (falsely) was also a KGB spy. Wright admits that these two ideas also came from him and Arthur Martin in the first place:

Arthur Martin and I discussed at length with him our doubts about the Penkovsky case. We also discussed the question of Harriman. We put the proposition that Harriman was a spy to him because there was someone in the US BRIDE who would appear to be Harriman. This was what provoked Golitsin to tell his story of Harriman to Angleton.[39]

One CIA officer who saw the files says:

In September [Golitsin] told this to John McCone [Kennedy's appointee as head of the CIA]. His allegation was that Harold Wilson was a spy and that he believed Hugh Gaitskell had been killed by the KGB. He said Penkovsky had been under KGB control and he was a fabrication. Since Golitsin had just left the embrace of MI5, McCone fired off a rocket-like cable to Hollis asking how he explained this ... McCone thought: 'We ought to have been told about this. What's going on?'

An urgent ciphered cable was sent to the CIA station in London from McCone, addressed to Roger Hollis. It would have been taken round to Leconfield House in Mayfair by Cleveland Cram, who handled inter-service liaison. Within 24 hours Hollis had cabled a dismissive reply via his Washington liaison office:

Roger wrote back and said they didn't think there was anything to it. But by then, Mr G was well in with that Arthur Martin tight circle.

While Hollis attempted to soothe the Director of Central Intelligence, Angleton and his fellow-enthusiasts in the middle reaches of their two respective agencies carried on pursuing the 'Wilson case' behind their superiors' backs. Wright's next move was to try to get scientific backing for his theory. He had already visited Porton Down, the British gas and germ research laboratories, without progress:

I went to see the chief doctor in the chemical warfare laboratory, Dr Ladell, and asked his advice. He said that nobody knew how one contracted Lupus. There was some suspicion it might be a form of fungus and he did not have the foggiest idea how one would infect someone with the disease. I came back and made my report in these terms.[40]

In fact, he was not prepared to give up so easily. He now contacted Angleton direct, and asked him to use his superior resources to comb all Russian scientific papers for mentions of the disease. Angleton obliged, although the research took several months. Then, at last, it seemed they had struck oil. Angleton sent over a translation of an article in a Russian medical journal of 1956. It mentioned that a drug – hydralazine – had been found to produce Lupus-like effects in rats.

84

But even this promising lead was to end in disappointment. For the first time Wright now went to see Walter Somerville, Gaitskell's doctor, to ask his view. Somerville pointed out that hydralazine was a drug used in the treatment of hypertension; it was made by CIBA under the proprietary name 'Apresoline'.

I told them there was nothing new in what they were saying. The side-effects of hydralazine had been well-known in the West for ten years.[41]

Somerville added pointedly that not only was the 'pill in the coffee' theory mere speculation, but it would not have worked. Gaitskell would have had to have taken such pills repeatedly over many weeks:

They clearly did believe there was something in this theory that Gaitskell had been poisoned, and they were reluctant to let go of it.[42]

Consultations with Gaitskell's brother Arthur about the history of the Labour leader's disease provided no comfort either. Wright returned to Porton Down to ply Dr Ladell with frustrated questions. Yes, it was possible that if the Russians had secretly continued work on hydralazine they might have refined it into a 'one-shot' drug to give people Lupus symptoms. No, he was not going to spend Porton's money on a crash programme of re-search in an attempt to prove it. Wright's great coup had slipped his grasp.

Wright, however, was not a man to give up a suspicion merely because there was no evidence for it. Eight years later the story was to leak to the British newspapers in an attempt to throw suspicion on Wilson. Angleton, too, continued to brood about the 'communistic' Wilson; when, shortly afterwards, the Labour leader became Prime Minister, Angleton was to launch a dramatic new initiative against him.

He combined this with a witch-hunt against suspected 'moles' in the CIA's own rival Soviet Division who had been 'fingered' by Golitsin. This was to paralyse the CIA much as it paralysed the smaller MI5. The best remark on this period of Intelligence history is probably that which a woman CIA officer made to Cleveland Cram, at the time No. two in the CIA's London station:

The relationship between Angleton and Golitsin was like the meeting of two paranoids who then walked arm in arm off into the setting sun.

Despite the curt rejection by Roger Hollis of the 'Gaitskell asassination plot', the CIA were not prepared to leave the 'Wilson case' alone. Instead, at the behest of some eight to ten agency counter-intelligence officers, John McCone went to see President Kennedy in 1963. McCone told Kennedy there was concern about Wilson and his connections with 'international socialism'. Walter Eden, McCone's staff officer, says:

85

It was unease about ... the relationships through the International Socialist movement ... Every time the West created an international trade union movement, the Soviets came up with one. When we had a Peace Congress, they had a Peace Congress.

Kennedy's reaction was brusque: 'He said, if you have specific proof, you pursue leads ... In the meantime, as President of the US, I will deal with Wilson if he becomes Prime Minister of the UK. And let's hear nothing more about it until something crops up.'

If elements in MI5 and the CIA were prepared to believe that Hugh Gaitskell had been assassinated by the KGB it was almost certainly a case of what is known in psychology as 'projection'. For at the time the theory was current the CIA itself had entered the assassination business.

They had been learning from the British. There is now a mass of unanswerable evidence that Anthony Eden, as Prime Minister, twice tried to have Nasser, the President of Egypt, assassinated by MI6 after he expropriated the Suez Canal in the 1950s. A Foreign Office minister, Sir Anthony Nutting, has testified that Eden shouted down a telephone to him at the Savoy Hotel, 'I want Nasser murdered.' And Peter Wright has told how, as one of the Secret Service's few 'boffins', he had joint talks at Porton Down with MI6 technical staff about the murder plan. Nerve gas, as developed by the pilot plant at Nancekuke, Cornwall, was to be inserted in canisters into the ventilation system at one of Nasser's HQs. Wright says it was he who pointed out that this would kill everyone in the building. The scheme was dropped as insufficiently 'deniable' after the Foreign Secretary, Selwyn Lloyd, found out and became distressed. When a direct Anglo-French-Israeli military invasion had failed, Eden returned to the murderous idea. According to Anthony Verrier, an author with excellent MI6 connections, 'Before leaving for Jamaica to recover from the worst effects of his fevers, Eden ordered Nasser's assassination. The MI6 station officer in Beirut packed up hurriedly and left for London.' CIA representative Wilbur Eveland confirms that MI6 officers subsequently told him in Beirut that, 'teams have been fielded to assassinate Nasser.' The plan failed – either through Nasser's good Intelligence, a faulty weapons cache, or deliberate MI6 'sabotage', depending on which MI6 channels one chooses to believe.

In 1961–3, around the time of Harold Wilson's rise to power, the CIA itself began to consider assassination as a tool in achieving their political and Intelligence aims. Wright claims that, on a visit to Washington, he offered Angleton and his pistol-toting colleague William Harvey technical tips on murder methods. It was later officially established that intended victims of the ZR/RIFLE programme, tucked away in a covert signals-eavesdropping department called 'Staff D', included both Castro in Cuba and Lumumba in the Congo. An agent, a deniable foreigner code-named WIN, was recruited on November 1, 1960 to assassinate Lumumba. A fatal virus, designed to mimic a tropical disease, was flown in for him in the diplomatic pouch, accompanied by syringe, mask and surgical gloves. The scheme foundered; Lumumba was killed shortly afterwards by his opponents.

There were dozens of unsuccessful plans to assassinate Castro, which included poisoning his cigars, and enlisting a Mafioso, Johnny Rosselli, to do the dirty work. On May 30, 1961, the CIA had been an accomplice to the shooting of Dominican ruler Rafael Trujillo. On November 1, 1963, the South Vietnamese leader Ngo Dinh Diem was assassinated by generals mounting a coup at America's behest.

So, all in all, it was unsurprising that these Intelligence men should jump to the conclusion that Harold Wilson had got where he was through assassination. That was a game they understood. But in the minds of men like Wright, the 'Russian plot' went even deeper. Having first put their agent in power at the head of the Labour Party, the Russians' next move would clearly be to ensure he became Prime Minister. How could that be done? Only by destroying the ruling Conservative Party. And was that not happening even at that very moment . . ?

The Profumo affair was one of the first domestic events to follow Harold Wilson's accession to the party leadership. John Profumo, the War Minister, was forced to resign after telling lies to Parliament about his relationship with a girl called Christine Keeler. Keeler had, it would appear, also been sleeping with Captain Eugene Ivanov, a GRU officer from the Soviet embassy. At the centre of the affair was a society osteopath, Dr Stephen Ward, who had been manipulating Keeler, and who was incautiously recruited by MI5 in the hope that Ivanov could be compromised.

One of the secret servicemen who appeared earlier in these pages, Harry Wharton, was by now working for MI5 in Britain, running a mixed stable of agents – journalists, prostitutes and policemen. He figured at the edge of the Profumo affair, having been tipped off by the vice squad at an early stage that things were going horribly wrong. Hollis' MI5 picked up their skirts and ran from the situation, leaving it to collapse: they only narrowly survived a judicial inquiry by Lord Denning into their failure to inform the Prime Minister of events.

Who had suffered from the Profumo affair? MI5 and the Conservative Party. And who had benefited? The answer was just as simple: Harold Wilson and the KGB. Peter Wright circulated the idea that the Labour Party had been deliberately tipped off about Profumo by a KGB 'mouthpiece', Victor Louis, and that this therefore proved that the entire situation had been orchestrated by the KGB in order to bring Harold Wilson to power. Twenty years later, he was still peddling this classic conspiracy theory:

When one remembers how the Russians were involved in the Profumo affair, the whole thing, to say the least, is suspicious.[43]

When the Labour Party won the General Election in October and Harold Wilson became Prime Minister for the first time, that only confirmed the suspicions of Wilson's enemies in MI5.

CHAPTER 5

The Labour Party, with Harold Wilson at its head, narrowly won the 1964 election having adroitly exploited 'security' issues. Would they get loyal service from MI5? Peter Wright, by this time ensconced in the counter-espionage branch of MI5, attempts in his memoirs to blame the Americans for any negative feelings towards Wilson.

> There was deep-seated hostility in the US intelligence community to the accession to power of Harold Wilson and the Labour Government in 1964. Partly this was due to anti-Labour bias, partly to the Labour government's plan to abandon Polaris – a pledge they soon reneged on.[1]

But Walter Eden, CIA chief John McCone's staff officer, says:

> I learned through normal liaison . . . that there were people in MI5 who were uneasy at the prospect of Wilson becoming Prime Minister.

Charles Bates, the resident FBI 'legal attaché' in London, recalls the hostile reaction to Wilson's victory of his own British colleagues in MI5:

> I do recall that when the Labour government came in, there was a general groan. The old school in MI5 didn't like Wilson's politics or his philosophy. There was a feeling which said, 'Wilson will screw up' . . . On my usual daily trip to MI5, it was comments like . . . 'The Empire is going down the drain'.[2]

One of Harold Wilson's first appointments after taking office was a meeting with Roger Hollis arranged by his inherited Whitehall Principal Private Secretary Derek Mitchell. Mitchell had already pointed out, no doubt with some amusement, that the Home Office exerted no real control over MI5. Lord Denning, who had carried out the official inquiry into the Profumo affair, had announced in his report that since the 1952 reforms by the then Cabinet Secretary, Sir Norman Brook, the chief Home Office official, the Permanent Secretary, had been in a position to supervise MI5. Mitchell told Wilson that this was news to him. As Wilson wrote later: 'Ministerial responsibility [for MI5] was blurred and I had to issue a new Directive.'[3]

He told Hollis that he was appointing his trusted colleague, the Labour MP George Wigg, as a ministerial link-man between MI5 and No. 10

Downing Street, and that he expected to be kept informed of any 'security developments' with political implications. He asked if any MPs were being run as MI5 agents: Hollis reportedly assured him that any such activity would cease. He certainly did not confide in the new Prime Minister that Tom Driberg had been run throughout the whole of the Attlee administration. Nor did he think fit to mention that on a golf-course a few years earlier, he himself had tried to recruit Wilson's new Navy minister, Christopher Mayhew, to spy on Labour MPs.

Nor, one imagines, did Hollis confide in the new Socialist Prime Minister that Captain Henry Kerby was an MI5 agent. Kerby was yet another Conservative MP linked to the Intelligence services. A large, bald man with a safe parliamentary seat at Arundel in the heart of the 'Tory shires', he had worked as an MI6 agent-runner in the war. He spoke fluent Russian and kept up many Soviet trade contacts on MI5's behalf. Peter Wright recalls a 1956 plan to use Kerby's links with the Russians to present the Soviet ambassador with a new bugging gadget – a silver model of the Kremlin artfully designed to reflect microwaves and thus function as a microphone. At the time of the Profumo affair, Kerby had successfully ingratiated himself with George Wigg, and with Harold Wilson's office, by offering scurrilous 'Intelligence' about the Tory party. He had subsequently managed to establish himself as Wigg's undercover henchman.

Wilson also asked Hollis whether the phones of MPs were currently being tapped. Hollis said 'Yes'. Wilson, by his own account, ordered it to stop forthwith. He said that no investigations were to be carried out on MPs or members of the House of Lords without the Prime Minister's personal approval. He then told Hollis that he wanted the young political advisers in his office, including his political secretary Marcia Williams, to be 'positively vetted' so that they could have access to secret papers, but he was not prepared to let his ministerial appointments be positively vetted. He would submit lists of the names of ministers he proposed to appoint so that MI5 could check them against their files – the process known as 'negative vetting', but that was all. George Wigg, probably backed by the Intelligence-minded Richard Crossman, had tried to persuade the new Prime Minister to trawl through his colleagues' private lives according to positive vetting methodology, but had failed to persuade him.[4]

Wilson no doubt imagined he was taking a firm line with MI5 by laying down rules at the start of his term of office. In fact his aims were probably based more on political expediency than on any point of principle: he wanted to avoid the kind of embarrassment Attlee had experienced when MP George Thomas had complained of being put under MI5 surveillance and, more to the point, prevent anything like another Profumo affair. The idea of introducing positive vetting for ministers was totally unpractical – how could any Prime Minister form a government while waiting several weeks for referees to be followed up and personal inquiries made? Who would run the government departments in the meantime? – but Wilson's rejection of it was seen in a bad light in some quarters, especially when coupled with this new policy of firmer political control of the Security Services. Charles Bates of the FBI recalls a general sullenness about Wilson's attitude: 'They weren't a bit happy ... it restricted their movements and the cases they were handling.' He agreed with them: 'I felt rather strongly that it was too much of a political intrusion into the operation of the Security Service.'

In fact Hollis managed with little difficulty to conceal from Wilson what the true state of affairs was within MI5, particularly the Blunt scandal and its repercussions. Hollis also concealed from Wilson, just as he had concealed from Macmillan, that MI5 was riddled with internal suspicion. The Prime Minister's hand would have been greatly strengthened had Hollis admitted that paranoia had reached such a level that, in the vain hope of proving his own deputy to be a Russian spy, Peter Wright's cameras were being rigged up behind one-way mirrors to study Graham Mitchell groaning to himself in his office on wet afternoons. According to Wright, while Hollis kept his own Prime Minister in the dark, he had already flown over in person to tell the agent of a foreign power – John McCone, head of the CIA – about the inconclusive Mitchell situation. The US Intelligence agencies were of course already aware of the Blunt confession, as was, in outline at least, one Conservative politician, the former Attorney-General, Sir John Hobson.

Hollis gravely abused his position in order to keep the Prime Minister in the dark: the key to the future, as his retirement approached, lay in keeping the Security Service out of the hands of a Labour nominee who might find out what had been going on. Wilson's failure to defeat – or even understand – MI5's manoeuvres, was a significant error. He was to pay dearly for it.

Of the original Labour government which Wilson appointed, at least six of his ministers were to be accused by elements in MI5 of being Soviet spies or 'security risks'. So was the Prime Minister himself together with one ministerial candidate, two back-bench MPs, and one senior party official. With the exception of the insignificant Will Owen, the spying allegations were all false. The eleven victims were (with the jobs to which they were initially appointed):

Harold Wilson: Prime Minister
John Diamond: Chief Secretary, Treasury
John Stonehouse: Parliamentary Secretary, Aviation
Sir Barnet Stross: Parliamentary Secretary, Health
Judith Hart: Under-Secretary of State for Scotland

Stephen Swingler: Parliamentary Secretary, Transport
Niall MacDermot: Financial Secretary, Treasury
Tom Driberg: Labour Party National Executive
Bernard Floud: MP for Acton
Will Owen: MP for Morpeth
Arthur Bax: Labour Party Press Officer

The following eight prominent Labour supporters were also defamed, without any justification whatsoever, by Peter Wright and those who sided with him:

Jack Jones, General Secretary of Britain's biggest trade union, the Transport and General Workers Union

Hugh Scanlon, General Secretary of the Engineers' Union

Lord Zuckerman, the Labour government's chief scientific adviser

Robert Maxwell, Labour MP, publisher and later owner of the *Daily Mirror*

Lord Bernstein, chairman of Granada Television

Lord Kagan, head of Gannex Textiles and Labour Party backer

Lord Plurenden (Rudy Sternberg), head of the Sterling petrochemical group and also a Labour backer

Lady Falkender (Marcia Williams), Wilson's long-serving political secretary.

It was an astonishing campaign, which undoubtedly weakened Wilson's governments and, as will become clear, had vicious effects on individuals. During it, MI5 officers repeatedly committed serious criminal offences by leaking supposedly top secret – and highly misleading – material from their files to the press and to the government's Conservative opponents. Needless to say, no MI5 officer has ever been prosecuted for such crimes. The Official Secrets Act, it seemed, only operated one way.

When Wilson's raw new ministers came to office (hardly anyone except Wilson himself had had Cabinet experience) they split into two groups: those who were infatuated by the idea of MI5, and those who were intensely suspicious of the hunch-backed, saturnine Hollis and his men. Their first contact with MI5 was when they received a booklet prepared in the wake of the Profumo affair by the convivial Dick Thistlethwaite, who had been the first post-war link-man with Hoover's FBI in Washington and who eventually rose to head, none too impressively, MI5's 'F' branch, the 'counter-subversive' department.

Entitled 'Their Trade is Treachery', this pamphlet consisted of a series of lurid case histories of officials and diplomats who had been seduced, compromised and blackmailed by Soviet Bloc Intelligence officers. In deference to the Foreign Office, many of the cases were not specifically attributed to the KGB, but the target was obvious enough. When the Wilson administration came in, Thistlethwaite toured Whitehall with his booklet, doing his best to frighten the new Labour ministers.

He certainly succeeded in some cases. The eager young Postmaster General, Tony Benn, was interrupted by Thistlethwaite's visit as he was installing telephone-answering machines, computers, photocopiers and other hi-tech gadgets in his office.

In his diary for October 27, 1964 he recorded (getting the booklet's title slightly wrong):

My first job this morning was the security briefing given by Mr Thistle-thwaite from the security services. With him was the Director-General [of the Post Office]; Tilling [Benn's civil service Private Secretary]; and Joe Slater [Assistant Postmaster General]. We had about an hour and a half and he went through all the material that is in the security services' book 'Their Trade is Treason'. It was a most unattractive hour and a half. This man, though very intelligent, was deep in the heart of the James Bond world, and whatever else one may think about espionage and counter-espionage, there is no morality in it either way.

Only nine days later, Benn and his wife were at the Soviet Embassy for anniversary celebrations of the Revolution. They found themselves regarding their old acquaintances among the Soviet diplomatic corps with new unease, particularly when one of them, Mikhail Rogov, made remarks suggesting he had been doing background research on the Benns' relationship with a CIA-linked businessman.

Coming so soon after MI5 had warned me about the number of Soviet intelligence agents operating in the Soviet Embassy in London, it certainly made us both more cautious about Rogov.

Benn's wife Caroline immediately suspected that Rogov might be linked to Soviet Intelligence. Thistlethwaite would have been pleased. Benn had not been 'vetted', but he thought MI5 might be following him about. That December, he became distinctly nervous about MI5 when Joe Cort, a physicist who had been hounded out of America by McCarthyism in 1954, made contact with him in London.

Benn's unease about the Security Services was shared by the young political advisers at No. 10. As soon as the government took office, he noted down a conversation with John Allen, a Labour Party aide who had moved into the Cabinet Office:

... John and I agree we both feel weighted down by the security side. We all had the feeling our letters were being opened and our telephones being bugged – though we suspected the security people were as inefficient as the government departments over which we had some control.

The 'positive vetting' of all the No. 10 aides filled him with distaste:

An MI5 man came along this morning to interview me about a political adviser who has given me as a reference for the positive vetting procedure in order to work at No. 10. The chap was a real pudgy, flatfoot police type and very friendly. But it is an odious business being asked to answer personal questions such as drinking habits, sexual deviations and private life.

When Vladimir Kirillin, the chairman of the USSR state committee for science and technology, came to London and dined at Benn's Holland Park home, the presents he brought were immediately removed by MI5 to see if they incorporated Peter Wright-style microphones.

Not all the new ministers shared Benn's views. With the new Home Secretary, Frank Soskice, who was nominally Hollis's immediate superior, and of White Russian background, the 'service' had very little difficulty. 'Soskice is an impossibly reactionary man entirely in the hands of his civil servants,' Benn noted. His view was confirmed by a story he was told by Labour's new Lord Chancellor, Gerald Gardiner, at the Labour Party Conference in 1965. Gardiner related to his companions at lunch:

I was once told years ago that Cabinet ministers were allowed to see their own MI5 files. So I asked my department to get hold of mine, thinking that this would give me a good opportunity to judge the efficiency of MI5. After all, I would be able to judge what they said about me, in comparison with what I knew about myself. However the civil servants hummed and hawed a lot and so I kept saying to them every week or so 'Where is my file?' In the end, I said I wanted it by tomorrow, and they said I would have to see the Home Secretary. Frank Soskice was embarrassed and said that he couldn't agree and that he wasn't allowed to see the files either. When they wanted to show him anything, they photographed a page and gave it to him, but he never saw the complete file. He was so upset about it that I just let it drop.

Gardiner went on to say that he had heard that one minister who had insisted on seeing his complete file had been told that it had been destroyed the day before. Gardiner drew his own conclusions: whenever he had sensitive matters to discuss with the Labour Attorney-General, Elwyn Jones, he took elaborate precautions:

I thought it more likely than not that MI5 was bugging the telephones in my office . . . I took him out on one or more occasions in the car, because I knew the driver . . . she would never have allowed the car to be bugged without my knowledge.[5]

Benn reacted predictably to Gardiner's tale of the files:

It was a most amusing story because not only did it reveal the essential naivety of Gardiner but it was a direct confirmation of what one suspects: that there is no political control whatever over the security services. They regard a Minister, even the Home Secretary, as a transitory person, and they would feel under no obligation to reveal information to him. Indeed, I do not know how the Home Secretary could physically get hold of an MI5 file short of sending a platoon of policemen along to take it out of the filing cabinet . . . It also said a lot about Soskice as I can't believe that a Home Secretary could be fobbed off with just a page from an MI5 file if he insisted on seeing the whole thing.

When Benn went on a Moscow trip he attended meetings in the British embassy's secret basement conference room, which was 'suspended from the ceiling so it does not rest on any foundations'. 'From a corner of the room came the recording of a cocktail party playing continuously.' Although MI5 had already tried to frighten him with tales of British visitors being bugged and compromised by the KGB, Benn had trouble taking it seriously:

Tommy Balogh [the government's economic adviser] . . . came into my suite and sat on the bidet in the bathroom while I was quietly having a bath and he told me what he hoped to achieve . . . It was only later that I realised we had disregarded all the warnings in the security briefings. The Russians would have photographs of me in the bath and the government's economic adviser sitting on the bidet! We had a laugh about that . . . I went to see Harold about the Russian visit . . . I told him the story about my bath, but he didn't think that was very funny.

There were, of course, Wilson ministers who had an entirely different view of the Intelligence community. Mayhew was Navy minister and, to the annoyance of the left-wingers in the party, Wilson appointed Alun Gwynne-Jones, a former military Intelligence officer, minister for disarmament. Gwynne-Jones, who had been working as defence correspondent of *The Times*, was dubbed a peer, Lord Chalfont. Not even a Labour supporter, he was in many ways a professional anti-Communist. Niall MacDermot, a Treasury minister, was far from leftist (he was a supporter of the right-wing James Callaghan and had been in MI5 in the war). The Foreign Secretary, who had responsibility for all the main Intelligence and propaganda organisations – IRD, GCHQ and Dick White's MI6 – was another right-winger, Patrick Gordon-Walker. George Brown, friend of CIA station chief Archie Roosevelt, and comparer of notes with MI5 about 'crypto-Communist' MPs, was also a minister, at the Department of Economic Affairs. Brown retained his fascination with the secret world and when he later became Foreign Secretary he insisted on breaking precedent by personally visiting the MI6 HQ, Century House in south London.[6] This caused consternation, because it was supposed to be a State secret that the Foreign Office conducted espionage – this 'aspect of our national functions' as Harold Macmillan had awkwardly referred to it.

But it was about one particular Labour Minister that the most interesting allegation has been made. It was said that Mr Z (as we shall call him) was in fact an agent of the CIA. (The author cannot name Mr Z for legal reasons.) Such a suggestion would raise few eyebrows about many US client states – King Hussein of Jordan, President Mobuto of Zaire and Anwar Sadat of Egypt have all been reputedly financed by the CIA, along with innumerable Latin American rulers. But in Britain . . ? One can only report that Arthur Martin, head of 'D1' (counter-espionage) in MI5 before his transfer to MI6, told friends, 'I did hear that [the minister] was a spy.' An MI5 officer who served in the counter-espionage 'K' branch in the 1970s repeated the same story independently to the author: 'We knew that [Mr Z] was a CIA agent, or, if not an agent, at least very close to the Americans.' The journalist Chapman Pincher picked up the rumour as well, writing in 1977: 'I know the identity of one former Labour cabinet minister who was in regular touch with the CIA.' A hint of what may have provoked Wilson to order MI5 inquiries on this topic surfaced at one of his Cabinet meetings in 1967. Barbara Castle noted in her diary:

> The key issue in cabinet was the proposed White Paper on defence. Harold began by saying he had had a telegram from President Johnson asking us to go slow on defence cuts East of Suez. This was the second time a foreign power had got to know cabinet business. In these two cases, being the US it wasn't serious. Nonetheless cabinet business was secret and we should none of us chat about it at embassies and so on.[7]

But it was George Wigg, a man with a face like a stretched Doberman and protruding ears, who was the Labour minister most completely in thrall to MI5. A former soldier, Wigg loved the world of 'security' and agents. During the Profumo affair, with the help of Henry Kerby, he mounted successful plots to discredit Macmillan and Profumo. He continued to use Kerby (or be used by him) in his new role as a sort of jug-eared Beria. He set out to cultivate Thistlethwaite and MacDonald, the heads of 'F' branch (counter-subversion) and 'D' branch (counter-espionage) respectively. MacDonald says:

> I recall Wigg asking to see me. It was something to do with a letter from a lunatic, but he said he felt he ought to know me because he was Wilson's security watchdog. He said the one thing he couldn't stand was traitors, and if he had his way, he'd kick them off Beachy Head.[8]

Wigg's military nature made him a trying companion in the No. 10

'kitchen cabinet', constantly barking at his colleagues to remember to use their telephone 'scramblers'. Benn and the left-wingers disliked him, and Benn confessed himself 'terrified that George Wigg may be made Minister for Security and given power over all our lives'.[9] Benn considered him 'a complete madman, and if, as Dick Crossman thinks, he will be the minister of State at 10 Downing St, we shall soon have a police state run by Col. Wigg on the security side.'[10]

This fear was not altogether misplaced. When Edward Heath became Leader of the Conservative Opposition in 1965, Wigg was fed malicious and unfounded rumours by Kerby (who professed to dislike 'pansies') that Heath was a homosexual and had had an affair with a Third Secretary at the Swedish embassy. There was, of course, no truth in the story of Heath's homosexual activities but it was duly fed to MI5, whose members recalled it later when Heath became Prime Minister and showed distaste for MI5's style of work. The story was also – inevitably perhaps – picked up by Czech Intelligence, who, having discovered Heath's passion for organ music, optimistically prepared a plot to compromise him with a handsome homosexual organist in Prague. It had, of course, no success. Again, Tony Benn's diaries perhaps shed light on this incident:

Peter Shore [a Labour aide in Wilson's office] said that George Wigg had told him: 'I could destroy Heath given three hours.' Peter asked him what he meant and he said he could destroy anyone within three hours, including Peter. It was a significant remark and I am slightly confirmed in my view that Harold would find it hard to get rid of George.

While Wigg was peddling smut and untruths, the management of MI5 was in such turmoil that the United States made a determined attempt to penetrate the agency and get control of it.

There had been ugly scenes behind the guarded doors of Leconfield House by the time Wigg arrived. MI5 had a peculiar structure. Half a dozen 'directors' formed the controlling board of the organisation, under the deputy director-general, Mitchell, and the 'DGSS', Hollis, who had a small personal secretariat along the lines of a ministerial private office. Hollis himself was not a distinguished figure. The son of a minor bishop, and educated at a minor public school, Clifton College, he appears to have been a boisterous Oxford undergraduate, with a reputation for getting drunk, telling lavatory jokes and playing a lot of golf. He left early without getting a degree, and 'to get away from the family and the Church' sought his fortune in China. A bout of TB brought him home, jobless, although he appeared to have some family shareholdings. The job in MI5 was secured through his tennis acquaintances back in England. He was physically not strong. His political views can be judged from his letters home from China. In 1936, while others were fighting in Spain or organising hunger-marches, he wrote to his fiancée about the abdication of Edward VIII:

> I have always had a passionate loyalty to the monarchy and the ideals and duties of an English gentleman. All my time abroad has strengthened that too, because I've seen how much other people do respect our code ... Staunch Conservative that I am, I feel Edward has let us down.[11]

At Oxford Hollis was briefly a contemporary of Dick White, a man of rather more substantial intellectual gifts. At MI5 White made Hollis his deputy. Then, in 1956, Hollis was suddenly pitchforked into the top job. The head of MI6, Admiral 'Sinbad' Sinclair, was sacked in a rage by Anthony Eden after the 'Buster' Crabb fiasco; Eden replaced him by White, the head of the rival service, at short notice. This meant that, for the next nine years, White had 'across the street' a man essentially subordinate to him who depended on his backing.

Hollis sent his son to Eton. His politics were vapid rather than fanatical – in later life he expressed the view that perpetual Tory rule was not necessarily good for democracy, and that he might have voted for Gaitskell had he lived.

This, then, was the head of MI5 – a man of limited education, vision and achievement. Under him, there were probably no more than 150 officers, plus, of course, a larger number of support and administrative staff. MI5 was roughly the same size as a national newspaper such as the London *Daily Telegraph* – and, indeed, was not dissimilar in its type of employee or its activities. MI5 was, it is true, far too small and circumscribed to bear comparison with the KGB or the Gestapo. It did not have police powers of arrest. It did, however, have enough power over the life of citizens to be legitimately called a secret police. MI5 could make life very difficult for those who became its victims – depriving them of careers, livelihood or reputation without any redress. It had, in practice, immunity from the civilian police when it broke the law: it could burgle people's houses, and photograph or tape-record them in intimate moments. Its officers could and did successfully claim 'national security' as a reason to breach the confidentiality of bank managers, doctors and psychiatrists. They could raid the files of all other government departments, obtaining, for example, medical and tax records. They could have foreign visitors kept out of the country. They could also pass on information they acquired to the police, the customs or the tax authorities, if they felt minded to make trouble for their targets. They could 'plant' stories in the press, and they could trade information in secret with foreign governments.

All this power was unaccountable. No MI5 official used his own name in dealing with the public or with agents (they tended to use 'light cover', often names with similar initials to their own, to avoid confusion). Only once in the entire post-war history of MI5 was an outside body allowed to publish a report on its conduct and methods – the Denning report on the Profumo affair, which was scarcely critical. No minister was prepared to answer questions in Parliament about what MI5 did. No independent political or judicial body had oversight over it. It was part of the secret apparatus of perpetual war with which the British populace had been blessed without ever being consulted.

The 'board of directors' of MI5 in those days did not include any departments handling science, computers or terrorism as it was to later. Nor did it meet in the same room with MI6, GCHQ, the Americans and Canadians, as did the 'Joint Intelligence Organisation' higher up the Whitehall tree. These directors had the only really powerful executive jobs in MI5: typically, one, Bill Magan, heading 'E' branch, was still concerned exclusively with internal repression in the rapidly diminishing British colonies. 'A' branch handled all technical services – this included the 'watchers' who followed people about (three to a car in best bureaucratic fashion – one to drive, one to work the radio and one to read the map). The same branch laid on bugs, poisons and their antidotes, phone-taps, break-ins and lock-picking. 'B' branch – personnel – was a relatively recent novelty: its standards of recruitment, monitoring and training continued to be primitive. As the veterans of the Second World War and the colonies moved towards the pinnacles of their administrative careers, they were joined by muscular under-achievers from the ancient universities. MI5 was not an attractive career, with its low civil service pay-rates, its limited promotion chances, and, above all, its sheer security-obsessed narrowness. A few people who joined with wide horizons got out again: John Cuckney, for example, spent ten years in the post-war MI5 before going into merchant banking and a variety of Whitehall roles. He finished up as chairman of a defence contractor, Westland Helicopters.[12]

There were three other branches – 'C', 'D' and 'F'. Of these, 'C' was the most dreary. It covered 'protective security', which meant helping vet the employees of government departments and the State corporations which ran the telephone system, broadcasting, power supply and the railways. This branch also liaised not only with defence contractors, but with other private firms on a more or less undercover basis. It was, in fact, running a system of institutionalised McCarthyism which had grown out of the original 1947 agitation to squeeze 'Communists' out of British life.

'F' branch – the old 'Political Parties' division – and 'D' branch, which covered counter-espionage, were the core MI5 departments. Broadly, 'F' monitored the political activities of the British Communist Party, strikes and trade unions, while 'D' attacked Soviet Bloc activities. This last was probably the only division of MI5 of which the British general public had any notion: the illusion that MI5 was exclusively concerned with 'catching spies' was one which its managers found attractive.

99

Both these departments had similar methods of working. They collected material in the form of reports from informers, often paid. These could range from a secretary infiltrated into a trade union office to a businessman having dealings with an Iron Curtain country, or to a full-blown 'defector-in-place'. Such informers were called 'agents' or 'principal agents'. They often had assistants, message-carriers, or informers they recruited in turn. These people were called 'sub-agents' or 'support agents'. Within MI5, such groups of agents were handled by a case-officer, known as an 'agent-runner'.

This system is no different to that used by policemen, who call their agents 'snouts' (informally) or, more officially, 'informants': they have their real identities kept secret, and are often paid surprisingly large sums of money for their services. Within MI5, agents, like police informants, were given pseudonyms. Their real identities were held on 'YPFs' – personal files kept apart from the main registry in 'Y-boxes'. The Registry itself covered the entire ground floor of Leconfield House, and contained about two million 'PFs' during this period. The difference between them and police criminal records was that the MI5 registry contained a farrago of unchecked 'Intelligence', much of which could never be proved right or wrong, or which was susceptible to different interpretations. Needless to say, it did also contain apparently factual material – membership lists, observation reports, and travel records for example. Events have also shown some of this material to be misleading or even simply wrong. MI5 was like any other government department with which the British public might be more familiar, such as the Gas Board or the Inland Revenue: it made bureaucratic mistakes.

The building was full of large numbers of young or middle-aged women, recruited as librarians, clerks and secretaries, and sometimes becoming case-officers. Their presence frequently led to intra-office marriages and affairs. Hollis had a long affair with his secretary, Val Hammond, and eventually married her. Arthur Martin married an MI5 secretary. Anne Last married another case-officer, Charles Elwell. Harry Wharton also married within MI5. Occasionally women had husbands outside the office – Anne Orr-Ewing, for example, a well-known counter-espionage officer, was married to Hamish Orr-Ewing, chairman of the office machinery firm Rank-Xerox. The building also had a bar, on the theory that inmates needed somewhere to unwind where they could talk secret shop. It was known as the 'Pig and Eye Club,' for reasons which have not been established. What has emerged, however, is that the gossip there could be of a poisonous nature.

Peter Wright's scientific empire-building had led to a devastating career disappointment. He lobbied to set up a full-scale science research laboratory for both Intelligence services, with himself as director. A secret science division was set up, at Hanslope Park, staffed by fifty naval scientists, but

100

Wright was passed over for the top job. That went to Hector Willis, head of the Naval Scientific Service. Wright had to content himself with being one of two deputies, and he hated it. It was, he said, 'undouotedly the most unhappy period of my professional life.' He lobbied hard to get back into the action, using as his passport his conviction that there was a 'mole' inside MI5. Attaching himself to Arthur Martin and pointing out to him possible suspicious failures in old bugging and radio interception cases, he won the support of the crusader from the 'Malayan mafia'. Ironically, it was Graham Mitchell, whom Martin suspected so strongly of being a 'mole', who later admitted having given the thwarted Wright his head. Mitchell formally approved his transfer to become a full-time counter-espionage officer. Not only that, but he was made a section head – of 'D3' (Research). In January 1964 at the age of forty-four, Wright now had real power. His appointment came a few weeks before the FBI turned over the first proof against Anthony Blunt to the British.

Arthur Martin, the head of 'D1' (Soviet counter-espionage) was the real driving-force behind the British mole-hunt. However extreme and tactless he was, he did at least know something of what he was talking about. A former Army signals officer, he had done much of the successful detective work following up the fragmentary code-breaks in the post-war Fuchs and Maclean cases. According to Wright, after the 1951 defections he was refused permission to mount aggressive investigations of all the 'Cambridge Communists', many of whom were now rising diplomats and officials. Instead, he was posted to Malaya as 'security liaison officer', in the colonial campaign which soaked up so much British energy. Now back in 'D' branch, he felt more than vindicated. Behind his unassuming manner, Martin was on a crusade. As MacDonald, another MI5 veteran of India, Malaya and Kenya, said of counter-espionage, in interviews before his death:

> The danger area is that if you become obsessed with somebody, something, there it is crawling inside your head all the time and you shut everything else out, and you just listen to what's going on inside your own head. And anybody that puts up the contrary side, you see, is guilty of sinning against your own special Holy Ghost.

Martin, too, was dangerously frustrated in his career. He wanted to be made overall head of 'D' branch and was resentful when the job went to the Old Etonian Malcolm Cumming, apparently on the principle that it was his turn. Martin chafed under Cumming. While he was engaged in the dangerous business of trying to prove that his own superiors were spies, he ran out of friends. When one of his ten case-officers, Hal Doyne-Ditmass, was suddenly posted to Washington, Martin had angry words with Cumming: Hollis called Martin into his office, and suspended him for a fortnight, military-style, for 'indiscipline'. And then, at an angry conference of senior

101

'D' branch officers in which Hollis again attempted to close down the Mitchell case, Martin directly challenged Hollis's authority. He said that if Mitchell was innocent, perhaps he was being run as a 'stalking-horse' for someone else. Those present, like Wright, thought the inference was obvious – Hollis himself was now being accused of being a Soviet spy. The suspicions about Mitchell had already led to appalling strains in the 'Office'. Furnival Jones later told the CIA that he had nerved himself to interrogate Mitchell alone and decided he was innocent. But 'It cost me a very dear personal friendship.'

By now, Hollis, the Director-General, was beside himself with rage at what he saw as Martin's veiled accusations. He decided to sack him on the spot. Dick White persuaded him to let Martin be transferred to MI6 until things cooled down. But it would be fair to say things never cooled down: twenty-five years later, Martin was more 'feverish and hawkish' than ever, in the words of one CIA officer who saw him. In 1964, Hollis ordered Martin to clear his desk and leave the building within three days or he would be sacked without a pension. Furnival Jones begged Martin to go up to Hollis's office and shake hands before he left. The farewell was counter-productive: Martin later grimly told friends that he found Hollis 'white as a sheet' with his head leaning on his arm – 'He knew that I knew.'

Meanwhile, Hollis was storming at MacDonald:

I've had my troubles with Arthur Martin, who's just gone. As far as I'm concerned, he wants to sit in this chair of mine. He thinks I'm a spy. To save you time, I am not a bloody Soviet agent, I'm the Director-General of MI5!

Martin's ejection in this atmosphere of hysteria had one dire consequence: it left the debriefing of Anthony Blunt in the hands of Martin's most enthusiastic and least rational supporter. Peter Wright now had his big chance: like his mentor Jim Angleton in Washington, he had got control of his very own defector.

While Hollis and his juniors snarled at each other, the Americans were also planning his downfall. Hoover at the FBI had never liked the British, and although the CIA was stuffed with East Coast Anglophiles, the drum-roll of penetration – Vassall, Philby, Blake, Blunt – had caused genuine shock. The structure of WASP links meant that the best things British spies had to betray were American secrets – submarine detection systems, eavesdropping tunnels, covert operations such as Albania. To top it all, a Labour government had come to power, whose members made noises about Vietnam, NATO and nuclear disarmament. President Johnson and his advisers, when they took over after Kennedy's assassination in 1963, were open to suggestions that, in America's interest, British counter-intelligence had to be brought under closer US supervision. It was a project close to Angleton's intriguing heart.

The existence of the 'Gray-Coyne Report' was perhaps the most genuinely surprising disclosure in Peter Wright's book *Spycatcher*. Wright described it as a deliberate act of US espionage, aimed at a wholesale takeover of British Intelligence in all but name. CIA sources have bridled at Wright's account, but describe it grudgingly enough as 'almost half-correct'. This would be in line with the general texture of Wright's memoirs, which have turned out time and again to be broadly true in outline, but unreliable on detail and occasionally deliberately misleading in emphasis. Wright himself blames the many admitted errors in *Spycatcher* on the publishers' unwillingness to let him have second thoughts about his manuscript.

As Wright tells the story, President Johnson commissioned the President's Foreign Intelligence Advisory Board (PFIAB) to carry out a thorough study of British Intelligence systems in the summer of 1965. The PFIAB had been resurrected by Kennedy after the Bay of Pigs debacle, and was to conduct some of its bitterest post-mortems over repeated Intelligence failures in Vietnam. The British study was carried out clandestinely. Two PFIAB members were given the job – Gordon Gray, the Governor of North Carolina, and Patrick Coyne, a former senior FBI officer. Gray, as Eisenhower's national security affairs representative, served on the President's 1955 '5412 Committee' set up to authorise CIA covert operations. He was the predecessor in that job of McGeorge Bundy, Walt Rostow, Henry Kissinger, and Zbigniew Brzezinski.[13]

The entire Anglo-US Intelligence relationship was up for inspection. Gray and Coyne came to London and were escorted around every single British secret establishment by Cleve Cram who, as resident CIA liaison officer, had a pass for free entry everywhere. According to Wright:

No one in British intelligence was told that the review was even taking place. In any other country, the review would be known by a cruder name – espionage.[14]

He says Angleton boasted to him of the report, saying, 'Everything'll change now. We're going to have a beefed-up CIA London station and half those officers are going to work directly inside MI5. We'll have access to everything and help you where we can.' The CIA men to be moved into London were, of course, to be hand-picked Angleton aides. Wright's version is that the report bitterly criticised Hollis and Cumming for failure of counter-intelligence leadership, and that Hollis and his new deputy Furnival Jones were enraged and frightened to hear that the US planned to make a formal approach to Harold Wilson via the US ambassador David Bruce, to 'brief him on the findings'. Cram was pressed by Angleton to take soundings with George Wigg, but Hollis threatened that Cram would be declared *persona non grata* and expelled if there was any more interference.

Obviously, the Wright version is only half the story. A full-scale review

103

of the Anglo-US link would have concentrated more on the sharing of Signals Intelligence, where a tremendous technological shift was on the way with the appearance of satellites. The Labour government was attempting to retreat from empire, with a corresponding reduction in the number of Intelligence bases it had available. There is evidence that this area was also reviewed, both by the British and the US. But, as Wright tells it, the US 'espionage' was an internal catalyst for the sort of MI5 reforms he approved of – 'D' Branch was expanded dramatically and Cumming eventually replaced as its head by MacDonald. CIA officers say that Hollis was so enraged that he refused to speak to Helms, the CIA chief, thereafter. The more diplomatic-minded officers in the London station persuaded Helms to drop the idea of direct political intervention in British affairs. Instead, they argued, why not simply wait for Hollis to retire at the end of the year? If Furnival Jones succeeded him, he would be a 'hawk' acceptable to the US and to Angleton. He could be relied on to make MI5 counter-intelligence much more powerful.

The most important change planned was the decision to set up a formal counter-intelligence machine on a multinational basis, to parallel the systems which bound GCHQ and MI6 to their English-speaking cousins. This was CAZAB – super-secret conferences every eighteen months or so, presided over by Angleton, at which the contents of counter-intelligence files would be freely shared between the Canadians, the Americans, the New Zealanders, the Australians, and the British (hence the acronym). So, it might reasonably be said, one of Wilson's first acts as head of the new Socialist government was to give away even more British autonomy to the US. Except that, according to Wright, Wilson was wholly unaware of CAZAB, which was set up behind the backs of the politicians in Britain.

If George Wigg imagined that the planned reforms in MI5, about which he was no doubt told, constituted an improvement in 'security', he might well have asked 'Whose security?' In the long run, Angleton, and Angleton's ideas, were merely given a free run in a process that was to do Harold Wilson great harm. The finest service Wigg could have done was to ensure that, when Hollis retired at the end of 1965, the Labour government put in their own man as Director-General of MI5. Wilson had the right to appoint the heads of the Intelligence services. Indeed, it was reported that he had his own candidate in mind – Eric St Johnston, Chief Constable of Lancashire, who had had many dealings with Leconfield House. But Wigg had been captured by those he had set out to control: he persuaded Wilson to let the 'professional' Martin Furnival Jones inherit the organisation.

CHAPTER 6

At first, Harold Wilson was able to exploit Furnival Jones's Intelligence machine for his own purposes. The most notorious example of this was the 1966 seamen's strike, which was having a severe effect on the British economy. Wigg was persuaded that, by bugging members of the seamen's executive, MI5 could expose a 'Red plot' which could be used to end the strike. He told Wilson the evidence was 'sensational' and, as Marcia Williams recalled later, 'The people on the ground came as a team to tell him of their work and how they bugged everybody and how they got tape-recordings.'[1] MI5 certainly acquired evidence to show that Communist activists were putting pressure on executive members to press on with the strike, but it was nevertheless a shock to Wilson's left-wing supporters when he used this evidence to play the Red card. Barbara Castle, by now a Cabinet minister, noted that Wigg was having 'a disastrous effect on Harold, seeking intrigues everywhere.' On June 21, Wilson told the Cabinet the strikers would go back were it not for 'outside pressures':

> This was received in pretty non-committal silence . . . I asked if we could be given more details of the conspiracy, to which Harold replied ponderously that there were some things which were better not revealed, even to the Cabinet (Shades of Wigg!).[2]

A couple of days later, Wilson found it politic to brief the secretary of the Trades Union Congress, George Woodcock, about a 'union official . . . interfering with the strike from the outside'.

> Frank [Cousins], looking like thunder, asked if we could be told who the official was since everybody else had been. Reluctantly, Harold named the Lighterman chap and Frank dismissed it contemptuously with 'Oh, him!'

Eventually, Wilson made a long speech in Parliament branding the Communists as 'a tightly knit group of politically motivated men.' He described meetings, dates, times, who had stayed in whose house, what the CP were privately planning – but he could not bring himself to quote from the surveillance transcripts, which made his accusations a little thin as a result.

While Tony Benn noted in his diary that Wilson's naming of 'the communists who had intervened . . . made me sick and reminded me of

McCarthyism'[3], Wilson, meanwhile, attempted to repeat the tactic which Macmillan had worked on him. He invited Edward Heath, the new opposition leader, to see him privately, and produced both Thistlethwaite, the head of 'F' Branch and 'one of the operators in the field' from MI5.[4] To Wilson's chagrin, Heath was not in the least awestruck. He walked out of the meeting and tabled a parliamentary question demanding that Wilson justify himself with more public information.

Wilson also turned to the Intelligence services during another crisis, when the white settler regime in Rhodesia declared unilateral independence in November 1965. He threatened unspecified MI6 sabotage if the Rhodesians interferred with electricity supplies from the Kariba dam, which also served a hostile black Zambia. As Barbara Castle noted in her diary, Wilson said that:

> If Zambia was cut off, we should cut off power to Rhodesia . . . He asked me not to press for details. 'There are ways of doing this which are best not discussed even in this cabinet, but which do not involve confrontation.' At this point he looked sternly round the room and said he preferred ministers not to take notes, 'not even for those diaries'. I looked up from my shopping list on which I had just written 'buy new lavatory seat' . . .

Generally, however, Wilson's Intelligence was so bad that Wigg rang round ministers asking rather desperately if they knew any specialists in psychological warfare (Crossman, who had been in PWE, noted acidly that people only talked about 'psychological war' when they had no troops). Wilson claimed on MI6 advice that economic sanctions would crush the Rhodesian rebellion in 'weeks, not months' (it only ended fourteen years later). Wigg, once again, attempted to come to the rescue, recruiting MI5's standby, Capt. Henry Kerby MP and a White Russian of his acquaintance to go out to Rhodesia and take covert soundings. It is scarcely surprising that Wilson's Rhodesian Intelligence was so poor. There was no machine to do the job. 'Rhodesian Intelligence' meant the anti-Communist organisation set up during colonial days by MI5, with support propaganda from IRD, in co-operation with the Portuguese and South Africans. Its head, Ken Flower, later recalled that throughout the 'rebellion' he travelled to London regularly to confer privately with his old friends in MI5.

The Rhodesians got more Intelligence on Wilson than he did on them. Wilson's own typing pool was penetrated. South African Intelligence (BOSS), acting for the Rhodesian Special Branch, recruited Helen Keenan, a typist, who handed over Wilson's cabinet minutes to an Intelligence officer she had met at the Zambezi Club in Earls Court. The British Special Branch interrogated her when she suddenly resigned, and obtained a confession. She and her controller were jailed for the very modest terms of six months and five years respectively.

During this early period, Tony Brooks, the 'war hero', was transferred over to MI5 from MI6 as part of the general boosting of 'D' branch numbers. One of his first jobs was to take part secretly in the Mountbatten Inquiry – the recently retired chief of the defence staff had to conduct an embarrassing inquest into how renegade MI6 officer George Blake had managed to escape from the prison where he was serving his 40-year espionage sentence, and turn up safe and sound in Russia. It was found that MI5 were not to blame. Harry Wharton, the MI5 agent-runner, was packed off to Nigeria where, as civil war loomed, both MI5 and MI6 now had stations. His role was presumably to ferret out Communism, in the interests of the stability of a regime which Britain supported. Communism turned out, however, to have very little to do with it. For the only time in his life, Wharton's name appeared in an official reference book. The new combined Foreign and Commonwealth List for 1967 has the entry 'First Secretary – H. D. Wharton'. It disappeared again from subsequent entries. Wharton met the Prime Minister when Wilson arrived in Lagos for the 1966 Commonwealth Conference, conducted, as he later recalled, to the crackle of distant small-arms fire. A few days after Wilson left, his host, Abubekar Balewa, was found dead in a ditch, which can have given the British Premier no great confidence in the MI6 reports which had told him it was safe to go there. Wharton was to meet Harold Wilson on a second occasion, five years later, in what were to turn out to be much more awkward circumstances.

Meanwhile, Wigg was also having to protect Wilson from enemies nearer at hand. The government was under attack not only from the Conservatives but from within Whitehall. The military, and military Intelligence within the Ministry of Defence, were Labour's bitterest enemies. One retiring Intelligence officer at the MOD, John Drew, proposed to right-wing journalist Harry Pincher that they write a novel together. Drew, says Pincher, had been in charge of 'cover-plans' there. Their novel, of which they wrote 30,000 words, was to be about a crypto-Communist Labour prime minister and what he did during his term of office 'to please his Russian masters' by way of cancelling military projects, closing colonial bases and cutting MI5 and MI6 budgets 'to ease the task of the KGB'.[5] This curious propaganda venture was never published. 'After about six months,' Pincher recalls, 'we had to abandon the project [for libel reasons] because as fast as we wrote a chapter, the Labour government actually did what we predicted.'

Another defence press officer, Colonel Sammy Lohan, regularly leaked scurrilous material to Pincher and others in an attempt to bring Wilson down. This included peddling an untrue story that Lord Chalfont, the disarmament minister, had been seen in the White Tower restaurant with his hand on the knee of a woman 'with Communist leanings' and was therefore a security risk. Wigg got reports of these disloyal absurdities from

Kerby. Wigg was also told by MacDonald at MI5 that Lohan had been suspected of leaking earlier stories to Pincher – when the imprisoned Soviet 'illegal' Gordon Lonsdale had been exchanged in 1964 for an imprisoned British MI6 agent, Greville Wynne, Pincher had been 'leaked' the story and 'D' branch investigations blamed Lohan. There is some evidence that Wigg was privately supplied with MI5 transcripts of taps on Lohan's phone. Pincher later said airily: 'Of course Wilson was right in saying that Lohan was anti-Labour, but then so are almost all civil servants who really care about defence and the Forces.'

Once again, Wilson's attempts to exploit Intelligence resources backfired painfully. Wigg's penchant for intrigues turned out to be a liability. Pincher eventually got hold of a mundane GCHQ story – that Signals Intelligence at Cheltenham secretly collected up all overseas cables for scrutiny. The secretary of the 'D-notice committee' – by now Pincher's friend Colonel Lohan himself – made no very strenuous attempt to stop him printing the disclosure, although the Anglo-US activities of GCHQ were normally regarded as a major Intelligence taboo. When the story appeared, it seemed to imply Labour were once again up to 'gestapo' activities – to Wilson, battling at the time to keep GCHQ's escalating secret budget under control, it must have been doubly infuriating. Egged on by Wigg, Wilson attempted to revenge himself on both Lohan and Pincher by setting up an inquiry to castigate them on 'national security' grounds, the so-called 'D-Notice affair'. Marcia Williams later said, 'We were told that fifty of our agents were lost as a result of the D-notice affair,' which seems hard to credit. Wilson found himself faced with an outcry over press freedom, and his perfectly truthful hints in Parliament that Lohan's activities had been of earlier concern to MI5 were condemned by *Times* editor William Rees-Mogg as 'a pitiless innuendo'.

Wigg – 'Harold's Rasputin' as Barbara Castle called him – had over-reached himself. He claimed later that he had also fallen out with Marcia Williams, Wilson's political secretary, over developments in her private life. She fell in love with a political journalist and they moved in together. They wished to have children and she became pregnant. Wigg misguidedly chose to regard the relationship as a potential 'security risk' and the pregnancy as a danger to Wilson's reputation. Marcia Williams later told friends she had attended a top-level meeting of security advisers at No. 10 and had been completely candid about her circumstances. But there was an atmosphere of secrecy in the Downing St circle. Marcia Williams was told – she does not specify by whom – 'You can't have an abortion: people will assume it was the Prime Minister.' No thought was, in fact, further from her mind. Marcia eventually had two children. After the relationship ended, she brought them up single-handed. There was later some embarrassment in 1969, when the five-year review of Marcia's 'positive vetting' was due. She showed no enthusiasm for a process which would put her private life on file to those she regarded as her enemies although she underwent it dutifully enough. It was as a result of this episode and Wigg's malice that yet more false stories about Wilson's relationship with Mrs Williams began to circulate within the Intelligence agencies. It was ironic in view of the discovery Marcia Williams later made – as she told friends – that Wigg himself had an unacknowledged son.

Within 'K6', the counter-espionage department where MI5's most secret files were kept one incredulous Intelligence officer recalls being told confidently many years later: 'Wilson has resigned because the KGB got evidence that he was the father of Marcia's children.' Naturally, these grotesquely untrue stories fuelled the paranoid digging of those like Peter Wright who had believed for years that Wilson was a Soviet agent. Such were the perils of Wigg dabbling in Intelligence matters. In 1967 he was kicked upstairs to the House of Lords, and before his death he was arrested and publicly convicted, to his shame, for attempting to pick up prostitutes in London's Park Lane. It was not inappropriate.

There was one final folly with which Wigg was associated. He stimulated the compilation within MI5 of the 'Worthington file'. This was not a 'PF' of a suspect individual, but a 'subject file', like those which dealt with a particular topic or an organisation such as a trade union. It had an individual's name on the cover, however – 'Henry Worthington'. This was a simple cover-name for Harold Wilson. Over the years the buff file grew, with an index and minutes on the left-hand side, and sheaves of 'source reports' stapled together on the right. One MI5 officer from 'K' branch who studied a volume of it in the 1970s says there were clearly preceding volumes which he was not shown. Peter Wright claims he saw a total of four volumes before he retired. The Worthington file was not kept in the main registry to be handled by the scores of 'registry queens'. Nor was it kept in the rows of locked 'Y-boxes' in the K6 secret registry, along with the identities of agents. It was kept permanently in the safe of Director-General Martin Furnival Jones, a practice which was continued by his successor Michael Hanley.

The file contained material about Wilson's friends and about his journeys behind the Iron Curtain in the 1950s. Most of it came from the sister-service, MI6, who said they got it from 'agents'. According to MI5 officers, one report came from an Anglo-US GCHQ-NSA code-break, possibly an old one from VENONA before the codes changed in 1948. It referred to Wilson speculatively as a Soviet 'asset'. Another came second-hand from a Polish defector-in-place, implying much the same. Wright says the file included agents' reports on Wilson's travels within the Soviet Union – probably from no more impressive a source than the MI6 station officer in the Moscow embassy. These disclosed that, for periods of his travels, there was no knowledge of his movements. In Wright's fertile mind, this meaningless information became transfigured into 'the missing weeks'. (He was to adopt the same reasoning process in trying to prove that his chief, Sir Roger Hollis, was also a spy, claiming his biography showed a 'missing two years'. It later transpired, to Wright's discomfiture, that there was plenty of documentation available about Hollis's period in China and immediately afterwards, including detailed letters home: Wright was merely unaware of it.) The Worthington file was to be swelled in time with an enigmatic 'report' from James Angleton in Washington, and an MI6 copy of the innocent photograph taken in Moscow in 1947. It was also to include background material on, at first, two, and later more of Wilson's friends.

MacDonald, the head of 'D' branch throughout Wilson's administration, said before he died in his retirement home in the South of France:

> Wilson had some dubious friends. Even the Labour Party were getting exercised about it, Wigg especially. I was asked to find out about Wilson's friends, which I did. There was nothing very sinister about it. I reported it back. We took it from there . . .

He added, a touch enigmatically:

> As far as Wilson was concerned, people had to be protected from themselves.

The 'friends' that were the cause of MI5's alarm were both self-made businessmen of Central European extraction. One was Rudy Sternberg, and the other was Joe Kagan.

Sternberg was one of the four sons of Paula Michel and George Sternberg, a corn merchant from Thorn, Austria, and his family were to suffer as much as most Jews from Hitler's persecution. He came to England in 1937 and studied chemical engineering at London University. In 1939 he joined the British Army as a non-combatant alien refugee. Demobilised on health grounds in 1943, he got work as a messenger delivering goods. In 1945, at the age of twenty-eight, Sternberg was granted British citizenship. In the spartan post-war years when Wilson was presiding over the Board of Trade, Sternberg bought old buttons and – using his chemical skills – dyed and re-sold them profitably to the garment trade. He saw early the possibilities of bakelite, a primitive German plastic, and in 1948 bought a disused mill in the North of England, at Stalybridge in Lancashire, to manufacture it as a raw material. By the time Wilson came to power, he had built up the fourth largest petrochemical company in Europe, the Sterling Group, and a firm of international traders, Dominion Exports. Sternberg had acquired a farm, Plurenden Manor, at High Holden in Kent, where he interested himself in livestock breeding. In 1951 he had married Monica Prust, the daughter of Major Robert Prust OBE of Vancouver, Canada. He was friendly with the

Plummers – Dick and Beattie – who were in turn among Wilson's closest intimates. One can judge how this unfashionable millionaire was regarded in Tory society by quoting from Sternberg's obituary in the Conservative *Spectator*. Ian Waller described him as:

> an unattractive little man, oddly enough not unlike Wilson in personal appearance with the same sort of conspiratorial mind . . . obsessed with winning the respectability Wilson gave him . . . his early release from the army had enabled him to start [in business] while his contemporaries were still under arms.

Sternberg early became somewhat notorious for his interest in doing business with Communist regimes and his obvious attempts to buy MPs. He had been at the centre of a political row whipped up in the Conservative press a couple of years before Wilson won the leadership of the Labour Party. In 1953 Sternberg had acquired a £3.5 million contract to import potash fertiliser from East Germany. He also acquired export agencies to sell goods to East Germany. In 1961, with the building of the Berlin Wall, the East German regime, which was recognised by few countries, embarked on a propaganda campaign to gain respectability. Sternberg seems to have been willing to be exploited in this regard: no doubt there was money in it for him. He put two Conservative MPs on his pay-roll – Burnaby Drayson and Brigadier Terence Clark. He was later found to have also been paying 'consultancy' fees to Labour back-bencher Will Owen and to Beattie Plummer after her husband's death. At the time, Sir Leslie Plummer became vice-chairman of the East-West trade parliamentary group, of which Owen later became secretary. Drayson also became 'adviser' to a PR firm employed by the East German regime to promote trade, and rather incautiously wrote a letter to *The Times* on their behalf, pleading the cause of an East German journalist who had been refused entry into Britain.

This parliamentary group financed tours to the Leipzig trade fair by MPs whom the East Germans referred to happily as the 'British parliamentary delegation'. Others, more hostile, referred to them as 'Sternberg's circus'. Sternberg drove around Leipzig in a Rolls-Royce flying a Union Jack pennant, but his patriotism was not universally appreciated. One of the PR men employed by the East Germans eventually resigned, making remarks about 'the activities of MPs who go to East Germany to ingratiate themselves with the East German government in the hope of getting contracts and agencies.' The visits became yet another Cold War scandal, much to Sternberg's surprise – even his political enemies admit he seemed genuinely bewildered by the fuss. He was later to develop similar trading contracts with Czechoslovakia and Romania. Of course the people who protested loudest about such politically tinged 'trade in human misery' were often to be found doing deals with South Africa or obnoxious Latin-American dictatorships.

Joe Kagan, by contrast, was not primarily an East-West trader; but he came from Lithuania on the Baltic, which had been forcibly incorporated into the Soviet Union after the war. His wife Margaret still had a number of relatives there. Kagan, too, was an 'unattractive little man' to those who looked down their noses at tough Middle European Jews with factories in the North of England. The son of a family of prosperous woollen manufacturers in Kaunas, the young Kagan was sent to Leeds University in England in 1933 to study textiles. He was in Kaunas when the Russians arrived at the outbreak of war. The family mill was expropriated and his father left for England. Kagan was a survivor, parlaying himself into management of the mill for the Russians. In 1941, the Germans arrived. They shot 7,000 Kaunas Jews on the spot. The 32,000 remaining were herded into the ghetto of Vilijampole. Fates varied. Margaret's ten-year-old brother Alexander was put into a camp, but escaped and lived rough. Pregnant women were executed by Nazi decree. Some Jews were worked to death in labour camps. All suffered starvation and absolute fear. Kagan had an 'able-bodied' labour certificate, was made to work in a foundry, and hid his new wife's family for almost a year behind a partition wall in the factory until the victorious Red Army returned in 1944. Although he later referred to his experiences in a 'concentration camp', this was largely said for effect. Kagan displayed a certain gallows humour about most things thereafter; one of his favourite jokes was about his wife: 'She had to choose between me and the Gestapo – and she took six months to make up her mind!'

Kagan stayed another six months in Kaunas after the Russians arrived. He and Margaret then walked across Europe, leaving a number of their relatives behind, and arrived as refugees in Romania, where Kagan made contact with the British mission. He claimed to be British, and got money and help from Douglas Morrell, a young SOE officer posted there from Spain, who came from a Jewish family in Leeds and was sympathetic. Morrell and he spent a year, by Morrell's account, black-market trading and helping smuggle Jews to Israel. Morrell stole radios for the Jewish resistance and gave them to Kagan who, reportedly, could not resist selling them on for a profit. It was the ugly side of his character coming out: Morrell, who twenty years later was to fall out with Kagan and inform on him for illegal trading, asserted: 'Joe Kagan leaves a trail of evil slime wherever he goes.' But this was a prejudiced view.

Eventually, having wheedled a British visa, Kagan and his wife rejoined his family in Britain in 1946. He worked in a garage; made and sold blankets for a while in a tin shed outside Huddersfield; and finally designed a new waterproof, insulated cloth, using wool on one side and the novel substance, nylon, on the other. This fabric, which he called 'Gannex', made his fortune. He lobbied extravagantly to sell it, ingratiating himself with North of England police forces, prominent local personalities, the Duke of Edinburgh

(Kagan got a 'Royal Warrant' for selling him shooting coats, which was worth a fortune in publicity), and the MP whose home town was Huddersfield – Harold Wilson himself. He first met Wilson, he says, in 1954. Wilson wore his coats, and made them something of a personal trademark, along with his pipe. Kagan's energy, his mordant cynicism, and his belief in the 'white heat of technology' made him an attractive friend to Wilson. Kagan was always willing to lend a hand – to provide financial support; to lay on a furniture van or have a fridge mended. In 1964, George Caunt, Wilson's aide, recorded in his diary that Kagan had donated £500 for election expenses. At the Adelphi Hotel in 1966, when Wilson won his second election with a convincing Labour majority for the first time, Kagan, along with Beattie Plummer, was at Wilson's shoulder.

The idea of investigating these 'Wilson friends' seems to have appealed to three groups simultaneously: MI5, MI6, and the opposition Conservative Party. Two of the most interesting agents concerned were a journalist on a right-wing paper – William Massie of the *Sunday Express* – and yet another Conservative politician who doubled as an intelligence officer – James Scott-Hopkins MP.

Over twenty-five years Massie claims to have had far better Intelligence 'contacts' than Harry Pincher, the British journalist who was much better known to the public for his links with MI5. An MI6 officer's wife was a close friend of Massie's wife, and he knew an MI5 officer – whom he declines to name – from his time as a naval cadet at Dartmouth. One of the young Massie's first reporting jobs was accompanying Wilson across the country during his victorious October 1964 election campaign: 'I first knew that MI5 were suspicious of Wilson because they showed an interest in him when they knew I was following him around,' he said in a 1988 interview. 'Somewhere in the back of my mind is a suggestion that the Americans had been worried about Wilson since the late 1940s or early 1950s, when a Congressman had wanted Wilson charged because he was trading with the enemy.'

Such MI5 links with journalists are much more common than the general public realises. 'We have somebody in every office in Fleet Street,' one MI5 officer says, 'I really mean every single office.' Given that the press will play such an important role in the story being told here, it is worth looking at these links more closely.

The best-known 'espionage expert' in Fleet Street at this time was the *Express* journalist, 'Chapman' Pincher. Between 1959 and 1961 he did his best to develop connections with Wright's 'D' branch colleagues. In 1959 he claims he 'was requested by MI5' to publish stories – 'and provided with all the evidence to do so' – about their discovery that groups of Polish students were being sent over in order to report on the Polish expatriate community. This publicity may have been organised by Harry Wharton, who was handling the Polish case, and who told friends he had met Pincher but had not revealed to him his true name 'because it would be in the papers the next day.' In connection with this affair, Wharton was also in contact with Auberon Herbert, an eccentric aristocratic MI6 agent who had embraced the cause of the emigré Poles (Herbert's nephew, Auberon Waugh, was to become a prominent columnist on *Private Eye*). Wharton functioned as MI5's 'Fleet Street officer' for some years in the 1950s. He met both Percy and Hugh Cudlipp, executives of the *Daily Mirror*, on an introduction from a publisher at Harrap, and used to attend meetings of the Paternoster Club, where journalists gave talks.

In 1961, Pincher met Michael McCaul, Wright's 'D' branch colleague, when he reported repeated contacts he was having with the Russian press attaché Anatoli Strelnikov (they had been arranged in the first place by the ubiquitous MI5 agent Captain Kerby); Pincher claimed Strelnikov was trying to bribe him. Pincher also published, at McCaul's request, lurid stories taken from MI5 card-indexes about visitors to Moscow who had been sexually compromised. The direct contacts then petered out; McCaul was posted to Washington in 1964, and Pincher's independent 'scoop' about MI5's arrangements for the Lonsdale exchange made Furnival Jones and MacDonald so uncomfortable that links ended. Later, however, Pincher was supplied with MI5 material indirectly via Victor Rothschild.

One of the most unlikely MI5 agents in Fleet Street was Raymond Jackson – 'Jak' – the veteran cartoonist of the *Evening Standard*. A small man with thick spectacles and a romantic disposition, Jak trained at Willesden School of Art and his only military experience was as a conscript in the Education Corps and then in the Intelligence Corps in Cairo between 1946 and 1948. He did, however, develop an admiration for military ways: 'I'm a great romantic – I admire the SAS and people like that,' he told the author in 1988. In the 1960s, Jak became friends with MI5 officer Freddie Beith. They lived near each other in Wimbledon, and met at the well-known Queen's Elm pub in the Fulham Road. They were soon in and out of each other's houses and attending rugby matches together, often in the company of other MI5 officers.

Beith was an agent-runner from the old days. During the war he was involved in the 'Double-Cross' recruitment of captured enemy agents in England – a ruthless business in which some of those who were captured or gave themselves up were 'turned' and others shot to keep up appearances. Talking about these executions in later life, Beith would say in his lilting Welsh accent: 'Well, they shouldn't have come here, should they?' He also ran agents in the Caribbean. A fluent Spanish-speaker who had been born in Latin-America and spent some time in Spain, Beith wrote books about Catalonia and Welsh mining. In MI5 in the 1950s, he was given the job of liaison with GCHQ. Beith has an extrovert temperament. He told Jak, who had a rather wistful longing to join the Special Forces Club in Knightsbridge, that he could not stand going there: it was 'full of middle-aged women with big bottoms sitting talking about how they'd been parachuted into Europe during the war.' When Wright's memoirs came out, Beith exploded, 'Wright was nothing! He knew nothing!' His reaction to being asked by the author about his journalistic connections was equally choleric: 'Get off the line, blast you!' he said, 'You haven't got any right to interfere with my life . . . I do not care for your profession.'

In the late 1960s, Beith became a member of a journalists' club, the City Golf Club in Fleet Street. He was introduced by Jak and gave his profession as 'author'. Those at the club remember Beith and 'other MI5 men who were named in *Spycatcher*' drinking and socialising there. The club had originally opened with an automated golf practice range incorporating a video screen in addition to its 50-foot bar. But it rapidly ceased to have any connection with golf. It was an ideal way to meet journalists: the club, run by a pleasant Old Etonian, Robin Arbuthnot, had about 200 members. Apart from a handful of lawyers and City businessmen, the majority were journalists from the Beaverbrook newspapers – the *Express*, *Sunday Express* and *Evening Standard*. The *Sunday Express* editor John Junor could be seen there. There was also a considerable contingent from *The Times*, including one of its political correspondents John Groser, the news editor Rita Marshall, the legal correspondent Marcel Berlins, and Christopher Walker, later to become Moscow correspondent. Beith and his friends were well-placed to hear gossip. Jak says:

> Yes, he tried to milk me . . . it's like journalists: they try and get more out of you than they give away. It's natural they want to extend their feelers everywhere, you never know what might come up. I mean, they are on our side, after all . . .

Wright says, 'Jak is a long-term MI5 agent who has worked for me.' Jak responds to the proposition with a not altogether displeased laugh: 'Why don't you print what he says? I won't sue you. It'll make me look like James Bond . . .' Wright also says, 'MI5 have agents in the newspaper and publishing world whose main purpose is to warn them of embarrassing publications, and directly they hear of any such publication due to come out, MI5 mount operations to get a preview.'

MacDonald, the head of 'D' branch, admits MI5's journalistic connections guardedly: there was, he says, 'very, very little' leaking of information to the press. But 'one or two' officers did have authorised contact with journalists. These were partly to probe the sources of sensitive stories, and, 'Sometimes one wanted to know what the press were thinking, and sometimes what line they were going to take on something.'

115

While MI5 was scouring the world of journalism, the Conservative MP James Scott-Hopkins was also digging into Wilson. He was an intermittent agent of MI6 from 1947 to 1973, apart from a short gap when he was a junior agriculture minister between 1962 and 1964. He also functioned as an inquiry agent for the Conservative Party into Wilson's personal life.

Educated at Eton and Oxford, Scott-Hopkins, the son of a colonel, served in the Army from the outbreak of war and in 1946 took a Russian course and specialised training in interrogation. He then stayed on as a military Intelligence officer until 1950. In 1947, he was first approached by Stewart Menzies' MI6, who wanted information fed back to them on the results of his interviews with Iron Curtain dissidents. Thereafter, over twenty-five years, he was available to provide information when asked on individuals abroad: after he left the Army he farmed an estate and became a Conservative MP, for North Cornwall, in 1959. Among the MI6 officers he happened to know personally were Stephen de Mowbray and Maurice Oldfield – although neither was apparently involved in the Sternberg-Kagan inquiries.

Towards the end of 1965, Scott-Hopkins was asked by the Conservative Party to 'investigate' Wilson. Scott-Hopkins told friends this was at the direct request of the defeated Tory Prime Minister, Sir Alec Douglas-Home. Home was understandably concerned to discover whether his opponent might be somehow 'vulnerable to blackmail'. Home and the Conservative Party were, of course, well aware of the gossip about Wilson and Marcia Williams: as we have seen, as early as autumn 1960, Conservative Central Office had been in receipt of false rumours that Wilson might have committed adultery with Marcia Williams since 1956, and with Barbara Castle as long ago as 1949. The gossip had re-surfaced during the General Election campaign, when Lord Hailsham had made pointed references to 'adulterers on both Front Benches'. The story circulated later that Wilson, faced with a weeping Marcia, had privately told assembled Labour MPs that his secretary was 'pure as the driven snow'. (Marcia Williams says this never occurred). To these untrue rumours were now attached the theory, of which Home was certainly aware, that, by going to the Soviet Union with Marcia Williams, Wilson may have 'laid himself open to blackmail' and thus become a 'security risk'. No doubt the Conservative Party, after its mauling over Profumo, would have shed many crocodile tears of patriotism had this turned out to be the case.

One of Scott-Hopkins' friends says:

He assumed that Alec [Douglas-Home] had been told about MI5's concern about Wilson when he was Foreign Secretary for Macmillan. It must have filtered down to him. Alec was certainly aware of all the gossip about Wilson, both about his marriage and the Soviet trips.

There was thus an interesting conjunction of rumours. Within parts of

MI5 and the CIA some people already believed that Wilson had come under Soviet control, as a result of which Hugh Gaitskell had been assassinated. Within the Conservative Party and the Labour Right, it was believed (or hoped) that Wilson's links with Marcia Williams were a skeleton in his cupboard which, had the Soviet Union discovered them, could already have been used to blackmail him.

What made sense of both stories? Why, the theory that it was during one of his numerous trips to Moscow for Montague Meyer in Marcia's company between 1956 and 1959 that the crucial act of blackmail must have occurred. This was the precise 'MI5 view' which was peddled ten years later and was given an airing in the pages of *Private Eye* and elsewhere. It bears the unmistakable hallmarks of the sometime MI5 Assistant Director D3 (Counter Espionage Research), Peter Maurice Wright.

One of these hallmarks is the complete lack of recognisable evidence; and the second is its inconsistency with subsequently known facts. For example, Wilson had first attracted the hostility of military Intelligence, as well as political accusations of acting in the Soviet interest, for his participation in the Russian jet sales, as far back as 1947. And the only evidence of NKVD interest in him as a blackmail possibility dates back to the same year. This was nine years before Wilson even met Marcia Williams; clearly some other explanation for his behaviour is required.

Back in 1965, Scott-Hopkins set about his MI6-style investigation into Wilson with zeal. He spent more than a year on the inquiry, and travelled both to Europe and Gibraltar. He set out to become acquainted with Kagan and Sternberg, who he pumped for information. In the process he discovered a great deal about them as well. Scott-Hopkins came to believe that Mary and Harold Wilson might have been contemplating separation at one point. He rapidly found out that Marcia and Ed Williams had got divorced by 1961. He heard rumours that Ed Williams had finished up with a financial settlement of £30,000 and had subsequently stayed out of Britain and resisted all demands that he be interviewed. Scott-Hopkins later told friends that he had heard that two of Wilson's supporters, Sidney (later Lord) Bernstein and Lord Kearton, had helped Marcia raise the cash for the settlement, and that the Jewish lawyer and 'fixer' Arnold (later Lord) Goodman, a friend and confidant of Wilson who played a prominent role during his government, had helped to make the legal arrangements. The only correct part of these rumours was that Lord Goodman had volunteered to help with some legal technicalities – free of charge – in 1963. Marcia Williams did not even meet some of these prominent figures until well after the formalisation of her divorce.

In democratic politics, politicians' sex-lives, real or imagined, become political footballs. Like Marcia's later love affairs and children, her divorce was her personal business, but Wilson's political opponents might

117

have seized on it. Indeed, Chapman Pincher later recalled that just such malicious rumours had been put about before the 1964 election – 'that Marcia's husband . . . had been paid a large sum by wealthy supporters of Wilson to withdraw a divorce action which could have been embarrassing.' The truth of it is that Marcia's divorce, although quite an innocent event, was treated as a matter of secrecy by the indefatigably conspiratorial George Wigg.

The 'Wilson divorce inquiry' did not lead to any political exposure of Wilson as a 'security risk'. This was partly because it became evident that such a thesis was nonsense. As Kagan was in a position to tell Scott-Hopkins, Marcia was far from having an adulterous affair with the Prime Minister; she was, in fact, having relationships, as she was perfectly entitled to do, with other people – a No. 10 political aide, John Allen, and later the political journalist, Walter Terry.

The following year, Scott-Hopkins continued his inquiries into the Wilson circle, but this time on behalf of MI6. The MP had temporarily lost his parliamentary seat in the March 1966 General Election, and did not return until November 1967. He was working as a consultant to an advertising agency, and was invited by Sternberg to accompany him on one of his regular trips to the Leipzig trade fair in East Germany. Scott-Hopkins told friends: 'Of course, I informed MI6 and they asked me to keep an eye on him . . . MI6 didn't know who Rudy was working for. That's what they wanted to know.' Scott-Hopkins reported back to MI6 that Sternberg had given the impression he was on friendly terms with 'everyone in the Politburo'; that the left-wing back-bencher Ian Mikardo, who was also involved in East-West trade, had been present at Leipzig; and that Wilson might have travelled in Sternberg's Rolls-Royce during one of his 1950s Meyer timber trips. There is some evidence that Furnival Jones now warned Wilson there were 'security concerns' about Sternberg.

In November 1967, Scott-Hopkins also found himself in a position to report on whether the gossipy Kagan was getting leaks of information as a result of his friendship with Harold Wilson. Scott-Hopkins knew a retired wing-commander married to a Hungarian woman called Liselle Johnson. She, in turn, was friendly with Margaret, Kagan's wife. Scott-Hopkins reported later that, in conversation with Liselle Johnson two or three weeks before the devaluation of sterling, Margaret Kagan had confidently predicted it was going to occur. Scott-Hopkins lunched with Mrs Kagan only to be told the same thing.

In fact, like so much startling 'Intelligence' information supplied in good faith, this incident did not prove anything at all about Wilson or his entourage. The devaluation of sterling was not in anyone's mind before the beginning of November 1967. Around that date, a forthcoming European Economic Community meeting placed on its agenda the question of what action to take if Britain devalued the pound. By November 4, Wilson and his Chancellor were forced to have an emergency meeting because the EEC agenda had leaked and continental Europe was awash with rumours that devaluation would occur in mid-November. The rumours were draining the reserves. Wilson dropped his opposition to devaluation; the markets continued unsettled, and by November 8 the Cabinet's economic policy committee had decided devaluation must occur shortly. There was a full Cabinet decision on November 15, followed by devaluation itself. So anyone who asserted at the start of November that devaluation would take place in a fortnight was merely repeating widespread European rumour, not 'insider' information.

Unfortunately for Kagan, Peter Wright of MI5 had already also picked up the suggestion from his own 'contacts' that the Lithuanian-born business-man might be a Soviet agent. Although they came from a much grander stratum of Anglo-Jewish society than him, Kagan was acquainted with the Rothschild family. According to Kagan, a woman he was friendly with, Judy Innes, had been on close terms with Jacob Rothschild during the early 1960s; indeed, the Rothschilds had expected them to marry. For whatever reason, Wright says that both Victor Rothschild and his wife Tess mentioned to him in the early 1960s that they thought it odd how Kagan had left Lithuania with such ease in 1945.

In fact, as we have seen, Kagan was a resourceful survivor, and certainly had no Soviet assistance whatever in getting to Britain. In 1945, as Morrell testifies, he was writing bogus IOUs on a New York bank in an effort to get cash from the British mission in Bucharest with which to eat. He wanted to go to Britain because his family were already there. And it would have shown supernatural foresight on the part of the NKVD to know that Kagan would become a very rich mackintosh manufacturer and make the acquaintance eight years later of an MP from Huddersfield who, ten years on from that, would become Prime Minister. But Peter Wright's speculations were equal to the situation. He recalled in later life:

We had been suspicious of Kagan for years because of the way he had escaped from the Soviet Zone after the war. Both Victor and Tess had independently pointed this out to me. It had all the symptoms of an escape arranged by the KGB. We became very concerned when it became very clear that Kagan was courting Wilson's friendship and patronage. Wilson was warned by successive Director-Generals of MI5 to beware, but took no notice. (Incidentally, the manufacture of raincoats is a well-known cover for Soviet intelligence operations. 'The Excellent Raincoat Company' was one of the main cover set-ups before the war for the Soviet network in Europe.)[6]

This material went on file. Years later, in 1971, MI5 officers repeated it, and it eventually appeared in British newspapers.

Behind these unattractive canvases of intrigue, the substantial Cold War realities of the Anglo-US Intelligence relationship and the Anglo-US power relationship continued to develop unabated.

The real Wilson is the one we catch a glimpse of during the visit to Britain of Soviet premier Kosygin in 1967. At Chequers, the Prime Minister's country house, he is locked in late-night negotiation with the Russian leader, trying to act as 'honest broker' to preserve the cease-fire in Vietnam. President Johnson has been constantly berating him for not sending British troops to Vietnam to support 'the West' – 'Johnson told me that if only I would put troops into Vietnam, my worries over sterling would be over.'[7] Meanwhile, members of his own party, and the outraged undergraduate heirs of Burgess and Maclean at Oxford and Cambridge, pelt him with eggs at bitter demonstrations because he refuses to dissociate himself from American policy in Vietnam. The role of secret 'peacemaker' is the only one which gives him any chance of credibility in a situation where he is powerless. Hidden in the 'prison room' on the upper floor where Lady Jane Grey's sister was once detained by Queen Elizabeth I is the senior CIA official, Chester Cooper, the same man who had served in the London station during Suez and who had brought the Labour Party its briefing material on the Cuban missile crisis in 1962. Cooper has an open line to the White House. Wilson has already done his best to strike up a rapport with Kosygin on the basis of his long links with Russia. Barbara Castle recalls the state dinner at No. 10, where Wilson asked her to keep Kosygin talking on the way out:

> Then Harold, who had been foraging, surfaced with an odd-looking chap who had something to do with timber [it was John Meyer]. Harold, who is in his unpretentious element on these occasions, started reminiscing about timber negotiations.[8]

Meanwhile, in Kosygin's suite at Claridges, the entire premises are 'bugged' as usual by MI5, and Wilson gets regular reports from Furnival Jones of anything significant Kosygin might say. (This bugging was confirmed later by Tony Benn: 'I know this because I got a mysterious memorandum from the security services reporting something they had picked up on tape that Kosygin had said . . . it indicated how very close Kosygin and Pompidou were, due to de Gaulle's Eastern policy.')[9] The secret mediation attempt over Vietnam fails, due to the 'hawks' in the White House, and Wilson continues to be dragged along in the wake of a disastrous US foreign policy.

The only lasting consequence of Kosygin's visit was one which had not been anticipated. Wilson did find time during the high-level negotiations to present Kosygin with a list of Soviet Jews who he requested to be allowed to leave the country. His friend and backer Joe Kagan had asked him to include on this list his brother-in-law, Alexander Shtromas: Shtromas had been with the family in the Vilijampole ghetto, but since then he had risen to become a legal academic working in Moscow. The Kagans wanted him to be allowed to come to Britain. Analysis of this list may well have led the KGB to conclude for the first time that the friendship between Kagan and the Prime Minister was worth exploiting.

Another snapshot from the world of genuine secrets shows Wilson trying, and failing, to curb the spiralling Intelligence commitments required by the American alliance. The price for GCHQ continuing to share in the US 'take' of Signals Intelligence was a sustained flow of British input from the communications monitoring stations round the world. But the game was changing in two respects. Firstly, Wilson had to withdraw from Aden, Singapore and the Far East as part of British defence cuts. But he was committed to funding the surveillance and code-breaking stations – the US badly wanted intercepts from Vietnam, had wanted to 'borrow' Aden if they were forced out of Ethiopia, and was making growing demands to eavesdrop in the Indian Ocean.

Furthermore, since the launch of Sputnik in 1957, the first US reconnaissance satellites in 1960, and the recent Intelsat civil communications satellites, a while new electronic world had appeared in space. The US was running spy satellites, and it also wanted to snoop on other people's satellite communications. There were some monstrously expensive political and hardware procurement decisions to be taken in complete secrecy – the British side of the UK-USA treaty already cost £100 million a year to run, probably much more if the various soldiers, planes and accommodation costs which were deducted from the direct military budget were counted in.

The US did not want Britain to leave Singapore – Michael Stewart told the Cabinet that they were 'terrified of another Cuba' – and they wanted Wilson to support the CIA-backed regime of the Greek colonels. While Wilson protested about the colonels' 'bestialities', Stewart told ministers, 'the only alternative would be a Communist coup which would weaken Nato's flank.' The Cabinet was told that the Cyprus base, with its bombers and GCHQ station, had to be retained. Castle noted, 'Yet this base, with its nuclear strike capacity against the Soviet Union, was one of the biggest irritants to the Arab world.' George Brown was completely accurate about the pressure Wilson was under:

He can't budge. Why? Because he is too deeply committed to Johnson. What did he pledge? I don't know; that we wouldn't devalue and full support in the Far East? But both of these have got to go.'[10]

Eventually, and painfully, reality partially broke through the pressure of US foreign policy requirements. Wilson was forced to devalue. The Aden guerrillas forced British troops to leave. Singapore was evacuated. Among the most important *quid pro quos* were that the Australians were persuaded

121

to take over the running of the Singapore GCHQ base, and to share the cost of the GCHQ station in Hong Kong. Furthermore, the inhabitants of Diego Garcia in the Indian Ocean were turned off their island so that it could be covertly handed over to the US as a satellite interception and naval eavesdropping base. Barbara Castle records, 'I approve the motive – to offload on to the US some of our responsibilities, but I don't like the method . . . The Foreign Secretary had put in a paper suggesting if the two countries [Mauritius and the Seychelles] didn't agree, we should transfer the islands to ourselves . . . I burst out 'Compulsory purchase? What legal right have we?'[11]

On the question of GCHQ's future, Wilson appointed an academic, Dr Stuart Hampshire, who had served in the war-time radio security service (spotting illegal transmissions), to carry out a secret review of the demands to spend large sums on getting into satellites. Hampshire resisted claims that GCHQ must build its own spy satellites in order to retain the right to share in the US 'take'. As a result, over the next decade, the US, came, in effect, to control the main source of serious Intelligence information. Hampshire recommended axing some of GCHQ's obvious smaller extravagances – such as the RAF Nimrod flights commissioned by Peter Wright to look for Russian 'spy' transmissions. But the US was allowed to expand its own NSA base at Menwith Hill, near Harrogate, to collect international cable traffic. And, after some strenuous lobbying by GCHQ officials who claimed that the US might otherwise cease to co-operate, Wilson paid up for the construction of a satellite dish at Bude in Cornwall to eavesdrop on the traffic of the new transatlantic commercial satellites. GCHQ's director Sir Leonard Hooper, wrote to his NSA opposite number, General Pat Carter, that he had 'leaned shamefully on you and sometimes taken your name in vain when I needed approval for something at this end.' The two 100-foot dishes at Bude should have been christened 'Pat' and 'Lou', he wrote, after Carter and Tordella, his deputy.

The cost of GCHQ was to continue to rise, to more than £600 million a year by the 1980s. This was the price of Wilson's yellow boxes in which the Intelligence reports were brought, courtesy of the US. They enabled Harold Wilson to pretend, like Ernie Bevin before him, as in a speech he made shortly after taking office in November 1964, 'We are a world power and a world influence.'[12]

CHAPTER 7

Meanwhile, behind the guarded doors of Leconfield House, Peter Wright was behaving like a Witchfinder-General. Under the nominal supervision of Mac-Donald, head of 'D' branch, he was chairman of the so-called FLUENCY committee, which tried throughout the rest of the Wilson administration to prove that either, or both, the Deputy Director-General of MI5, Mitchell, or the recently retired chief himself, Roger Hollis, were agents of the Soviet Union.

Wright's colleagues on this joint MI5–MI6 body were Arthur Martin (now under Dick White's wing at Century House) and the wheelchair-bound Patrick Stewart, who wrote analyses of Golitsin's views and even travelled to Canada to re-interview the truculent old defector Gouzenko. These activities were to lead, at the end of the decade, to Hollis being summoned from his golf-course and formally interrogated as a suspect spy. Even 'Jumbo' (as the sizeable Michael Hanley was known in boarding-school parlance) was also interrogated, with Wright listening intently through his headphones; and Wright went to Hanley's psychiatrist, hoping vainly to find evidence of treasonable tendencies in the unhappinesses of his child-hood. Half a dozen junior Intelligence service officers were 'purged' on the grounds that they had something unsatisfactory in their background. Wright, the amateur investigator, frequently went too far when he tried his own hand. MacDonald, in interviews shortly before his death, claimed:

> I don't think he was a very good interrogator . . . I know one officer, and a very able clever chap and very experienced, who Peter interrogated and the chap apparently broke down. Peter telephoned me and said: 'He's broken! He says he'll only tell you' . . . So I said 'Oh, well, you'd better send him over.' And of course it was just an enormous leg-pull. The officer concerned hadn't broken at all, he was just pulling Peter's leg . . . the officer concerned got a hell of a good wigging.

MacDonald asserts that he was uneasy about letting Wright continue to do interrogations. But he was certainly doing so up to the autumn of 1967. Perhaps, like a well-regulated bureaucrat, MacDonald was more concerned about Wright's lack of skills in man management than about any injustices he might be inflicting on members of the public. For he did sack Wright from his executive post:

I personally think he'd have been better to have stayed a scientist ... I inherited Peter as assistant director in charge of D3 and I wasn't happy about it, but I was told just to make the best use of him. He became a rogue ... There were too many people like Wright without any training in the service in those days. Peter's management of D3 was catastrophic. I had to get him out of it. I was frankly appalled by what I found – everything was behind. He had no genius at all for telling people what to do. He was just completely chaotic ... he wasn't an administrator in any sense of the word, he wasn't even methodical dealing with his deskwork ... He was always leaping on his hobbyhorse and riding off in several directions at once ... He had *folie de grandeur*: he wanted to be the counter-espionage big boy ... his big failing was that he didn't appreciate the value of evidence.

MacDonald disliked Wright's FLUENCY committee a great deal: 'There was a witch-hunt going on – they sat and they theorised, all for very different motives.' He preferred the ex-Indian policemen who still made up MI5's unimaginative backbone:

Peter, like so many people, wanted to cut a dash in the counter-espionage world and produce something that was really sensational ... And there were others who thought the same ... He could be very irrational at times ... You see, once you get bitten by this kind of bug, then you're on a crusade – right? And every bit that you can turn up of circumstantial evidence or any suspicion is immediately recorded. Anything that doesn't suit your thesis is pushed into the background and ignored.

The truth is that Peter Wright never caught a single spy. He disagrees vehemently, citing his many 'cases'. But none ever led to courtroom proof. The more Wright failed to get his work recognised, the more menacing and widespread his accusations of 'treachery' became. Deprived of his status as an executive, he spent more and more time closeted with the languid and dispirited figure of Anthony Blunt, the one stoolpigeon he possessed. It seems Wright was convinced that somewhere in the large selection of 'pansies' and 'pinkos' who had been Blunt's companions at pre-war Oxbridge, he would find his Big Fish; the Fifth Man whose sensational exposure would doubtless make his colleagues sorry that they had ever underestimated Peter Wright.

MacDonald noticed the number of hours Peter Wright started spending with Blunt, either at MI6 officer Maurice Oldfield's 'wired' premises or in Blunt's elegant study at the Courtauld Institute:

I don't think he did a good job. He was with Blunt morning, noon and night. He always came to me for a bottle of gin. He and Blunt used to drink it together. Peter was so bloody keen to do it. That's why I didn't put anybody else on it . . . Peter and Blunt were like a couple of homos . . . pussyfooting around each other, exchanging jokes . . .

The only concrete outcome of the Blunt 'interrogations' was the suicide of one of Harold Wilson's more talented MPs. Wright later tried to bluster his way out of this by saying, 'Rather than talk, he knocked himself off.' But, as we shall see, that was far from the truth.

There were a couple of minor 'spies' already in the bag even before Blunt confessed. Michael Straight in Washington had named Leo Long as a fellow underground Communist. Long had been in war-time military Intelligence (where he had passed material to Blunt). Blunt had tried to get him into post-war MI5 and he stayed with the Army in Germany until 1952. He had later got work with Sidney Bernstein, had been nowhere near classified information for a decade, and was told by Arthur Martin he would not be prosecuted. John Cairncross, a former treasury official who had access to ULTRA intelligence at Bletchley in the war, had been already incriminated back in 1951, when he promptly left for Rome and a job with FAO. Blunt had no qualms about incriminating him further, and Cairncross was black-mailed into 'helping' Wright with the threat that he would never otherwise be allowed to return to England. What price this red-haired working-class Scotsman paid for the political convictions of his youth can be seen in a rather pathetic letter he wrote to Wright from Rome as late as 1972:

Dear Peter,
A rather urgent question has come up on which some advice from you is necessary. I am scheduled to leave for Monrovia . . . If I am unable to go, there will be extremely serious complications as regards my position here . . . Since Liberia is in the US area, I am rather apprehensive, as you can imagine. Even if there would normally be complications, I would urge you to do what you possibly can . . . It is almost certainly the last time I am likely to need such intervention . . . With apologies and all best wishes, yours ever . . .[1]

'Yours ever,' indeed.

Wright also convinced himself that his own acquaintance, the scientist Alister Watson, was a spy. This suspicion was not due to his skilled inter-rogation of Blunt over the gin. Rothschild had mentioned that Watson was a former Party member to Dick White as long ago as 1954, and the fact was on his file. He had been repeatedly cleared for top secret work, and was doing research on submarine detection for the Admiralty – a highly sensitive activity. Patrick Stewart, Wright's 'great friend', as he claims, was in charge of the surveillance of Watson, while Cecil Shipp did the interrogation. After six weeks of continuous questioning, Wright concedes the scientist appeared drugged and unable to understand what he was being asked. Watson himself later said he was not a spy and that he was so confused he was saying things he did not really mean. Watson was debarred from secret work and moved to the National Oceanographic Institute. Wright describes how during interrogation Watson admitted meeting certain Russian Intelligence officers whose photographs they showed him. He also admitted to Communist sympathies. Neither Wright, nor Arthur Martin, have ever spelled out on what dates or on how many occasions these incriminating meetings were supposed to have occurred. However, Watson certainly did not admit to being a Soviet spy, and nor did Blunt confirm that he was one. The bugging and following failed to catch Watson meeting anyone untoward. Wright's reputation for wild allegations is so bad that one simply cannot take his word that Watson made any damning admissions at all. His life may have been ruined for nothing. On the other hand, perhaps he was a Russian spy. Wright says, and there is no reason to doubt it, that Watson's guilt was generally agreed within 'the Office'. As with so much of MI5's activity under Wilson, one ends up not much the wiser. As Watson is dead, the Intelligence officers and their journalistic outlets can defame him with impunity.

Wright had still not got a new spy out of Blunt. Surely, he demanded of him over the gin, there must have been others, perhaps not at Cambridge, but at Oxford? This new approach looked fruitful. Blunt agreed that his assistant (and possible accomplice) at the Courtauld Institute, Phoebe Pool, had known some of the Communists at Oxford. Regrettably she was a sick woman who had suffered a severe depressive breakdown and was in a clinic: the sight of MI5 might be too much for her. Wright continued to press Blunt. Eventually they agreed on a subterfuge. Another of Blunt's colleagues at the Courtauld was Anita Brookner – subsequently to become a distinguished novelist.

Wright says, smoothly: 'A degree of deception was inevitable.' It has never been explained how Phoebe Pool became so frightened, or why Blunt wanted to keep away from her himself. But Anita Brookner, writing after the publication of *Spycatcher*, corroborates the fact that she was manipulated in all innocence by Blunt into visiting her sick colleague at the psychiatric department of the Middlesex Hospital.

My function, as I now see it, was to glean from Phoebe's largely incoherent speech names that evidently had some significance for Phoebe, Blunt and Peter Wright . . . Blunt . . . as I saw it, was naturally concerned for her. These visits to the hospital were macabre. It was obvious that Phoebe was very ill, and her words did not make much sense. Although she was in a state of great distress, a little communication was possible. The few names she mentioned were, I thought, those of friends of hers

. . . Yet what I feel now is that I may somehow, unwittingly, have brought back a name that struck a chord in Blunt.[2]

Phoebe Pool, her condition unlikely to have been improved by this stressful episode, supplied, Wright claims, some names – Sir Andrew Cohen, the diplomat; Jenifer Fischer Williams; the brothers Peter and Bernard Floud. At last Wright had got his breakthrough – or so it seemed. It was, as he put it, 'An important new Ring at Oxford'. Andrew Cohen, the odd one out (he had been at Cambridge), had a heart attack and died shortly after this discovery – Wright does not volunteer in his memoirs whether he had the opportunity to threaten him first. Peter Floud was dead already. Both the others already had files on them in MI5. Jenifer Fischer Williams, daughter of a distinguished lawyer, had gone into the Home Office in 1936 and later married Herbert Hart, who had been a war-time member of – of all organisations – MI5 itself.

Wright started with her as the easier of the two. She had been a student at Somerville. She was approached via her husband, now an Oxford professor. As Wright concedes, 'She told her story quite straightforwardly.' Jenifer Hart has subsequently detailed her history herself, so there is again a check on Wright's account: it turns out to contain some significant elisions of fact. Like many of her former student friends, she joined the Party and went 'underground', just after she left the University in 1935. Jenifer Hart says it is false to say, as Peter Wright alleges, that she was 'recruited' by her fellow-undergraduate Bernard Floud. 'What in fact happened was I went to a camp organised by the National Unemployed Workers Movement in summer 1935. I found my stay there a most moving experience. It gave me a first-hand insight into the effects of unemployment, insecurity and poverty. Many people in the camp were Communist sympathisers: the natural thing to do seemed to be to join the Party. No pressure was put on me by Bernard Floud or anyone else. I was attracted by its apparent efficiency and its persuasive analysis of fascism and nazism.' Subsequently she was given instructions by Arthur Wynn, a trade union activist who later joined the Civil Service. (Wright was excited to hear this: Wynn was at that time still in the Civil Service and about to be promoted to Deputy Secretary at the Board of Trade.) Next, in 1937, she was approached by a 'man with a Central European accent,' whom she found 'creepy'. He expressed pleasure that she had joined the Civil Service, urging her to aim for one of the major government departments – 'where I would be useful to them.' He suggested she lie low as a 'sleeper' for as long as ten years. According to Jenifer Hart, by the time she had been posted in 1939 to a private secretary's job handling, among much else, the applications for telephone-taps, she was sick of being a secret Communist, and dropped all contact with the Russian. She later married, and later still became a History don at Oxford.

127

Two things are perfectly clear from Wright's questioning of Jenifer Hart. The first is that she did not name Bernard Floud as a Soviet spy and indeed did not regard herself as potentially one. She stressed that she thought she was being recruited to work for the British party. She saw herself perhaps, briefly, as subversive of the British state, but certainly not as an agent of a foreign one. It was a course adopted by many intelligent, politically immature people at that time. Denis Healey, later to become a robustly right-wing Labour Defence Secretary, joined the open Communist Party – and then left it. Hugh Gaitskell, the man who fought all his post-war life to empty the Labour Party of its 'Socialist' baggage, had been saying in 1932, 'the Labour Party must go straight out for socialism when it is returned to power.' When an undergraduate, the pacifist Michael Foot admired Stalin.[3] In those years, to be a revolutionary at twenty was a normal sign of intelligence.

The second important fact is that Wright came away from the interview with nothing that would justify a serious investigation into Floud, and he knew it. Floud was a Labour MP, and the Prime Minister had forbidden surveillance of MPs without special permission. Furthermore – and Wright must have realised this from the available files on Floud – his profile was not that of an active underground mole at all. He had been an open supporter of Communism after the war. As a consequence, he had been 'purged' from Harold Wilson's Board of Trade in 1948 under the blacklisting procedure for civil servants. And if he had only pretended to leave the British Communist Party subsequently, his name would have been on the 55,000 files looted by MI5 from the CPGB under operation PARTY PIECE in 1955. Wright does not mention these key facts in any of his variously ghostwritten memoirs. But, in 1967, Wilson, perhaps as an act of misplaced kindness, put Floud on the list of politicians whom he might promote to ministerial office, and circulated it for 'negative vetting'. Peter Wright saw his chance, and registered a strongly written objection to clearing Floud in view of the grave allegations against him on file – Wright's own file. With Wilson's permission, he was allowed to interrogate Bernard Floud to 'clear him'. It was thus Floud's extreme misfortune to be confronted by an MI5 'investigator' who was, at best, self-taught.

There was much that Wright did not know and never found out about the Labour MP for Acton, this apparently urbane, and upper-class figure who he summoned to the microphoned interview room in the War Office. The young Bernard Floud was overshadowed by his father, who was a prominent Establishment figure. Sir Francis Floud had been permanent secretary at the head of the Ministry of Labour, and High Commissioner to Canada. There was good deal of talk later about the 'puritanical' atmosphere of Cambridge which had led to Communism among the undergraduates, as distinct from the more worldly air of Harold Wilson's pre-war

128

Oxford. This was an unreal distinction: it was also the Oxford of Tom Driberg, Michael Foot and Philip Toynbee, which had notoriously voted in 1933 at the Oxford Union Society that it would refuse to fight for 'King and Country'. There were many different worlds at both places, and one of them was the world of 'underground' Communism.

'My father became a secret member of the Communist Party at Oxford,' says Bernard Floud's son, Professor Roderick Floud. 'Philip Toynbee told me before his death that so did every other member of the Oxford Labour Club executive. The only one of them who didn't was Christopher Mayhew, and he never seemed to have grasped that all the others were! Toynbee said you bought silk pyjamas from your tailor in the High Street, danced the night away, and then shot off to CP headquarters for your secret instructions. Although my father was, on the surface, a typical 1930s schoolboy who didn't let his feelings show, he was somebody who was insecure. It was like the Church: his friends said he loved being in the Party. It became very hard to leave.'

Bernard Floud was close to James Klugmann, the lifelong Communist from Cambridge who recruited many of his friends. In 1938 they went together on a League of Nations student association trip to China. Not only his circle, but his family links revolved around the Party. His elder brother Peter was a Party member; he later became a keeper at the Victoria and Albert Museum, and an authority on William Morris fabrics. He was at Gresham's School alongside Donald Maclean, who kept in touch with the Peter Flouds on leave from his diplomatic posting in Washington. Peter's wife Jean, later to become Principal of Newnham College, Cambridge, was also in the Party. The woman Bernard Floud married – Ailsa Craig – was also a convinced Marxist theorist. In turn, her sister, Priscilla Craig, joined the Communist Party for a time: Priscilla married an engine-driver, Bill Allan, whose own Communist convictions sprang from a different pattern of experience. Of them all, oddly enough, Bernard Floud seems to have been the one with the most superficial intellectual commitment.

The young Floud qualified as a lawyer, but on the outbreak of war was called up and joined the Intelligence Corps. Malcolm Muggeridge, subsequently enrolled in MI6, recalled later in an unpublished letter:

Bernard Floud and I became friends in 1940 at Mychett Hutments when we were both privates in what was then called Field Security and became the Intelligence Corps. There was, I know, some sort of hold-up in his getting his commission but in due course, to the best of my knowledge, full clearance came from MI5 and he appeared in a particularly smart officer's uniform ... Certainly he had strong Leftish views to which he gave ardent expression. Yet I never detected, and cannot looking back recall, any intimation in our talks that he had any special fancy for the

USSR under Stalin. He was an attractive and gifted person. When our military service paths separated, we corresponded and occasionally met ... Undoubtedly there was some sort of conflict going on inside him, and this may well have concerned divided loyalties.[4]

Muggeridge may have been prescient. The young Floud had been approached by Douglas Springhall, the British Communist Party national organiser who functioned as a link-man with the Comintern, and asked to spy. His friends say he refused point-blank. This approach by Springhall was very much in keeping with his pattern of war-time scouting on Stalin's behalf. It was ended by a seven-year jail sentence after an in-camera trial in Britain in 1943: Springhall was then convicted of getting information out of two other sympathisers, Olive Sheehan, an Air Ministry secretary, and Captain Ormond Uren, who had been posted to SOE. The Springhall incident does not square very sensibly with the idea that Floud was already a fully participating Soviet 'mole', of the Philby/Blunt/Maclean/Burgess class.

Nor does the recollection of Philip Toynbee's first wife, Anne Wollheim. She says:

We saw quite a lot of him at Wilton in 1941, where Philip was in Intelligence at the Southern Command HQ. Bernard was in the Security side of Intelligence in the Southern Command then and still a member of the Communist Party. Philip had left the Party at the time of the Soviet–German pact and was violently anti-Russian, but his relations with Bernard remained very friendly. I remember them both thinking how funny it would be if Bernard got Philip sacked for being a security risk. I find it impossible to believe that Bernard would have had these very open public discussions if he was a Russian agent.[5]

Later in the war, Floud was moved to the Ministry of Information. As an 'expert' on China, presumably on the strength of his 1938 trip, he was used to provide advice on the Chinese resistance and on the handling of Chinese visitors.

At the end of the war, he followed his father into the Civil Service, as a principal in the Board of Trade. In 1947, the 'Civil Service Communists Group' used to meet at the flat of the Marxist intellectual Eric Hobsbawm: his then wife was a member and so was Floud. As a result of these open Communist associations, Floud figured on the 1947 lists of Communists being compiled in each Whitehall department with a view to blacklisting them off secret work. Shortly after Harold Wilson became head of the Board of Trade and concluded his controversial trade agreement with Moscow, Floud was one of his staff who was privately told they had no future. They were ineligible for 'secret work', which meant in practice that they could not be promoted. Floud would never now be able to emulate Sir Francis, his father.

As the Cold War deepened, and news began to emerge of Stalin's brutalities and purges, Floud's convictions, such as they were, appear to have further weakened. The breach between Stalin and Tito in 1949 caused a crisis among his friends and relations. James Klugmann, who had exploited his position in SOE to promote Tito's cause, had little apparent heart-searching and stayed in.[6] Bernard's brother Peter, on the other hand, decided to leave the Party, and so did his wife Jean. In 1951, Floud threw up the civil service and attempted to run a farm at Ongar, just outside London. Ailsa, his wife, suffered from very severe attacks of asthma and it was thought that the move to Essex might help. They were joined by her sister and brother-in-law, Priscilla and Bill. Roderick Floud says:

> When we were living on the farm, Priscilla and Bill subscribed to the *Daily Worker*. But my father would never read it.

Floud was later to make censorious remarks within the family about these two diehards, saying they were misguided to believe 'all that dogma'. His wife Ailsa, too, later confided in her daughter-in-law: 'What fools we'd been!' Roderick recalls:

> I knew he had been in the CP, but he didn't talk about it much – neither he nor my mother, who certainly shared his opinions. There was no conscious effort by him to convert me to the CP – I was in the Labour Party from a young age. I think his political views had simply changed. We had lots of discussions and political arguments, so I would have known his attitude.

In 1953, Floud joined the Labour Party. This was regarded by some of his relations as an activity beneath their intellectual dignity. He fought Chelmsford unsuccessfully in the 1955 General Election, having explained to the Labour Party when they were selecting him that he had ceased to be a Communist some years before. In 1959, he stood as a Labour candidate at Hemel Hempstead, again unsuccessfully. There had already been a precursor of what Muggeridge calls 'his rather drastic ups and downs of mood': he had a relatively brief breakdown.

Finally, in 1964, Floud entered Parliament for the first time for Acton, as one of Wilson's narrow Labour majority of MPs. By this time he had given up the farm, which had not been a success as far as he was concerned: he had been kicked by an animal, and suffered from back pain. His wife Ailsa had problems too: she developed agoraphobia, a psychological anxiety about meeting people and going out. Floud got a job as personnel adviser to Granada, which was going into the new field of commercial television. This was the firm run by liberal-minded Jewish entrepreneur Sidney

131

Bernstein. He also became a director of ITN, the news organisation funded by the commercial TV companies. For thirteen years, Floud had been doing nothing of any conceivable interest to the Soviet Union, even had he not long left the British Communist Party.

For the first time for many years, he must have briefly felt his career was picking up. Then full-scale tragedy overtook him. His wife Ailsa's asthma worsened dramatically, and in January 1967 she died in the Middlesex Hospital after her lungs collapsed. Bernard Floud was plunged into severe depression. His sister-in-law Jean said:

> The violent grief and the suicidal despair of this normally robust man shocked and frightened us all. [7]

In March, Floud was still so distraught, and talking of suicide, that he was persuaded to see a psychiatrist, a Dr Gould. Eventually his twenty-five-year-old son Roderick was phoned from ITN to take his father home – he had broken down in the middle of a board meeting, saying he could no longer go on. In the middle of June he was admitted to a London nursing home in Primrose Hill where for several weeks he was given electric shock treatment – electro-convulsive therapy – in an attempt to lift his depression. The recipient of ECT is anaesthetised, and strapped to a trolley; electric current is passed through electrodes placed on the head until epileptic convulsions are stimulated. Although this often causes short-term memory loss and other side-effects, it is sometimes effective in treating severe depression.

Towards the end of July, Bernard Floud was released from the nursing home. Both the Labour Chief Whip John Silkin and his old ministerial friend Tony Greenwood (one of the old Communist 'October Club' at Oxford and now housing minister) knew of his condition. They may have thought – and Harold Wilson was always generous to those in distress – that a new interest in life would help speed his recovery. With Parliament due to adjourn, towards the end of July, the evidence suggests, Wilson had pencilled in Floud's name on a list of those he intended to promote after the long summer holidays, and who therefore needed MI5's 'negative clearance'. The list came back with three names to which were appended details of 'MI5 objections' by Martin Furnival Jones. One name was Floud's. Wilson agreed that he could be 'interrogated' to clear up Wright's allegations that he was a potential Soviet spy. He removed Floud's name from the promotion list for the time being and went off on his own family holiday, to the Scilly Isles.

At the end of August, Bernard Floud returned from Iran where he had gone to recuperate with his fourteen-year-old daughter (his brother-in-law, Sir Denis Wright, was ambassador there). He wasn't back on his feet,' his son says. 'He'd been talking about killing himself since mid-summer. He could hardly carry out any constituency work in September, let alone take a government job. He managed to open a fête in Acton, I think, and that was about all.'

It is impossible to establish exactly when or how many interrogations Bernard Floud underwent in the autumn of 1967. He himself apparently told no one he was being required to see MI5. The leaks from MI5 are of no help. The Conservative MP Rupert Allason, whose best source was Arthur Martin, says the interrogations definitely did occur, 'in the afternoons at the War Office,' and that Floud was interviewed 'in the week preceding his death.' He claims to have got this information from two MI5 officers. He asserts confidently in his books (written as Nigel West) that there was 'a series of interviews' and that 'Floud returned home from an interrogation and killed himself.'[8] Allason's source, Martin, was not on the case himself, however, and should not have had any need of access to the Floud files: although he stayed in close personal touch with Wright and his FLUENCY colleagues, he was in the employ of MI6 by now, not MI5.

Furthermore, one's trust in Allason as a historian is diminished when, in the passage in his book *MI5: 1945–1972* dealing with Floud, one discovers two gross errors. Allason asserts, with his usual self-confidence:

> Jenifer Hart . . . had come to MI5's attention after being denounced by Mrs Flora Solomon, the Marks & Spencer executive who had offered proof of Philby's duplicity in 1962.

This seems to have been simply wrong. As the novelist Anita Brookner was later to confirm and Peter Wright to describe in some detail, Mrs Solomon had nothing to do with it. Jenifer Hart's name was first mentioned by the lowly Phoebe Pool, in quite a different context. Was Allason being supplied with disinformation? Or was he just guessing? Allason goes on to record that Floud killed himself on October 27, 1967. In fact, he killed himself on the night of 9 October: this date has some importance in view of the claim that it was on the very day of his interrogation. Allason's second mistake further undermines his belief that he got these facts from the horse's mouth.

But the alternative source of MI5 leaks, Peter Wright himself, is no more satisfactory. He initially told Chapman Pincher, with whom he was collaborating on the 1980 book which first stigmatised Floud as a 'Soviet agent': 'Floud was interrogated closely for two weeks . . . after an unproductive session in October 1967, Floud went home . . . and killed himself.' Seven years later, for his *Spycatcher* memoirs, Wright told the journalist Paul Greengrass a different story – that the interrogation had taken not two weeks, but two successive days. It consisted of one interview followed by another the following day. 'The next morning I got a message Floud had committed suicide.' Wright cannot be telling the truth for the simple reason that the night of October 9 was a Monday. Wright was working office hours, and cannot conceivably have started his formal White-hall interviews with Floud at the weekend, on a Sunday afternoon. The single, melodramatic, common factor in these varying accounts is that Floud killed himself on the day of one of his interrogations – with the implication that he was on the point of exposure. That cannot be true either, as we shall see.

At the beginning of October, Floud's son and daughter-in-law were at work during the day: Floud was going out of the house regularly to see his psychiatrist. It was thus possible that these interviews might have taken place unbeknownst to his family.

We only have Wright's word for what occurred, and that is worth little. We also know that Wright was desperate to get results; that he was a clumsy interrogator; and that he would have tried to conceal what he was truly driving at, because the Phoebe Pool/Anthony Blunt connection, and Blunt's MI5 confession, were 'official secrets', too embarrassing to disclose even to the Prime Minister. We can also assume that Wright would have picked up and misapplied standard interrogation techniques – these include putting the interviewee at a psychological disadvantage, by acting as if one knows every intimate detail of his life, and thus establishing 'dominance'. It is also worth bearing in mind that the 'subject' was entirely alone, without a friend present, let alone a lawyer. His son says, 'If I had known such interrogations were planned, I would immediately have put a stop to it.'

The unintentional admissions Wright makes about these 'interrogations' are telling:

> Floud's attitude, when I began the interview, was extraordinary. He treated the matter as of little importance, and when I pressed him on Jennifer Hart's story, he refused to either confirm or deny that he had recruited her: 'How can I deny it if I can't remember anything about it?' he said repeatedly. I was tough with him. I knew that his wife, an agoraphobic depressive, had recently committed suicide . . . I explained to him in unmistakable terms that since it was my responsibility to advise on his security clearance, I could not possibly clear him until he gave a satisfactory explanation for the Hart story. Still, he fell back lamely on his lack of memory. The session ended inconclusively . . . the following day I did not make any progress with him, he maintaining he had no recollection of 'recruiting' Jenifer.[9]

Wright was ill-informed (Ailsa Floud had not committed suicide, for example); but he knew well enough that Floud, his victim, had just lost his wife; Wright felt exasperated by Floud's inability to recall thirty-year-old events which Floud seemed to regard as 'unimportant'; he threatened him; he warned that he would continue to exert pressure; and he gave Bernard

134

Floud to understand that he had no future. One assumes that Floud's doctor, had he been consulted, might have said that there was little prospect of getting any sense out of a man in such a condition. He might have added that such treatment was unlikely to improve the mental state of a recently bereaved middle-aged man who had already been hospitalised and was severely – suicidally – depressed, who was suffering from the usual symptoms of such an illness, including inability to recollect or focus his mind, and who was fearful of attempting to resume his career. One might be tempted to conclude that Wright's over-zealousness had helped to kill the man.

For Floud's mental health certainly deteriorated during this period. He was being urged by his psychiatrist to try to resume work at Granada, and this had been planned for Monday, October 9. On the preceding Friday, Floud woke up in an extremely distressed state. Saying 'Life's not worth living', he took his car keys and said he was going to kill himself with his car. His son says:

> I was with him most of that Friday. He was suicidal. He kept debating whether he should marry again, and was obsessional – he would repeatedly clean the grill-pan. There had been similar threats since the summer. He was terribly depressed and he couldn't really concentrate very well.

After what must have been a painful weekend for the family, Floud nerved himself to resume his Granada job on the Monday. He could not have been interrogated in Whitehall on that date either, for he spent the entire day at one of Granada's motorway service stations, on the M1 at Toddington. Lord Bernstein confirms: 'After his first day at work, he said he was unable to go on, despite our urging him to do so.' And when he returned home, his son recalls, 'He was in a terrible state, saying he couldn't work. He was depressed about my mother's death and his inability to work.'

When Roderick Floud came downstairs the next morning, he found that his father, having carefully arranged his bank statements on the desk and wrapped himself in a blanket, had turned on the gas poker and killed himself with it. Shortly after hearing the news of Bernard Floud's death, the distraught Phoebe Pool, who had unwittingly given his name to MI5, threw herself under a Tube train. Wright does concede that he was now stopped from carrying on his witch-hunt. He claims, although one is disinclined to believe him, that Martin Furnival Jones said, 'All these suicides. They'll ruin our image.'

What he does not mention is that, two years later at the height of hostility to Wilson's premiership, MI5 attempted to re-open the investigation: they sent other officers from 'D' branch to Floud's mystified sister-in-law, the academic Jean Floud, and also for the second time to Jenifer Hart. One was a middle-aged ex-classics master from a Midlands grammar school, who confided that he had failed to gain 'mature entry' into the civil service proper. On the pretext that he was compiling a history of the student movements of the 1930s, he took Jean Floud through her own Communist involvement from when she and her husband left the Party back in 1949 to incidents she had completely forgotten, which Wright's 'research' section had laboriously compiled. 'He knew, he said, I had gone from the London School of Economics as delegate to a 'Youth Peace Conference' in Brussels. I denied it and then remembered – it had been in 1933 when I was seventeen years old!' Only at the end of the interview did he gingerly raise the real topic – Bernard Floud's name – and only afterwards did it occur to Jean Floud that he had been hinting at something which had never occurred to her: that Bernard's suicide had been connected to his activities as a student Communist. When nothing incriminating was discovered, 'D' branch sent along a second officer – a brusque military type, who barked accusingly, but made no further progress. The Floud family were unaware of the reasons behind this badgering.

There was a second name on Wilson's ministerial list in July 1967 who was subsequently ruined by 'D' branch of MI5. This was a relatively prominent Treasury minister: Niall MacDermot. He was quite innocent.

The MacDermots, married for 22 years, now live in a pleasant post-war apartment block in Geneva. The peeling paint of the building reveals that it is showing its age – that of the era of post-war optimism when the European office of the United Nations was established in the old League of Nations building, up on the slope overlooking the Alpine shores of Lake Geneva. MacDermot's wife, Ludmila, a warm and voluble women, still attends out of sentiment the Easter services of the small Russian orthodox church in Geneva: they remind her of her childhood, and of her mother who lived with them until she died recently, after long years of exile from her beloved Russia.

The Cold War seems very distant: although MacDermot, aged 71 now, still works at the respected human rights organisation, the International Commission of Jurists, which he heads, and of which the British section is the well-known 'Justice'. The ICJ has turned out streams of reports over the years, from a critique of the building of the Berlin Wall in 1962 to the need for legal services in rural areas of the Third World. One is led to reflect that MacDermot was a loss to the British Labour government, which has usually been short of talented lawyers. But he decided to resign when MI5 insisted, falsely and secretly, that his wife could be a Soviet spy.

In 1967, Harold Wilson was so alarmed by Furnival Jones' claim that towards the end of July he ordered his private secretary to remove the mystified MacDermot from his position on the cabinet's defence committee, which handled top-secret military issues, pending an investigation. He crossed him off the list of ministers who might be promoted to Cabinet rank or made law officers. Wilson asked MacDermot if his wife would agree to be interrogated by the security authorities. Meanwhile, the Prime Minister decided that in the forthcoming autumn reshuffle he would switch MacDermot from his job at the Treasury to become a Minister of State, assisting Richard Crossman in passing through Parliament the Town and Country Planning Bill and the Countryside Bill.

Ludmila's interrogation lasted longer than was expected. It was conducted from his wheelchair by Wright's colleague on the Hollis-hunting FLUENCY committee – the implacable Old Rugbeian, Patrick Stewart, by this time the assistant director in charge of 'D1' (Soviet counter-espionage).

Niall MacDermot was an Old Rugbeian too. Stewart remarked, when he eventually got MacDermot's wife in front of him, that he had been 'following his career with interest'. MacDermot was an idealistic lawyer. Like Floud, he was no particular intimate of Harold Wilson. He was a supporter of the right-wing James Callaghan. As a former MI5 officer, he had the misfortune already to have a fat 'security file': MI5 officers, who lived in a world of secret files, seem often to have thought that individuals were more interesting, or more potentially dangerous, because they had a sort of electrical charge from already being recorded in those rows of buff, official, 'PFs'. There was a little more to it than that, however: as we have seen, he had already attracted attention as a backbencher by asking uncomfortable questions about Philby, who he had known from the war years as a senior man in MI6. There were people in MI6 who regarded any attempt to expose this private grief as the work of an 'enemy'.

After leaving Rugby, MacDermot had been involved with a utopian political group which was outside the left–right mainstream. His mother was one of its backers. The 'New Britain Group', which flourished in 1933 with calls for European Federation, was inspired by the Yugoslav philosopher Dimitrije Mitrinovic and heavily influenced by syndicalist ideas.

MacDermot read law, first in London, then at Balliol. When the war came, he enlisted. Anxious to get to France, he soon found himself in 'Field Security' in Marseilles. Recalled in February 1940, the young second lieutenant married Violet, a fellow member of the New Britain movement. Illness knocked him out of the fighting war: he developed a duodenal ulcer and was moved to military Intelligence to work on deception. On the Inter Services Security Board (ISSB) he sat alongside the Intelligence agency planners who coordinated the various schemes to confuse the Germans – the phantom armies, 'turned' agents, and disinformation documents which culminated in the successful D-Day landings. In early 1942, MacDermot was transferred to a new military liaison section of MI5 as a major. There

MacDermot met, among others, Dick White, Philby briefly, and Furnival Jones, the man who was to head MI5 twenty-five years later, when he turned on MacDermot himself. MacDermot comments:

He was handling security, I think, at defence contractors. A rather dull fellow, I thought. But MI5 as a whole were very brilliant. They were having these fantastic successes with the Double-Cross system. At the time of the Normandy landings in 1944, every German agent in the UK, bar one, was under control.

MacDermot found his work in MI5 tedious. There was barely enough work for one person in his section, let alone the three employed.

He was glad to be transferred a year later: working under an American colonel, he prepared the counter-intelligence plan for the invasion of France, coordinating the different secret British and American Intelligence organisations.

In April 1944, he was promoted at the age of twenty-seven to be the counter-intelligence Lieutenant-Colonel in charge of the Normandy landings, for which he received an OBE. 'At the end of the war, Dick White traced the Abwehr dossiers. They had infiltrated 105 agents: we had identified over eighty and of the others, only one had ever actually reported back to the Germans. It was a quite remarkable score.'

The captured Heinrich Himmler's belongings were distributed among the Intelligence team as souvenirs.

One barrister I knew had Himmler's braces. I had his spectacles – Years later, I threw them away in disgust.

Declining the offer to become Brigadier in charge of counter-intelligence for occupied Germany, MacDermot qualified as a barrister and built up a considerable practice over eighteen years, sitting as a part-time judge. He was not even a member of the Labour Party when, in 1954, he met, and fell in love with Ludmila Benvenuto, a half-Italian, half-Russian girl. She was staying in England, in Richmond-on-Thames, learning English.

Ludmila recalls: 'Our eyes met in the mirror of a car. There was a "coup de foudre": we hadn't spoken. Niall was very modest, and not wealthy. I didn't speak English very well. But we were involved with each other from then on.' It was a painful romance – they lived apart for the next thirteen years. MacDermot took the decision that he would remain married for the sake of their son. 'I came from a divided home, and I grew up without a father. So I decided there would be no divorce until my son left school.' Ludmila had only come to England temporarily, in the hope of qualifying in the language to obtain a job as a UN translator at Geneva. From then on, Niall MacDermot travelled to Geneva and she to London when they could for short meetings.

The whole relationship was nothing to do with espionage. It was a love story.

Ludmila herself had had a tragic history. It started with the unusual destiny of her mother, which began about 1906 on the beach in the North Italian village of Sestri Levante, near the picturesque cove of Portofino. A bare-legged girl of eight or nine, Ludmila's mother Laura played on the sand with a boy her own age: he was a son of a well-known Russian writer, Alexander Amfiteatrof, living with his family in exile in Italy.

The two children became close friends. So much so that Amfiteatrof proposed they take the little girl into their household. No doubt the prospect of one less mouth to feed persuaded her poor family to agree. After the 1917 Kerensky revolution, Amfiteatrof decided to return bringing Ludmila's mother with them. By that time, Laura Benvenuto spoke perfect Russian. She was present in Leningrad during the insurrections which led to the Bolshevik seizure of power. In 1920, disillusioned by the revolution, Amfiteatrof broke with Maxim Gorky and other friends of his exile, and fled with his family again, leaving their furniture and other belongings behind. They were a wedding present for the young Laura, who had met and married a Leningrad engineer, Vassily Patrikeev. When they married, Laura was advised by family friends to keep her Italian passport. They said: 'Soon it will not be easy to pass our frontiers.' The infant Ludmila was born in 1920. She became an Italian citizen. It may have saved her life, but cost her a great deal of suffering thereafter.

She grew up in a non-Communist household. At school in Leningrad, there were posters on the wall saying Easter celebration food was 'poison for children'. But every Easter festival, her father would send a note to school saying 'Ludmila is staying home because of domestic circumstances.' Her father was running a small car business. After 1927, the Bolshevik regime began to harass him as a 'capitalist'. He was accused of breaches of regulations. Huge fines were imposed; his enterprise closed down; and the possessions in their flat confiscated, including the furniture Amfiteatrof had bequeathed to her mother. The 1934 assassination of Kirov, the senior Party official in Leningrad, led to a major new wave of terror. Ludmila Benvenuto and her family kept as quiet as they could. She passed the competition for entrance to Leningrad University but one month later discovered that her name had been omitted from the list of students. Both she and her mother were to be separated from her father and expelled from the Soviet Union as 'foreigners'. It was one of many thousands of such brutalities.

In 1938, mother and daughter arrived as penniless exiles in Mussolini's Milan. They had an unfriendly welcome, as both refused to sign a document denouncing the Soviet Union. They were thus listed on the files of the fascist secret police as Communist sympathisers. To sign would, of course, have been an act guaranteeing that they were never allowed to return. 'To make the denunciation would have been an idiotic thing to do; although it might have made life temporarily easier,' Ludmila says. She had never been a Communist and never joined the Italian Communist Party. She had no conceivable incentive to do so.

Ludmila got poorly paid work as a draughtsman in a Siemens factory. Later, the family of Nicola Benois, the senior director of the Scala Opera in Milan, who was Russian by birth and a strong Russian patriot, befriended the two women, and they were invited to join the household.

The one ambition of Ludmila and her mother was to return to Russia as soon as possible and to rejoin their father and husband. For this they needed to be granted Soviet citizenship. Ludmila went to Rome to hand in applications to the Soviet consulate. In May 1941, a young member of the consulate came to Milan and suggested they would probably receive their passports shortly. His name was Nikolai Gorshkov. Only one month later, Germany invaded Poland and Russia, and Italy entered the war on the German side. Further communication with Russia was impossible.

Ludmila and her mother struggled to survive, knowing they were regarded by the Italian authorities almost as traitors. Ludmila, however, showed herself ready to take risks. A young Soviet doctor, Abram Polonski, who had been studying in Padua, was stranded in Italy by the outbreak of war. Ludmila persuaded him to go with her in an attempt to reach the Soviet embassy. Mussolini's police arrested him on the embassy steps, and attempted to arrest Ludmila too. Cursing the police in fluent Italian for trying to manhandle her, she was released but followed from a distance the detachment taking Polonski to the police station. In a tram, he managed to slip her a piece of paper with an address on it. It was the home of an Italian professor, an anti-Communist, but an even stronger anti-Fascist. This remarkable lady reported Polonski's plight to the Swedish embassy and consequently to the Red Cross, who sent him parcels: he survived the war in an Italian camp.

Through Benois they met an elderly Russian opera producer, Alexander Sanin. Invited to become producer of the Rome Opera, he asked them both to join him for the duration of the war, Ludmila's mother keeping house for him. Ludmila found a job there as a draughtsman with a ship-building firm.

Soon afterwards she joined an underground escape organisation for Allied prisoners of war. It was run by a Roman Catholic priest of Russian origin. She also had contacts with another anti-Fascist underground organisation which she used to help sporadically. She remembers vividly a house-to-house search by German police at a time when two Russian escapees were in the kitchen of the flat where they lived. Ludmila blocked the stairway one floor lower, chattering desperately in a perfect German with the two

German military police until their commander impatiently called them away. Without her intervention, she and her mother and the women with whom they lived would all have been before the firing squad.

'There were different types of people in the resistance,' she recalls. 'I met many anti-German White Russians. The war had changed their feelings: it was a question of the survival of Russia.' She also met a Russian priest and Madame Gallone, a Polish–Jewish underground activist who supplied her with false papers. There were rumours at the time that Madame Gallone was a British agent, and her name was to recur in MI5's subsequent inter-rogations. 'They wouldn't give me a gun!' Ludmila recalls. 'They were afraid I would go out there and then and shoot Germans.'

With the liberation of the southern half of Italy, a Soviet mission moved into Rome. Ludmila began working as a factotum for Nikolai Gorshkov, who remembered her applying from Milan for Soviet citizenship. Abram Polonski, on his release from internment, sought repatriation and was glad to find Ludmila already installed at the Soviet mission. His testimony about the help she had given him increaseed her bona fides. There was nothing more in life that Ludmila wanted than repatriation for herself and her mother. They still wanted to be allowed to return home and find her father. Gorshkov, although only First Secretary, appeared to wield considerable power. Among his duties was the import of Soviet films into Italy, and Ludmila contacted Italian film distributors on his behalf and generally ran errands: 'It was publicly known that I was working for the Soviet repre-sentation. Gorshkov, who was very intelligent, wanted to know everything about the Italian film industry. He wanted me to work full time for him on Russian films.'

Ludmila made a fresh plea for Russian citizenship and permission to return. A ship arrived from the Soviet Union in 1947 to collect returnees: but no visa documents arrived. Gorshkov and his colleagues professed themselves puzzled.

It took several years before she learned what had become of her father. After she and her mother were expelled from Russia, he was arrested and tortured. Later released, he took part in the defence of Leningrad. After the war, he was again arrested and was to be exiled to Siberia. Tortured so brutally that he could not survive such a journey, he was thrown out of a prison camp in Central Russia, a dying man. Ludmila later found his grave.

All her numerous relatives in Russia died, as victims either of the Stalinist terror or of the war, and the siege of Leningrad. Ludmila and her mother, perhaps unsurprisingly, no longer sought to return.

But it is clear from subsequent events that the energetic American hand of James Angleton in Rome, busy re-establishing and funding the Italian

141

secret police, would have fallen on Ludmila Benvenuto's activities with the Soviet mission. The Italian police files would have recorded that Gorshkov was an NKVD Intelligence officer and that Ludmila was a suspected 'Communist sympathiser'. Had not Mussolini's police been vindicated by subsequent events? In fact, Ludmila knew nothing of Gorshkov's Intelligence work until she learned it from the MI5 interrogators.

Ludmila had no incentive to remain in Italy. Her work in Italian films had come to an end. Sanin, the opera producer, was seriously ill and could not work any more. She was annoyed by continuous visits by the Italian police, and she had to find a proper profession.

In 1952 she was advised by a friend, who was an Italian interpreter, to go to the interpreters' school in Geneva to add French and English to her languages. With the help of a Russian staff member there, she was given temporary contracts as a UN translator. But despite passing the UN linguistic competition, they repeatedly refused to give her a permanent contract. Eventually, she was tipped off: the Italian authorities had reported that she was 'not loyal towards Italy'. They would no doubt have preferred the post to be given to an Italian nominated by them. It was only in 1961 that her contract was made permanent.

It was more than two years after Ludmila and MacDermot began their long-distance relationship that MacDermot joined the Labour Party and it was in February 1957 that he won a parliamentary seat at a by-election. He was forty-one: a career in politics had been at the back of his mind, but he had been anxious to get an established law practice first.

In 1961, Ludmila and her mother returned to the Soviet Union for the first time as visitors. They learned then that no member of their family had survived the war and its aftermath. Ludmila made two further visits to Russia in 1963 and 1965 to bring to the Bakrushin Theatrical Museum the archives of Alexander Sanin, concerning his work with Toscanini and other famous people in Europe and the Americas. On her second visit she spent most of the time classifying and describing the material she had brought. A book about Sanin is now in preparation based largely upon these documents.

On her visit in 1963 she found their old dacha had been turned into a state orphanage. In the brief Krushchev years of de-Stalinisation, the Russian local authorities were anxious to demonstrate a return to 'Socialist legality':

When I got home, I was so excited. I told my mother 'I've found the house! We're going to get it back!' But my mother didn't want it any more. She said, 'What need of the house? These children – their parents were killed in the war. Let them keep the house . . .'

As to Ludmila's feelings towards Russia, she says:

I cannot say that I feel a hatred, but a bitterness and deception I will carry in me for ever. In spite of everything I continue to love my country. I keep a warm feeling towards it and the Russian people. My generation shared with me a not less tragic destiny. During my short visits to the Soviet Union everyone was kind to me and I found a human understanding and warmth.

In 1964, after the victorious General Election, MacDermot became a British government minister. Ten years after the two had first met, Mac-Dermot now formally told his wife Violet of the situation. She agreed to a divorce. MacDermot made an appointment towards the end of 1965 with Harold Wilson and told his Prime Minister of his pending divorce, in order to marry a half-Russian woman who worked at the UN. He offered to resign his post.

Wilson said: 'Is she anti-Soviet, then?' I replied 'No – from time to time she goes to Russia. Ludmila was never a communist, of course. She went through enough never to want to be.' Wilson would hear nothing of me resigning. He brushed it all aside and said I could carry on – 'There'll be talk, but never mind. It'll be a nine-days wonder.'

The marriage plans went ahead. Ludmila started looking for work in London and in August 1966 the wedding took place in Geneva, with Mac-Dermot breaking off from his ministerial duties for 48 hours to fly there. He had not told the press in advance as he was not sure if she would be able to get away that weekend. As a result, there were headlines in the newspapers – 'Minister's secret wedding.' It may have been these which piqued the interest of MI6, which would ask the Italians for 'reports' from their files. Or it may have been another irrelevant and embarrassing incident which give MI5 the opportunity to pry. Wilson had been obliged to ask for an official investigation into McDermot's background after an Irishman approached Downing Street – perhaps for blackmail or some unexplained reason – and claimed bizarrely that MacDermot and his pre-war New Britain group had been engaged in 'ritual murder'. The police files had been bombed in the war, but the basis of this was eventually traced. The young MacDermot had been involved in an unfortunate accident: in a quarrel, he had struck one of his friends who turned out to have had an unknown heart condition. The man died. Mac-Dermot was forced to go through the formality of a prosecution for manslaughter, at the end of which he was acquitted, without the jury even needing to retire to consider their verdict.

By 1967, MacDermot expected to be promoted – Wilson had hinted that he would be made Solicitor-General. The job went instead to the distinctly undynamic barrister Arthur Irvine.

He was puzzled to read the English papers in Paris on his way home from holiday, and find he had not got the job in the reshuffle. The mystery was soon explained. Back in Geneva the next day, there was an urgent call from No 10 Downing Street for him to present himself:

> I was convinced it was because of the publicity after our marriage. I saw Wilson on his own. It was his habit to meet people in the cabinet room. There was a long table with his seat in the middle. He gestured to me to sit next to him and said: 'MI5 have received reports ... there are allegations from abroad.' They wanted to interview Ludmila, who would no doubt be able to clear up things. He seemed quite optimistic, and gave the impression they could be satisfied. But I realised until it was cleared up, there was no question of promotion.

MacDermot says he felt fairly optimistic about the likely outcome 'because I knew the facts of the case'. He was taken aback by what happened. Ludmila recalls:

> When Niall came back, he said: 'Are you prepared to go for vetting?' We understood: it seemed understandable. I thought that perhaps one of my colleagues in the UN at Geneva had made some allegation: there were a number of very reactionary White Russians there. Niall said: 'You have to write something first', so I sent them a biography of several pages. I explained how I got into the confidence of the Russians and how I met and worked under Nikolai M. Gorshkov.

There was a delay until February 1968 before arranging the formal interview: largely because Ludmila had her work to do in Geneva and had to wait until a time when she could make herself free. There is some evidence that MI5 spent the interval in the usual way – bugging, following and burglarising. Ludmila's desk drawers in her Geneva office showed signs of interference. A date was fixed for Ludmila to attend at the MI5 room in the War Office by a private secretary at No. 10. MacDermot's own ministerial private secretary was kept in ignorance of this 'security matter'. Both Ludmila and her husband seemed to have approached this vetting process, as they thought, in a sensible spirit. He had been, after all, a colonel in military counter-intelligence and knew exactly what was involved:

> I stressed to Ludmila that she should be absolutely truthful in her answers, no matter how awkward or embarrassing the questions were. I dropped her off from my official car on the way to my Ministry in the morning.

Ludmila takes up the account:

> There were two of them, a man and a woman, both sitting behind a desk with their backs to the window. I thought it was an opportunity to clear up any foggy parts of my biography. Niall had said to me: 'If you want

144

them to understand the whole picture, you must tell all the truth.' I was concerned about Niall, that I would break his career, so I wholeheartedly intended to cooperate. But I seemed to be an accused person to them . . . It was the first time in my life I had been questioned in this way. At the beginning they just looked at me, saying nothing. So I started: 'I imagine you would like to know everything about me – where I was born and so on. I was born in Leningrad . . .' I would speak and the woman would suddenly interrupt, put questions in the middle of my explanation. . . .

English was not Ludmila's first tongue, or her best tongue. Although her grasp of the language had improved greatly since her first attempts to learn it in Richmond 13 years before, she says:

On the first day I just didn't realise what the situation was. On the second day I realised Stewart was very hostile. I had felt a little pity for him because he was in a wheelchair. He was dark-haired, looked rather Italian. I felt the woman was more intelligent and understood more than the man. To my surprise she once gestured towards the ceiling when we were alone for a few minutes, as though to say that the room was bugged.

Ludmila was correct: the room was bugged. It was often Peter Wright, who would be seated upstairs listening through the headphones. Later that day, the recording would have been played over and over again, while 'D' branch tried to detect signs of hesitation or what they fancied might be lies. The woman with Stewart used a cover-name – 'Old'.

MacDermot says: 'That evening Ludmila told me the interrogator was Patrick Stewart, who had been "following my career with interest." He was a friend of a cousin of mine and we were in the same house at Rugby. A year junior to me – a good fly-half, I think . . .'

The interrogation had lasted all day, from 9 a.m., with a brief break for lunch. The next morning it resumed:

They tried to shock me by telling me about the manslaughter charge and how Niall belonged to this group, and how he was prosecuted. I said, 'Yes, I know', and spoiled it for them.

I became inhibited in answering them. I was not against them . . . I was helping Niall to clear it up – but their attitude was so hostile that I felt uncooperative. Nevertheless, I continued with the interrogation sessions. The implication was that I was guilty of something because I loved my country. For instance, at one moment, I was told almost without reproach, 'But you love your country.' I replied, 'But certainly.' If they had been intelligent, they would have realised that I hadn't come into the room with any antipathy towards them. I had nothing to hide. . . .

I soon realised that Gorshkov was the key question for them: Why did the Russians, normally so secretive, allow me into the mission?

145

I explained to them that Gorshkov knew from our 1940 application for Soviet citizenship, and for permission to return to my father in Leningrad, that I was not hostile to the Soviets and, on the contrary, wanted to return to my country. I could be of use to him as I spoke fluent Italian and from my resistance work I could advise him on matters such as who should be invited to receptions, and so on. As I was never employed on confidential work and was unaware of Gorshkov's Intelligence role, this was quite sufficient 'clearance'.

I told them about the work I did for him, such as helping to organise receptions at the representation, showings of Russian war films, and other odd jobs of that kind. I explained that I was soon fully engaged in finding an Italian firm and helping to set up an organisation for dubbing and distributing foreign films, and at first especially Soviet films, which at that time were very popular in Italy. After a time, a representative of the Russian 'Sovexport Film' arrived from Moscow, and from then on I worked under him in a separate villa and had no more work under Gorshkov.

They asked me about a meeting I was supposed to have had with Gorshkov in Switzerland. I told them there was no truth in this, but Stewart continued to insist that I had met him. He gave no details about the time or place of the supposed meetings. This made me furious. I pounded the arms of my chair, I was so cross. When I got angry a smile as though of satisfaction would appear on Stewart's face.

I cannot remember whether they told me in fact that Gorshkov was a Russian Intelligence officer, but as the questioning continued I understood that this was so. This had never occurred to me during my work with Gorshkov. I explained to Stewart that my relations with Gorshkov were rather cool at the time my work for them ended. Sovexport terminated my employment after a few months as they felt I was not sufficiently pursuing Soviet as opposed to Italian interests. I was severely embittered by this insinuation and by Gorshkov failing to intervene on my behalf.

After that, I was employed on this work by an Italian film distributor until his firm went bankrupt in 1951.

Stewart asked me if I had tried to go to the United States. I said I never did. It was only at home that night that I recalled that after I broke with the Russian representation and was working at the dubbing studios, which included some American as well as Russian films, I was urged by my colleagues at work and by some Russians in the Hollywood film industry, to spend my holiday in the United States. I applied for a visa, but it was refused. I assumed this was because of my work in the Russian representation. I thought no more of it, and did not recall it when this question was put to me. That evening I remembered it. I did not bother

146

to correct it. I felt there was no point, as by this time they had made it obvious that they were not believing my answers. I thought they would not believe that I had forgotten it when asked.

When Ludmila indignantly returned to their Dolphin Square flat that night, MacDermot's heart sank:

When she told me about Gorshkov being head of Intelligence – from that moment I became very gloomy. I thought: 'They simply will not take the risk of giving clearance to someone who had worked under a KGB officer.' I knew what fools they'd made of themselves over security in the past. I didn't tell Ludmila my thoughts. These interviews were bound to be a terrible strain for her. But I just felt disgusted and hopeless.

The interrogation dragged on for a full week. At one point Ludmila was asked the odd question: 'Are you tidy in your office drawers in Geneva?' She had been puzzled earlier in the year that her drawers had been obviously straightened out by someone. This appears to have been a ploy to throw her off-balance by implying that she was being searched or having her phones tapped.

I felt inhibited, especially after the muddling of their questions. They asked me about numerous people and I would tell them what, if anything, I knew about them. I never understood the purpose of this questioning, but the tone of it was always insinuating something negative.

On one occasion they produced a card relating to one Masoyedov, and asked me: 'What about *this* man?', holding up the card without attempting to pronounce his name. That provoked *my* sarcastic smile, but it showed how inaccurate their information was. I did not know him personally, but he was an elderly man, an ex-consul in Rome in the time of the Czar – so anti-Soviet and pro-German that he had to flee with the Fascists and Germans to Venice when the allied troops were approaching Rome.

They showed me photos of Russians they said I must have known. On one occasion, Stewart handed me a photograph of a man and asked if I knew him. I said I could not recognise him. He said his name was Grishin and that I must have known him in Paris. I said I knew a Russian singer in Paris called Grishin. For some reason this seemed to irritate him. I told him they could check it at the Russian conservatoire in Paris.

On another occasion, Stewart showed me a photograph and asked: 'Who is he?' I replied it was Mr Rogov who worked at the Russian representation in Rome. He asked his nationality. I said I always considered him Russian. I told him I had never heard of his having any other name. Again, I got the impression that he did not believe me.

They gave me a real grilling about all sorts of things. They asked how Niall and I had met 13 years earlier: but they didn't seem to grasp that we had met before Niall had even become an MP. At one point, Stewart jumped right out of the chronology and said: 'How did you meet Madame Gallone? Who put you in contact with her?' I suppose he knew about it because she was rumoured to have been a British agent. Right at the end, when we got to the question of how I got to the UN, Stewart asked about the person who had originally recommended me. [This was a Russian staff member, unknown to Ludmila, but who had been pestered by a mutual friend to recommend her.] She was the Russian wife of an elderly Swiss doctor in whose flat I was living as a student.

There are some interesting features of this interrogation. One can see the textbook ploys – the attempt to establish psychological 'dominance', the prolonged silences, the air of omniscience, the sudden changes of topic. One can also see an apparent textbook failure: from very early on in the 'interrogation', Stewart managed to antagonise his subject. On Ludmila's account, he also made no attempt to produce the 'evidence' which would jog her memory of, for example, the US visit, or contradict her claims that she had not met Gorshkov in Switzerland. Nor does he seem to have addressed himself to the point that it was a logical nonsense for the KGB to have sent Ludmila to recruit a British politician: for at the time she fell in love with him and began their long affair, he was neither a Minister nor an MP, nor even a member of the Labour Party. The KGB had been accused of many demonic traits but not – so far – of clairvoyance. Moreover, shortly before her marriage, there was an article about her in the Lenignrad press, and her name was mentioned on Russian television, expressing gratitude for her work in aid of Russian prisoners during the war. It seems strange for a country to give such publicity to one of their secret agents.

The question of motive, too, must have been a puzzle to any reasonable person. Ludmila was scarcely subject to blackmail when her only close relative behind the Iron Curtain – her father – had already been tortured to death under Stalin. Her mother lived with her in the West. By the same token, her maltreatment by the Soviets was unlikely to have made her a convinced Communist. Killing one's father rarely has a positive political effect. Ludmila appears to have spent the war risking her life in the same cause for which her interrogator won a Military Cross, and his colleague Tony Brooks was venerated as a war-hero. Even if knowledge of Mac-Dermot and Ludmila's affair reached the KGB, there was no possibility of blackmail over the 'scandal' – for they had married and regularised the position. It was a case built on thin air.

Nonetheless, at the end of a full week's 'interrogation', Stewart shuffled around the desk in his wheelchair, formally shook the hand of the Minister's wife and said: 'If you want to tell us anything more, you know where to find us.' He and his colleagues then returned to Leconfield House with their tape recordings. After some weeks' deliberations, during which the case would have gone across the desk of MacDonald, the 'D' Branch head, Furnival Jones approved the preparation of a report denouncing the Minister's wife as a liar and a suspect Soviet agent.

There was an uncomfortable interview between MacDermot and an obviously embarrassed Prime Minister. Wilson had a sheet of paper in his hand. He said that MI5 did not seem to be satisfied. But he hoped that MacDermot would stay on in the government. He said he would show MacDermot a 'report' he had from MI5. Disgustedly, MacDermot said: 'I don't want to see it.'

Personally, the Prime Minister was very nice, but it was obvious to me that if I stayed on, I wouldn't get a law officer's or cabinet job. And then, at the very end of the interview, suddenly, obviously awkward, Wilson said: 'I must ask you, did you ever tell your wife any confidential information?'

MacDermot felt bitterly wounded. He said curtly: 'Of course not', and on that insulting note his political career was ended.

Later, MacDermot made a private approach to his ministerial friend and colleague, James Callaghan, who had been newly appointed Home Secretary and was therefore presumably in Furnival Jones' confidence. He asked him what on earth MI5 thought they had against his wife. 'She gave three answers which were false and which she knew to be false', Callaghan knowledgeably replied. He then refused to say what they were. Deprived of knowledge of the charges, and deprived of a right of appeal, MacDermot and his wife puzzled for days over what these 'three lies' could be.

Judging by the interviews, it seems that one of the supposed 'lies' was her denial of having tried to go to the United States. Another might be the denial of knowing the mysterious Grishin, or the other for Rogov. But it seems obvious that the major issue was Ludmila's denial that she had met Gorshkov in Switzerland. Presumably, MI5 had received a report to this effect from someone they considered credible. It is human to err, and MI5 had made many errors. But, like all security authorities, when challenged, they hide behind the need to protect their sources. Consequently, there is no way in which the victim of an error can explain the error and establish the truth.

MacDermot and Ludmila abandoned their house-hunting in London. MacDermot decided to resign from the Labour government. He felt he had no wish to remain in British politics at all if this was the attitude towards him and his wife. He preferred to seek work abroad, if possible in Geneva so that Ludmila could at least continue her job there. MacDermot made a second appointment at Downing Street with Harold Wilson to tell him of his decision. He agreed to stay on to finish the outstanding legislation and

149

they agreed what should be said to the press. In September 1968, a small announcement appeared in the newspapers that the Housing Minister was resigning and returning to the Bar 'for personal reasons'. 'D' Branch had claimed their second victim.

CHAPTER 8

MI5's aggression towards Wilson's ministers in 1967 was part of a pattern. In the final years of his first government Wilson began to fall out with both the US and British military Establishment. At the same time the Intelligence agencies on both sides of the Atlantic feared increasing internal embarrassment: there was a danger that they themselves would become exposed and discredited as a result of the Philby affair and their own continued internal witch-hunting.

The CIA and its friends were also starting to go out of fashion in the 'revolutionary' mood of the late Sixties. Long-haired student demonstrators, unwilling to be drafted to Vietnam, chanted, 'Hey, hey, LBJ, how many kids did you kill today?'

One of the least-remarked but eventually most seismic events of the period occurred in the summer of 1968 when a young officer called Philip Agee angrily resigned from his secret desk in the CIA station in Mexico, saying afterwards, 'Everybody I knew was against the Vietnam war.'[1]

The years from 1967 to 1970 were the years in which James Angleton was further humiliated by Philby; in which MI6 was thwarted by Wilson; and in which talk began for the first time of a 'coup' against Wilson, of the kind recently carried out with CIA backing by the Greek colonels. They were also the years in which, for the first time, MI5 began to peddle rumours which had the aim of discrediting the Labour government.

Lyndon Johnson wanted Wilson to send troops to Vietnam; to hold the value of the pound in order to protect the stability of the dollar; and to maintain Britain's military and Intelligence bases in the Far East. In American eyes, Wilson was becoming a 'bad ally'. The British Prime Minister dared not send troops to fight in an unpopular American war, although he supplied some covert Signals Intelligence on the UK-USA link. As the British economy collapsed he was forced to devalue and make sharp defence cuts in mid-1967. Nonetheless, Britain had 54,000 troops in Malaysia, in the 'confrontation' with Indonesia (where the gung-ho General Walter Walker was allowed by Defence Secretary Denis Healey to conduct 'deep unacknowledgeable raids' across the border). There were also British bases strung out across Aden and the Gulf.

That summer there was a 'gathering of the left-wing clan' at Wilson's country house, Chequers.[2] Among those present were his friend Beattie

Plummer and the increasingly influential Marcia Williams, who reputedly strode in and ordered fresh air in imperious tones, despite the 'security risk' of opening the windows (she says she did no such thing). Two weeks before, Wilson had complained to the Cabinet that Intelligence of his plan to make a statement on defence cuts had already been leaked to Johnson – 'a foreign power' – who was objecting to it.

Meanwhile, on the other side of the world, in Melbourne, Australia, another clan was gathering. The security precautions were far tighter than at Chequers, for the Intelligence agencies of the Atlantic axis were meeting to decide their own priorities. This was the first of the CAZAB conferences organised at the United States' behest. Present were the most senior figures of the CIA, the FBI, Furnival Jones' MI5, Dick White's MI6, the New Zealand Secret Service (NZSIS) and the two Australian agencies, ASIO and ASIS. They swapped warnings about 'penetration'. One of the titbits Wright had to share was his latest successes in breaking old radio traffic which might be used against the German Social Democrat Willi Brandt. He had found his name mentioned in wartime coded Soviet signals. According to Wright, it was at CAZAB that Furnival Jones caused a scene at the airport, when the occupation 'Gentleman' in his passport was queried by the irreverent Australians.

The tone of the gathering can be judged by the fact that the defector Anatoli Golitsin was allowed to address the meeting. Golitsin (who had by now added to his conviction that Harold Wilson was a Soviet spy the thesis that the Sino-Soviet split was a deception organised by the KGB) appears to have treated the occasion as an opportunity to set up his stall once again. He claimed that if he was allowed access to British files he would be able to detect even more British penetration. Furnival Jones invited him over for a second visit, at the usual rate of £10,000 a month tax-free.

By now some of the old scandals were showing signs of leaking out. In Britain, a group of investigative journalists working for Harold Evans of the *Sunday Times* dug up and published the basic facts about Philby. Until then, they had been quite unknown to the British public, for whom the whole subject of Intelligence activities was taboo. The Foreign Office and George Brown tried, unsuccessfully, to lean on the newspaper not to publish. In October 1967, the American newspaper the *Saturday Evening Post* identified Dick White as the current head of the British MI6. Then, in Moscow, Philby and the KGB, stimulated by the *Sunday Times* disclosures, decided to stir the pot by producing Philby's own 'memoirs'. Attempts to suppress these in the West also failed: they appeared in Paris in December and were published in Britain and the US the following year.

The effects were traumatic. Sir Stewart Menzies, the aristocratic head of MI6 who had been responsible for Philby at the time, lost his reputation as the enigmatic spymaster, which had been based almost wholly on public ignorance. He wrote pathetically to a colleague that, at the time, 'One could not have thought Philby to have been an out-and-out traitor.' His wife, Lady Menzies, later drunkenly denounced Menzies in a crowded restaurant for 'having let the side down'.[3]

Angleton, too, who made a fetish of his anonymity and mysterious aloofness, felt humiliated by what appeared in print.[4] Philby publicly identified him, and dwelt sadistically on the intimacies they had shared during the war and in Washington. 'We formed the habit of lunching once a week at Harvey's . . . Our close association was, I am sure, inspired by genuine friendliness on either side . . . For my part, I was more than content to string him along . . . the real nature of my interest was something he did not know.'[5]

Philby's book *My Silent War* was designed to work on several levels. The KGB were studiously presented as 'an elite force' and there were some items of crude disinformation, such as the suggestion that the CIA had killed Ukrainian emigré Stepan Bandera (who was certainly assassinated by the Russians). But the real deadliness lay in Philby's informed jeering at the CIA and 'British Intelligence'. It spoiled their reputations. (Professor Hugh Trevor-Roper, a war-time MI6 officer, soon published a telling attack on MI6 in Philby's wake.) Philby included some subtle points, designed no doubt to raise the level of mole-hunting paranoia. One of the choicest was an apparently throwaway mention;

> The quality of MI5 in wartime owed much to its temporary recruits. There was a particularly good haul from the universities, Hart, Blunt, Rothschild, Masterman and others . . .

Blunt, of course, had been secretly exposed as a spy three years before, although MI5 did not dare tell either Labour ministers or the public. As Blunt was still entirely at liberty and the wash from his 'defection' had spread over dozens of other interrogatees, it was virtually certain that Philby and the KGB knew all about it by now. The three other names, mentioned so casually, also had alarming implications to MI5 'insiders'. Professor John Masterman, former secretary to the war-time 'Double-Cross' Committee, was never suspected of disloyalty, but he was privately causing trouble in Whitehall at the time. He was again demanding the right to bring out his long-censored memoirs, saying he was 'depressed by the low state of the reputation of the British Security Service.'[6] Herbert Hart was the husband of Jenifer Hart, whom Peter Wright had so recently pronounced to be part of the pre-war 'Oxford spy ring'. And as for Victor Rothschild . . .

It was known to very few people that Rothschild was still active in agent-running in Iran and China and in technical research for his old war-time friend Dick White. (Rothschild, with his banking links, had joined MI5's commercial section at the outset of the war, identifying Nazi-linked businessmen.) And it was known to still fewer that he had had embarrasssingly close links with Anthony Blunt. Blunt had given Rothschild's name as a reference when he joined MI5. Blunt had shared Rothschild's leased-out war-time premises in Bentinck Street, Mayfair, with Tess Mayer. The two had become very close friends, and the friendship continued after Tess married Rothschild himself. Tess Mayer had also been acquainted with Brian Simon, a Communist academic who had served in a 'phantom' unit in the war, sending deception signals. Golitsin, in his wilder moments, used to speculate that 'David and Rosa' in the KGB war-time radio traffic, might be Victor and Tess Rothschild. Both Rothschilds were entirely innocent patriots, and Rothschild's friendship with mole-hunter Peter Wright certainly helped to ensure that speculation did not get out of hand. But there was plenty to work on for those who wanted to see Rothschild as a 'security risk': Rothschild himself became increasingly anxious over the years as a result. All in all, Philby had made as much mischief as he could by blandly linking these four names in public.

While tension rose in the Intelligence communities, Wilson pressed on with devaluation and the defence cuts. He did not endear himself to the military Establishment by doggedly refusing to boost the economy with arms sales to 'anti-Communist' South Africa. This was a matter of principle from which the normally flexible Wilson would never be deflected, thereby adding South African Intelligence to the long list of covert agencies which regarded him as an enemy.

In December 1967, at an angry meeting of the Cabinet Defence Committee, Wilson fought off demands for South African sales by questioning the need to 'humour US prejudice':

If all matters with an economic bearing were to be called into question . . . regardless of moral issues, then I must insist the Foreign Office submit to our scrutiny the . . . indefensible and anomalous restrictions on trade with Eastern Europe . . . The FO might still find it desirable to humour US prejudice, but. . .'[7]

In the New Year, the defence cuts went through the Cabinet. The British generals and admirals were furious at the refusal to buy the US F-111 'strategic' plane and at the 'scuttle' from Aden, which spelt the end of their pretensions (and also a military defeat by raggle-taggle Arab guerillas). But the real fury came from America. George Brown told the Cabinet, 'I had a bloody unpleasant meeting in Washington this morning with Dean Rusk.' Brown said that relations with the US were now critical. A senior State Department official had accused Britain of going 'neutralist'. The next day, as Barbara Castle recorded in her diary;

Harold . . . circulated to us two telegrams from LBJ to him marked 'For Secret Eyes only' in which the President's sense of outrage at our decision to withdraw came clearly through. As for the F-111, the threats of retaliation if we cancelled went as far as the international proprieties allowed.[8]

The only item which came through unscathed was the nuclear weapon system, Polaris. Smaller British nuclear weapons – the home-made WE-177 bombs and depth-charges – were also kept in production, in an unpublicised decision. Wilson also agreed to keep the Aldermaston nuclear research laboratories in business by a secret programme of 'hardening Polaris' and adding 'penetration aids'. This was against the warnings of his scientific adviser, Solly Zuckerman, and of left-wing ministers like Benn. Wilson had been curiously soft on nuclear weapons, ever since Lord Mountbatten, as Chief of the Defence Staff, had urged him in 1964 to keep them as an insurance against US unreliability in Europe.[9]

There were other covert pay-offs in an attempt to appease the US. The decision to hand over Diego Garcia as a US base was pushed through in August 1968. That summer, Wilson became highly evasive in the Defence Committee when asked about US chemical warfare in Vietnam. Barbara Castle demanded:

Wasn't it true we were sharing chemical warfare know-how with the US? ... Of course, Harold went all secretive at this point and said the information I asked for couldn't be given even in OPD [the Overseas Policy and Defence Committee].'[10]

When George Brown resigned as Foreign Secretary a couple of months later, there was a furious upset in MI6. Wilson, acting on recommendations from the recently departed Wigg, and alarmed by MI6's failure to provide a coherent Intelligence picture about the August 1968 invasion of Czechoslovakia, moved Dick White to a novel job as Cabinet Office Intelligence co-ordinator.

There was nothing wrong with that: but instead of giving White's seat at MI6 to the deputy, Maurice Oldfield, Wilson appointed an 'outsider'. This was Sir John Rennie, a Foreign Office man – who in 1953 had been head of IRD, the anti-Communist propaganda department. It is hard to observe anything revolutionary in the appointment of such a colourless patrician as Rennie. Indeed, Oldfield's self-appointed biographer, Donald McCormick, protested, fatuously, that it would surely have been more in keeping with the spirit of Socialism to have given Oldfield the job, because he was less socially exalted – 'a member of the Athenaeum rather than of White's.' Oldfield, the ousted contender, was, unknown to Wilson, in fact a secret homosexual who had lied during his 'vetting'. Like Hollis, the adulterous head of MI5, and Rothschild, the man with the unfortunate friends, he was, in the savage parlance MI5 normally reserved for Labour men, a

155

'security risk'. Nevertheless, some in MI6 saw the move as a Foreign Office plot to strengthen their bureaucratic influence and keep out their MI6 colleague 'Moulders'. Others saw it as a characteristic misdeed by a Labour government, prejudiced against 'insiders'.

It was in this context that various peculiar events now began to occur. According to Peter Wright, James Angleton made a special flight to London to see his friends in MI5. He told them he had

> some very secret information from a source he would not name. This source alleged, according to Angleton, that Wilson was a Soviet agent. He said he would give us more detailed evidence and information if we could guarantee to keep the information inside MI5 ... The management of MI5 were deeply disturbed by the manner in which Angleton passed this information over. After consideration, they refused to accept Angleton's restrictions on the use to which we could put the information, and as a result we were not told anything more. However, Angleton's approach was recorded in the files under the codename OATSHEAF.[11]

There is corroborative evidence that Angleton did develop a fanatical belief that Wilson was under Soviet control. Otherwise this would be a hard story to swallow. Wright, in the various versions he has given, has embroidered every detail over the years (perhaps through failures of memory), leaving only the bare outline intact. In February 1981, he wrote:

> In 1968-9, Angleton approached Furnival Jones to say that he had information which pointed very strongly to Wilson being a Soviet agent ... he [wanted] an absolute guarantee that no action would be taken on it. He was clearly worried any action would blow the source (I suspect that it was a source in position behind the Iron Curtain or in an embassy in N-S America). FJ refused to accept the condition.[12]

Three years later, Wright had changed the date to 'in Hollis's time' (i.e. before 1966) and the condition was 'not to pass it on to the Administration', which is somewhat different from 'no action'. At around the same time, he told another journalist the codename was not OATSHEAF, but OAKLEAF or OAKTREE. None of Angleton's immediate colleagues in Washington have admitted to hearing of this story – although that proves nothing – and no records of it were found after Angleton's dismissal (which is even less surprising, given Angleton's habits).

In the original draft of *Spycatcher*, Wright added a new speculation – 'I am now pretty convinced that it came from an Israeli source. My reason for saying this is that Victor Rothschild, who had many contacts with the Israelis, had got a hint from Mossad that they were suspicious of Wilson. However, they were not forthcoming in any details to Rothschild about this matter.' In *Spycatcher* itself, the dates given are simply impossible. The

156

event is now located at a time when Furnival Jones was head of 'D' branch and after Wilson came to power. But Furnival Jones never was head of 'D' branch after 1963; Wilson did not become premier until 1964.

However, there are fragments of collateral evidence from MI6 officers that in the 1960s they received some ambiguous remarks from a Polish defector-in-place to the effect that Wilson was regarded as a 'Soviet asset'. This may be the source of OATSHEAF. Angleton may have stolen this material by eavesdropping on MI6 and felt he wanted to provoke some wider interest without betraying that it had come from another department of the British Security Services. This would explain his extreme anxiety not to have the raw material circulated. Alternatively, he may have made up the 'source' to stimulate MI5 into disloyal thoughts. It is unlikely that Wright himself invented the entire story, although none of the details can be regarded as reliable.

Around this time, Cecil King, the newspaper magnate, embarked on a campaign to overthrow Wilson and replace him by a 'government of national unity' backed by the Army.

On May 5, 1968, Hugh Cudlipp, one of King's executives on the *Daily Mirror*, went to see Lord Mountbatten, the recently retired Chief of the Defence Staff. Mountbatten had started off cordially enough with the Labour government – Major Denis Healey, the Defence Secretary, used to salute him at meetings. But he had become disenchanted by the recent defence cuts, believing that plans to scrap the aircraft-carrier fleet would imperil the nation.

Cudlipp engaged the disaffected Earl in conversation about the decline of the country and the desperate state of things under Wilson. Curiously, both parties knew MI5 men who were later to become worried about the types of people who were Harold Wilson's friends. Harry Wharton had met Cudlipp years before when he was the 'Fleet Street officer'. His colleague Tony Brooks, the 'war hero', had recently served with Mountbatten on the inquiry into George Blake's prison escape. This proves that such men moved in such circles: it proves nothing else. Subsequently Cudlipp arranged a meeting between Mountbatten and Cecil King. Cecil King was a 'long-term agent' of Harry Wharton's, according to Peter Wright. This is most unlikely to have been true. Wharton denies it, and there is no reason to doubt his word. King's nephew Michael King was a foreign correspondent on the *Mirror*: MI5 may well have approached him, as they approached many journalists, quite reasonably, for information about the activities of Russian diplomats they encountered. Any hostility to Wilson on Cecil King's part was more likely to have been because Wilson, as he later told colleagues, had refused to give the self-important King either a Cabinet post or a hereditary peerage.[13]

157

Mountbatten appears to have felt he was being drawn into something dangerous, because he asked his confidant Solly Zuckerman to come along and witness the encounter. Zuckerman, as we have seen, was Wilson's scientific adviser, and no friend of the profligate British generals. Mountbatten, Zuckerman and Cudlipp all say that at the meeting, King painted a picture of the breakdown of government, rioting in the streets and the need for Mountbatten to take over as leader of some kind of government of national salvation. At this point, Zuckerman walked out of Mountbatten's house, saying it was 'Rank treachery!' But he kept the incident to himself. In King's version, Mountbatten tells him there is anxiety about the government at the Palace, and that the Queen has had an unprecedented number of letters protesting about Wilson. Mountbatten's biographer says the royal Earl did no more than 'toy' with the idea of becoming head of government in some coup.[14]

Next, King addressed young officers at Sandhurst, astonishing them by his calls for the Army to rise up. He plastered a huge statement in the *Mirror* saying 'Wilson must go'. There were reportedly other meetings, one at the Defence Ministry itself.[15] One senior Army officer at the Ashford Intelligence services, said privately at the time that planning had reached the stage of designating the Shetland Islands, in the far North of Scotland, as a home for 'internees'. Lists of 'acceptable' trade union leaders, such as Clive Jenkins of the white-collar union ASTMS, were also being drawn up.

George Kennedy Young, who had left his powerful position as vice-chief of MI6 seven years earlier, just before the Philby scandal broke, was increasingly dabbling in far-right politics. He claims:

> In the first Wilson administration . . . there were five Ministers of the Crown whose membership of the Communist Party is not known to have been renounced, and overlapping with them, other Ministers whose ultimate allegiance is outside Britain.[16]

He later backtracked a trifle on his implied allegation of a Jewish-Bolshevik conspiracy – based apparently on counter-intelligence files – saying in his book *Subversion and the British Riposte* (1984): 'There were Ministers of the Crown who had never broken their links with the CPGB *or its front bodies . . .*' (author's emphasis)[17] The book also contains the following passage, which gives a good indication of the way the minds of people like Young tend to work:

> Under threat of invasion . . . a security counter-action need cover no more than 5,000 persons, including some 40 MPs, not all of them Labour; several hundred journalists and media employees, plus their supporting academics and clerics; the full-time members and main activists of the

158

CPGB and the Socialist Workers Party; and the directing elements of the 30 or 40 bodies affecting concern and compassion for youth, age, civil liberties, social research and minority grievances. The total internment could easily be accommodated in a lesser 'Gaelic Archipelago' off the West Highlands.[18]

To these fantasies Young adds his own faint but rather chilling euphemisms about the fate of the blacks:

One fundamental change since that analagous 1940 situation would be the presence of those 3.5 million non-Europeans whose loyalties centre round their own communities, and whose conduct would be unpredictable under threat of conquest. *National survival demands that this delicate factor be fully evaluated and taken into account.*[19] (author's emphasis)

Furnival Jones at MI5 clearly picked up some reverberations of all the talk about a coup. He later insisted that the Home Office had been briefed, although not Harold Wilson himself. 'You can't go round to ministers every time there's loose talk by gin-sodden Generals,' he is reported as saying.[20]

The 'loose talk' of a coup apparently subsided, not least because no one could be found to lead the revolt. But the rumours about Wilson continued to seep out. William Massie, the *Sunday Express* journalist who had been approached by MI5 as soon as Wilson was elected, recalls that this was 'a particularly busy period' for contacts with his MI5 friends. They told him that there was security concern about Wilson's friend Rudy Sternberg and gave him a 'full account'. They also told him an outrageous story about the Treasury minister Jack Diamond, who had just been promoted to the Cabinet. They said he was a 'womaniser': many years later, they produced a photograph said to show Diamond in the company of two Yugoslav women in Venice in April 1964, and implied it was a KGB entrapment attempt. (It was in fact quite innocent.) Meanwhile, Chapman Pincher, not to be outdone, published a story exhuming the Arthur Bax case, to show there were Communist agents in the Labour Party.[21]

Peter Wright, inside 'D' branch, claims to have been involved in all this: 'Cecil King ... made it clear that he would publish anything MI5 might care to leak in his direction.' Wright does not back up this dramatic claim with any detail: it is much more likely that Wright and his friends merely debated whether they should push material in Cecil King's direction, without doing anything about it. What is much more serious and interesting is that rumours about the Soviet connections of Wilson and his friends should now start to circulate privately for the first time.

Solly Zuckerman, who had had the temerity to storm out of the meeting with Mountbatten and was no friend of the military establishment, was perhaps lucky not to be smeared. Peter Wright later summarised to a right-wing journalist what purported to be Zuckerman's MI5 file. It was a web of anti-semitic defamation:

> Solly Zuckerman had a cottage in the wilds of Essex. It was called 'World's End'! He used to hold very odd weekend parties there ... There were also suspicious left-wing people there ... Solly had a considerable file in the office and many people were very suspicious of him. As you know, he is a South African Jew, with no fundamental loyalty to the UK. A lot of his defence decisions, as Sir Ben Lockspeiser's before him, were extremely suspect. He was considered to be untrustworthy basically because he was considered to take decisions popular to the Labour Party, particularly to the left wing, and not to the best interests of the UK. We never proved any Sov. Bloc connection, but he was certainly a black-mailable character.[22]

Every one of these allegations was wholly untrue. Wright identified other targets:

> Other people who were associating with Harold Wilson right from before he became PM in 1964 were Sternberg and his East European friends and Maxwell of Pergamon. We were very suspicious about these people and warned Wilson repeatedly about the risks ... Bernstein was a very suspicious character and had a file.[23]

'Maxwell' was the tycoon and Labour MP Captain Robert Maxwell, who had been born in Czechoslovakia, had a number of trading links with Eastern Europe, and ran a very successful publishing company, Pergamon Press. Sidney Bernstein was the distinguished chairman of Granada TV. Both were Labour backers and both were 'snips' – as Wright, like George Young, used to refer to Jews.[24] Neither were Soviet agents of any kind: Wright's attack on Bernstein was based on nothing more than the fact that Leo Long and Bernard Floud had both once worked for him. The hostility towards Maxwell was mere prejudice and quite unfounded.

At an official level, MI5 targeted a third Labour minister, and prevented him getting into the Cabinet. This was Stephen Swingler, a political friend of Wilson's and a left-winger of many years standing. There was little doubt that, during and after the war, he had had links with the Stalinist adherents of the British Communist Party. Oxford undergraduate and public school-boy, he belonged to the Labour Party from 1933. He was the son of the rector of Cranbrook, Kent; his mother was the niece of an archbishop. But his brother Randall was a Communist until shortly before the Hungarian uprising of 1956 and, as literary editor of the Communist paper the *Daily Worker*, was in its London office in 1941 when it was closed down by Churchill for interfering with the war effort. Randall was refused a commission in the war, although he won the Military Medal twice. In the post-war years he visited Czechoslovakia several times to research a book on the Czech resistance.

Stephen Swingler, by contrast, was granted a commission during the war. But he fell foul of the military mind. William Deedes, later editor of the *Daily Telegraph*, recalls a visit by 'security' when Swingler was due to lecture to the unit of which Deedes was education officer. The security men said Swingler had been making 'defeatist remarks' after giving such lectures, and was involved in Eastern Europe. They asked for consent to put in a spy who would attend the mess dinner and take notes, but Deedes' colonel indignantly refused.[25] After the war, Swingler led the campaigns against German re-armament and the H-bomb. He was one of the founders of the 'Communist-dominated' Campaign for Nuclear Disarmament.

But by this time, as Barbara Castle's protegé, he was serving under her at Transport as Parliamentary Secretary and then at a higher level as Minister of State. Barbara Castle, a woman against whom there was no whisper of 'subversion', even from the diehards of MI5, says: 'He was a skilled parliamentary performer and a prodigious worker, and was to prove an invaluable ally.'[26] The old group of left-wing 'Bevanites' had frequently gathered at the Belsize Park home of Ann and Stephen Swingler for drinks and discussions. Wilson, after his 1951 resignation, had first joined Labour's finance and economic group of MPs in a carefully planned Bevanite faction, alongside Ian Mikardo, Harold Davies, Marcus Lipson, and Swingler himself. Swingler had been one of Wilson's campaign backers for the Labour leadership.[27]

After Swingler's sudden death from viral pneumonia in 1969, Wilson, who went with his wife to the funeral at Golders Green, publicly thumbed his nose at MI5. He published a generous tribute to him in his memoirs, saying his death was a deep loss to the government and the party. He described him as 'one of the most successful of our ministers'. Because of his 'untiring work and mastery of his subject' Wilson had long thought of him for promotion, and was actually considering Swingler for a Cabinet post at the time of his death, when he was a junior Social Security minister. 'I had earlier thought of him as a possible successor to Barbara Castle in Transport.'[28]

Wilson had not been so brave at the time. Barbara Castle recalls that in April 1968, after an 'urgent summons to No. 10' to discuss the pending Cabinet re-shuffle, she had urged Wilson to replace her as Transport Minister with Swingler himself: 'The trouble here, Harold said, was security. Stephen had been doing some "very stupid things".' The following day, Barbara Castle, together with her ministerial colleague Richard Crossman, sat down with Wilson again:

Marcia came in too, and we sat around talking brutally frankly about the power set-up in the Cabinet. I . . . begged him again to put Stephen in my place. Harold said he would check up on the record again and see how black it was, but Stephen really had been dabbling in Eastern Europe too much. He couldn't risk giving Jim Callaghan, who had access to the security records, a weapon against him by bringing Stephen into the Cabinet if Stephen were in any way a security risk. Dick agreed with him on this.[29]

What Castle was unaware of was that this 'brutally frank' discussion came only a week or two after Furnival Jones had put in the final report pronouncing Niall MacDermot a ministerial 'security risk', a report that was copied to James Callaghan, Wilson's chief rival for power in the Cabinet. Furnival Jones' activities were beginning to be an impediment to the Labour administration.

While 'D' branch sniffed out KGB plots, Thistlethwaite's 'F' branch flooded the industry departments in Whitehall with news of Communism among the British trade unions. Their interminable briefs read very oddly to Labour ministers who knew the men in question well. Most of this material came from 'agents' or was the result of laborious monitoring of left-wing meetings and the press. It was predicated on the assumption that the two main trade union leaders, Jack Jones of the Transport Workers and Hugh Scanlon of the Engineers, constituted the 'enemy within'. But ministers were never shown the speculative counter-intelligence files on which such assumptions were based.

Barbara Castle found herself the recipient of these 'ministerial briefs' when she took over the Department of Employment and was attempting to enforce restrictions on pay rises. She records in her diaries:

One of my discoveries in my new job is that the Minister of Labour has always been furnished with security reports on the trade unions. The first one on my desk was about the inner Communist clique in the engineering unions. Say Security, of the 52 members of the AEF national committee, 10 are Communist Party members and 9 more are sympathisers. They have been holding secret meetings under the chairmanship of Ramelson, the Party's chief industrial organiser. All very James Bond, but I gather that Denis Barnes [her Permanent Secretary] doesn't take these Security boys very seriously . . .

31 October 1968 . . . Another glorious document has been circulated to me by our Security boys. This reports on the attitude of the Communist Party during the engineering negotiations. Scanlon, it says, did not seek the advice of the Party, and had departed from that advice by agreeing to talk about productivity before pay. He had consolidated his position as President and had to some extent freed himself from Party direction. Interesting!

By the following year, she was becoming impatient with these briefs:

162

Another Security Service report on the Ford dispute. The more I read these reports, the less confidence I have in our intelligence. To begin with, the material is always mighty thin and and most of it would be obvious to an informed politician. I'm not surprised to read, for instance, that Scanlon was anxious for a prompt settlement. As for his over-ruling Reg Birch and Bob Wright on the AEF executive, he had as good as told me that himself. Or take Jack Jones: I don't need a Security Service to tell me that he succeeded in giving the impression he was more militant than Scanlon, or that he hadn't been in direct touch with the Communist Party during the dispute, or that Harry Urwin is Jones' protegé. It is mildly interesting, if true, that Urwin has a record of Communist Party membership, although he isn't currently a member. But it is a blinding bit of the obvious to say that the CP is finding it difficult to counter its critics on the Left who will contend that it has conceded the very point of principle – the inclusion of 'penal' clauses – on which it supported the strike in the first instance. Altogether, I really wonder what we pay these people for. I bet I could find out more myself in a few weeks, if I were given the job, than they do in a lifetime.

Barbara Castle, dealing only with the bland products of 'F' branch, underestimated the potential of counter-espionage to cause turmoil.

On July 21, 1969, Josef Frolik came down the stairs of a US Air Force transport plane in Washington, with his wife and son. The CIA had already relieved Frolik of his entry-ticket – a sheaf of amateurishly coded files listing every Czech Intelligence operation since the war that Frolik had managed to memorise. What was happening now was a purely formal, celebratory moment. Richard Helms, the CIA director himself, was produced to perform the big handshake. He did it in a gratifying manner, announcing:

'Joe, the telegrams are going out from Prague to your embassies and intelligence agencies throughout the world. And do you know what they're saying? I'll tell you: 'Stop all activity. Frolik has defected!' Joe, you've brought the Czech service to its knees![30]

This made the burly junior officer, with his heavy cheekbones and receding hair, feel good. He had made it. Frolik was appreciated. But the truth was that to the CIA's counter-espionage division, Frolik was small potatoes. Lots of Czechs had come over in the past year, since the Russian tanks had rumbled across the borders, crushing the 'Prague Spring' while the West stood by. No fewer than seventeen officers of Czech Intelligence were on the Russian blacklist, for lack of 'fraternal spirit', when the tanks arrived.

Some, like Robert Husak, Frolik's old boss, had swallowed their dismissal gamely, and gone to work on such menial heavy labouring as digging tunnels for the Prague underground railway. Others had defected to the United States, taking most of the secrets of the HSR, the Czech espionage service, with them to Langley, Virginia.

A general, Jan Sejna, had come over, in the backwash of coup attempts against Dubcek's predecessor as head of the Czech regime, the brutish Nowotny. Captain Marous had come; and Ladislas Bittman, of the disinformation department, and Frolik's old colleague, Captain Frantisek August, who had quickly seen which way the wind was blowing when he was tipped off that he was about to be recalled home from his field post in the embassy in Beirut.

Frolik was late, and he was junior. The value of a sudden defector is low: he freezes enemy operations in the wake of his departure for months or perhaps years, making arrests and evidence hard to get. He is of low value compared to the 'defector-in-place', who can be forced to stay in his post, risking his neck for as long as his eventual hosts dare squeeze him.

Frolik had not been bothered about that: he had hung on in Intelligence headquarters in Prague until the whispered word came that he, too, was about to get the sack. Then, and only then, on his own account, did he seek out the CIA. It is a measure of what Angleton and the CIA thought Frolik was worth to them, that they eventually settled on him the princely lifetime sum of $150 net a week. And they even groused about that.

And the best Frolik had to sell concerned not the Americans themselves, but the British. He had been on the British desk from 1961 to 1964, and then had done the obligatory tour of field duty between 1964 and 1966, posing for snapshots with his wife and child on Westminster Bridge, with Big Ben and Parliament in the background. The milieu was apposite: Frolik had collected a good deal of dirt on the British Labour government and its friends, and it was this which he sought to stammer out in his fractured English almost as soon as he arrived. He recalled later:

> ... I found myself on the other side of the fence and my first words to the appropriate CIA member concerned three Members of Parliament and that Minister.[31]

He denounced as a 'Czech agent' the Postmaster General and former Aviation Minister John Stonehouse. He also named the junior Health Minister, Sir Barnet Stross; the Labour party official Tom Driberg; and the obscure back-bencher Will Owen. The CIA moved fast on these names. They had to. There was no hope of catching the politicians in the act of meeting any more Czech contacts. The Czech embassy in London would be keeping its men indoors and rapidly having their bags packed. But there was always a good chance that the British 'traitors' would not have been warned. Contact was too dangerous for the Czechs – after a defection exposed agents had to be left

164

to sink or swim. As a result, quick raids might find money, code-pads, cameras, all kinds of potentially incriminating equipment. Furthermore, the security leaks had to be stopped quickly – suspect British government ministers could not continue to be in receipt of secret papers, including US or NATO material, for one further unnecessary moment.

Consequently, at the end of July, the cipher teleprinters between London and Washington clattered out the four surnames – Stonehouse, Owen, Driberg, Stross. One can imagine what Sir Martin Furnival Jones felt at this moment: his worst suspicions about the Labour government he was employed to serve were coming true. Stross had in fact been dead since 1967, but Driberg was prominent in the Labour Party National Executive Committee (and supposedly an agent of MI5, not of the other side), Stonehouse was a very senior minister handling sensitive military-technical issues – and Owen – surely there was a *David* Owen who had recently been appointed to take charge of the Royal Navy, no less . . ?

If Harold Wilson is to be believed, the excitement of the head of MI5 overcame him. Furnival Jones exercised his right to see the Prime Minister directly and rapidly. Under the circumstances, he could scarcely have simply gone to James Callaghan at the Home Office with such allegations about his own ministerial colleagues. Furnival Jones told a hostile and disbelieving Harold Wilson that the Americans had now discovered that 'Stonehouse and Owen' were Czech agents. Furnival Jones later maintained that he had never accused the talented young Navy minister by mistake: he had merely 'exchanged information'. Wilson, on the other hand, got the impression that David Owen was indeed the man under suspicion. Wilson kept his sour recollection of this muddle to himself for the next eight years, but he did not forget it.

When the confusion was resolved, Wilson authorised surveillance on the obscure back-bencher Will Owen – his phones were to be tapped, his letters opened, his parliamentary locker rifled and his home burgled to see what could be found. As far as Stonehouse was concerned, the evidence suggests that Wilson demanded to have the Czech defector brought over and personally interviewed by the British before authorising any action against the Postmaster General.

This was a remarkable demand. But it was a remarkable accusation. The CIA received a report back from Furnival Jones that Frolik had to come back to Europe and convince a sceptical Harold Wilson before any steps would be taken against Stonehouse. Frolik says he had been in Washington no more than a week before he was bundled back on a military plane, flown to a US air base, and taken to London.

There, accompanied by a CIA 'handler', he told his story to Furnival Jones and the men from 'K' branch. 'D' branch had now been enlarged, rechristened 'K' branch and split into two, partly because of the growing load

165

of 'mole' allegations, and partly because of the sinister reputation Wright and his friends were beginning to acquire. MacDonald says: 'D was regarded as a crack outfit. But it had become unpopular because it was so secretive.' Wright says more vividly that at an annual MI5 conference at the Civil Service College at Sunningdale, Berkshire, his colleagues had launched 'bitter attacks' on the men from 'D1' and 'D3', saying there were 'innocent men suffering'. At his own suggestion, Michael 'Jumbo' Hanley, who had survived the investigation into his own 'loyalty', took over a new, more orthodox section, 'KY'. This tried to work out the Soviet bloc 'order of battle' with CIA help using the computerised 'movements analysis' programme to chart which Communist representatives at the embassies and the trade delegations might be Intelligence officers. Barry Russell-Jones, one of Wright's closer friends, went to this 'ORBAT' work which was, in time, very successful.

MacDonald, meanwhile, continued to run the 'KX' half of the branch, and it was this which handled Frolik. Charles Elwell, an officer with a clipped military bearing, ran 'K2', which dealt with investigations concerning the Soviet satellite countries. Elwell, whose wife Anne Last was a former MI5 secretary, had a long history as a case officer on specific investigations. He had organised the search of naval clerk Harry Houghton's house during the Portland spy case. And, according to Wright, he had also handled one of the most futile investigations to arise out of Wright's interpretations of Golitsin's innumerable speculative 'serials'. This was the surveillance and burgling of the Suffolk farmhouse owned by an English writer, Shiela Grant Duff and her husband Micheal Sokolov Grant.

Wright's account of this episode in *Spycatcher* is even more misleading than usual. Golitsin had mentioned – says Wright – that there might be a 'Russian sleeper' near an RAF airfield defended with batteries of guided missiles; the Sokolov Grants farmed on the edge of RAF Stradishall in East Anglia, which fitted the description. Wright claims – incredibly – that this hapless couple were picked on merely because Sokolov Grant had a 'Russian-sounding' name and was in the electoral register in the right district.

Shiela Grant Duff left Oxford in 1934, where like many undergraduates she had been a member of the left-wing 'October Club'. As an undergraduate she had a close relationship with Goronwy Rees, the academic who was later close to Guy Burgess and Anthony Blunt and was eventually ruined by the connection. She married Micheal Sokolov Grant after the war, and they farmed together for the next thirty years.

He was not, as Wright asserts, a 'Russian refugee' who had arrived in Britain five years previously. He had been born in France, educated in England, and served in the Royal Navy in the war. They did not have a 'Queen Anne' farmhouse from the rear of which, 'You could see the end of the runway stretching across the swaying fields of barley.' Their farm was

166

near Needham Market, twenty-five miles away from the airfield. They did not move away after Charles Elwell 'asked a few questions in the village.' In fact the house that Wright and a man from GCHQ broke into, which Wright describes as 'unbelievably untidy', had been sold by the Sokolov Grants earlier that year. It was uninhabited, but still contained some furniture waiting to go into storage. The Sokolov Grants knew nothing of Wright's burglary until Wright described it in *Spycatcher*, wringing his hands over how unfair it was that an ordinary, innocent man could fall under suspicion.

The Stonehouse case was – on the face of it – a much more grave affair. Frolik told Elwell, Peter Wright and Michael McCaul that the Labour minister had apparently been recruited as an MP 'in the late 1950s' after a sexual entrapment in Czechoslovakia. The head of the British desk in Prague at the time, Vlastimil Kroupa, was posted to service in the field in London around 1961. Frolik, a junior member of the British desk from 1960 onwards, did not have any detailed information involving Stonehouse during these early days, but after his own posting to London as one of the team of thirty Intelligence officers working under cover in the embassy, he had witnessed something significant:

I had known he was working for us since 1965, when I had been the chance witness of his being contacted at a reception on Czech Army Day.[32]

Major Robert Husak had arrived from Prague in 1965 as No. 3 in the Intelligence team, with instructions to 'take over control' of the new minister. Husak barged up to Stonehouse at a Czech embassy function and introduced himself, so Frolik had gathered, 'by means of a password'.

As he was an aviation minister and was one of the few people to have test-flown in the planned TSR-2 British fighter-bomber (later cancelled), the Czechs hoped to get some details out of Stonehouse. They had entered into talks with him about a civil aviation purchase for the same reason. Frolik himself had not handled Stonehouse. He had been engaged in relatively menial tasks such as following civil servants around London for hours, hoping to find them womanising, or frequenting homosexual bars. He had also been trying to cultivate trade unionists.

But more recently, while he was amassing information back in Prague with which to defect, Frolik had picked up further evidence about Stonehouse. In 1969, Husak's successor, Kalina, boasted to Major Kerel Trsek, of the courier service, 'who passed it on to me in the Savoy Restaurant on Kepler Street in Prague in the second half of May 1969, that he was running "the biggest operation of our service in Europe" . . . Kalina is controlling a minister in London . . . we have a cabinet minister in our network.'[33]

(As Postmaster General, Stonehouse was not, in fact, in the Cabinet, although he did have sensitive technological information about, for example, the new network of microwave towers being built for telephone links, which included GCHQ international tapping arrangements and some military communications.)

Frolik says he was excited at hearing this news, which he did not immediately connect with Stonehouse. He sought out the by now disaffected Husak, and on May 19 asked him what he thought of Kalina's claims. Husak replied scornfully, and rather to Frolik's disappointment:

'As to that Minister, you know him very well. You were present when Ambassador Trhlik got involved in conversation with him at the military reception in October 1965. I had instructions to contact him by means of a password . . . I had no choice but to go up to them myself and get rid of Trhlik and tell him to leave me alone with the Minister . . . everything Kalina has he took over from me!'[34]

Frolik says he had a final chance to check the information when he encountered the former London station chief, Major Josef Minx, at the Intelligence corps holiday camp in Bulgaria. Minx confirmed in conversation that Kalina had not scored a new coup: 'Prague handed that Minister over to Robert by means of a password in October 1965.' Frolik maintains that Stonehouse had also been paid cash – but it is unclear where he got this information from.

All the problems about 'defector information' stare out from this account of Frolik's. It sounded good, but what did it add up to? All Frolik really knew was that his colleagues boasted they were 'controlling' a minister. He had never seen any secret information supplied by Stonehouse. He had never seen the file on Stonehouse. He had never had any personal dealings with him, collected information from him, or paid him money. As Frolik himself describes it, his colleagues vied with each other to boast how successful they were. He also mentions how unscrupulous this process of amassing 'informants' could be: he says one of his more gorilla-like colleagues in London constantly treated them all to expenses-paid sessions in London night-clubs – 'Jan Koska had invented an "English policeman" who cost Prague £1,500 in bribes to cover Koska's drinking bills.'

There was one snippet of collateral information, according to Peter Wright. Frantisek August, who had already defected, had himself had some dealings with Stonehouse in the 1950s, when the MP was supposedly first recruited. Wright later said, wildly:

The most important witness is Frantisek August – Stonehouse's handler in Czechoslovakia during one long debriefing and briefing session in a secret hideaway by a lake in the country, well away from Prague.[35]

This was a wild assertion because August had already been in US hands

168

since the previous year. If he had had any concrete evidence against Stone-house of that kind, the investigation would have been launched in 1968. It would scarcely have needed to wait for the arrival of Frolik. Of course, the problem is that the words 'long briefing and debriefing session' could mean much the same as 'a lengthy conversation with someone who happened to be a covert Intelligence officer'. It all depends on the inter-pretation put on the event.

Nevertheless, the case against Stonehouse looked alarming.

It was all deeply embarrassing and annoying for Harold Wilson. He was pre-occupied with another planned arrival at a US air-base – the new US President Richard Nixon had decided to pay a flying call on Harold Wilson on the way home from a world tour. It was characteristic of the relative importance of the two men that Wilson was informed that the US president had only a short time available. He would be landing on territory under US control, at the US air-base at Mildenhall, Suffolk, on 3 August, and did not have time to visit London. Wilson would have to take himself down to the air-base and speak to the president while his jet was being refuelled.

With Stonehouse on his mind, Wilson flew to Suffolk from Chequers by helicopter. After the meeting with Nixon Wilson drove to Beattie Plummer's nearby country home where Marcia Williams and Lord Gardiner were waiting to be regaled with news of Nixon at a late supper. Back in London, and due to set off shortly for his holidays, Wilson had a personal session with Frolik – or so the Czech defector claims. He says he spent two hours going over his story with the Prime Minister, and spent the rest of the day being ferried around London by 'K' branch, looking for a 'safe house' where he thought Stonehouse and Husak had held meetings. He could not find it.

Wilson took a rapid decision about Stonehouse. It was a much more dangerous situation than that ever posed by Floud, MacDermot or Swin-gler. He did not really trust or believe MI5 and their CIA defector. But he did not altogether trust Stonehouse either. He is later reported to have said, 'I never thought he was a spy but I always knew he was a crook.'[36] Oddly, Stonehouse was something of a professional anti-Communist in his public attitudes. He had also, however, left an air of corner-cutting behind him in his business and political career which was closer to sharp practice than to conventional political opportunism. The one thing Wilson did not want was for the witch-hunters of MI5 to decide on his guilt or innocence, and then, as with Ludmila MacDermot, present him with a *fait accompli*. The arrest of a minister, Wilson's personal appointment, as a Soviet Bloc spy ... few Labour Governments would be likely to survive such a furore. Wilson sent for Charles Elwell, the case officer from 'K' branch.

When he arrived the Prime Minister said, 'I have decided you can make these charges to Stonehouse's face, and say what you have told me.' To

Elwell's astonishment, the Postmaster General was then shown into the Cabinet room. Michael Halls, Wilson's Principal Private Secretary also came in to make notes. There is broad agreement as to how the interrogation now went. Stonehouse gave his own version of it later, and Frolik was subsequently shown the transcript of it by MI5. According to Stonehouse:

> The Prime Minister said: 'There has been a statement made by a Czech intelligence officer who has defected, in which you have been named as an informer . . . As head of security, I have to take an interest in these matters.' Elwell then proceeded to read from a report. 'We must get to the bottom of this,' said the PM. 'You will appreciate how important it is that you co-operate in investigating these allegations.'[37]

Frolik's version of how this bizarre meeting opened is similar, although written in Americanese:

> At the beginning of the conversation they were saying something like: 'Listen buddy, we have received information that you are supposed to be a spy. You will have to make some statement about it.'[38]

Stonehouse's reaction, said Frolik, 'was that of an educated, logically thinking man. He had visited Czechoslovakia, he said, at Czech expense, and he had met Husak and others, but it had been simply a matter of pure friendship. He had never been a spy . . .' After reading Stonehouse's entire version of events, a rather crestfallen Frolik wrote later:

> I felt very odd and it made me think how naive people could be and what strange friendships there were . . . I have no reason to believe anything to the contrary. It is possible that all the people with whom I spoke were not telling the truth or were exaggerating. I don't know. I never personally had anything to do with this Minister.[39]

Stonehouse's story covered much the same events as Frolik had picked up, but there was no sex, no spying and no 'password'. His first visit to Czechoslovakia had indeed occurred in September 1957, about six months after becoming an MP. He had been on a London Co-operative Society delegation with Harry Clayden, a director of the LCS and a Communist. They had a week in Prague of 'red carpet treatment'. Stonehouse had been taken on a trip to Lidice, the village destroyed by the Nazis twenty miles outside Prague. He had visited the town of Kladno, to discuss a 'twinning' plan with his own constituency, which subsequently led to many friendly contacts. On the last day of the trip, there had been an official lunch, and something of a drinking contest. Stonehouse had boarded the plane, fairly drunk, giving a revolutionary clenched-fist salute of farewell.

On the continuing contact back in London with his 'control', Stonehouse said there had indeed been a 'pushy diplomat' called Vlado Koudelka. 'I was glad to have a London contact to help the "twinning" relationship. I had several lunches with him.' Koudelka had tried hard to establish a special relationship and was particularly persistent in seeking information on Labour Party activities. 'Whatever I told him was innocent enough.' Koudelka had pushed for odd scraps of political information, 'most of which I regarded as totally irrelevant.' Koudelka once invited him to a party, but Stonehouse did not go. 'I subsequently learnt it was for male guests only and there were girls provided.' In 1961 and 1962 Stonehouse went to the Leipzig trade fair in East Germany – one in the same series to which Rudy Sternberg had led 'parliamentary delegations' causing such scandal. In 1962, he had made a stopover in Prague where Koudelka, now posted home, made contact and dined him. He offered Stonehouse free holidays. Stonehouse declined them. Koudelka urged him to keep up contact with his successor in London and Stonehouse had 'one or two cursory meetings' with him, although he claimed not to recall his name. He had been sent bottles of drink that Christmas but had returned them unopened.

As to the 'hand-over of control' to Husak by means of a password, Stonehouse gave an alternative explanation of the events. He had had little contact with the Czechs again until he became a government minister. Then, at a cocktail party given for some visiting delegation, the suave figure of Husak appeared. 'He was trying to push his luck with me. He knew all about Koudelka and Kladno – and started trying to make a date for lunch. I allowed myself to be pushed forward in the party melee – but he pushed an obviously prepared note into my hand with the word "Husak" on it, and begged me to have lunch. I did. But I reported the conversation through the Ministry security officer.' Stonehouse said he saw Husak at 'several diplomatic functions afterwards'. When he was involved in negotiations on the possible sale of VC10 aircraft to CSA, the Czech airline, Husak turned up again as interpreter to the minister negotiating for the Czechs.

This only left the story of the final 'controller', Kalina, who had boasted that he had a British cabinet minister in his network. Stonehouse agreed that he had gone to Czechoslovakia again at the beginning of the Dubcek era – the 'Prague Spring'. He went to sign a technological agreement. He had paid another visit to Kladno, the 'twin town'. A 'small party' had been arranged. Stonehouse had made a presentation of tools made, ironically, by Charles Elwell's family firm, which was located in Stonehouse's constituency. A free skiing trip had been laid on to the Low Tatra mountains. To Stonehouse's astonishment, Husak materialised in the hotel room late at night with his 'successor' – who was about to be sent to London. They sat and drank wine together until about 1 a.m. The next day, on the ski slopes, the new man, whom Stonehouse found rather sinister, suddenly arrived and skied alongside him, making him feel uncomfortable. In July

171

1968, at a formal dinner at the house of the Czech ambassador, 'hovering in the background I saw the sinister man on the mountain and several times he tried to approach me.' The following month, the Russians invaded Czechoslovakia.

Stonehouse said: 'Elwell seemed impressed I had submitted a report on my first lunch with Husak . . . heaven knows what would have happened or how it would have been interpreted if I had not. Perhaps I would have been charged like poor old Will Owen . . .' Having listened to Stonehouse's explanation, Wilson showed him out the back door, to avoid any journalists. To Stonehouse's chagrin, Wilson also forbade him to go on any more holidays to Czechoslovakia that summer – he did not want a defection.

Was Stonehouse's story true? There were people in both the CIA and MI5 who were convinced it was a pack of lies. They were furious that Wilson had not allowed a 'proper' interrogation, MacDermot-style. Frolik was certainly told by someone in MI5, 'Wilson's not going to do anything about it because it would bring the government down.' According to Stonehouse, Elwell was allowed to have several more follow-up meetings with him to check points in Frolik's story, on the minister's home ground, in the leather armchairs of the RAC Club. This was not at all the same thing as the repeated grillings, with the microphones and the backs to the light, to which lesser figures were subjected.

At the end of the day, MacDonald's 'K' branch went back to Wilson and reported that they were intensely suspicious of Stonehouse, who they believed had been making undisclosed trips to Czechoslovakia in the past. There was no proof of it on his passport, but nothing would have been easier than for the Czechs to give him detachable visas in Paris. Wilson demanded to know whether they had any substantial 'evidence' that Stonehouse was lying. No, they did not. Wilson said much later that the allegations had been 'fully' investigated by MI5 with Wilson's 'full approval':

> The security services advised me at that time, that there was no evidence to support the allegations . . . I had them very fully investigated and there was nothing in them . . . Mr Stonehouse gave every possible help at the time . . . If there had been a scintilla of evidence in 1969, he would not have remained a member of the Government.[40]

Frolik meanwhile had been told by his handlers that Wilson had 'hit the roof' at the disclosures, and that Stonehouse would certainly be removed from the House of Commons. When he discovered that it was all being hushed up, he railed bitterly to the sympathetic men from MI5 about Wilson's insistence on 'evidence':

> Unfortunately I could not order an American Van Lines company van to be in front of the intelligence centre in Prague before my flight, into

172

which I would load the agency files and deliver them to the appropriate places. That would not fit even into a scenario of a crazy spy serial. However, what would not get into a TV serial seemed obviously normal to a high political personality of Great Britain.[41]

Stonehouse was allowed to continue in his position as Minister for Post and Telecommunications throughout the rest of Wilson's term of office. But Wilson clearly remained uneasy about him: he was quietly excluded from any position as Labour spokesman after 1970, and went off into a series of business ventures. He was still very much an MI5 target – it is one of the most puzzling and troubling aspects of the entire Wilson affair that virtually all the friends and colleagues of Wilson who attracted MI5's attention found their financial activities coming under official scrutiny. Stonehouse was to be the first who attracted the attentions of the police, but not the last.

Peter Wright and his colleagues on both sides of the Atlantic thought Wilson's behaviour confirmed their belief that Wilson himself was a Soviet Bloc agent ... What other explanation could there be of his refusal to let MI5's inquiries take their course? But the reality was that MI5 had no supporting evidence at all. Stonehouse's story was, at the very least, curious – but it was not inconsistent with the facts. Wright wrote later:

We read a lot of Czech traffic at the right time, but we were never able to prove that a particular cryptonym was Stonehouse. I am pretty certain it was, but we were never allowed *by either party* to interrogate him hostilely.[42] (author's emphasis)

The tacit admission here is that Edward Heath, when he became Prime Minister, also found the evidence too negligible to justify re-opening the case. And so the Stonehouse affair, as Wilson hoped, was secretly buried for ever.

However, just as the Sternberg investigations had been whispered into the ear of journalist Bill Massie, so the word about Stonehouse was now passed surreptitiously to Chapman Pincher. Pincher recalls:

In 1970, I was warned by an Intelligence contact that Stonehouse, then Minister of Post and Telecommunications, who was known to be a friend of mine, had been in difficulty with his Prime Minister, Harold Wilson, over a security issue. No further information was forthcoming and for libel reasons I could not report it. The tip did help to explain, however, why Stonehouse had assured me more than once that he would never get any further in government under Wilson and for that reason was going into the business world.[43]

If he got to the point of being prevented from publication by the libel laws, Pincher presumably made inquiries about the story: this may be what Harold Wilson referred to some years later when a full-scale 'leak' was orchestrated. He then said, bitterly, 'In this case, there has been I believe, a very serious press campaign based on stories that go back to 1969 when I had the responsibility for those matters.' Who was Pincher's 'Intelligence contact'? Michael McCaul, his former 'D' branch handler, had been out of touch since the early 1960s. It was certainly not him. One of Pincher's few 'Intelligence contacts' was Victor Rothschild, who certainly was to feed Pincher material in the future, and who kept up private contact with the MI5 counter-espionage branch as well as with senior officers in MI6. Another was Bruce Mackenzie, a white Kenyan politician who was heavily involved in MI6 maneouvring to service and stabilise the pro-Western regime of Jomo Kenyatta (while Czech Intelligence, according to Frolik, were trying to recruit Kenyatta's student nephew). Mackenzie, who was on close terms with Oldfield and other senior MI6 officers, fed Pincher anti-Wilson material later. As we shall see, MI6 de-briefed Frolik for their own reasons, and would have heard all his stories.

Whoever tipped off Pincher was behaving disgracefully: the fact that Blunt, for example, was a real spy, was kept an official secret; the fact that a Labour minister had had nothing proved against him was circulated as a smear. This was the reality, over the years, of the 'Wilson plot' by members of the Intelligence agencies. Much worse was to follow.

Meanwhile, Frolik spent a week with 'K' branch in London, trying to substantiate the Stonehouse allegation, and passing over enough details to enable a police investigation to start into the Labour back-bencher Will Owen, who, he said, had also been 'run' by the ubiquitous Husak and Kalina. There was much more concrete detail about 'Granpa', as the Czech Intelligence officers derisively referred to the veteran MP for Morpeth in the industrial North of England. Owen was making money out of East-West trade – he ran a travel agency specialising in East German tours. His official code-name was LEE. They also described him, said Frolik, as a 'greedy bastard' and 'the little miser': not only did he take £500 a month from the Czechs, but he repeatedly demanded expenses-paid holidays. At embassy functions he stuffed his pockets with free cigars. Owen was clearly such an embassy joke that Frolik had picked up a lot in conversation about him. Although Frolik had not 'run' him personally, he knew Owen met Husak once a week, while taking his dog for an early-morning walk in a park near his home. He also knew he had started taking money fifteen years earlier from Lt.-Col. Jan Paclik (also known as Novak), the then embassy Second Secretary.

Owen had mentioned to the Czechs in 1962 that a Conservative MP was recruiting British scientists for the US 'brain-drain'. They had cunningly

174

suggested, said Frolik, that he ask hostile parliamentary questions about the MP's activities and thus 'discredit' him. 'It was one of our most successful coups which helped sour Anglo-US relations.' If this was the height of Czech subversion in Frolik's time, it seems clear the West had little to worry about. As a 'caper', it was on the same level as 'Operation Wales' of the same year, when men were hired with pots of paint to daub swastikas on Jewish graves in Wales. It was hoped that this would be blamed on a German NATO battalion training there and cause 'anti-Nazi' sentiment.

But Frolik also provided one piece of direct 'evidence' suggesting that Owen had carried out espionage. With his own eyes, he said earnestly, he had seen in the embassy safe-room 'top secret material of the highest military value' handed over by Owen from the Commons Defence Committee. It concerned the Rhine Army and British contributions to NATO. Frolik's facts were not wrong – but he exaggerated the importance of the material. As a back-bencher, the 'Estimates Committee' of which Owen was a member had no access to top secret material. It did, in theory, have access to material for briefings classified 'Secret', which then appeared in published reports decorated with rows of asterisks. But nothing really sensitive was ever shown by the defence ministry to this committee, which they regarded as a body of interfering and probably insecure outsiders. The committee had none of the powers of a US Congressional Committee, and certainly not of the real 'Defence Committee' – the Defence Committee of the Cabinet, chaired by the Prime Minister.

The usual MI5 procedure, according to Wright, would now have been for Owen's house to be burgled. Kalina, Owen's current handler, had been hastily withdrawn in the autumn of 1969, but surveillance continued. The 'A' branch burglars found packets of money scattered around the house, in desks and holdalls. There were sixty bottles of spirits in the cellar. Wright says:

Owen had . . . more money from the Czechs than he ever admitted receiving. Apart from what Frolik told us, we found thousands of notes in Owen's house and a large sum in his family's bank account . . . he claimed it was from business and stock exchange dealings, but could not tell us what they were. We got him in the end by tipping off the Inland Revenue who succeeded in removing most of it.[44]

To their intense interest, they also found that Owen had been on the payroll of the enigmatic Sternberg, as a 'consultant' to the Dominion Export Company. More links to Harold Wilson! MI5 decided it would try to bring a criminal case against Owen, when the time was ripe, using Frolik as a courtroom witness, with a hood over his head if need be.

A team from London now accompanied Frolik back to America and the embrace of the CIA – 'A number of MI5 and MI6 officers came to Washington for three months,' Frolik recalls. Closeted in a Georgetown motel, 'I repeated, analysed, talked *ad nauseam*.' His most alarming revelations concerned the past. Once again MI6 operations were revealed to have been riddled with penetrations up to 1961. The emigré Czech Intelligence organisation, launched and funded by MI6 in 1948, had been sold out to the Czechs for a total of £40,000 over five years by one of their number, Karel Zbytek, who then retired to run a seaside boarding house on the proceeds. The close links with Dick White's MI6 had compromised a number of British agents as well, including Mohammed Hamdi, an Egyptian diplomat in Prague, run by the MI6 station in Vienna. MI6 later made successful moves to censor disclosures of this scandal in Britain, through the 'D-Notice' secretary.

Frolik also revealed some information embarrassing to the Tory Party – about the unsuccessful plots to entrap Edward Heath and the wife of minister Maurice Macmillan – which was also to be censored. And Frolik knew of a real spy. Ten years earlier, he disclosed, Nicolas Prager, a young RAF technician with a Czech background and a wife who turned out to have been provided by Husak, had been persuaded to hand over the entire plans for 'Blue Diver' – the radar-jamming device to be developed for Britain's nuclear V-bombers. There may have been problems with tracing and surveillance, but it is an indication of priorities that Prager was not arrested until January 1971 – a year after the trivialities of the Will Owen case. Prager was sentenced to twelve years in jail.

The eventual criminal case against Owen collapsed, by contrast. When Frolik was flown back to England to give anonymous testimony, it was ruled out as hearsay. As a result, Owen's lawyers successfully argued that there was no evidence he had passed classified documents. However, he had admitted taking money from the Czechs, he was forced to resign his parliamentary seat and was discredited. All this occurred shortly before the 1970 General Election which the Labour Party lost. The affair cannot have improved their standing.

As mentioned earlier, Frolik had also named as 'agents' two other Labour MPs. One was Sir Barnet Stross, who Frolik said was code-named GUSTAV. It is impossible to say whether there was any truth in the allegation. It is quite possible Stross merely had friendly contact with the Czechs and made ordinary political conversation. Frolik never published any evidence of free holidays, cash payments, or even fees for 'articles' (a popular Czech ploy). One man's 'agent' is another man's lunch-guest.

Frolik's own claims are downbeat. He says: 'GUSTAV was bought for money. He was recruited by my old chief Vaclav Taborsky, also in the mid-50s. He was not as important as LEE, but he was in a position to deliver interesting information about the domestic and foreign policies of the Labour Party while it was in opposition, and later, when the Wilson government came to power, about defence matters.'

A young Harold Wilson with colleague Barbara Castle in 1955

Below Harold Wilson comes to power. As Prime Minister in 1965 with Marcia Williams (left) and Mary Wilson (note the Gannex raincoat)

James Jesus Angleton,
head of CIA
counter-intelligence

Below Peter Wright towards
the end of his career in
1976 (right) with Barry
Russell-Jones (left) and
another Intelligence
colleague

Top left: Harry Wharton, head of 'K5', MI5's counter-espionage branch

Top right: George Kennedy Young, vice-chief of MI6 until 1961

Below: Tony Brooks, the MI5 'War Hero' who investigated Kagan

Right 'Jak', the newspaper man who was befriended by MI5 men

Below left James Scott Hopkins, the Conservative MP who conducted inquiries into Wilson's friends for MI6

Below right Auberon Waugh, nephew of the writer Evelyn Waugh and columnist on *Private Eye*

Top The old order: Douglas Dodds-Parker, Conservative MP and SOE officer, sharing a joke with Lord Tedder, Marshal of the RAF, General Gruenther, and Admiral Tully Shelley, at a ball at the Dorchester, 1956

Below left William Massie (in 1965), the *Sunday Express* journalist with Intelligence friends
Below right Lord (Victor) Rothschild, MI5 officer and friend of Anthony Blunt and Peter Wright

Wilson's Jewish friends: *above left* Joseph Kagan and *above right* Rudy Sternberg

Below left Robert Maxwell and *below right* Solly Zuckerman: unjustly defamed by Peter Wright

Named by the defector Frolik: *right* John Stonehouse, Postmaster-General 1968; *below left* Sir Barnet Stross, junior Health Minister; *below right* Will Owen, back-bench MP; and *top left opposite:* Tom Driberg, Labour MP, Communist Party member, agent for MI5, the KGB and Czech Intelligence – and tormented homosexual – at a 1971 Labour Party conference

Top right opposite Stephen Swingler: kept out of the Cabinet

Below left opposite Hounded by MI5: Ministerial candidate Bernard Floud when he entered Parliament in 1964 and *below right opposite* Treasury Minister Niall MacDermot when he resigned in 1968

The available facts are that Stross was a doctor, an expert on industrial diseases who represented a mining constituency in the Staffordshire Potteries. His parents came to Britain as refugees from Poland at the end of World War I. As a junior health minister, he was scarcely in any position to know much about defence matters. But he was something of a public 'friend of Czechoslovakia'. He was the founder of the movement to rebuild Lidice, the Czech mining village razed by the Germans in 1942. More significantly, perhaps, as chairman of the British-Czechoslovak Society, he was able to make representations to the Stalinist Czech government on human rights issues. One of his friends was Elwyn Jones, later Labour Lord Chancellor, who recalls that in 1955 Stross had used his position to lobby unsuccessfully on behalf of Dr Ernest Singer, head of the Jewish community in Bratislava, imprisoned in an anti-Semitic show trial.

As for Driberg, supposedly code-named CROCODILE, the 'evidence' is even more peculiar. As has already been demonstrated, the one confirmed fact is that, unbeknownst to his comrades in the war-time Communist Party, Driberg was reporting to Maxwell Knight, his fellow-homosexual in MI5, and was thrown out of the Party in consequence. After Knight's retirement in the mid-1950s, Driberg had an urgent need to keep up his British Intelligence links. It provided him with some protection against prosecution for homosexual activity, which was then a crime. He hit on the idea of going to Moscow and persuading Guy Burgess, another homosexual, to disgorge some 'memoirs'. A KGB-inspired confection, this manuscript was then submitted by Driberg for MI5 vetting in advance of publication.

After that, Peter Wright is the only witness to events. He claims that the KGB blackmailed Driberg with homosexual photographs all over again in Moscow, and forced him to provide information about the Labour Party. If he did so, there is no evidence available as to whether Driberg told them anything true or useful. To judge by what happened later, he probably did not. Frolik, the Czech defector, claimed to have heard second-hand of an MP called CROCODILE being 'run' by one of his colleagues. On being shown photographs, he picked out Driberg. Frolik has never made any reference to the CROCODILE case in any of his subsequent memoirs, testimony to Congressional committees, or private letters. This may be because Wright is faking the story, or because there was good reason for suppressing the information: on Wright's own account, he personally bullied a confession out of Driberg that he had been taking money from the Czechs and then – in effect – pressurised him into supplying Wright himself with tittle-tattle about the Labour Party.

All one can say about this claim is, firstly, that it would constitute the first confession Wright ever successfully got out of anybody; and, secondly, that if he did, Driberg went on to make a thorough fool of Wright. For he solemnly told him – to Wright's considerable excitement – that he could reveal a piece of scandal about Harold Wilson. He, Driberg, had been in the habit of lending his flat to Wilson for assignations. One day, rooting about afterwards, he had discovered down a sofa a letter addressed to no less than Barbara Castle! This was an ancient and untrue story, of course, which had been circulating since the two young politicians had made a trip to Canada together in 1949. Whoever Driberg had been lending his flat to, it was not Harold Wilson. But Wright was delighted. It all went into the grab-bag of allegations against the Prime Minister which Wright now constantly carried around with him.

Frolik had a few more recollections which could be used to discredit the Labour movement, if handled unscrupulously. But his attempts to implicate the trade union leaders Jack Jones and Hugh Scanlon as Soviet Bloc agents have a thin air, even with the best effort his US-backed ghost-writer could make later.

Frolik used to cultivate trade unionists, he said, as part of the general task of attempting to penetrate the British Left, and as a distraction from his dreary official Intelligence duties, pounding the London pavements or trying to think of a way to suborn refuse-men into letting him steal bags of classified waste from NATO buildings.

In the first draft of his memoirs, Frolik describes how he met Jack Jones:

Husak arranged a couple of cocktail parties for him at the Czech embassy: then I invited him to my flat at 34 Bayswater Rd . . . he turned out to be a friendly, sociable man with whom, I think, I got on famously. I started to cultivate him. But such things cost money. My expenses started to mount. They were forwarded to Prague from whence, a little later, I got the brisk order: 'Drop the Jones project, he's a horse of friends.'

Frolik – or his CIA-approved ghost-writer – attempted to imply by this that Jones was already being run by a KGB officer of Frolik's acquaintance, Nicolai Berdenikov. It implied, of course, no such thing. First of all, satellite services were never allowed to attempt to recruit figures such as Jones. Secondly, any contacts he had with Berdenikov were innocuous. And thirdly, as Frolik was certainly unaware, Jack Jones, for all his left-wing sympathies, used punctiliously to report to MI5 any attempts to recruit him as a foreign agent.

The same applied to Frolik's fatuous account of how he tried to recruit Hugh Scanlon – or rather, how he would have tried to recruit him, had he been given the opportunity. At one of the innumerable embassy parties for trade unionists, Frolik invited Ernie Roberts, a left-wing engineering union official, home for a drinking session. He presented him with a bottle of brandy, hoping it would function as a bribe – 'He looked so poorly dressed that I thought I was doing him a favour by giving him the drink . . . he looked a little surprised.' Roberts later invited him to a party at his home,

178

where he showed him his holiday slides. 'It was a real villa, of the type once owned by the richer classes in my country. And this place belonged to the man to whom I had so generously given one lousy bottle of brandy! Even today I blush at what a fool I made of myself.' Eventually, Frolik persuaded Roberts to introduce him to Hugh Scanlon himself: Frolik succeeded in shaking the hand of the man he called 'the most powerful person in the whole of the United Kingdom'. That, however, appears to have been that. Frolik says he was instructed to leave British trade unionists alone, and stop submitting optimistic expense claims for 'cultivating' them. Frolik's tales of why he thought the late Ted Hill of the Boilermakers' Union and the late Richard Briginshaw of the Printers' Union were also Soviet Bloc agents, were even thinner than this.

All in all, as his publisher later conceded, Frolik was very much in the 'Third XI' of spies. What is important is that his tall tales and his bitter complaints about Stonehouse were poured into the paranoid ear of Peter Wright. In the spring of 1970, Frolik was brought over to England for a second time, to testify – unavailingly – at the committal proceedings against Will Owen. He recalls being taken on a picnic to a Berkshire beauty spot, the White Horse at Uffington, by two MI5 officers. One of them was almost certainly Wright, who recalls:

Most of the debriefing of Frolik was done by the CIA and the tapes relevant to the UK passed to us. But we did have him in the UK for the Owen case and talked to him ourselves ... I do remember over dinner one evening, Frolik telling McCaul and myself that he believed we were penetrated and that he would tell us about it later, but he was deeply involved with the Owen case at the time and was furious that his testimony had been rejected as 'hearsay' because he could not produce the file in court! (The file was still in the StB [the Czech security police] in Prague).[45]

Even small spies are of great importance to counter-intelligence departments, however. Frolik did provide a mass of technical recollections down the years, from Czech techniques for beating the polygraph, to the bizarre incident in which a bloodstained dummy had been tossed in front of a car driven by a British embassy secretary in an attempt to persuade her she had killed someone. From the middle of 1969 until 1972, Frolik was in quarantine, under armed guard and in some fear of assassination, until he was squeezed absolutely dry. He said:

I was talking, talking, talking, for about three years, five days a week for hours on end, I sat in a room over a glass of beer, just talking and answering questions ... they want to know the names of the officers, how you worked, how much you were paid, the operations, where you were recruited, even what the office looked like. My God, they are interested in everything.

Frolik may have felt like a squeezed lemon, but to the group of MI5 officers and CIA men with a special interest in Britain, he was more like a crammed dustbin. One day, they promised themselves, they would tip the noisome contents all over Harold Wilson's front lawn.

CHAPTER 9

It was Joe Kagan, the Lithuanian raincoat manufacturer, who unwittingly laid the fuse which ignited the Harold Wilson conflagration.

A number of Kagan's relatives – or rather his wife's relatives – were still left behind in the Soviet Union. One was his wife's brother, Alex Shtromas, who was now a Law lecturer in Moscow. Shtromas had not done badly in Stalin's Russia. After his escape from the Vilijampole ghetto, he had completed his schooling at Vilnius, in Lithuania. He was adopted, he says, by a Soviet family. Not only did he read Law, but he was also allowed to study in Moscow, where he graduated with high academic honours in 1952. For someone of Jewish extraction, from a forcibly occupied Baltic state with a family of refugee 'capitalists' in the West, this suggested he gave the Communist Party little reason to doubt his loyalty. After running a forensic science laboratory for the Ministry of Justice in Vilnius, Shtromas returned to Moscow as acting head of the Comparative Law department at a Ministry of Justice research institute. He also gave law lectures at the Institute of Foreign Relations in Moscow. In the Soviet context, Shtromas was not only an academic – he was a fairly high government official. Exiles like Roy Medvedev thought later that it would have been difficult for Shtromas to rise so far without at least an appearance of co-operation with the ubiquitous KGB. Shtromas' published views, however, after his eventual arrival in the West, were vociferously 'anti-Soviet'.

Another relation of Margaret Kagan was her cousin Yasha Bum, who was thought to have a daughter Irina. They still lived in Lithuania, in Kaunas. Yasha was in the process of separating from his wife Elana. She was friendly with a Moscow film director, Gresha. Elana was also acquainted with a Lithuanian party official, Richardas Vaygauskas. Joe Kagan, always a resourceful opportunist, no doubt used his close relationship with Harold Wilson to further his wife's ambition to re-unite her family. It is common practice for Western politicians at summit talks to present Soviet leaders with lists of names of 'humanitarian cases', no doubt compiled originally by the Foreign Office.

Shtromas, and probably Yasha Bum and his daughter, had already been on the list presented to Kosygin by Wilson on Kosygin's 1967 London visit. When Wilson visited Moscow the following year, he presented the list of names again. Wilson would not have been human if he had not mentioned that he was personally acquainted with Joe Kagan. The Russians may well have known it already: in a piece of typical commercial self-promotion, Kagan had persuaded Wilson to present a Gannex raincoat to Khrushchev on Wilson's visit to Moscow as Leader of the Opposition in 1963.[1]

One must assume the KGB saw this as a situation they might be able to exploit. That would certainly have been the reaction of any of the Western Intelligence agencies had they been in the KGB's position. Or perhaps the KGB seized on the circumstances later. In the autumn of 1969, Richardas Vaygauskas suddenly turned up in London, listed as the Soviet Consul. He lost no time in making the acquaintance of Joe Kagan – was he not a fellow Lithuanian, from his wife's home town, and a great chess player to boot, just like Kagan?

One of the questions they began to discuss was whether Joe and Margaret Kagan might not return to their birthplace, as guests of the Soviet Union, and negotiate a private Lithuanian trade deal. Kagan later described it as, 'A know-how deal with Lithuania which would involve them modifying existing factories to manufacture our range of Gannex products under licence.'[2] It seems inconceivable that the question of Margaret Kagan's relations and the favours that could be done in that regard did not also come up in Kagan's conversations with the friendly Lithuanian. Jewish emigration from Russia, whether of relatives or otherwise, was a cause close to the heart of all good Jews. By the spring of 1970, Kagan and Vaygauskas were frequently in each other's company: Kagan's managing director from the North of England, Bill Atack, first saw them together in around February of that year.

Opinions differ as to what Vaygauskas was like. Kagan says he was a simple-minded, congenial sort of character, who was so unsophisticated that he needed to be taught Western styles of managing a knife and fork. John Parker, on the other hand, the son of Kagan's London agent and less worldly-wise than Kagan, describes him as 'very well-educated, with a good command of English.' There is little doubt Vaygauskas was treated to Kagan boasting of his friendship with the Prime Minister. Kagan once struck up a conversation with a businessman on a London-bound train and finished up taking him into No. 10 Downing Street to meet Wilson. Another of his colleagues recalls Kagan once impressing the company by conducting a long, friendly telephone conversation with 'Harold', purportedly on the other end of the line, when the phone-line was in fact dead. This would be in character: in later life, Kagan would make a habit of sitting in the House of Lords tea-room waving affectionate greetings over his guests' shoulders to various peers and dignitaries – the point of the exercise was that it was impossible to see whether the recipients of these greetings ever acknowledged him in return.

He maintained his entrée to Downing Street by doing humdrum tasks. If a plumber was wanted for one of the staff, he would produce one; if Wilson was thought to need new shoes, Kagan would send round a consignment of shoes and slippers. He also attempted to intercede with Marcia Williams' personal problems. Not all the malicious stories about Kagan were true, however: for example, when the campaign to vilify him was at its height, the *Sunday Times* alleged that Kagan had crudely threatened the father of one of the No. 10 secretaries who had had a breakdown. He would get the girl's father the sack from his job unless she went to a psychiatrist of Kagan's choice, the story went: 'because of fears that she might be indiscreet about the turmoil at No. 10'.[3] During research for this book, the author traced the girl concerned who said this was 'simply not true'.

It was natural that Kagan should try to impress Vaygauskas by introducing him to the Prime Minister in person. Kagan admits this occurred. Vaygauskas later claimed that he persuaded Kagan to visit No. 10 one evening, after Kagan offered to provide some piece of political information. Vaygauskas waited in his car, and when Kagan came back, persuaded him to return once again and get further details. Kagan says he does not recall such an episode, but does not regard it as impossible. This incident, the nearest Vaygauskas apparently ever got to successful 'espionage', would have been more impressive if Vaygauskas had ever specified what the information was; whether it was supposed to be secret; and who Kagan proveably talked to at Downing Street. He could have been speaking to any one of the Downing Street staff, or to no one there of consequence at all.

In a statement he issued later, Wilson made clear: 'At no point ... did [Kagan] raise any matter of government policy with me deriving from his acquaintanceship with Vaygauskas. Nor was he in receipt at any time of classified government information or any other material of the slightest interest to the Russians.'[4]

Wilson also implies, and Marcia Williams supports him in the claim, that he felt Kagan needed an unofficial 'minder' to keep an eye on what these Russians were up to. Certainly Wilson, with his long experience both of Russia and of 'security' issues, ought to have felt the need to watch his back. He turned to one of his favourite policemen, Arthur Young. Young had already known Kagan since 1966, probably thanks to the Wilson connection, and the small City of London police force which he controlled had bought Kagan's lightweight rainwear.

Young was that rare figure, a 'counter-subversion' expert who retained the trust of Labour politicians. He had been seconded in 1952 to the show-piece imperial 'anti-Communist' campaign in Malaya, where, according to his biographer, John Cloake, the commander, General Templer, found him 'transparently honest with no axe to grind ... a real leader and enthusiast.' Young professed distaste for the Malayan 'police state', in which his men were under the direct orders of the government and not in touch

183

with the 'community'. Anxious to return home in time for the Coronation, he set out to train a new 'special branch' of political police: Templer came to sympathise with his ideas, saying, 'It would be a poor victory if in rooting out terrorism, we were to substitute one fear for another.'

Young was next sent out to the Kenya colonial insurgency in 1954, where he won the warm respect of Barbara Castle: 'a brilliant and unusual police-man ... he had been of great help to me when I was trying to expose the excesses of the security forces in Kenya during the Mau Mau emergency.' Wilson had called in his services in Northern Ireland: in October 1969, he had appointed Young to take over as Inspector-General of the Royal Ulster Constabulary. The long upsurge of Irish 'troubles' was about to begin, with the whole colonial secret apparatus of propaganda, surveillance, 'covert operations' and armed undercover squads. For the time being, Young was sent to take a liberal approach to communal violence. The largely Protestant police were to be reorganised, and the 'B-Specials', a sort of Protestant militia, were to be brought under coherent military control.

These tasks would have been unlikely to have left Young with much time for supervising Kagan and Vaygauskas. But Wilson says Kagan arranged meetings between the Russian and the policeman, and that Young subsequently introduced Vaygauskas to the Commissioner of the Metropolitan Police – presumably on some social occasion.

In any event, Vaygauskas's links with the 'Prime Minister's friend', however impressive they may have looked on reports to Moscow, were short-lived. In June 1970, somewhat to the surprise of political commentators, Wilson failed to win his third General Election, and was out of office. He repaid Joe Kagan for his loyal service by giving him a knighthood. In the British context this was an unremarkable piece of patronage which attracted little comment – British premiers are expected to bestow titles and honours on their cronies and colleagues as a matter of course, just as senior civil servants receive knighthoods automatically 'with the rations'. Rich businessmen, party political hacks, the occasional prosperous actor or cricketer, 'helpful' journalists and the heads of government departments frequently end up as 'Sir' and their wives as 'Lady', whether they deserve honour or not. Knighthoods are cheap to give – they cost neither the Prime Minister nor the taxpayer anything – and are regarded as correspondingly cheap to receive.

At the moment of receiving his honour, Kagan and his wife were just making the final arrangements with Vaygauskas for their trip to Russia. The Kagan-Vaygauskas connection was far from being regarded as a secret matter by them. Arthur Parker and his son John Parker, who ran the textile company's London agency from Kagan's rather ordinary Bayswater flat, within walking distance of the Soviet consulate, cheerfully told journalists all about it:

'Kagan's Lithuanian by birth, you know. They're very proud of him over there.' Mr Parker knew this because he'd been getting Mr Kagan's visa for Lithuania (or rather Russia) from the Russian Consular Mission in London, whose chief is a Lithuanian . . .[5]

Kagan must have known Richardas Vaygauskas was an Intelligence officer: indeed he says he assumed it. Why, then, did he make such a friend of him? John Parker, who was able to see the relationship develop between the two at first hand, says:

I don't think even Joe knew. It was partly to get his relatives out; it was partly commercial; it was partly because Joe knew it would not be approved of so he'd do anything to upset people for the hell of it; partly ego; and partly chess. Who was using who is difficult to say . . . I was in and out of the embassy quite often, as was my father . . . Joe was always delivering presents to people. Once I had to deliver one to Vaygauskas . . . It was, as usual with Joe, very very lavish and Vaygauskas seemed overwhelmed and embarrassed . . .[6]

None of these comings and goings would have mattered very much, but for one melodramatic event. In February 1971, MI5 acquired Oleg Lyalin, their own KGB defector in London – a 'catch' of such rarity to the British that they were beside themselves with excitement. It was a triumph for 'K' branch, and once again Peter Wright, whose position was increasingly precarious, managed to get into the act. He says:

While Lyalin was still in position, I was involved in the day-to-day running of the case. As the scientist involved, I was also responsible for providing the people involved with Lyalin with the necessary antidotes for any poisonous attempt to assassinate him, and briefing them on what method had been used.[7]

This did not prevent Wright later getting the dates wrong. Both his subsequent ghost-writers, Pincher and Greengrass, were told that Lyalin was under MI5 control in early 1970 – a year too early. Like so many of these apparently insignificant slips, this error is seriously misleading. For it suggests that it was during Wilson's premiership that these events occurred.

Lyalin was, in Wright's words, a 'low-level thug'. Based at the Trade Delegation in Highgate, north London, he did not have diplomatic immunity. His job was contingency planning for sabotage inside Britain in the event of hostilities. He was recruited by the counter-espionage agent-running section, 'K5'. It was an operation controlled by the overall head of the Soviet investigations branch, 'KY', who had succeeded Alex MacDonald in the post on his retirement in 1970. This was Christopher Herbert, described by Wright as 'calm and dependable'. Herbert was fifty-eight; he had served before the war as an administrator in India, and during the 1950s as a colonial 'security Intelligence advisor'. His reward for the successful handling of the Lyalin case was to be a two-year posting to Northern Ireland as 'DCI' – Director and Co-ordinator of Intelligence – in the war with the IRA, and the almost equally compelling war for supremacy in the province between MI5, the rival service MI6, the military and the police.

Herbert's two agent-runners, who culminated their careers with this recruitment, were equally veterans of the old days when the British lion roared. One was Harry Wharton, now fifty-one, the gnome-like Yorkshireman who had recruited informants for the British internal security interest in Palestine, Nigeria, and the bars of Fleet Street. And the other was Tony Brooks, now forty-nine, the hard operator from SOE who had survived three years in Occupied France, and fifteen years buccaneering for MI6 during its wildest, least realistic days of perpetual war. 'One of the toughest and nicest people in MI6,' says Wright. 'He was kind of roguish,' says one CIA man who worked with Brooks. In the office, the two were known, respectively, as 'Buddha' and 'the War Hero'. From now on, although strictly in the line of duty, they were required to be inextricably involved in the affairs of Harold Wilson.

The whole Lyalin operation was under the ultimate command of Furnival Jones. According to Wright, he decided for security reasons not to tell even the Americans, let alone any politicians or British outsiders, even though this contravened existing rules regarding the use of sexual entrapment. Instead, once the operation succeeded, it was used as dramatic proof of the need to realise Furnival Jones' true ambition – the expulsion of the enormous number of Russian Intelligence officers picked out by Hanley's painstaking computer analysis of daily movements, and Wright's statistical extrapolations with GCHQ, of how many spies the average resident Intelligence officer might be expected to control.

It is hard to see why Wright is so defensive about 'sexual entrapment' in his book. All he says is that Lyalin was having an affair with his Soviet secretary, Irina Teplakova, and that when Wharton and Brooks made contact via her, he said he wanted to defect. Perhaps there is a clue in Wright's later statement that when Lyalin was due to return home, MI5 planned to arrest him at the airport to 'force his hand'. Why did his hand need to be 'forced'? It may be that the Lyalin recruitment was more of a sexual blackmail operation, like other unsuccessful ones Wright describes, and less a case of the couple 'choosing freedom'.

Lyalin agreed to act as a 'defector-in-place', on the promise of safe-house facilities to conduct his affair, and an eventual new life for both of them. He appeared to have had a remarkably extensive programme of subversive activities on his job description. Wright says, in briefs he later leaked to Harry Pincher:

186

Lyalin's job was to do reconnaissance for sabotage before the outbreak of war and to set up communications agents with radios, etc. The actual saboteurs would be infiltrated by sea just before D-Day. He had only set up one group of communications agents before he came over to us. They were a bunch of Cypriots in the East End of London. They had radio communications with Moscow. From Lyalin's information we were able to arrest them while they were actually in communication with Moscow ... Lyalin had supplied detailed maps and photographs of Fylingdales [the radar early warning domes on the north Yorkshire coast] and had found landing places ... for the saboteurs. He was to go up there and command the operation. As regards the V-bombers, each squadron had to have two quick reaction aircraft loaded and armed with nuclear weapons, ready to go at 30 seconds notice, the crews waiting in a hut alongside. Lyalin had to discover the exact location of these aircraft on each airfield and plan a route for saboteurs to get to them by D–1. I went on a tour of inspection of these aircraft and found that most of them were not even behind a barbed wire fence. You could drive by public road within 100 yards of them! Other plans not yet developed included flooding the tube system in London and causing panic in major cities by guerrilla threats of the use of clandestine nuclear or nerve gas weapons.

This was interesting. So were Lyalin's detailed 'order of battle' lists. But what was truly riveting was the information he for some reason volunteered about his former colleague at the Soviet Consulate, Richardas Vaygauskas, who was shortly due to go home to Lithuania:

While Lyalin was still in position, he continuously described Vaygauskas' relationships with Joe Kagan (Vaygauskas was a personal friend of Lyalin). He reported on Vaygauskas' briefings of Kagan to visit No. 10 and obtain information and on one occasion, he reported that the *previous evening*, Vaygauskas had given a particular briefing concerning certain EEC and Nato affairs. Kagan had gone to No. 10 at about 10p.m. and had seen Harold Wilson. He had met Vaygauskas an hour later. Vaygauskas had required answers urgently to supplementary questions. Kagan had returned to No. 10 at midnight and got the answers. Lyalin was able to warn us of the activity and we had been able to check it. The movements were correct. (author's emphasis)

This is Wright's account of Lyalin's version of what Vaygauskas boasted that Joe Kagan had asserted to him about Harold Wilson. Eventually it was to percolate in an even more garbled form into Fleet Street. As we have seen, evidentially it is trash, and fourth-hand trash at that. Even as it stands, the account is impossible. Wright's memory had slipped again. The event could not have taken place on 'the previous evening'. Wilson was not in power when Lyalin was being run in position' Subsequently, Wright changed his story, and said he meant 'the previous year' (when Wilson had still been Prime Minister). The incident, he said, had been checked and found to be consistent with Vaygauskas' known movements and the entries for that evening (or some likely evening . . .) in the 'Security Book at No. 10', more than a year previously. Wright's cavalier approach to the details of such grave 'allegations' is chilling.

Inside MI5, however, this discovery was regarded as shattering. Tony Brooks was sent up to Huddersfield to recruit agents from among Kagan's friends and colleagues. Kagan was put under full surveillance as a potential Soviet spy. The picture looked dramatically black: for not only had Kagan himself long been under suspicion but so, of course, had the former Prime Minister. Here appeared, to the more paranoid mind, confirmation of the way in which information had been flowing from Wilson, a Soviet agent, via his friend Kagan, another Soviet agent, direct to the KGB. The fact that Kagan probably saw as much of Marcia Williams as of the Prime Minister only went to prove that she was part of the chain too. Here, suddenly exposed, was the enemy within – a Communist cell in Downing Street itself! 'Wilson,' says Peter Wright emphatically (but without foundation), 'was a traitor.'

It was only a few weeks after the recruitment of Lyalin – March or April 1971 – that Tony Brooks, using his 'light-cover' identity of 'Colonel Brewster', recruited Arthur Parker, Kagan's London representative, as an agent. Parker in turn recruited his son, and then Kagan's managing director, Bill Atack, and his wife Betty. Parker rang Atack: 'Brewster is in MI5,' he said. 'He wants to see you. Can you be at the Post House Hotel?' When the Atacks arrived, Brooks was already sitting waiting for them in a corner. 'You obviously know who I am and what I do,' he said. 'Kagan has been watched for a long time before I came on the scene'. All these people that MI5 approached were innocently patriotic, and it was quite right of them to feel they ought to assist their country. But in the process, their attitude to their employer was changed.

Brooks was to 'run' the people around Kagan for the next five years as he pursued what became a considerable pre-occupation with him. One might wonder whether he was the wisest choice for an inquiry involving the close friends of a Labour Prime Minister – Brooks' personal political sympathies were, after all, with the Conservative Party. But that was probably considered normal. John Parker recalls:

One of 'Brewster's' concerns about Kagan was the Palace. He had connections there – travelling rugs for the Royals, coats for the Queen's corgis, Prince Philip wore a Gannex coat – also the fact that I and my father – Father especially – had been in and out of Downing Street all

188

the time. My father was Kagan's London salesman – I was in charge of the south. I'm not saying the Palace was the trigger for 'Brewster's' interest – he was concerned about Kagan over everything. He really didn't trust him.[8]

After six months, the Lyalin operation stalled abruptly. The increasingly distraught KGB man heard that his wife, who had returned to Moscow, was making some trouble about him and his girlfriend, and that he was due to be recalled. The worse for drink, he was stopped by a passing police constable while driving uncertainly up Warren Street, near the Tottenham Court Road, and put in the cells at Marlborough Street police station. 'K' branch hastily got the charges dropped, and rounded up his agents – the two Greek Cypriot brothers and a Malayan called Abdoolcader, who had been supplying lists of MI5 car numbers from his clerical post in the London vehicle-licencing department. Lyalin was now 'blown': his defection was trumpeted and used as the ostensible reason for expelling 105 Soviet diplomats and trade representatives.

Vaygauskas' name was on the list of those who would be *persona non grata* if they ever tried to return to Britain. The public naming of Vaygauskas as a spy caused some alarm to both Wilson and Kagan – neither of whom, of course, had had the least idea that during the previous six months their contacts with each other and with Marcia Williams had been under intense surveillance.

Both, it seems, had the same idea – to call in the good offices of Arthur Young. Kagan says that he consulted Young, and as a result attended a two-hour interview at Room 55 in the War Office. All he recalls, he says, is that the room had double locks, and that an MI5 officer told him bluntly that Vaygauskas was definitely an Intelligence officer: he had been kept under surveillance emptying 'dead-letter drops' before his recent departure. 'I was surprised,' Kagan said later. 'I didn't think he was sophisticated enough to be KGB.' In other moods he says, 'Well of course I knew he was KGB – they all are.' Wilson himself has never disclosed that he too sought an explanatory interview with MI5, but Wright's account of this has been confirmed by Harry Wharton to his friends. Wright says in his letters:

Wilson approached Arthur Young, a personal friend ... I would emphasise Young was nothing to do with Special Branch or us. He was a good ally when we had problems in the City, but that was all ... Wilson said he wanted to talk to somebody about Kagan's relationship with the Russians. Young expressed surprise that Wilson had not spoken to Furnival Jones, but offered to act as an intermediary. Furnival Jones was furious [at not being approached directly] but asked the case officer for Lyalin to see Wilson.

This was Harry Wharton, who was now in the odd position of conducting an MI5 interview with the former Prime Minister and Leader of the Opposition, who a number of his colleagues believed to be a Russian spy. It is the only occasion, as far as can be established, on which Wilson was ever personally questioned by MI5. He probably thought he was behaving very punctiliously, having met Vaygauskas socially at least once. Kagan, though, is very probably correct when he says: 'By now, Harold had no time for MI5. He didn't think anything of them.' Wright was his usual hostile self about the interview:

> Wilson tried to convince us that he had had no idea of Kagan's relationships, other than trading, with the Soviets, and that he was sure he, Kagan, was acting in the best interests of the country. All this, despite the previous warnings!

Wharton's friends say that he was guarded throughout the interview, and did not feel obliged to reveal all he knew of the Vaygauskas affair because his 'loyalty was to the government of the day' and not to the ex-Labour Prime Minister. This presumably means that Wilson was not enlightened about the claims that Kagan had been a conduit for information from Downing Street. Wharton certainly did not confide his private attitude that the personal friends of the ex-Prime Minister were 'an unsavoury bunch' and that he regarded Kagan as 'a menace' – both views which he expressed later. According to Wright, Wharton broached the subject of whether Wilson himself had ever been put under KGB pressure. Wilson, claims Wright, replied tersely: 'I can assure you, I kept my trousers buttoned up while I was in Moscow.' How fanciful this anecdote is it is hard to tell.

The note of the Wilson interview went into the bulging 'Henry Worthington' file kept in Furnival Jones' safe. Kagan did nothing to assuage his hidden watchers. His wife kept up friendly relations with the exiled Vaygauskas, making visits to Moscow. Arthur Parker, too, went on a cruise with his wife to the Soviet Union – their ship sailed from Tilbury Docks to Leningrad and then up the Baltic to Lithuania. They called on Vaygauskas, who appeared to have resumed his domestic existence as a high party official. Parker briefed his 'control', Tony Brooks, before departing, and he gave him a full account of the meeting on his return. Kagan's dealings with the Soviet embassy continued to be intriguing – one of his employees says he saw Kagan put £25,000 in a suitcase in this period, for despatch to the Soviet embassy. The most likely explanation is that Kagan was passing funds through black-market channels to his brother-in-law, Alexander Shtromas. At about this time, Shtromas told his friends in Moscow that he had managed to get money from his relatives in England, with which he bought a luxury flat.

Eventually, in 1972, Yasha Bum and his daughter Irina were given permission to leave Russia for Israel. In September 1973 – Kagan says after a further humanitarian intervention from the Conservative minister Robert Carr – Shtromas was allowed out. He was given an academic post at Bradford University, of which Harold Wilson was Chancellor. At least one other Jewish emigré was helped to leave Russia by Kagan during this period. Kagan says he was a dentist called Voscinus. A 'Kagan Trust Fund', chaired by Menachem Savidor, an Israeli parliamentarian, also operated to fund such emigrés. Savidor testifies that 'Kagan has extended direct and substantial help to many immigrants.' Kagan himself says: 'To get a Jewish family out of Russia is not only a question of getting a visa for a few thousand pounds . . . they had to support them while they were waiting to get the visas. And when they arrived absolutely penniless in Israel, you had to set them up . . . if he was a dentist, he needed dentist's tools and a dentist's chair . . .'

Meanwhile, Kagan's links with the Wilson ménage were much diminished, those at No. 10 say. This was despite the coincidental fact that Tony Field, Marcia Williams' businessman brother, who played golf with Wilson and worked for him in his office in opposition, married Kagan's own secretary in 1973.

Tony Brooks appeared to regard all the financial activity involving the Russians with the utmost suspicion – he probably would have argued that it was his job to be suspicious. He discussed with the Parkers and the Atacks whether it was possible that Kagan was 'planting illegals' – the old theory, to which Angleton had been so attached in the years after the war, that Jewish refugees could be easily recruited by the KGB as the price of their freedom, and given documents for Israel, England or the United States, as ready-made spies. Another possibility was that Kagan was acting as a 'support agent', transferring funds for 'illegals' in Britain or Europe. Yet another possibility, of course, was that Kagan had nothing to do with espionage at all, but Brooks' superiors seem to have been wedded to these suspicions.

The 'Worthington file' also continued to fill up with details of Wilson's long-established dealings with Sternberg, who was by now discreetly funding the Opposition leader. Wilson had also made Sternberg a knight in his farewell honours list. Marcia Williams is insistent that Wilson had at first heeded MI5's warnings, and refused on two or three occasions to recommend Sternberg for an honour, saying 'He's a spy.' But finally, he had ordered a full security check and had been informed that 'Sternberg was using his contacts in a way helpful to British Intelligence.' If this was so, then one branch of British Intelligence was not liaising with the other, for elements in MI5 like Wright continued to regard Sternberg with immense suspicion. Around this time William Massie's anonymous MI5 friend showed him 'a glimpse' of their Sternberg dossier: he said Sternberg had always willingly briefed the Foreign Office and MI6 about his impressions of Soviet Bloc officials he had met, including Khrushchev. Sternberg's trade deals had by now expanded into Romania and Czechoslovakia. The 'Agricultural Export Council' which he chaired, and on which Beattie Plummer sat, was selling irrigation plants to the Soviet Union itself. When Lady Plummer (Wilson had made her a member of the House of Lords in 1965) died in 1972, Wilson wrote a *Times* obituary tribute on June 5, 1972, saying:

> She was a founder-member of the Agricultural Export Group and travelled widely, especially in Eastern Europe, promoting the sale of farm products, livestock, agricultural equipment and the know-how and services needed for great irrigation schemes. She was passionately devoted to improving East-West relations not so much by speeches and organised movements as by personal relations. In recent years she was engaged in a real practical sense in the development of far-ranging farm irrigation schemes in Romania and the Soviet Union ... A great hostess ... but above all, a loyal and understanding friend.

One of her last services to Wilson had been to help organise the funding of his office in opposition. At the time, the Opposition received no support from public funds. The impoverished Labour Party itself provided only nominal sums and wanted to control what Wilson did with them. So he had to grub and scrape to pay for a modest secretariat. Wilson himself never showed any sign of personal greed – indeed, the reduced way he lived after his retirement would suggest he did not devote enough thought to lining his own pockets. Selling his memoirs to his personal friend and publisher Lord Weidenfeld raised some money for his office. The rest came from a fund set up by rich businessmen. Prominent among them, to the chagrin of some in MI5, was Rudy Sternberg.

Marcia Williams says Sternberg was one of the three chief organisers of the trust fund. The others were Lord Wilfred Brown and Lord Fisher – two well-known Labour businessmen. According to her:

> So discreet were they about the organisation of the trust fund that, although Wilson knew of its existence, neither he nor anyone else knew the full details about it. It operated quite separately from the Private Office and we did not know at any one time exactly who contributed to it.[9]

By now, Wilson was much more trusting towards Sternberg. In 1973, Sternberg reportedly organised and financed a visit to Czechoslovakia made by Wilson. This was anathema to the Cold Warriors – understandably – because the post-Dubcek Czech regime, like the Ulbricht regime in East Germany when Sternberg had opened trading relations with it, was regarded as a pariah. Wilson used the visit to get the release of a Cold War clergyman, the Rev. Hathaway, who had been imprisoned for distributing political tracts and bibles – but this little publicity coup did not make the Intelligence services feel grateful. Frolik, the Czech defector, was later to attack Wilson for making this trip, particularly as, on the plane back, Wilson incautiously remarked that he thought the 1968 Russian invasion of Czechoslovakia was 'best forgotten'.

The most remarkable outcome of the Lyalin affiar was that stories began to be leaked in quantity for the first time, implying that Wilson was a 'security risk'. The summer and autumn of 1971 was when the 'Wilson plot' really achieved momentum. None of the stories directly referred to the Kagan case – this was so top secret that it could scarcely have been leaked to the press without a major internal inquiry. Instead, it was the old case-histories that began to seep out.

One of the clearest examples comes from William Massie, the *Sunday Express* journalist. It was even before the Lyalin case, after Wilson's defeat in 1970, he says, that a CIA officer and an MI5 officer met him together and showed him transcripts of the raw debriefing tapes made in Langley by Josef Frolik. These 'revealed', of course, that a senior Wilson minister, Stonehouse, had been a Soviet Bloc agent. They went on to tell him how Wilson had refused to let Stonehouse be interrogated, and had deliberately hushed the matter up. The implication was that Wilson too, had something to hide. As we have seen, it was the second attempt made by Intelligence men to 'expose' the Stonehouse story and thus discredit Wilson. The two Intelligence officers added that President Johnson had already been warned to treat Wilson with 'circumspection'. Massie's newspaper was – not surprisingly – unwilling to print the story. But Massie told his editor, and others. It began to circulate underground in Fleet Street.

It was in 1971, in the immediate wake of Lyalin's defection, that the opportunity was seized to 'plant' the eight-year-old story given credence by Peter Wright and Arthur Martin, that Gaitskell had been assassinated by the KGB in order to bring Wilson to power. Readers of the *News of the World*, Britain's most raucous Sunday newspaper, which existed largely on a diet of 'kinky vicars' and rape stories, were taken aback on October 24, 1971 to see the blaring front-page 'splash' – 'WAS GAITSKELL MURDERED BY THE KGB? SPY OLEG'S AMAZING CLAIM'.

There is nothing to show that the particular hand of Peter Wright lay behind the story. It was credited to Peter Earle; he says he picked it up in the Palace of Westminster. This is possible, as there were plenty of Tory MPs, as we have seen, who had intimate links with MI5. Ultimately, though, the tale could only have originated within the Intelligence services. The story was full of misinformation and carefully written to stay within the libel laws, but the subtext was unmistakable to anyone in the know – it planted the idea that Wilson was connected to Soviet skulduggery and that Lyalin was somehow involved:

> Fantastic evidence is emerging which suggests that prominent Labour Party figures, Russian emigrés and others hostile to communist policies who died from 'heart failure' or mysterious symptoms were in fact murdered by Russian killer squads. The evidence has come from the continued interrogation of Oleg Lyalin, the KGB defector ... Incredibly, one name on the list, I understand, is Hugh Gaitskell. As Labour leader of the opposition ... Gaitskell was responsible more than any other leading figure for directing the movement away from communist doctrine at home, and Russian policies abroad. He died in January 1963 from an unknown virus ... No Conservative names are on the list. The theory is that a Tory would be replaced with one just like him. But in the Labour Movement, right-wingers hostile to communism could be replaced by left-wingers with very different views ...

Simultaneously a long campaign was launched by *Private Eye*, the scurrilous magazine which in those days had a considerable reputation for muckraking. The magazine had always poked fun at Wilson – its feature 'Mrs Wilson's Diary' had appeared all through his government. Previously the attacks on Wilson had been largely facetious. Now a new element appeared – a sustained attack which lasted until Wilson's resignation five years later, implying in tones ranging from the comical to the deadly earnest that he was a 'Soviet agent'. It was accompanied by violent attacks, some true, some not, on 'Wilson's friends'.

From May 1971, the name Kagan began to appear repeatedly in *Private Eye*. He was portrayed as the *eminence grise* and secret paymaster of the Wilson entourage. Marcia Williams was another target. The magazine unfairly accused her of insinuating members of her family, such as her brother Tony Field, into powerful positions, and made hints about the existence of her children. This could all easily be put down to gossip as the tensions and jealousies of the Wilson 'kitchen cabinet' spilled out. George Wigg was preparing his memoirs, clearly designed to get his own back on Marcia Williams. Others in his office, like George Caunt, who had failed to get a high honour in Wilson's resignation list, were sour and resentful. Joe Haines, Wilson's press secretary, was clearly jealous of Marcia Williams' influence too.

But in July 1971, Auberon Waugh, *Private Eye*'s humorous political columnist who wrote under the name 'HP Sauce', launched a remarkable and lengthy campaign. In a column headed 'BLACKMAIL', he wrote:

> Enough is enough ... Patriotic Britons will look to the Leader of the Op-

position with anxious eyes. At this stage it would be inappropriate for me to say more than that the present Leader of the Opposition seems inadequate to the task with which destiny has entrusted him. However, if Mr Harold Wilson has not resigned from the leadership of the Labour Party before 30 October this year, I give due warning that my organ, HP Sauce, will publish the entire range of information which it possesses on the past and present behaviour of this man. This warning will not be repeated.

He went on to give some hints of what he was talking about by saying (incorrectly) that Victor Rothschild, newly appointed by Edward Heath to head his Downing Street 'think-tank', had failed to achieve top-security clearance. He 'has been discovered by vetting to have once been a Communist Party member and also more recently associated with the Israelis':

Politicians are exempt from this McCarthy-style indignity, of course, which explains . . . the presence of a known Moscow stooge close to the centre of power in fairly recent history.

A couple of months later, in September, when Lyalin's defection had finally been made public, Waugh returned to the attack in a long piece sneering at the 'disclosures' of other papers, which he attributes to 'Ogilvie's bum-boys' (a fairly unmistakable reference for 'insiders' to the homosexual Maurice Oldfield, the day-to-day head of MI6 under the Director-General, Sir John Ogilvie Rennie).

No, the thankless and hazardous task of unmasking the senior KGB agents in high places must remain on the shoulders of your political correspondent . . . The poverty of the late Mr Harold Wilson continues to mystify . . . His latest trip to Moscow can hardly have helped his finances much, since he has lost the job he used to have as economic adviser to Montague Meyer, a firm of timber merchants who frequently required their economic adviser, for some reason, to visit the timber people in Moscow. Nor is it likely that my old friend Yuri Andropov, who heads the timber export business from the Moscow end, was very pleased that Wislon [sic] chose to *pose for photographs* with a vodka-swigging junior clerk in the lingerie exports departments called Oleg Lyalin. It rather lets the side down, don't you know. If only Wislon had delayed his trip by a few days, he could have discussed possible reprisals against the [Foreign Secretary's] bombshell when [he] decided to expel so many honest KGB timber advisers from the country. (author's emphasis)

Yuri Andropov was head of the KGB at the time.

Who were Auberon Waugh's sources for this impressive piece of invective? It was in line with the hints being dropped to the *Sunday Express* and the *News of the World*. But it also accurately mimicked the precise obsessions of 'K' branch about Wilson's repeated Moscow trips, just at the moment when there seemed to be sensational secret evidence from Lyalin pointing in the same direction.

One good speculative candidate would be Waugh's uncle, Auberon Herbert. Waugh was fond of him, and his various passions for anti-Soviet emigré groups had led him to be recruited as an agent not only for MI6, but even for Harry Wharton of MI5 twelve years earlier, the man who was now actually 'running' Lyalin. There is no suggestion that Wharton himself was doing any improper leaking, but Auberon Herbert certainly had the right sort of Intelligence contacts.

There are even faint stylistic similarities between Waugh's sarcasms about 'timber advisers' and an indignant letter on the same theme that Herbert had written to the *Daily Telegraph* in 1950 during the Korean War. It was Harold Wilson's Board of Trade, of course, which had made the Soviet trade deals in question. Herbert protested that if Russian inspectors were to be allowed into British factories then Britain should inspect the 'slave labour areas of Siberia' where the timber was cut:

> It would do the Ministry of Supply no harm to know how Soviet timber is cut, and the British public would, no doubt, benefit by a closer knowledge of the really modern methods employed in exploiting the endless forests and 30 million foresters of Siberia.

A second, more important source for Waugh and *Private Eye* was one of Wilson's own political aides at No. 10 Downing Street – David Candler. Candler worked for Wilson from 1967 to 1970. Oddly enough, just as he was arriving there, he had repeated contact with MI5. Candler decided to report to them that, in his previous job at Labour Party HQ, he had been the subject of suspicious interest by a Czech diplomat (no doubt one of Frolik's colleagues). Candler had no fewer than three friendly interviews with MI5 officers from 'D2', the original Soviet satellites branch.

Candler says that he had no further direct contact with MI5 counter-espionage. But, he says, he picked up hostile gossip about Wilson's former days at the Board of Trade, which ultimately emanated from Wilson's own Principal Private Secretary, the senior civil servant Michael Halls. Halls had been intimately linked to Wilson then – he had been Private Secretary to the young Cabinet minister in the late 1940s. Halls was also, in his current job, No. 10's official link-man to MI5.

Halls was, in fact, being specifically cultivated by Peter Wright's MI5 colleagues. Halls' widow, Marjorie, says a number of the officers identified in *Spycatcher* were known to her as officials in 'the government'. They would meet on social occasions, in London clubs, and go to the theatre together. It was claimed after his death that Michael Halls had a grudge against Marcia Williams. He was alleged to have regarded her as a potential 'security risk' because of her children, and to have wanted her to be forced to resign. This gossip made Marcia Williams understandably furious. She says there was no shred of justification for it. After Halls died of a heart attack, his wife opened legal proceedings for compensation, and publicly documented these allegations to Chapman Pincher. This coincided with Wilson's return to power in 1974. Was Halls merely a conduit for the MI5 smears, which were transmitted via Candler to *Private Eye*? Or did he inadvertently go further and help his MI5 officer friends with more titbits of historical information for their files? Either way, the picture of disloyalty is not a pretty one. It did occur to Candler that MI5 might be using individuals like him to get information out.

A third source was, of course, William Massie himself. Frustrated by the reluctance of his newspaper to print his stories, he began attending *Private Eye* lunches and feeding them Intelligence material gathered from his MI5 friends, some of them by now, he says, 'senior'. From now on, items in the back of the magazine by Waugh tended to be paralleled by unsigned articles in the front 'news' section about MI5 and MI6 internal politics, provided by Massie.

Waugh returned to his theme in 1973, when Wilson went to Czechoslovakia:

Cord Meyer ... the new CIA chief in London should take a long hard look at these repeated attempts by Iron Curtain countries to secure Wilson's re-election. The Czechs' recent stunt with a Methodist minister is only the latest in a series which includes Wilson's Soviet invitation to visit Russia as prime minister after the next election. I am not of course suggesting Wilson may be a Russian agent, which would be completely absurd, or that there could be any connection between these events and his close relations with various Russian leaders after Mr Wilson's numerous visits to Moscow as 'economic consultant' to Montague Meyer, the timber merchant. There are Labour men who say Wilson is 'best forgotten' ... the point is that Wilson is only waiting in the wings to do it all again ... It is high time the CIA took an interest in this curious man, if only to counter the efforts being made on his behalf from the other side of the Iron Curtain.

For a supposedly humorous column, it was hard, at first sight, to see what was meant to be the joke. Two months later, however, Waugh had recovered his sense of fun. In a column about Wilson's relations with the political correspondents, he dropped in a little paragraph:

Unless Wilson apologises immediately for the fright he has given these amiable elderly gentlemen, I shall release certain photographs which have come into my possession taken long ago and apparently overseas.

197

And three weeks later, there was the merest throwaway line, commenting on the appointment of the secret homosexual Maurice Oldfield as the new head of MI6:

I have no doubt that Maurice, who is still a bachelor at 57, will make a much better job of it than his predecessor, the wretched Sir John Rennie, and we will have fewer communist agents in Downing Street . . .

While these 'official secrets' were merrily seeping out, the head of MI5, Sir Martin Furnival Jones, also did his discreet best to raise the temperature. He gave evidence to the Franks Committee, which was making a vain attempt to reform the Official Secrets Act. Some of his evidence was published in the Committee's Report. Furnival Jones, who had just authorised an operation against the personal friend of the recently retired Labour Prime Minister, did not put his own name to his opinions. They were published anonymously as from the Director-General of the Security Service:

The Soviet Bloc intelligence services are very active among political parties around the Palace of Westminster. I can certainly say that very many MPs are in contact with very many intelligence officers . . . No doubt many MPs, many people, enter the House of Commons in the hope of becoming Ministers. If the Russian intelligence service can recruit a back-bench MP and he continues to hold his seat for a number of years and climbs the ladder to a ministerial position, it is obvious the spy is home and dry.

Although the general public did not get the point, his subordinates at Leconfield House knew exactly what Furnival Jones was driving at – Harold Wilson, John Stonehouse, Bernard Floud, Niall MacDermot, Stephen Swingler, Tom Driberg – and, bringing up the rear, the only one who had been publicly denounced, the hapless nonentity, Will Owen. In the wake of the Lyalin affair, 'K' branch must have felt gratified by this obscure but menacing pronouncement. It had in fact nothing to do with the subject under discussion by the committee, but Furnival Jones was trying to persuade them to keep the Official Secrets Act in its full rigour. The Franks Committee transcripts record that he wanted even non-secret information of the kind picked up by journalists to be covered by the legislation:

Q: How would that sort of information be involved with the Official Secrets Act in any sense?
A: Oh, very readily. Every government department, I presume, I am sure, keeps a personal file in respect of its employees.
Q: But it is an official secret?
A: It is an official secret if it is in an official file.

Harold Wilson might have been forgiven for thinking Furnival Jones could have done a better job in keeping secret the contents of his own organisation's defamatory 'personal files'.

The Lyalin case was strictly British. He was a source not shared with the US until after the event, and then only partially. Ironically, according to Wright, Angleton was so irritated by this attitude that he pronounced Lyalin to be yet another 'fake defector' and refused to circulate the reports when they did come over. Angleton's refusal to admit the authenticity of any defector other than his own pet megalomaniac, Golitsin, was already becoming notorious within the CIA.

But it is worth spending a moment to ask if Angleton might not have been correct. Lyalin produced some lurid and unlikely 'sabotage' plans which were never going to happen short of World War III. Taking them seriously involved re-casting British domestic strategy to tie up a great many troops in contingency plans for guarding hundreds of 'key points', thus diverting NATO resources. The agents 'blown' by Lyalin were of almost ludicrous triviality – the two Greek Cypriot brothers had no access to any sensitive information and Abdoolcader was already a wasting asset who was becoming recalcitrant and unco-operative. Lyalin's most forceful impact was that he tied up MI5's counter-intelligence in a long and futile operation to hound Joe Kagan, and sowed further unjustified suspicion about the loyalties of Harold Wilson. This was bad for the Atlantic Alliance, always supposedly a central target of Russian policy. There was some later evidence, as we shall see, which could be used to suggest that the whole Kagan affair was nothing more than a Russian 'provocation' from start to finish.

Such a theory has the amusing consequence that Peter Wright, his attendant anti-Communist journalist friends like Chapman Pincher, and James Angleton himself, become nothing more than 'useful idiots', unwittingly dancing to the Kremlin's tune all the time. And nor is this mirror-image technique entirely an intellectual game: in the US, a CIA counter-intelligence officer, Clare Petty, finally sought to discredit Angleton by turning his byzantine suspicions upside-down in just this way and writing a long paper to demonstrate that Angleton himself was a 'mole'. After all, he had virtually paralysed the counter-intelligence agencies of the Western world singlehanded. If that was not a Russian Intelligence service objective, then what was? The point is that, as the Russian defector games of the 1960s so harshly demonstrated, it is very easy to get to a point in the counter-intelligence business when no one has the least idea any longer what is true and what is false. At that point 'intuition' has to take over – a word which sometimes means bureaucratic self-interest, or even mere political prejudice. Wilson may have been partly a victim of deep structural incompetence on the part of the British secret police.

Despite Furnival Jones' reticence, the CIA were soon tipped off unofficially about Kagan and Wilson. It was a secret too good not to share with the avuncular 'foreign power'. There was one damning piece of documentary evidence left in Angleton's files after his departure, which his colleagues discovered. It proved that the British had leaked material about Wilson – it was a half-sheet of paper on which Angleton had handwritten: 'Who is Kagan?' CIA executive Steven Schram[10] recalls:

> One of our guys was returning from an overseas meeting and he called up a friend in London around 1973. He was either in MI5 or MI6. They went out for a few drinks and he told him there were worries about Harold Wilson. Wilson had been keeping odd company. He told him all about someone called Kagan who owned a raincoat factory, and asked him, 'Have you heard anything about this?' Our guy says: 'Jesus, no!' Within a month of getting home, our guy wrote all this up, saying, 'There's some suggestion Wilson may be a bad guy.' He didn't get the facts very straight, as I recall, but the report was circulated to Angleton. This was definitely the first Angleton had heard of Kagan. We thought, 'Should we ask for a trace?' and we decided no, because it would have betrayed our guy's source. But we were fascinated by it all. There was a bit of a stir around. Kagan's name was looked up in *Who's Who*. Angleton's counter-intelligence team prepared a file of five pages of notes stapled together.

Angleton sucked this Intelligence into his growing conspiracy theory, which it appeared to confirm. By now, this had three elements. The first was that the whole of Europe was rotten with Communism and could be virtually written off as a bulwark of the free world. De Gaulle's France had been manipulated move by move by cleverly placed Kremlin agents – Golitsin had identified several, including the NATO information officer Georges Paques. Italy, as Angleton knew from his time there, was only precariously prevented from going altogether Communist by CIA subsidies to politicians and 'front' organisations. The United Kingdom of Harold Wilson – where Angleton himself had grown up and been educated – was a rat's nest of subversion. Interviewed later, one of his colleagues, Leonard McCoy, recalls Angleton expounding his view of the KGB as being rather like the rabies virus, moving inexorably westwards:

> His umbrella theory was that the KGB is controlling most of the world and they'll get here soon. The Red Menace is spreading, and they've got Europe.

The second element in the thesis was that the Kremlin would send streams of 'false defectors' to the West, in order to discredit Golitsin and, in effect, Angleton himself, by casting doubt on their theories. The disastrous consequences of this belief have been thoroughly documented in the United States since Angleton's downfall, but they still seem grotesque. The most notorious example was the hapless Yuri Nosenko, who claimed he was a KGB officer when he defected in Geneva. He was kept in solitary confinement for more than three years, latterly in a cell, subjected to repeated lie-detector tests, and accused of being a 'plant'. One of those involved recalls:

> When they put Nosenko on the machine, they used to say to him quite falsely, 'This machine says you're lying – now you confess.' It was quite disgraceful. Poor Nosenko got so nervous that the machine used to register false readings. It was all Angleton, he was behind all this. He could be very extreme.

Nosenko was eventually 'rehabilitated' and released.

The final element in Angleton's paranoia was the conviction that the CIA was penetrated by a high-level 'mole' – a view echoed in Britain, of course, by the receptive Peter Wright, who did his part by denouncing hs own Prime Minister and the head of MI5 itself (Wright was also instrumental in circulating mistaken accusations against the head of Canadian counter-intelligence, an Englishman called James Bennet, who was only cleared after being forced into retirement). Golitsin told Angleton there were thirty-five spies in US Intelligence. Eventually he insisted there were at least six. Joint investigations by the FBI and the CIA on the lines of Wright's British FLUENCY committee, found evidence of none. But this did not deter Angleton. His suspicions fastened mistakenly on David Murphy, head of the Soviet division, who had refused to co-operate with Golitsin's demands to see all his files, but passed lie-detector tests. Angleton only began to overreach himself in 1973 when Murphy was posted to Paris. The gaunt, conspiratorial counter-intelligence chief flew to Paris and, despite the fact that Murphy had been cleared, told his French opposite number that Murphy was a Soviet agent. In the resulting diplomatic ructions, the new CIA chief, William Colby, was forced to apologise to the French. Angleton's days were numbered. But he and his supporters still had much mischief to make.

CHAPTER 10

'Moulders' and 'Jumbo' were the two men who did best out of Edward Heath, the new Conservative Prime Minister. He appointed these two insiders to head MI6 and MI5. They were known as Oldfield and Hanley to those in the government who had not been to boys' boarding schools. They were not known to the general public by any names at all. Heath was also to agree to the expulsion *en masse* of 105 Russian diplomats.

But that apart, Heath was a disappointment to MI5 and MI6. As a bachelor, vulnerable to smears that he was a homosexual – both MI5 and Soviet Bloc agents had circulated these false stories – Heath was acutely aware of the dangers of unchecked Intelligence 'dirt'. He is on record as saying that, to him, 'the internal control of the security services' was a matter of vital importance[1]:

> That was one of the matters on which I took a firm stand. I instituted machinery which dealt with these aspects. I have always believed there must be severe limitations on the work of the security services internally, to say nothing of their activities overseas. From 1970 to 1974, I believe that control was firm . . . We are dealing with people, and it is the choice of people that matters. In the inner control of the security services, the first point to remember is the selection of people and their admission to them . . . I . . . met people in the security services who talked the most ridiculous nonsense, and whose whole philosophy was ridiculous nonsense. If some of them were on a tube and saw someone reading the *Daily Mirror*, they would say 'Get after him, that is dangerous. We must find out where he bought it . . .'

Heath may well have been referring to Wright and his friends, with whom he came into contact. Whilst manoeuvring him into appointing their chosen men at the top, the Intelligence services did not choose to confide in Heath about the continuing rows and accusations over Hollis. Nor, having discovered his reluctance to allow no-holds-barred 'investigations', even of his political opponents, did they open up their Wilson files to him. Instead, they tried to make their manoeuvres through those they thought of as Intelligence 'friends', like Victor Rothschild and Maurice Macmillan. At the same time links were forged between the extreme Right of the Tory party, who were determined to replace Heath with someone tougher, and the madder elements in the Intelligence services. Heath was correct that – uncontrolled – these secret officials were dogs who would bite anybody. Fifteen years later, he had become an opponent of the secrecy fetish:

We are in an extremely silly position: we do not even admit the existence of the security services. There is no such thing as MI5 or MI6. There is no budget for them, because the House never discuss them. What a contrast that is with the United States! ... I am beginning to realise that there is a period of history in which I moved, about which I shall never know the truth. I find that disconcerting and, to say the least, worrying.[2]

Ironically, it was Heath who ceremonially dubbed the chief proponent of MI5's 'ridiculous nonsense' a Commander of the British Empire. In November 1971, Robert Armstrong, his Principal Private Secretary, wrote the customary confidential letter to Peter Wright, saying Heath was to give him the CBE and 'would be glad to be assured that this would be agreeable to you.' (These letters are sent out in advance so that the number of people who refuse such 'honours' can be concealed.) The order, invented as recently as 1917, has as its motto 'For God and Empire'.

Wright probably owed this preferment – the high point of his career – to Victor Rothschild. The millionaire scientist and dabbler in Intelligence rose to a position of power under Heath as head of the Central Policy Review Staff, Heath's new 'think tank'. As such, he was part of Heath's 'machinery' for attempting to control the Intelligence services, acting as his eyes and ears rather as George Wigg had done for Wilson.

Rothschild provided a back-channel for Peter Wright to feed reports of the 'Red Menace' in the trade unions direct to the Prime Minister. These went behind the back of Philip Allen at the Home Office, and over the heads of 'F' branch, whose job it was to provide political briefs on trade unionists via Allen's department. Wright's behaviour was disgraceful. He supplied an outrageously false report, untruthfully accusing both Jack Jones and his wife of being Soviet agents. This was done by reading all forty volumes of Jack Jones' file (it took Wright two days) and extracting anything which suggested a Soviet link, whether well-founded or not. For good measure, he also put in the wilder stories from Frolik about his attempt to recruit Jones and other 'Czech agents' in the Labour Party.

Wright claims that after a series of National Economic Development Council meetings between the Prime Minister, Jones and Scanlon, Heath complained that Jones 'talked like a Communist' and demanded to see the information on file. In a record later compiled for Victor Rothschild in 1980, a copy of which he kept, Wright puts it this way:

At the height of Heath's troubles with the Unions, the PM was not satisfied with the Security Service reports on Jack Jones ... The reports only gave the subversion information. The PM discussed the matter with Rothschild. Rothschild said that he might be able to get more information. He consulted Peter Wright, who knew the case. Peter Wright consulted the DG (E.M.F.J) who told him to 'give Rothschild what he wants'. Wright gave Rothschild a note summarising the evidence of Jones' Soviet connections, which were damning (but not legal proof). Rothschild was attacked by the Permanent Secretary, Home Office, for going outside his terms of reference, despite the PM's request.

Wright's 'note' on Jack Jones, whom he called 'a classic example of the cancer in our midst', went as follows:

Jack Jones was brought up in and around Liverpool. He became a dock worker and a political communist agitator in the ISHA [International Seamen's and Harbourworkers' Association], a Soviet front organisation. He married a girl who was a Comintern courier. They both appear in the pre-war Comintern radio traffic [known as MASK] which we read for a number of years. JJ went to Spain during the civil war as political commissar with the International Brigade. We knew of 19 such commissars. 17 of them have been proven to have become Soviet agents later: the only 2 not proven are JJ and Will Paynter the miners' leader who is best described as being a 'latter-day saint' and much too overt for a Soviet agent. After the Spanish civil war, JJ returned to his political Trade Union activities. He was an overt communist until the autumn of 1941, when after the German attack on Russia he publicly left the party and became a left wing Socialist. (All the Burgess, Blunt, Philby galere were so instructed.) I am sure this was done under Russian orders. JJ maintained secret underground contact with the Party and, with Hugh Scanlon, had secret meetings with the industrial officer of the Party, then Peter Kerrigan, and the Russian KGB officers en poste in London, to my knowledge right up to the early 70s. In the 60s, JJ was in frequent contact with the wife of a Swedish diplomat, Mrs Hammerling. Mrs Hammerling and her son were Soviet agents used as communications agents i.e. acting as a cut-out between Soviet intelligence officers and their more sensitive and important agents. We were never able to prove she was acting in this role between JJ and the Russians, but it was very likely. Mrs Hammerling was interviewed by us, and was dropped by the Russians. At this time, Frolik, the Czech defector, cultivated JJ with a view to recruiting him. When he asked HQ in Prague for clearance to proposition him, he was told that their Russian friends were already in touch with JJ and were working with him. Frolik was to close his file and return it to Prague for handing over to the Russians. Frantisek August was also aware of the interest in JJ.

This was an absurd tissue of untrue smears and innuendo. To Wright's immediate discomfiture, Heath knew it. Jones had never been in the Communist Party and nor had his wife, Evelyn. His soldiering in Spain as a political commissar in the Major Attlee company (he was wounded) is described in great detail in his autobiography. Even more to the point, Edward Heath, as a member of a sympathetic student delegation, had actually met Jones out there in 1937. Heath wrote of the encounter: 'One could not but admire these men, civilians at heart . . . They would go on fighting as long as they could, that was clear.'[3] The only clandestine element in the Spanish excursion was necessary because the then British government had declared that enlistment for Spain was illegal. Mrs Hammerling and her son were not Soviet agents (they had been interviewed in 1961 as coincidental contacts of Antonin Buzwk, the defecting Czech journalist who had been giving money to Labour official Arthur Bax). Scanlon, the engineering union leader, was not a Communist agent. Wright's exaggerated account of the Frolik story, as we have seen, did not add up to anything. Any social contacts Jones had had with Russians who made recruitment approaches had always been reported to MI5. Jones was a left-winger and not anti-Communist – but he was by no stretch of the imagination a Soviet agent. Even Wright recognised there was no 'proof'.

What was particularly absurd was that Jones, in 1972, complained that Heath did not sufficiently appreciate that he and Scanlon had to stick doggedly to a tough line when meeting the Prime Minister, because their union colleagues objected to them having such negotiations with the Tories at all. Jones was in fact remarkably sympathetic to Heath. He recalled later:

No Prime Minister, before or after, could compare with Ted Heath in the efforts he had made to establish a spirit of camaraderie with trade union leaders, and to offer an attractive package which might satisfy large numbers of workpeople . . . Those of us who had got to know him well felt keen disappointment when he lost the leadership of his Party. At the outset, I thought he represented the hard face of the Tory party, but over the years he revealed a human face of Toryism at least to the union leaders who met him frequently.[4]

It was Wright's kind of rumour which had previously attempted to block Jack Jones from taking over Barbara Castle's planned Ports Authority in 1967. 'I suggested Jack Jones . . . the Department were a bit nervous about "security" – they obviously think he is a Communist', Castle recorded in her diary. 'But we cleared all that: I spoke to Harold, who thought it was an excellent idea.'[5] And, three years later under the next Labour government, as Tony Benn recorded, MI5 objected once again to his plan to make Jones chairman of the National Enterprise Board, on the grounds that he was a 'subversive'.[6]

205

Wright was clearly not alone in his paranoia about trade union leaders. Chapman Pincher recalls:

Maurice Macmillan told me that when he was Minister at the Department of Employment in 1973, two MI5 officers called to see him to complain of the inroads being made by communists into the unions. They suggested that MI5 would welcome the introduction of legislation to curb communist activities. Macmillan reported the visit to Heath, who said he would do what was necessary – but no legislation ensued.[7]

To use such back-channels suggests that the secret policemen were feeling surprisingly confident. One can argue that what Victor Rothschild in fact did in his role as MI5 link-man was to ensure MI5 kept out of anyone's real control. There were major skeletons in MI5's cupboard, and one of them was the Rothschild/Blunt link. The one thing that frightened Rothschild was that the Anthony Blunt affair might leak, with damaging publicity for him. In 1972, Blunt developed cancer. Wright says:

Victor and Tess Rothschild became alarmed that Blunt might die . . . and might leave a testament about his [Blunt's] spying, including his long association with them (innocent I'm sure). Blunt at the time was a bit out of his mind and vindictive against society.[8]

A long review of Blunt's late-night bottle-sessions with Peter Wright was carried out by Ann Orr-Ewing. It came to the uncomfortable conclusion that he had never been a genuine stoolpigeon, but had always dodged and weaved to avoid giving information which would implicate anyone who mattered. Contact with the elderly renegade was broken off. It was decided that disclosure – if it had to come – had better be managed carefully. The Conservative Home Secretary, Reginald Maudling, was gingerly briefed by Dick White, on the verge of retirement as Cabinet Office Intelligence Co-ordinator.

The news was not well-received by Home Office Permanent Secretary Philip Allen (later Lord Allen). That MI5 had found an upper-class spy in their own ranks eight years earlier, had hushed it up, and had given him and half his friends blanket immunities from prosecution must have seemed incredible. Meanwhile wretched clerks and sergeants had been appearing at the Old Bailey and had been jailed for long terms for espionage offences. One of Maudling's men says: 'The whole thing appeared to have been done without regard for the potential political consequences. They just did not seem to be aware of the political dimension.' Fortunately, Blunt recovered, and Rothschild was spared the 'exposure' he dreaded.

There were other embarrassments: MI5 was discovered attempting to negotiate immunities for the criminal Littlejohn brothers, who were employed as MI6 agents to cause trouble for the IRA in Northern Ireland.

And one of Edward Heath's own ministers, the Air Minister, Lord Lambton, was suddenly implicated in a sex scandal. He was photographed in bed with a pair of Maida Vale prostitutes, one white, one black. He was also smoking marijuana at the time. The story was sold to the newspapers and Lambton had to resign. The Home Office thought it unlikely that MI5 had not been aware of the activities at the brothel and felt they had been taken by surprise. One of Allen's senior colleagues says:

> MI5 seemed to have no caution for political realities, no political antennae. When the Lambton case blew up it became clear to James Waddell, the deputy secretary in charge of MI5 liaison, that an MI5 informant was involved in the case. But although Waddell and Allen were the Home Secretary's men, they just could not get any steerage or guidance out of MI5.

The Home Office were right. The ubiquitous agent-runner Harry Wharton had been efficiently doing his job. One of his MI5 colleagues says:

> His superiors got their fingers slapped over Lambton. It wasn't Wharton's fault. He was running a prostitute at some club. One of her friends said Lambton was her client and Harry told her to find out. The girl was promised she'd be 'alright' and she was under the impression she was an agent. When the police investigation took place, they got very resentful at what they termed 'MI5 meddling'.

The friction was not just over demarcation disputes. One senior official complains:

> ... The quality of the intelligence was not there. They were splendid at telling you what had happened after it had happened, but we used to bang the table and say, 'You are supposed to be there to give us some warning.' Terrorism from the Middle East was a particular problem in this regard. We had to press and press to get them to take a real interest.

The Home Office was worried about the growing spread of domestic amateur revolutionary groups as well as of international terrorism. The civil servants were frightened and puzzled at the sudden eruption of the 'Angry Brigade' – a group of anarchistic students from good homes who were causing explosions at the premises of politicians.

Allen and the Home Office had never succeeded in dominating the stubborn Furnival Jones, despite their nominal right to supervise his activities. A succession of MI5 bureaucrats had passed before their eyes on committees since the mid-1960s – Malcolm Cumming, the former incumbent of 'D' branch under whom Wright had first been given his head; Dick Thistlethwaite, whose 'F' branch political summaries left ministers so lukewarm; the successive Deputy Director-Generals Ronald Symonds and

Anthony Simkins; the reticent 'Jumbo' Hanley; younger men from 'F' branch such as the doggedly unimaginative miner's son, John Lewis Jones. None of them impressed.

As the time approached for Furnival Jones' retirement, Allen made a determined effort to have Waddell appointed as the new head of MI5.

The warriors of Curzon Street already found Waddell finicky over applications for telephone taps – requests had to go up to the Home Office with a 'short reason' attached proving to the Permanent Secretary that some 'major subversive activity' was involved. Such a man was unlikely to be relaxed about 'K' branch's regular buggings and burglaries (or 'illicit entries' as they were prudishly described in the office.)

He thought little of the 'K' branch obsession with Russians. 'We weren't terribly impressed with them,' he later recalled, 'They seemed to live in a world of their own.' Whitehall mandarins involved in this affair say Peter Wright's unpleasant account of it in his memoirs, while as usual faulty in detail, is not wrong in substance. Rothschild did MI5 a favour: he kept Waddell out by strenuously lobbying the Prime Minister in person, on behalf of MI5's own candidate – 'Jumbo' Hanley. Dick White was lobbied too to use his influence. In Wright's record of events composed later for Rothschild's private consumption, he recorded:

> Victor Rothschild discussed the matter with Peter Wright, who said the Service wanted Hanley. Peter Wright arranged a meeting between Rothschild and Hanley. As a result, Rothschild had a private talk with the Prime Minister.

Heath was eventually persuaded not to leave the recommendation to a small committee of Permanent Secretaries, but to interview the two candidates in person. Hanley, well-primed, performed impressively. Meanwhile, Wright himself was busy circulating false rumours in an effort to discredit Waddell, rumours about a 'nest of Communists' inside the Home Office. He used his 'D3' research to good effect, by spreading stories of the 'Leighton Group' – a band of left-wingers who had been undergraduate Communists in the 1930s and who were now inside Whitehall. Tipped off by Rothschild at one point that another deputy secretary, Francis Harrison, might be a compromise candidate, Wright's reaction was to claim to Rothschild, quite falsely, that Harrison might have been a homosexual friend of Guy Burgess. As he put it in his later record for Rothschild: 'Fortunately, Peter Wright was able to give the security doubts about the . . . candidate to Victor Rothschild.'

Hanley thus got control of MI5 at the end of 1972. Bowing to the preoccupations of the Home Office, he switched the organisation's targets dramatically. 'K' branch was downgraded and its expensive plans to computerise 'watcher' communications were scrapped. Its anti-Soviet agent-running sections were combined with MI6. From now on, 'F' branch was king. Money was poured into it, and officers who had cut their teeth on robust operations against the Soviet Union and its spies were transferred into the much more delicate field of 'domestic' work.

Charles Elwell was moved over to head 'F' on Thistlethwaite's retirement. His deputy was Keith Thomas. Michael McCaul, the most energetic counter-espionage officer from the old 'D' and 'K' branch days, was posted to a new anti-terrorist section, 'F3', which expanded at speed. Barry Russell-Jones, Wright's close friend, who had worked on Soviet order of battle lists, was eventually promoted to be 'FX' – in charge of agent-running into the domestic political scene: unions, universities, political parties, pressure groups, the media.

New names from the world of the 'industrial desk' – John Jones, David Ransom, John Woodruffe – began to rise to prominence. MI5 fought – and beat – MI6 for control of Intelligence in Northern Ireland, under a succession of 'DCIs' on two-year tours to this new, uninhibited career-posting – Ian Cameron, Jack Credock, John Parker. Old war-horses like Patrick Stewart had retired through ill-health; Arthur Martin retired as head of the MI6 registry in 1970, still convinced that either Hollis or Graham Mitchell had been a Soviet agent and the beneficiary of a cover-up. All the talk now was of schemes to computerise the Registry, and link it directly to the personal files of government ministries like the Health and Social Security Department at Newcastle. The new research projects were on domestic Trotskyite groups like Gerry Healey's Socialist Labour League or Ted Grant's Militant. The new agents were being recruited and run direct into the universities, to spy on long-haired student activists like Tariq Ali and Bruce Birchall. Journalists and producers were being blacklisted out of the BBC and newspapers for being 'radicals'.

This switch-over was one which was very dangerous to make with an unreformed staff used to bugging, burglary, entrapment and harassment. As even Wright recognised, what was acceptable against agents of the Red Menace became distinctly dangerous and distasteful when turned on domestic 'radicals'. There was no open political debate and no real political control of MI5. They therefore continued to find their own solutions to bureaucratic pressure.

But these new moves left Wright out in the cold. He was becoming a dinosaur, with his clutch of yellowing files about old men who had been left-wing homosexuals before the war. Wright's reaction was characteristic. Having decried Jack Jones and James Waddell, he now made a fresh attempt to prove that Harold Wilson was a Soviet agent. He claims that Furnival Jones, on the eve of his retirement, gave him permission to fly once more to Washington and try to prise further details out of James Angleton regarding his 'source'. Wright would probably have made the bid, permission or no permission: CIA officers involved say he was flying over to see Angleton and discuss technical advances in bugging and radio 'three or four times a year' anyway. It was a coup Wright badly needed – the DG-designate, Hanley, was no friend of Wright and his 'Gestapo', having suffered an embarrassing grilling himself about his 'loyalty'.

Angleton's 'source' is regarded with scepticism by his fellow CIA officers. No traces of it exist in other departmental files. They point out that Angleton's counter-intelligence department did not run agents directly. He had a history of personal contact only with a few Italian sources, for historical reasons, and with Israeli Intelligence. But if Mossad had ever got anything hard on Wilson, it would have been passed from government to government, over Angleton's head. There was certainly no CIA source in Mexico saying anything about Harold Wilson. Wright was doomed to disappointment, but he was loath to admit it. He late claimed that he had succeeded in getting some details out of Angleton's staff over a drinking session. But on his own account, this was merely a playback of the 'Kagan' allegations.

Just how contradictory Wright has been over this Angleton episode is shown by two statements he made about it in 1984, within a week of each other. On 28 June, he said in an interview with one journalist, John Ware:

> Eventually I managed to get it out of Angleton's people. The information was, basically, that Wilson was asked by a friend – a Soviet – to check if he had met a certain person. I know that the information was fairly hard.

But on 6 July, in an interview with another journalist, Paul Greengrass, he said:

> At first Angleton wouldn't tell me, but in the end, after a couple of bottles of gin, he said: 'I think there is somebody in Mexico who had a pact with Kagan and Wilson and that this person in Mexico was without doubt a Soviet agent.'

Both of these stories cannot be true. In fact, one must conclude neither of them are.

What is true is that someone in the CIA now decided to activate Frolik. The gloomy Czech had been wrung dry after the standard three-year de-briefing. The tapes of his exhaustive interviews were handed over to him and he was told to start writing his memoirs. The Agency would translate them into English, would remove what was necessary for 'security reasons', and have them published, not in the United States where interest would be minimal, but in Britain. There, of course, they would have the effect of embarrassing Harold Wilson severely: even if Stonehouse's name could not be published because of the British libel laws, enough gossip would be caused to bring the story to life. Frolik was told, as he lamented later, that he would make a great deal of money.

210

Defector memoirs are a specialised art-form. They are invariably manipulated by the host Intelligence agency – and sometimes entirely ghost-written by staff CIA or MI5 men. This has been a long tradition from Alexander Foote's 1947 memoirs, written for him by MI5's Courtney Young, to Golitsin's eventual book, which was put together by Arthur Martin and Stephen de Mowbray.

Frolik set to. By the middle of 1973, he had turned the transcripts into a 600-page manuscript called *Camorra*. It was translated, vetted and doctored by the CIA, who removed 100 pages they thought unsuitable. They put Frolik in touch with a jobbing British writer, Charles Whiting. Breezy and prolific, with a silver-grey crew-cut, Whiting specialised in military subjects and had a long association with the US Army. He had experience teaching languages to their officers in Europe, he says. Frolik, who opened their correspondence by pointing out errors in Whiting's recent book on the war-time Heydrich assassination, sent him one of the CIA de-briefing tapes. In September 1973, Whiting wrote to the British publisher Leo Cooper about his 'find':

His name is Major Frolik and he was a senior officer in Czech intelligence from 1952 until he defected in 1969. At present he is in Arlington Va. were his own account is being vetted by the CIA prior to publication . . . I know nothing of his ability as a writer, but that's no problem . . . his story sounds a winner . . . He's preparing at the moment to come to Europe to sell his account.

Frolik responded promptly to the publisher's approach, via 'Olga Malina', a CIA pseudonym and postbox: 'I would like to visit London around the end of November . . . To various Western intelligence services, I gave the names of approximately 400 citizens who worked for Czech and Soviet intelligence.' He listed twenty-one selling points. Chief among them was the story of the attempt to compromise Edward Heath and 'The astonishing success of the communist services in the penetration of the British government, social and trade union institutions.'

Whiting wrote excitedly to Cooper in November: 'The outline of Frolik's book which he sent me seems to contain a certain amount of dynamite, especially Heath and the Red business with the UK unions. . . . His selling-pitch was largely about the trade unions. He didn't mention Stonehouse by name at this point, though he did talk about the Heath caper and about Maurice Macmillan's wife . . . He said "twelve MPs" . . . something like that . . . had been in Czech pay – I thought it was rather sensational.'

Frolik duly arrived in November 1973, and was put in a hotel in Bridlington, Yorkshire, where Whiting was currently based. He carried around a tape-recorder disguised as a cigarette-packet, and had a suspicious air. He turned over his manuscript. As he said later:

The CIA was not too much happy about my trip – not because of the book, but because of the timing of the trip. They tried to convince me to postpone the trip to early summer 1974. I did not know why, but later when I read some articles in the British press that the hordes of CIA agents flooded London with the aim to penetrate the British trade unions, the bell rang.[9]

Leo Cooper approached Admiral Farnhill, Secretary of the D-notice Committee, which exercised an informal censorship over co-operative publishers. Cooper was unsure whether Frolik was genuine, and he did not want to get into trouble. Hanley's MI5 and Oldfield's MI6 do not seem to have found this CIA initiative altogether welcome. In January 1974, Whiting wrote an interesting letter to his publisher, urging him on:

It strikes me that the authorities are giving you the run-around probably because they are getting cold feet. They know all about our friend, what he knows and what he doesn't know. After all, he's been over here 4 times 'helping them with their inquiries'. Now I should like to see the book published a) because the sooner some of the public knows what's going on the better – I've got a vested interest in doing my little bit to help make our people aware, b) I'd like to help our friend who naturally has a pathetic desire to justify himself, c) I'd like to see you get a book on the market which will make you a lot of money . . . The big money is in the US and once the thing gets on the market there, there is little that can be done to stop it here . . .

Cooper started to float the defector around town, to nudge Farnhill with publicity. He put him in the way of the London *Times*, who interviewed him. They stressed his claim, by now a little more moderate, that three MPs were foreign spies: 'The three MPs had not been arrested because evidence was not found to stand up in court – but the three were confronted and their usefulness diminished: the London people have other means up their sleeve to damage these men and they have already done so.'

The publicity immediately attracted the attention of Josef Josten, the emigré Czech who ran the 'Free Czech Intelligence Office'. He contacted the publishers and offered to help. Josten, although he had personal reason to be interested (the Czechs had tried to assassinate him) had extensive links with MI5, and with right-wing political groups, including the National Association for Freedom.

Farnhill and the British Intelligence services decided to be co-operative. They agreed that Frolik was genuine, and said Cooper could publish, provided he removed about 50 per cent of the manuscript.

The items Farnhill wanted deleted were significant. Many of the objections had clearly come from Oldfield's MI6, which did not care to be reminded of its past embarrassments. Frolik's stories about MI6 officers or their agents were to be removed, no matter how old. Nor did MI6 wish its penetration in the 1950s via a Soviet Bloc agent in the exile 'Czech Intelligence Office' in London to be discussed. This could give 'a very damaging impression'. Admiral Farnhill also expressed pain at the slights against Heath and Macmillan. Other than that, 'the authorities' gave the book the green light.

Cooper signed up Whiting as the ghost-writer and told Frolik: 'We should be prepared to put up at least £1,000 advance.' News of Frolik's planned disclosures began to seep around Fleet Street, just as the General Election campaign began which was to oust Heath and return Harold Wilson to power for the last time.

Leo Cooper, a civilised, impecunious figure, had a few qualms about what he was being sucked into: 'Frolik volunteered right from the off about Stonehouse . . . When we asked for more details he had to go back and see what he was cleared to say. He also mentioned "someone who was connected with the Royal Family" and "someone in the Labour Cabinet". I was scared, frankly. I was a little publisher with no resources. And I had a feeling Frolik was going to turn out less important than we thought . . .'

Frolik's 'hordes of CIA agents' were part of a large propaganda and infiltration machine. Just as *Socialist Commentary* and *Encounter* had fought for Gaitskellism with CIA backing, so the propaganda work of Britain's 'Information Research Department' was supplemented by a large London-based news agency, Forum World Features. This was backed by the CIA. At the same time the CIA started to put its own agents into British trade unions. This was all seen as 'defence of the West'.

Meanwhile, as industrial conflict increased in Britain, largely because of the strains of high inflation, a group of domestic 'patriots' were gathering, preparing to take matters into their own hands. They saw an Armageddon coming, in which Communist agents, spearheaded by men like Harold Wilson and Jack Jones, would have to be fought on the streets. It was the last spasm of Empire, after all the disappointments and retreats of the post-war years: prominent among the new 'citizens' ' groups were retired MI6 officers and Army men.

George Young, the ex-deputy director of MI6 and indefatigable conspirator, was at the back of it. With a small group of far-right extremists, he tried to take over the Conservative group, the Monday Club, at the beginning of the 1970s. In 1972, he delivered an anti-immigration petition to Heath, the Prime Minister, for whom he had the utmost contempt. One of his associates, Harvey Proctor, later became an anti-immigrant Conservative MP, before being convicted of sex offences against teenage boys. Young and his petition were accompanied by a group who had links to the virulently anti-immigrant National Front. Young wrote at the time: 'The wogs are going to come in, whatever we do. My thoughts are on a wider national action, looking to a more distant future.'

The next year, Young was behind 'Unison'. This was a shadowy group which soon made contact with and recruited General Walter Walker, the recently retired Commander-in-Chief of the British Rhine Army. Another Unison backer was Anthony Cavendish, the former MI6 officer turned businessman. Both Young and Cavendish tried simultaneously to get into Conservative politics, although their views were unwelcome to Heath and the relatively moderate Conservative administration. Young obtained the Conservative nomination for Brent in north London: while a candidate, he produced a twenty-three-minute film called 'England, whose England?' which was generally agreed to be an extreme piece of racialist propaganda. Young was concerned about blacks, Jews and Communists, not necessarily in that order. He says: 'A group of us formed a committee. The issue was what to do if the government lost its grip . . .'

In February 1974, the government did indeed lose its grip. Heath, faced with a miners' strike over pay, took bad advice from the hardliners in his cabinet and called a snap election. He lost. By the narrowest of margins, Harold Wilson became Prime Minister again.

The 'Soviet agent' had returned to power. But there were many people determined that he would not last for long.

214

CHAPTER 11

There is no doubt that as of March 1974, James Angleton, serving as counter-intelligence chief under the DCI William Colby, and under the President of the United States Richard Nixon, still believed absolutely that the new Prime Minister of Britain was a Soviet agent. He said so, to anyone who would listen.

Interviewed in 1988, Leonard McCoy, who was to become deputy head of CIA counter-intelligence, remembers how the cadaverous Angleton briefed him in a 'set speech ... to senior officers' during Wilson's final premiership:

> The speech he gave me was to introduce me to the sophisticated world of counter-intelligence. It dealt primarily with the massive Soviet deception campaign. In 1959, the KGB decided it was going to create a worldwide deception operation and completely deceive the West ... Eurocommunism ... Wilson as a servant of the Soviet Union ... Soviet, Romanian, Albanian and Yugoslav ideological disagreements were all KGB deception operations ... it was not to be questioned, it was given. 'The earth revolves around the sun and everyone knows that'. It was in that spirit.

Hardened case officer as he was, McCoy confesses to some shock:

> I certainly wouldn't have dared to ask him for evidence. Angleton over the years had developed a reputation which almost precluded questions ... it was something like the J. Edgar Hoover phenomenon – that when he said something, it was coming down from a very high place and one accepted this. One doesn't say, 'Well, Sir, ah ... that sounds to me like a wild theory, what is the evidence for that?' One just didn't do that with Mr Angleton ...

Angleton had fitted the recruitment of Wilson perfectly into his picture of a Sovietised continent. First, he said, the KGB had moved into Eastern Europe on the back of the Red Army. Then it had fanned out into the Communist Parties of Western Europe. And finally, where the Communist Party was not in the ascendant electorally, as in Britain, 'other approaches' were used. The entrapment and recruitment of Wilson was part of this third wave of KGB subversion. McCoy continues:

215

What he said was that . . . Wilson was a Soviet agent. That control of Wilson was exercised by a senior KGB officer or officers, and that this relationship with the KGB went back to the time when he was travelling in and out of the Soviet Union on commercial assignments . . . the basis of Angleton's knowledge was that the KGB had a confidential relationship with a senior official of a West European Labour Party. And that this . . . party was on track to take over the government . . . and in order to ensure that the individual the KGB controlled would rise to the top of this party, his strongest competitor at that time would be dealt with with extreme prejudice by the KGB's 'wet affairs' department.

This, of course, was the theory about Gaitskell's 'assassination' plot broached by Peter Wright and Arthur Martin of MI5 thirteen years before, and taken up so enthusiastically by Golitsin. For all these years, Angleton had believed in it – not only believed in it, but built on it. He had tantalised his best British disciple, Peter Wright, with hints that there was further evidence. But there was none. The credulity that Philby had spotted in him in Washington in the 1940s was still present.

At some point in the preceding twenty years, the head of CIA counter-intelligence had gone mad. As McCoy shrewdly points out, a clinical definition of a paranoid state is the inability to distinguish between that which is possible and that which is probable. What, then, other than 'mad', is one to call a man who refused to distinguish between what was impossible and what was certain?

McCoy says:

Angleton and Golitsin's mentalities were similar. Golitsin was a deep person who was able to assimilate a large amount of material and synthesise a hypothesis from that. Angleton was the same way. The problem was that there seemed to be no governor on the mechanism in either case. And so, once Angleton had, so to speak, input this into his hypothesis about world domination by the KGB, it was there. I can't imagine what cataclysmic political event would have shaken that out of Angleton's theory . . . He certainly would not admit you had information or logic superior to his own, or which in fact meant anything, when one realised the vast territory that his theories covered. He thought, well, not cosmically, but at least *planetarily*, and one was a bit cowed in the man's presence.

As McCoy says, 'Angleton picked his audience carefully.' Peter Wright, too, was unshakably wedded to the belief that Wilson was a Soviet spy. Faced years later with the complete failure of corroboration to surface, his reaction was similarly entrenched:

I still believe Wilson was an 'agent of influence', briefed only occasionally.[1]

CIA officers who worked with Angleton are confident that he was certainly the dominant personality in his relations with Peter Wright. While the official heads of MI5 and MI6 were never warm towards US attempts to influence British politics, in Peter Wright, Angleton found a malleable fellow-spirit. Wright was always something of a hero-worshipper: in later life he used to tick off proudly the list of 'my powerful friends' – Victor Rothschild, Maurice Oldfield and James Angleton. It is a reasonable inference that Angleton – crab-like in his manoeuvres as always – sought to use Wright as a stalking-horse to spread doubt and suspicion, and foster renewed investigations of Harold Wilson. Wright's vanity and frustration could be appealed to: so could his belief that as an MI5 officer he was above the law – or at any rate above British democratic politics. As Wright insisted in a 1988 interview:

I certainly didn't, and most people in MI5 didn't have a duty to Parliament. They have a duty to the Queen . . . It's up to us to stop Russians getting control of the British government.

Wright was not the only one to come under Angleton's influence, of course. It is hard to say how many of the other British counter-intelligence men – Martin, McCaul, de Mowbray, Russell-Jones, Stewart, Elwell, Brooks, Wharton – who were exposed to these toxic rays from Langley, succumbed in some degree to their effect. It would have been their duty to consider seriously what the long-serving head of CIA counter-intelligence thought and said.

CIA and MI5 derangement with regard to the Prime Minister was paralleled – parodied is perhaps a better word – by the moth-eaten would-be junta which surrounded 'Unison' and George Kennedy Young. Some of these people could be found in the Carlton Club, home of traditional Toryism. Others had a natural habitat in a lesser-known building in Knightsbridge, near Sloane Square. This was the Special Forces Club at 8 Herbert Crescent, which has no name-plate and a discreet buzzer for entry.

Originally established for underground resistance veterans like Tony Brooks, the club was founded by Gerald Holdsworth of the Special Operations Executive immediately after the war. Thirty years on, it still had 1,800 members. Some were old SOE hands, or members of FANY, the peculiarly British ladies' Secret Service auxiliary, the 'First Aid Nursing Yeomanry' (the 'women with big bottoms sitting talking about how they were parachuted into Europe during the war,' as Freddy Beith of MI5 used to put it to his Fleet Street friends).

217

The membership lists were regularly topped up with newcomers, not all of whom were relatives or descendants of resistance fighters. The club bar tends to be populated by Lord Lucan lookalikes, with moustaches and blazers. A recent membership analysis, circulated to club members and seen by the author, showed that of 329 new members the largest subset (70) came from the Special Air Services – the crack undercover soldiers who go on Intelligence missions and kill terrorists. From the United States came twenty-six members, including twelve from the 'special forces'. And another twenty-two came from 'various Intelligence organisations in the UK and kindred organisations'. There were also a handful from the Marines, the Royal Air Force 'special duty squadrons', the Paratroops, Royal Navy 'special duties', Naval Intelligence, the Foreign Office, the Special Boat Service, and the police, ranging from a Chief Constable to a member of the Special Branch. In the category of honorary members ('Of such character and spirit ... that they might have served in the Resistance ... had circumstances allowed') were seven mercenaries from the forces of the Sultan of Oman, a British client state.

It was, as the club's Committee Chairman Hugh Verity puts it, 'a special people's club' (Verity had piloted a Hudson of the King's Flight into landings in occupied France, collecting and dropping agents). It also constituted a roll-call of the militarised side of the British 'Intelligence community' – there were probably very few Labour voters among the members. They had £30-a-head annual dinners at the Hyde Park Hotel, where guests ranged from the Prince of Wales to Al Haig. At reunions, mythical figures from the past would materialise, like Roy Farran, the hero of the SAS in Palestine. Reagan's CIA chief, William Casey, was an honorary member until his death.

Here, in rooms hung with portraits of old MI6 freebooters like Colonel Harold Perkins, and 'Jak' cartoons of hulking SAS men, could be found disaffected colonels left over from the past. One such was Colonel Robert Butler. Colonel Butler, too, believed that Wilson was a traitor. He confided – absurdly – to the author:

A Special Branch officer told me. He said 'We're trying to get him. He had £100,000 of Kremlin money via his friend Kagan. It's only a matter of time.'

This was the latest variant of the story that Kremlin gold had put Wilson into power. William Massie's MI5 friend gave him a version which said Sternberg had funded Wilson to the tune of £8,000 before the election. As such rumours have a tendency to do, it changed as it spread. At Army HQ in Northern Ireland, a press officer working on black propaganda, Colin Wallace, was in a good position to pick up gossip from the sizable MI5 contingent operating in the province. He scribbled down for future reference: 'Wilson had £60,000 for his election campaign from East German sources.' The basis of this, of course, was Sir Rudy Sternberg and his trust fund. Wallace also picked up gossip about Vaygauskas, the KGB man cultivating links with Wilson via Kagan. The Wilson stories were surfacing at every turn.

Butler, like many fighting men, has an engaging simplicity of mind. He sprang from a military family and is proud of it. His retirement home, 'Long Orchard', is in the Hampshire village of Sway, deep in the heart of the New Forest; there he keeps the family medals. They commence with his wife's Victorian forebear, General Sawyer, who beat down the Indian Mutiny. Next come the decorations of his father-in-law who won the Victoria Cross, followed by those of an uncle who served in the Punjab Rifles. Butler's own row of medals starts with the Military Cross.

Public school – Oundle – was followed by military cadet school at Sandhurst. He cut his teeth, like so many of the figures in this story, on Britain's attempts to suppress the Jews. He was in the Army during the pre-war riots of the Palestine mandate, and in 1944, as Israeli guerrillas bombed both the Arabs and their British masters, Butler's job was 'internal security'. He ran a bomb-disposal course for the military and the beleaguered Palestine police, to pool their knowledge of 'terrorist devices'. He personally defused eighteen captured Israeli bombs.

Butler moved on to fight a losing war in the old Empire's main theatres. There was a spell as a military adviser to the diminutive emperor Haile Selassie in Abyssinia where, he recalls, he became 'champion white jockey'. He was sent on a course in London in 1953 at the Joint Services Staff College – the mark of a high-flier. It is a difficult world to re-capture now, in which Suez and the dominance of the United States were yet to come. Butler and his Army friend Bobby Wynford, now Lord Wynford, stood loyally at the gates of Buckingham Palace during the Coronation of the young Queen Elizabeth. While at the staff college, Butler was among those treated to a lecture from a supposedly distinguished outsider – Sir Vincent Tewson, General Secretary of the Trade Union Congress. Butler stood up and attacked trade unions–no doubt to the applause of his fellow-officers– for tending to interfere with government. He was a right-wing, polo-playing athlete and yachtsman with a private pilot's licence – an ornament to a fading Empire.

Butler was posted to the colony of Kenya as a G1 – a senior military Intelligence officer – to fight the Mau Mau uprising. The guerrillas, led by Jomo Kenyatta, murdered white settlers in their beds. The British rounded them up: the deaths of detainees at Hola Camp led to a major scandal about British atrocities. Butler composed, for Army use, the 'Handbook on Anti Mau-Mau Operations'. His view of the insurrections was simple – the Russians were behind it. His contemporary Alec MacDonald, out in Kenya

219

and later to head MI5's 'D' branch, and the MI6 officers alongside them, probably did not dissent. Butler and MI6 worked closely together: he was to pick up the threads with them twenty years later.

He was posted to Cyprus, at the personal request of the new Prime Minister, Anthony Eden. One of the youngest Lieutenant-Colonels in the British Army at thirty-seven, he was to advise the governor on the growing Eoka insurgency. All the Intelligence professionals were clustered there now – Lord Chalfont, later to become a Labour minister; Stephen Hastings of MI6, later to become a Conservative MP; Tony Brooks; even Peter Wright from MI5, trying to spot the radio aerials of the guerrillas' leader, Grivas, so the Army could assault his HQ. It was there that Butler's luck ran out. In February, 1957, the guerrillas threw well-aimed bombs at his Landrover twice in a day. He was badly wounded. He still has the scars and shrapnel in his leg. His military world collapsed, and he was not to get the chance to re-live it for another eighteen years – until Harold Wilson came narrowly to power in 1974.

When Butler retired from his trailer business some years later, his views of the trade unions, foreigners and Communists had not mellowed. 'He had the experience of a walk-out by his work-force due to the subversive activities of a worker – a card-carrying Communist,' recalls his friend Wynford. Back in Sway, he began to brood on 'the forces of subversion', when Heath's pay conflict with the miners led to power-cuts. The Colonel puts it colourfully: 'I realised the Russians were behind it. I declared a one-man war on the Kremlin.' He felt the same, muddled, way about Heath:

I ran the ruler over him. He went with Hugh Scanlon to visit people in Spain during the civil war. I found that out. It was before he was a Tory. He was a penniless reporter on the *Church Times* . . . and then in 1974, he surrendered to the miners!'

As Wilson scrambled into office, Butler bombarded leading Tories with his paper on the 'Russian threat' – the right-wing back-bencher Anthony Kershaw, the aristocratic William Whitelaw, and Airey Neave, the barrister and Intelligence operative who had run MI9 – the 'escape line' service – after breaking out of Colditz himself.

After the war, Neave had continued to be involved with MI6 and emigré Poles. His wife Diana, who was in 'a secret underground organisation' during the war (probably the Polish section of SOE), also subsequently joined MI6. Neave, who was the shadowy backer of the campaign to oust Heath and put the rightist Margaret Thatcher into power, very much kept up his Intelligence connections. Butler's efforts to reach Neave were headed off: in the ramrod accusatory figure of the colonel, it was easy to smell a political liability. But he was pointed towards another one-man warrior against the Kremlin. This was recently retired General Walter Walker.

On the face of it, General Walker was a much more substantial military figure. He had fought the Indonesians in Malaya in the 1960s, and had recently held one of the most important military posts in NATO, as head of Northern Command until 1972. Yet his views on Harold Wilson – which Butler says he was responsible for – covered familiar ground. He privately told journalists that Wilson was a proven Communist. There was a 'Communist cell' in Downing Street. He had seen filmed interviews of Wilson on his return from official visits to the Soviet Union. The man was visibly shaking. This suggested to General Walker that Wilson had been compromised by the KGB.[2]

Walker had been working with George Young and his ultra-right 'Unison Committee for Action' group since 1973. He invited Colonel Butler to sign on. He said Unison were the best organised of the 'patriotic' groups then being formed. 'They have finance and are involved in many parts of the country.' An inner committee of bankers, businessmen and barristers met regularly, ready to act when 'there was a collapse of law and order'.

This committee included Ross McWhirter, a Conservative anti-trade union activist and, in a supporting role, Young's friend and admirer, the romantically patriotic former MI6 officer Anthony Cavendish, who was a great friend of the serving MI6 chief Maurice Oldfield. Butler says this small group was interested in 'high-level planning – putting pressure on the Tories to – how can I say this? – make *arrangements* in the event of emergency.' Walker's role, as it evolved, was to enrol a corps of thousands of 'volunteers' throughout the country.

Another supporter was Colonel Ronnie Wareing, who has the triangular moustache, like a shaving-brush, that one sometimes sees on elderly military men. He was an MI6 agent who had fled the 1974 collapse of the dictatorship in Portugal. Wareing, who had been wounded behind enemy lines in war-time, had been living in retirement there for twenty years. He gave lectures in counter-subversion to officers at the Portuguese staff college who were struggling to hang on to the colony of Angola: they had no recent battle experience to compare with the British, and Wareing went out to Angola in 1972 to advise. At the same time he reported to MI6 on the state of the Portuguese military. After the regime had tumbled, his 'controller' said, 'I'm getting out: you'd better do the same.' Wareing fled, and offered to help Butler fight Communism at home.

This group of self-appointed national saviours were in touch with serving Army men. Butler, for example, thought nothing of seeking out a general, Sir Hugh Beach, and asking him a curious hypothetical question:

Whether there was not some point at which a senior officer's conscience would preclude him from obeying an order which was patently not in this country's interests.[3]

221

To Butler's chagrin, Beach seemed perfectly loyal to the idea of obeying orders. He said that the Conservative *Daily Telegraph*, from which Butler was quoting, was a 'right-wing rag'. Exasperated, Butler said that, surely for example, he would disobey an order to shoot the Royal Family. As Butler himself records, 'Beach stroked his chin reflectively and said, "It would depend on the circumstances."'

The colonel's reaction to what he termed this 'amazing display of left-wing thought' was interesting. Through Colonel Wareing, he contracted an old friend still serving in MI6 and asked what the Secret Service files had on Beach. Butler and Wareing refused to disclose the MI6 officer's name to associates because in Butler's words, 'He was acting illegally.' In his late sixties, this officer had been parachuted behind German lines in the war, and was still in service, lecturing to young MI6 officers. Butler claims:

Back came the reply that they believed both Beach and his wife to be Marxists, and that Beach's career had benefited from a friendship which he had developed with Harold Wilson.

Sir Hugh and his wife were not, of course, 'Marxists' or anything of the kind. The interest of this story lies in the Colonel's thought processes: when General Beach refused to interest himself in what some might regard as questionable propositions, Butler reacted by suspecting him of being a Soviet agent. Butler had no more success in approaches to General Farrar-Hockley and Field Marshal Lord Carver. As a consequence, Butler regarded them both with grave suspicion ('Carver never spoke out against defence cuts sufficiently,' he said.)

Butler's question about disobeying orders was significant. An unknown serving Army officer wrote in 1974 in *Monday World*, the journal of the right-wing Tory Monday Club, about the Army's political role, saying some soldiers believed they would be 'called upon to act in England'.

David Stirling, founder of the war-time SAS, also had long-standing Intelligence connections, and was 'exchanging ideas' with Unison. In July 1974 he said: 'Moving into installations owned by the government is a very delicate business, and that is one reason for the secrecy surrounding those people who have already made positive plans.'[4] Stirling, who later felt impelled to set up a parallel and more presentable volunteer body called 'GB 75', said he felt 'uneasy about the highly militaristic and very right-wing nature of Unison's management, and therefore of that management's long-term intentions.'[5]

The minds of George Young and his friends turned repeatedly to the idea that the Queen's name could be invoked to overthrow a 'traitorous' Labour government. In one of his books, *Subversion and the British Riposte*, Young spelled out the theory that the heads of the Intelligence services could con-

222

ceal their doings from the government. He quotes approvingly Professor R. V. Jones, war-time MI6 scientist, who around this time gave an address to the US Defence Department saying most Intelligence chiefs should have discretion in what they chose to reveal to 'the highest elected authorites' because:

> The chief of an intelligence service might have cause to suspect the minister concerned not merely of indiscretion, but of a positive sympathy for some foreign power or some dissident element in his own country.'[6]

Young went on to suggest Intelligence chiefs could confide in the Queen and urge her to use her power to dismiss 'corrupt or revolutionary Ministers'. The aim would be to overthrow 'treason in high places'. In a passage headed 'When Treason Can Be Right' he asks rhetorically, 'What of a government willing to pursue détente to the point of complete surrender? At that stage, the officers of a special operations executive and of the security service may feel that the only course of action is to grab their Top Secret files and head – if not for the hills – at least for the United States embassy.'

The idea that the Secret Services worked for the Queen was the justification MI5 men also gave to themselves for acting above the law when they carried out burglaries. They liked to see themselves as 'the military servants of the Crown' who did not have to obey the government. The British Army had proved itself remarkably reluctant to enforce the Labour government's policy in Northern Ireland in May 1974. They pronounced themselves unable to break an insurrectionist strike by Protestant 'loyalists', and keep essential services going. This was then used as justification for preparing an elaborate contingency plan which Army officials in Belfast recall seeing.

It drew on the 'transition to war' blueprints which already existed for a Soviet conflict. The scenario went: another strike in Northern Ireland would require a flow of supplies across the North Sea. The mainland ports might be crippled by sympathetic strikes, and this would require the introduction of protective 'control zones' around them. Meanwhile, terrorist attacks could be expected from groups like the Baader-Meinhof gang as British troops were withdrawn by plane from Germany. It would be necessary to guarantee their passage as well, and this would require a 'control zone' around Heathrow airport.

The 'control zones' were originally in the 'transition to war' schemes to protect the East Coast from 'saboteurs' on behalf of the United States, which would use the Liverpool area as a major reinforcement staging-post for a Hot War in Europe. There was one other aspect of the 'transition to war' book – British passenger liners, 'including the QE2', would be immediately requisitioned by the military (exactly as occurred at the outset of the 1983 Falklands War). Curiously, in the summer of 1975, when the secret agitation against Wilson reached its height, just such a proposal was made by three 'Army and secret service people', who asked Cunard officials if they would be prepared to make over the liner as a floating detention centre, apparently for the Cabinet.[7]

Clearly, as in 1968, the smell of a coup was in the air.

Airey Neave, the Tory intriguer with Intelligence connections, took a carefully provoking line. While publicly deploring the danger of 'an unofficial force', he and other Monday Clubbers put their names to a call for the next Conservative government to create a 'voluntary reserve' of citizens. The Labour Defence Minister Roy Mason responded with a violent speech in August 1974, attacking what he called a 'near-fascist groundswell'. He asked Wilson to have the 'private armies' investigated by Hanley's MI5.

It was Peter Wright of MI5 who got himself involved, and he seems to have been playing a double game. Wright had been hanging on rather precariously in Leconfield House since the arrival of Hanley. 'Jumbo' had moved him out of harm's way, as he thought, by making him his 'personal consultant' on counter-espionage, with access to all the files. He encouraged him to take extensive round-the-world trips in search of obscure caches of VENONA material, and to spend as much time as he liked in Northern Ireland, looking into phone-tapping prospects. It seemed that his career was simply to fizzle out.

Wright already knew Airey Neave. He had been to quiz him about one of his fellow Colditz inmates, a journalist named Michael Burn, whose name had surfaced as a friend of a friend of Anthony Blunt. Wright imagined, or hoped, that Burn might have said something Communistic during his imprisonment in Colditz Castle. He was disappointed, although 'Neave gave me a lot of valuable information about inmates who were either traitors or potential ones.' This gave Wright a good excuse discreetly to approach Neave again, as one of the suspect 'plotters' against Wilson. He says: 'The . . . interview with Neave was whether he knew of any secret armies or proposed ones in the UK. He came out of the interview very well, showing himself to be loyal to the Crown and to British democracy. I do not believe that he was a conspiratorial type of man.'[8]

This was scarcely a surprising conclusion. Wright was, if anything, even more extreme than Neave in his personal views. And the words 'loyal to the Crown' had a special double meaning for people like Wright. As he said later: 'Officers of MI5 were not Government employees. I do emphasise this; it's a very real point.' Loyalty to the Queen but not to Harold Wilson was the motto of the plotters.

Wright now presented himself as an infiltrator. He circulated the information that he was a 'patriotic officer' who wished to blow the whistle on treasonable Labour ministers – Wilson himself, Stonehouse, Mac-Dermot. He thought of approaching the financier James Goldsmith

224

using a cover-name. He knew Goldsmith to be concerned about the state of Britain, and also to be interested in Intelligence and security – he was later to aid his nephew, Antonio von Marx, to set up a British security firm, Zeus, employing many ex-Intelligence and military figures. (There is no reason whatsoever to think, of course, that Goldsmith was involved in any misconduct: indeed he became acquainted later with Marcia Williams, and was knighted by Wilson.)

Wright claims he managed to get an introduction to the Unison committee, headed by George Young. When Young and Goldsmith were named in British parliamentary proceedings as contacts of Wright, both said they had never heard of him.

But it was only partly true that Wright was engaged in an Intelligence operation. He was bitter about the fading of his career and the meagre pension he seemed likely to get. He was looking for security work, for which he would no doubt have been prepared to exploit his access to secret files. Victor Rothschild offered him money to 'moonlight' for him: he wrote in a letter which Wright preserved, offering to pay him to 'keep himself up-to-date' on terrorist intentions which might endanger members of the Rothschild family or the family firm. He made it clear that Wright would need to 'renew certain acquaintanceships' after retirement for the deal to work.

Wright admits in his memoirs that he tried to get a group of businessmen to hire him, but that he did not succeed. The story seems to have circulated in garbled form afterwards: Chapman Pincher says he was told by a Tory peer and former Cabinet minister, who 'was keen to get rid of the Labour government', that a 'dissident MI5 officer' had been put in contact with him, and that he had sounded out several large companies on his behalf, after hearing that the MI5 man was 'so incensed by the activities of two particular Ministers that he decided it was urgently in the national interest for them to be exposed.'

Was Wright just gathering Intelligence, as he told Hanley (and no doubt Rothschild), or was he trying to make contact with the 'private armies' to do a deal on his own behalf? Either way, his behaviour put into even wider circulation the rumours that Labour ministers were 'traitors'.

Meanwhile, Mason, who had asked for the inquiry into the 'private armies', was told there was nothing to worry about. He banned contact between serving officers and the 'volunteer' organisations, which eventually petered out. Mason promptly became the victim of a 'security' smear: in December 1974 William Massie in the *Sunday Express* retailed the false story he had been given that MI5 were anxious about Mason's own social indiscretions.

The 'private armies' added to the strange atmosphere surrounding the new

Wilson administration. But they were ultimately unreal. There was no evidence of CIA backing, which would have been necessary for any serious coup. Nevertheless, there were serious points of tension between the Wilson government of 1974 and the US Intelligence community. The transatlantic loyalties of all the military/Intelligence link-ups – ABCA, UKUSA, CAZAB – meant that British soldiers and secret servicemen were often more influenced by the opinions and needs of their American senior partners, than by those of their own government. This was the legacy of the perpetual war.

Wilson thwarted the secret Anglo-US Intelligence marriage over four matters: satellites; the renegade CIA officer Philip Agee; Southern Africa; and détente. During his first administration, Wilson had commissioned the academic Sir Stuart Hampshire, on Dick White's recommendation, to write a review which headed off GCHQ's costly demand to keep up with the US by launching its own spy satellites. It was a reasonable decision – the UK had no space launchers of its own and could never afford them. Hampshire's reward had been to be questioned and smeared by Peter Wright as a 'security risk', because he had known Blunt, Burgess and James Klugmann in the 1930s.

But the result was that technology was leaving GCHQ behind. Although UKUSA provided for full sharing of information and research and development, as the US made dramatic leaps in the quality of satellite technology, it became understandably reluctant to make a gratuitous present of its fruits to a country which did not pull its weight, and whose leader was someone about whom successive US administrations had long had secret 'reservations'.

The dramatic leap in satellite technology had just occurred as Wilson came to power. The first two RHYOLITE launches took place in 1970 and 1973 from Cape Canaveral. Their key feature was that these satellites could hover and continuously intercept Soviet and Chinese high-frequency radio transmissions, ranging from missile telemetry data to Moscow phone calls. The Soviet Union was, it was believed, unaware that this could be done. They made obsolete the simple photographic spy satellites and low-level satellites which could only make a pass over an area of interest for a few minutes daily.

The US did not propose to share its RHYOLITE take with the Wilson government, although US Intelligence satellite ground stations were based in Britain, at Menwith Hill, Oakhanger, and Croughton. Only after Wilson left power did the new CIA director, George Bush, negotiate an agreement with Wilson's successor, James Callaghan, to share the satellite 'take'. A new pair of advanced RHYOLITES were developed and launched in 1977, after Wilson had left office. The protection of the RHYOLITE secret from interference by both Britain and Australia (where there was also a CIA satellite receiving dish at Pine Gap) was a high CIA priority.[9]

During Wilson's last government, the US consequently concealed 'sources'. One example was when a Soviet pilot defected to Japan with the latest 'Foxbat' fighter. The Soviet Union planned a retaliatory raid on a Western airbase in Germany to steal a NATO plane. Although the US discovered this, US officials say it decided to conceal the threat from the British, to protect sources. The US had also set up, by 1965, an intercept station at Vint Hills Farm, Virginia, to intercept and successfully break British diplomatic transmissions.[10]

If satellites were one issue, Philip Agee was another. The young CIA officer, who resigned in 1968 after the collapse of his marriage, had finally finished up in London, where he was working on a devastating unauthorised biography exposing the CIA – the first of a series of books that ended with *Spycatcher*. While MI5 trailed him at the behest of the CIA, they could do little to harass him or have him expelled – at any rate, while Wilson's liberal appointee as Home Secretary, Roy Jenkins, was in power. All they could do was code him 'J' in the ports watch-list – an instruction that MI5 were to be phoned, discreetly, as soon as he presented his passport for travel abroad.

While Agee was given a free hand under Wilson to wage his war against the CIA, the Agency was experiencing the backwash of the Watergate investigations at home, and the wholesale disclosure of 'CIA secrets' by the Pike Committee and the Church Committee. Agee finished his book in Cornwall in summer 1974. The CIA, meanwhile, 'planted' stories that he was a drunken operative who had leaked information to the KGB in Latin America.

As Agee later discovered, the CIA briefed the State Department more or less accurately on him, but prepared a very different account for propaganda purposes. The accurate briefing said:

It was inevitable that sooner or later the CIA would be faced with the problem of a disaffected staff employee such as Philip Agee. He is the first one in the Agency's history and has written a book about his Agency experiences . . . Agee's overall performance as an operations officer was competent . . . he was regarded as bright, aggressive and well-motivated . . . there is no definitive evidence that Agee's activities are sponsored by opposition intelligence services.

For the guidance of the press, however, the line suggested on Agee included the following elements:

Egotistical . . . essentially shallow . . . always borrowing money . . . consummate preoccupation with sex . . . stole the children from their mother . . . recently acquired mistress . . . grandiose schemes for making money . . .[11]

By autumn of 1974, six months into Wilson's government, Agee was gathering like-minded radicals around him in London and saying at press conferences: 'There are good reasons, we believe, for waging a campaign to destabilise the CIA ... today we begin the campaign of exposure.' Only after the departure of Wilson from the premiership were Hanley and MI5 able to oblige their CAZAB partners by having Agee expelled by a new Home Secretary.

The third point of conflict was over Chile, Angola and South Africa. Despite the steady unravelling of CIA malpractice on Capitol Hill, William Colby's Agency was still being asked to perform 'covert operations'. Just as Richard Helms had been ordered to 'make the economy scream' in Chile in the process that led to the overthrow of Allende, now Angola was the target. The collapse of the Portuguese regime, and the subsequent likelihood of her African colonies gaining independence, led to a covert decision to fund a civil war in Angola, to deny leftists 'an easy victory'. This operation, code-named IAFEATURE, required, ideally, the use of two 'surrogates', Britain and South Africa, to provide Intelligence support in the region and, eventually, some 'deniable' fighting men. Africa was traditionally in GCHQ's zone of responsibility – since the fighting had begun in earnest in southern Africa, GCHQ had broken the codes of the DGSE, the Portuguese security police, and was targeting Angola from a base in Ascension Island, and Mozambique from Mauritius. South Africa, meanwhile, had successfully solicited GCHQ and CIA liaison to operate its own listening base at Silvermine, the surveillance station near the Simonstown naval base, and in return got information on 'revolutionaries' from the US.

Wilson refused to have anything to do with South Africa – he stopped selling arms and broke off liaison with Silvermine. Nor would the British government assist the Angola project. In 1975, they closed down the Mauritius base and turned Ascension over to the US. The CIA finished up recruiting British-based freelance 'mercenaries' in 1975, and shipping them out from London behind Wilson's back. The CIA operation was both immoral and pointless: but once again there was a complete mismatch between the Western Intelligence agencies, with their fixation on doing down 'Communists', and a British Labour government which had some sympathy with the leftists in Portugal, Angola, and indeed Chile. Wilson's more idealistic ministers also wanted to refuse to sell arms to the CIA-backed colonels' regime in Chile.

The upshot was yet another attempt by MI5 to push one of Wilson's ministers out of office – this time it was the leftist Judith Hart, who had been in Wilson's 1964–70 Cabinet. In the summer of 1974 London was awash with untrue rumours that Judith Hart was part of the 'Communist cell'. MI5 officers hinted to their journalist friends that there were 'certain ministers' who could not be relied on to see Intelligence information because they might pass it to 'freedom fighters'.

The truth was that, in mid-1974, Judith Hart was intensely concerned about the arrest of anyone in Chile who opposed the regime. Many of them, of course, were Communists. Hart phoned British Communist Party headquarters in London, knowing they would have the best picture of the situation. MI5's 'A' branch were, as usual, tapping the party's phones. The transcript of Hart's innocent contact was excitedly circulated within MI5, and throughout Whitehall.

Hanley felt constrained to report these matters to Wilson. He claimed that there was evidence which might also show that Hart had attended a Communist-backed international peace conference in Warsaw in 1950. At the back of it, it eventually transpired, was a twenty-four-year-old blurred photograph from the *Daily Worker*, captioning among others a Mrs J *Tudor* Hart, the wife of a prominent Communist Party member.

Some original bureaucratic confusion might have been understandable. The names and the appearances were similar. But the affair had odd features. When her 'blacklisting' was investigated afterwards by two journalists, Roger Courtiour and Barrie Penrose, they discovered that a Special Branch inspector had made field inquiries about Judith Hart back in 1950 when she was a Labour candidate in the seaside town of Bournemouth, and had been told by her agent, Freddy Reeves, that there had been a mistake about the photograph . . . Yet the picture had remained on file.

Secondly, Mrs Hart had already been a minister for ten years. This meant that she had survived 'negative vetting' at least twice already, whilst four other ministerial candidates, some if not all quite innocent, had been denounced to the long-suffering Labour Prime Minister. Clearly, someone in 'K' branch had tried their luck with a much more denunciatory report to pass up to the new Director-General, who had little personal experience in counter-espionage. When Wilson was succeeded by Callaghan as Prime Minister, MI5 tried their luck again, claiming to him there was still a 'security query' about Mrs Hart. This was after Wright's retirement.

On the evening of Thursday October 17, 1974, Wilson was obliged to send for Judith Hart in a scene reminiscent of the interview seven years earlier with the equally indignant Niall MacDermot. It delayed her arrival at the weekly 'husbands and wives dinner' of left-wing ministers at the London house of the economist Thomas Balogh. Barbara Castle records:

Judith came in late, obviously upset. Halfway through the meal she disappeared, and Tony [her husband] said she wasn't too well as she had just had a great shock. Harold had sent for her and told her she was

229

being positively vetted. When Judith came back, she poured out her heart to me. The very idea that anyone could consider her a communist! It was all no doubt to do with her contacts in Chile. Didn't the fools realise there were even more non-communists in gaol than communists? Harold had accepted her assurances, but she was clearly shaken to the core.[12]

The episode left Hart, who was later made a peeress, convinced of one thing. As she said later of Wright's confessions of an MI5 plot against the Wilson government: 'I am one of those who know that the allegations in his book are true.'[13]

The last issue on which Wilson and the CIA did not see eye to eye was détente. Wilson took seriously the efforts to put together a European security and co-operation agreement at Helsinki in 1975. When he became Prime Minister, he informed a shocked and resentful 'K' branch that they were to suspend efforts to suborn and recruit Soviet diplomats: he did not wish to prejudice the 'Basket 3' negotiations on human rights by some diplomatic incident. Wilson also made it clear that he had a low opinion of the 1971 expulsion of 105 Soviet 'spies', which had disrupted trade relations. At Helsinki, where he was conference chairman, his Foreign Office advisers caused a considerable row by repeatedly trying to delete the phrase 'peaceful co-existence' from his speech. They said it was Leninist double-speak favoured by the Soviets and which they in fact regarded as giving them a licence to attempt world domination. This pressure to interfere with Wilson's speech came from the US.

Wilson would have been reckless to underestimate the potential effect of these conflicts and 'security' questions on the stability of a government disapproved of by the CIA. There is evidence that it was CIA initiatives which discredited and ousted both Willi Brandt, the Socialist Chancellor of West Germany, and Gough Whitlam, the Labour premier of Australia in this period. Brandt was discovered to have a Soviet agent, Gunter Guillaume, as an aide in his office. The information came from code-breaks and investigations by MI5 and the CIA. Whitlam clashed openly and repeatedly with the CIA about their unacknowledged use of Pine Gap: he was eventually dismissed by the Governor-General.

Gunter Guillaume was arrested on April 24, 1974 in Bonn. A refugee from East Germany who joined Brandt's Social Democrats, he had been originally regarded as a security risk, but was eventually taken on to Brandt's personal staff. When new evidence emerged against him in 1972, Brandt was advised to keep him on his personal staff while enquiries were made, but to exclude him from access to secret material. Brandt's willingness to follow this advice from the West German security services proved to be a mistake: when Brandt was eventually forced to resign as Chancellor, he said that Guillaume had inadvertently been allowed to see secret material, and there had been signs that 'my private life would have been dragged into speculation'. He denied that he had been subject to blackmail and later protested that a campaign of defamation had been set in motion against him. The affair had involved at least four of the West's Intelligence agencies, working in partnership with each other – the West Germans, the French, MI5 and the CIA. Peter Wright, who played a part in the traffic decipherment which preceded Guillaume's exposure, regarded Brandt as yet another of his 'enemies'.

Wright's disclosures in fact throw a remarkable new light on the discrediting of Brandt, whose 'Ostpolitik' had softened relations with the Soviet Union. In his private correspondence, Wright makes it clear that elements in MI5, sharing their information with the CIA, claimed that old war-time Soviet ciphers threw suspicion on Brandt himself of being a Soviet agent.

This allegation, while as absurd as all Wright's other 'interpretations' of his material, shows there was much more to the Guillaume affair than was realised at the time. In the early 1960s, the British got hold of a pile of wartime coded radio traffic intercepted by the Swedes. Sweden interpreted her 'neutrality' as meaning that she was willing to pass Intelligence material over to the UK, but not to the Americans. Britain and the US shared the material behind Sweden's back nonetheless, and, using VENONA techniques, broke out lists of individuals' names spelled out in the radio messages between Moscow and the war-time resistance groups in Scandinavia. Brandt's name was among them. This was scarcely surprising, as he was fighting in the Scandinavian resistance at the time. But Wright decided this made Brandt a Communist:

> Brandt . . . himself is very suspect. In the war, he left Germany and was firstly in the Danish resistance and then the Norwegian. He was one of the leaders of a big communist network run by radio from Moscow. In the second half of the sixties, we broke most of the traffic between the communist resistance in the war and Moscow . . . With the help of Danes, we definitely identified Willi Brandt in the traffic.

Wright goes on to describe how the British code-crackers of GCHQ subsequently broke into East German Intelligence cyphers as well, and identified a woman spy: 'As a result of this success, we had a conference with the BfV [the West German security service] who explained there was another agent in the traffic who appeared to be more important. I briefed GCHQ . . . they managed to get some more out which showed the agent was very close to Willi Brandt.' Guillaume was thus identified, and Wright adds, menacingly: 'I believe Brandt resigned to stop further inquiries into himself and his associates.'

One cannot demonstrate direct CIA involvement in the Brandt case: one can merely observe that the CIA were parties to the Intelligence manoeuvring which occurred, and that the upshot was that Brandt himself was discredited and forced out of office: from 1967 onwards, Angleton and Wright were not only in and out of each other's offices: they attended the formal CAZAB sessions where the world's 'White Commonwealth' swapped techniques and gossip.

There is more evidence in Australia of direct conflict between Whitlam and the CIA, involving the British as junior partners. After coming to office in 1972, Whitlam ordered the Australian equivalent of MI6, ASIS, to stop co-operating with the CIA. Whitlam addressed a party meeting on 4 May 1977 at which his former ministerial colleague Clyde Cameron took careful notes. Cameron's notes show that 'Whitlam told . . . how, shortly after he came to office, he discovered that ASIS had been employing agents in Chile to work with the CIA and the military junta . . . to bring about the downfall of the Allende government. He had told the head of ASIS . . . "to stop, in short order" . . . ASIS had done the same thing in Cambodia.' He opposed the Vietnam war: he also objected to ASIO (the equivalent of MI5) security probes into his staff. His Attorney-General 'raided' ASIO offices in March 1973 and carried away files on the grounds that ASIO was concealing material from the government. James Angleton himself made clear his views about this: in a later TV interview quoted by William Blum in *The CIA – A Forgotten History*, he said the CIA seriously considered breaking Intelligence relations with Australia at that point. 'This bumbling Attorney-General moving in, barging in – we were deeply concerned as to the sanctity of this information which could compromise sources and methods and compromise human life.' When his interviewer protested, 'But it was done by the elected Attorney-General of the country,' Angleton cut in, brusquely and revealingly: 'I am not disputing the fact that he was elected. I don't understand the point of your question.'

In August 1974, Whitlam fulfilled an election pledge and set up a Royal Commission of Inquiry into the Intelligence services, under Mr Justice Hope. It was a more restrained version of the US Church Committee, but such a move caused chills among British Intelligence men.

Peter Wright of MI5 had a further, personal reason to feel hostile to meddling Labour politicians. The head of ASIO, Peter Barbour, was moved to be Consul-General in New York in September 1975 (the head of ASIS had already been removed). The head of MI5, Sir Michael Hanley, had promised Wright that after he retired to Australia, Barbour – one of the old Intelligence regime – would be persuaded to give Wright a chance to earn money as a 'counter-espionage consultant'. With Barbour's removal, Wright faced life out in the cold. Meanwhile, as Cameron's diary records, 'Whitlam told [us] that the CIA was upset by us appointing new heads of ASIO and ASIS and [with our] having Hope looking into it.'

After Whitlam ousted the heads of both ASIO and ASIS, he threatened not to renew the lease of Pine Gap – the CIA's most important satellite base. His concern was that CIA men were funding opposition parties, fomenting strikes and trying to undermine his government. The CIA adopted a threatening tone, and tried to work through sympathetic Australian military men. There is continuing controversy about what contacts there were between the military, the Governor-General Sir John Kerr, the British and the CIA in this period. But there is no doubt that on November 8, 1975 the CIA again threatened, through Washington liaison with ASIO, to cut off all Intelligence links with Australia. On November 10, the ASIO station in Washington telexed Sydney at CIA behest, saying, 'CIA cannot see how this continued dialogue with reference to CIA can do other than blow the lid off these installations [Pine Gap].' Whitlam said later, 'The CIA cable to ASIO was on a service-to-service basis ... the information was to be kept from the government.' But Whitlam's new ASIO head immediately showed it him. Whitlam later said that the British were also spying on the Australian government – 'the Brits were actually decoding secret messages coming into the Foreign Affairs Office.' Whitlam's knowledge did not help him. On November 11, the Governor-General used an archaic constitutional right to dismiss Whitlam as Prime Minister in the Queen's name.

The CIA had a lot of power if a left-wing politician played into their hands. A Guillaume or a Pine Gap would rapidly finish Wilson off, and he knew it.

There were two reasons why Wilson's relations with the US Intelligence community did not develop into a full-scale crisis. The first was that the US administration was itself in turmoil: during 1974, President Richard Nixon was driven to resign by the revelations of the Watergate cover-up, and by the end of the year, in the parallel series of exposures of CIA misconduct, James Angleton himself was ousted by CIA chief William Colby. The second reason was that Wilson himself did not last as British premier for very long. The new CIA chief, George Bush, subsequently mended fences with the British.

Why, then, did Wilson go? It was an uneasy time for him. He was unpopular with elements of the CIA. He was badgered by MI5. The illwill within his own 'kitchen cabinet' led to a spate of uncalled-for leaks about Marcia Williams, her children, her temperament, her family and her friends. Some of the Conservative Party, cheated, as they thought, of office, tried to spread and magnify every rumour they could (an enormous furore was kicked up in the Conservative press, for example, about the 'Land Deals' affair, in which it appeared that Marcia Williams' brother Tony Field had been having some perfectly legal business with land developers while working in Wilson's office at No. 10).

Within eighteen months of regaining power, Wilson decided to put a date on his resignation. He had certainly taken the decision to quit by the summer of 1975, when he took practical steps, after his holiday in the Scillies, privately to notify the Queen at Balmoral and to organise a time-table for departure. The last eight months of office were a characteristically Wilsonian period of manoeuvring to present his eventual announcement in the most artistic light – 'so no one will be able to say I was pushed out,' as he later told Barbara Castle.[14]

But Wilson actually decided to organise his resignation immediately after a blazing confrontation with Michael Hanley, the head of MI5, in early August 1975. He accused members of Hanley's MI5 of plotting against him. This accusation the evidence shows to have been perfectly true. The chief plotter was Peter Wright, trying to achieve, as he later admitted, 'what would have been the biggest thing in my career'.

The only mistake Wilson made was in thinking that the 'plot' had only recently come into being. Officers of MI5, together with colleagues in MI6 and the CIA, had been plotting against Wilson, one way and another, for more than fifteen years.

At the time Wilson decided to resign, his close friend Joseph Kagan was under renewed full-scale investigation by 'K5'. Kagan's flat in Queensway, near Hyde Park, was bugged and if he spoke to Marcia Williams on the phone, his conversations were tape-recorded. What 'K5' feared and what Peter Wright hoped, was that they might find evidence of the Prime Minister's political secretary passing government information to Kagan, who in turn would be passing it on to the KGB.

Simultaneously, Peter Wright was trying to exploit the impending publication of the CIA-inspired Frolik memoirs to discredit Wilson. He was passing MI5 information to journalists to suggest that Wilson had deliberately concealed the spying activities of John Stonehouse when he was a minister. Other material was leaked to journalists recalling the time twenty-five years before when Wilson had sold jet engines to the Russians, and worked for Montague Meyer; the implication was that he was a Soviet agent.

At the same time, MI6 officers under Oldfield stirred the pot by making available the old NKVD photograph of Wilson in Moscow, which they passed to MI5 for the 'Worthington file'.

Finally, Peter Wright tried to get his hands on the full 'Worthington file' and to whip up his colleagues into joining him in a deputation to Wilson which would secretly blackmail him into resigning, by presenting him with detailed documentation of all his mysterious trips to Moscow.

This was an impressive collection of MI5's sick fantasies. They went hand in hand with the continuing public cover-up of the Blunt affair, and an awkward admission to the US – at the May 1974 CAZAB conference – that the former Director-General of MI5, Sir Roger Hollis, had still not been cleared of suspicion that he too was a Soviet spy. Had these facts come tumbling out into the light of day in 1974, there would have been a second Watergate on the British side of the Atlantic. Like the CIA, the British Secret Services would have been exposed, purged and reformed.

Instead, the truth was suppressed. This was partly because Wilson himself became lost in conspiracy theories – he launched a bizarre attempt to blame his misfortunes and those of the Liberal leader Jeremy Thorpe on South African Intelligence. He was encouraged in this belief by MI6, in Wilson's last and least successful bid to exploit the resources of 'Intelligence'.[15]

Thorpe was homosexual, and lost the party leadership after a police investigation into a plot to assault Norman Scott, a fellow-homosexual. Marcia Williams had now been made a peer, as Lady Falkender. Wilson's attempts to 'save Jeremy Thorpe's skin' (as she put it) were assisted by Lady Falkender. Wilson proudly described her as 'Detective-Inspector Falkender'.[16] The Liberal leader was charged with conspiracy to murder, and, although acquitted, he was completely discredited, as was Wilson for his support of him.

Even with the publication of *Spycatcher* thirteen years later, the truth did not come out. Wright's book was the first admission of MI5 'plotting', but the self-serving work of this 'fuddled old farmer' (as his colleague Harry Wharton called him) was far from truthful. It downplayed his own role severely.

What happened in the real world was, in fact, less complicated than subsequent disinformation made it out to be. As Frolik's defector memoirs proceeded towards publication, his CIA-approved ghost-writer and his British publisher Leo Cooper had what appeared to be an enormous stroke of luck. Just before their trip to Washington in September 1974 to take Frolik through his Stonehouse allegations again, a menacing paragraph appeared in *Private Eye*:

Delicacy and good taste prevent me from mentioning the names of two Labour MPs who are at present under investigation by the Special Branch for their connections with an Eastern European Embassy. However, I should point out that the Czech Embassy, which covers espionage and 'dirty tricks' for the whole Soviet bloc, allocates £20,000 a month for 'gifts', 'retainers' and consultancies to politicians, journalists, civil servants and others who might prove useful.[17]

When Charles Whiting arrived in the States, he recalls: 'I spoke to Frolik's CIA handler on the phone . . . Frolik told me "One of your Ministers" – I thought he said "in the Treasury" actually – is going to defect ... He definitely said, "One of your Ministers is going to run away".' He also spoke at length about Stonehouse, 'under the watchful eye of the CIA' as Cooper put it. Whiting recalls: 'He said that Stonehouse sold the Czechs knowledge of the war-time microwave communications system for a great deal of money, and that the damage to the UK had been irreparable.'

Frolik's knowledge about Stonehouse seemed to be increasing by leaps and bounds. Sure enough, in November, John Stonehouse, who must have been under continuing surveillance, suddenly disappeared. He was under growing financial pressure from a law-suit over his unsound banking venture, the British Bangladesh Trust, and decided to abscond. Having obtained a dead man's passport, he left his clothes in a pile on a Florida beach.

It is tempting to accuse the CIA of bringing about Stonehouse's financial downfall in order to discredit him. But apart from the odd hints shortly before his disappearance, and the mysterious vulnerability of many of these Wilson-related Intelligence targets to financial harassment, there is no evidence of it. What is indisputable is that it led to maximum embarrassment for his Prime Minister, Harold Wilson.

It was now only a matter of time before the story came out. Frolik was given a further big financial incentive to talk freely and boost his sales. His advance on royalties was a modest £1,750, split with his ghost-writer. But, just before Stonehouse absconded, the CIA cut off his $150 weekly pension. Cooper's files show that he wrote: 'My friends from the Washington company probably got the idea that I could become rich through this book and broke off all previously given promises and stopped all payments to me.' Even before the Stonehouse disappearance, Cooper was trying to catch the interest of *Times* columnist Bernard Levin. He told him Frolik's material 'would make your hair stand on end ... he names three trade union leaders who are household names as being directly in the pay of either the Russians or the Czechs and has also named to me nine MPs.'

But when Stonehouse absconded, Whiting said excitedly: 'It could be our sensation.' They wrote to Frolik demanding more details and asking, 'Is this the scandal you were warning us about?' According to Frolik, two MI5 officers flew out again to see him in December 1974 – he does not name them, but clearly they, too, were stimulated and excited by Stonehouse's disappearance. They must have hoped he had defected.

Leo Cooper sold the Stonehouse story to the *Daily Mirror*. There was nothing political or conspiratorial in what he did: the *Mirror* were the biggest payers.

Consequently, on December 16 and 17, 1974, Harold Wilson was faced with two successive front pages, blaring out the 'security sensation' that Wilson's former minister had been a 'contact for a Communist spy ring'. This was much better news for the CIA than the imminent publication in

London of Philip Agee's *Inside the Company*. But it was bad news for Wilson. Wilson demanded of Hanley and MI5 the same day whether there was any fresh evidence against Stonehouse since the uncomfortable session in Wilson's Cabinet room five years before. Hanley said 'No'. Wilson immediately made a fighting parliamentary statement that 'No evidence to support these allegations has come to light.' He said:

> One of the reasons I made this statement was because of the publicity. Since I know the facts, I thought it right, particularly in the interests of the family, that these should be said. It is causing great distress. His mother, I understand, has had a serious heart attack due to the anxiety and pressures. I really think that the Press in question, or some of them, are really hounding them . . .[18]

Wilson also took a dig at Frolik which was accurate enough, but not calculated to make the affronted Czech feel any more appreciated:

> One has always got to face the possibility of defectors when they come out of the country where they were and find their capital diminishing – intellectual capital – trying to revive their memories. But nothing has been said this week that was not said in 1969 when the most rigorous inquiries were made. Not only was it proved there was no evidence, but there has been no evidence since . . . Yards of newsprint have been devoted to the lie I have disproved. I hope they will use their newsprint in printing the truth instead of the lies.

Nothing could have been more alarming to the beleaguered Wilson than what happened next. The right-wing Conservative back-bencher Winston Churchill immediately dashed off a handwritten private letter to him (a copy was preserved by Wilson):

> Dear Prime Minister,
> In case he may be unaware of the fact, I think your friend Sir Joseph Kagan should be informed that his houseguest, a delightful Russian, Victor Lessiovsky, is a senior serving officer in the KGB.
> May I congratulate you on your statement in the House today. The innuendoes to which Mrs Stonehouse is being subjected are intolerable.

Churchill clearly meant well: he said later, 'I was just passing on a message to someone who had been very kind to my family' (Wilson had always been admiring of Churchill the elder). Churchill was almost certainly unaware of the significance of what he was saying: there was no reason for him to have known of the history of the Kagan affair. It appeared that Churchill had met Lessiovsky in the summer of 1974 when on a family visit to the Soviet Union, and he had been pointed out to him as a KGB officer. How did he know he had been visiting Kagan? Churchill said later that an acquaintance

237

had mentioned to him in the Commons that Lessiovsky had been visiting, and wanted to send Churchill his regards. But he never knew for sure whether Lessiovsky had been in the country or not.

There were several extremely strange aspects to this incident. Kagan says he never had a visit from a Russian called Lessiovsky, although he admits to dealings with various other Russians. Douglas Houghton, one of Kagan's MP friends, whom Churchill had mentioned as a possible source of the story, says he does not recall any such thing. If the KGB were really making covert contact with Kagan, the last person they would have sent was Lessiovsky, and the last thing Lessiovsky would have done was gratuitously advertise his presence to a Tory MP. For Victor Lessiovsky was notorious. The previous year, he had been 'blown' in the US in a CIA-approved book by John Barron listing dozens of identified KGB officers. A former assistant to UN Secretary-General U Thant in New York, Lessiovsky was an 'active measures' propaganda and deception operator. His photograph and an unflattering description of his activities had recently appeared in the London *Daily Mail*.

This leaves only two possibilities. Lessiovsky could have been a Soviet 'provocation', a sinister presence designed to throw suspicion on Kagan and hence on Wilson. Such activities were, after all, Lessiovsky's job. The Russians were not to know that Churchill, instead of circulating malicious gossip about Wilson, would behave in an honourable fashion and send him a private warning.

Alternatively, the Lessiovsky story could have been untrue, but put into circulation as an MI5 'provocation', designed to encourage Churchill and his Tory colleagues, acting in good faith, to think the worst of Wilson. One argument in favour of this is that Peter Wright mentions Churchill as one of the MPs he wanted to 'prime' to stir things up. But Tony Brooks and his colleagues in 'K5' must have been unaware of such a plot, if it existed, because Wilson punctiliously passed the Churchill letter on to MI5, and Brooks shot up to the north of England again with photographs of Lessiovsky, anxiously asking his amateur agents if they had seen him.

Like many of the counter-intelligence conundrums which so confused MI5 officers, the Lessiovsky question is unanswerable without new evidence. Churchill's role appears to have been totally honourable. Only one thing is certain – that it was not evidence that Joe Kagan was a Soviet spy, only that someone wished him to appear that way. 'K5' were soon to be plunged into a new and bizarre Kagan investigation; but first the Frolik 'caper' had to work itself out.

Right-wingers who wished to hear more about the Frolik material now materialised. Stephen Hastings, the Tory MP and former MI6 officer, approached Leo Cooper. Cooper remembers: 'I went with Jilly, my wife, to Hastings' flat. His wife took Jilly off to the kitchen and then Hastings turned to me and asked me if I could tell the bits that I wasn't able to publish . . . It was an unsubtle attempt to get ammunition, particularly about the trade unions.' Hastings later wrote to Cooper that it was 'a matter of the highest importance': he eventually got hold of the deleted parts and read out Frolik's passages about trade unionists under parliamentary privilege, with the air of exposing a great scandal. He no doubt thought he was performing a public service.

Two days after Wilson's angry statement about Stonehouse, Josef Josten, the Czech emigré who had helped with the manuscript, received a 'confidential' approach from Geoffrey Stewart-Smith of the 'Foreign Affairs Research Institute', a far-right body with South African links. Stewart-Smith offered him and Frolik money to provide evidence that Wilson was 'lying':

> Mr Wilson has publicly stated that he [Stonehouse] was not working for the Czechs. Your colleague, Mr Frolik, says that he was . . . I happen to be going to Washington in mid-January, and I was wondering if you would very kindly consider writing to Frolik . . . and asking him if he can produce any hard evidence that Stonehouse was working for Czech intelligence . . . While my financial position is weak, I may well be able to pay both you and him for services rendered. I am sure you are aware of the potential political significance of the fact of the public reaction if we could prove that Wilson was lying to the House of Commons – a British Watergate cover-up?

This letter was passed to Cooper, who kept it. Josten himself, who was linked with the right-wing National Association for Freedom, thought the Frolik story could destroy Wilson. He wrote later: 'I must admit that when I was entrusted with the original ms of [Frolik's] book I kept it safely locked in a bank. Disclosure of its contents might have brought down a government – a step that even a very outspoken national daily decided not to take on itself.' He also advised Frolik to tone down any criticism of MI5 in the book 'so as not to antagonise them.'

At Christmas, to the acute embarrassment of the Labour Party, Stonehouse was discovered with a woman friend in Australia, disguised as a Mr Muldoon. He was arrested and brought home, charged with fraud. A certain amount of silence fell in Britain pending his trial, for legal reasons. It was eventually scheduled to open in April 1976 – by which time Wilson had resigned, and absented himself from the firing-line.

In the spring of 1975, an MI5 officer travelled to Atlanta, Georgia, ostensibly to re-interview Frolik about his Stonehouse recollections. Frolik does not name him – it may have been Peter Wright; it was certainly one of his friends. This MI5 officer, knowing Frolik was in touch with the media, dropped veiled hints about Wilson into his ear. Frolik dutifully relayed

239

them to Leo Cooper when he visited him shortly afterwards to make the final preparations for publication of his memoirs and Cooper passed them on to Bernard Levin of *The Times*:

> He claimed MI5 had been to see him ... he said there was one senior member of the Government under suspicion at this very moment ... a senior member of the Board of Trade in past years had been successfully subverted.

Cooper says scornfully, 'It was all teasing. Frolik always knew somebody who had seen a dead donkey.' But one would only have to collate this 'Intelligence' with the rest of the gossip circulating in Fleet Street to point the finger at Harold Wilson. It is reminiscent of the concise description of propaganda as practised by the war-time 'Political Warfare Executive', given in Philip Warner's history *The Secret Forces of World War II*:

> Information of this type, now known as disinformation as it is designed to mislead, is usually spread through the press of neutral countries. The process of deceiving neutral journalists is not, however, simple ... he must be given the impression that he is making important discoveries for himself.

A month or two later, on the eve of Frolik's publication, it was undoubtedly Peter Wright who was responsible for a much more blunt approach to the press.

The second Czech defector, Frantisek August, whom Wright regarded as a corroborative witness, was suddenly brought over to England – for unexplained reasons. Wright, as he later admitted in a private letter to Pincher, encouraged Lord Rothschild to tip Pincher off. Pincher recorded in 1977 (deferring to the libel laws as Stonehouse was still alive):

> In the summer of 1975, I was summoned to see a former MI5 officer to be given some most intriguing information about an MP [Stonehouse]. A defector called Frantisek August ... was about to return to London under a false name for a brief and secret visit ... If I could induce August to talk, he could give me a most interesting story concerning the activities of a well-known Labour MP who for libel reasons must be nameless. It was said that this MP was not just an agent of Czech intelligence but an officer of the KGB.[19]

Wright's admission to Pincher that he was behind this 'planted' story in 1975 is the most direct confirmation of the 'Wilson plot'. Yet, oddly, Pincher does not appear to have made this fact public.

In November 1975, Frolik was put up by the CIA to testify to the Senate judiciary sub-committee. By now, it was clear just how many words were being put into his mouth by interested Intelligence parties. He delivered a

240

long statement denouncing CIA agents who blew the whistle, in terms clearly aimed at Agee. He also mentioned a number of British Intelligence embarrassments which had been kept out of his book. Among the other titbits was mention of a Prague film director who was 'a personal friend of Princess Margaret and Lord Snowdon' and whom the Czechs had planned to approach.

But the CIA also authorised Frolik to assert loud and clear what the Labour Prime Minister of Britain had already officially denied: that successful Czech operations 'which because of their significance constituted a danger to the security of the US and the NATO states' included:

John Stonehouse, a member of the British House of Commons, former Minister of the British Government (Minister of Aviation, Minister of Technology, Postmaster General) – subject is under investigation today for embezzlement, fraud and insurance fraud. His case officers are Capt. Robert Husak and Lt.-Col. Josef Kalina.

Depressed by the pressure he was being subjected to, the wretched Frolik eventually wrote to his publisher with an authentic cry from the heart:

I am not an exhibitionist who wants to see himself on TV or read his name in the newspapers. All I ever wanted from all this was to make some money . . .

The defector had been used to embarrass and perhaps alarm Wilson. Wilson was not frightened that the pending trial of Stonehouse would reveal the Prime Minister's double life as a Soviet agent – but it was reasonable of him to think that MI5 and the CIA would dig up as much public dirt about Stonehouse as they could. What, for example, if Stonehouse had been taking bribes from US aircraft companies while he was a minister? This was something Wilson later expressed unease about.

Wilson was being 'de-stabilised'. Those hostile to him would no doubt have said it was all Wilson's fault in the first place for appointing shifty characters to office. Those of his cynical friends like Joe Kagan would say: 'Give me a name – just give me a name and I'll make a case against anybody.'

Kagan himself was next in the firing-line. Peter Wright lurked in his own office or his laboratory, having dark private sessions with middle-aged sympathisers about 'the traitor, Wilson'. But the real action was going on on the fourth floor, where 'K5' was based.

This joint counter-espionage section was the glamour department of MI5. Since the merger with MI6 counter-intelligence, it ran about 150 agents, not just in Britain, but all over the world. There were KGB majors in Copenhagen and GRU captains in Geneva. Liaison with the CIA was maintained through Thomas Russell Blackshear of the London station, who had a pass to walk in and out as freely as he pleased (at least until 'K' branch dis-

241

covered the full extent of CIA disingenuousness about information-sharing under Wilson.)

The section was big – it had about thirty officers, many seconded from MI6. For bureaucratic reasons, it was jointly headed by MI5 and MI6. This meant that any rumours and activities in the one organisation rapidly got back to the other. Harry Wharton – 'Buddha' – was the MI5 section head. His MI6 counterpart was a veteran, James Speirs. Aged fifty-one, he had been in the Army or MI6 all his life. He stayed on in the military after the war in Singapore, and Stewart Menzies' MI6 put him under the Far East region – with diplomatic cover in Burma and then in Indonesia. His Cold War experience came in Berlin and Munich at the end of the 1950s: he was Sir John Rennie's station chief in Tel Aviv under Heath in 1970–72 and was now on his last posting. He retired at the end of Callaghan's Labour government in 1979 with a classic set of political-industrial connections: a member of the Special Forces Club, he became 'Group Security Adviser' for the Gallahers international tobacco company and then an Intelligence 'adviser' to the Sultan of Oman.

Speirs, under instructions from MI6, does not like to talk about the Wilson case: he says he did not have 'very much' to do with it. The section worked closely with 'K6', the secret registry where agents' 'Y' personal files were held. This was headed by Ray Whitby and Robert Holden. The other old war-horses of 'K' branch had been dispersed – some, like Charles Elwell, Barry Russell-Jones and Michael McCaul, to 'F' branch's big new domestic revolutionaries and terrorism department; others, like Hal Doyne-Ditmass, the veteran of Movements Analysis, to computerise the 'watchers' charts in 'A' branch, or, like former colonial policeman Martin Fleay, to serve in Hanley's personal secretariat.

There was what one 'K5' officer calls a 'Wilson coterie' in the section. Wharton had run the Lyalin case himself, back in 1971, and had personally interviewed Harold Wilson. His chief agent-runner, Tony Brooks, had been continuously running a stable of informants around Kagan for four years now without getting anywhere. This was why the Lessiovsky case had caused such excitement. Kagan persisted in associating with Russians – for example, he was now regularly entertaining the chief Russian trade representative, Victor Ivanov, at his North of England home. Ivanov was a senior KGB officer, as Brooks knew very well. When 'agents' like Arthur Parker said excitedly, 'Why don't you *do* something about these Russians?' Brooks would reply grimly, 'Ultimately it's a matter for the Prime Minister.'

If Brooks had been doing his surveillance job thoroughly, he would have made an extremely interesting discovery in 1974 about the Prime Minister's friend. Throughout this period a new figure had appeared on the scene at Kagan's offices in Elland. This was Douglas Morrell, Kagan's old associate from the days in Bucharest after the war. Oddly, he and Tony Brooks had

242

something important in common – they had both been in SOE, Brooks in occupied France, Morrell in Spain. Morrell was helping Joe Kagan organise a tax avoidance scheme. The pair of them were setting up a dummy company in Europe with a Panama registration and a Swiss bank account. The idea was that Kagan's company would ship out enormous quantities of denim cloth, sold at artificially low prices as 'seconds'. The Panama company could then sell it throughout Europe at full price, and the resulting profits would disappear into a Swiss bank, free of British taxation.

Brooks ought to have noticed something: as he told Arthur Parker, he and his wife, while on a 'Fly-Drive' holiday in Switzerland, had actually bumped into Kagan at a Swiss airport. Morrell denies that he was ever recruited as an agent by Brooks, or that he ever met him. But his activities could scarcely have escaped Brooks' attention. Once again, as with John Stonehouse, the exposure of financial malpractice was eventually to have dramatic consequences.

In 1975, the Kagan situation took a startling new turn. One of Doyne-Ditmass's 'watchers' from 'A4' reported excitedly that he had been following the Soviet Embassy's main KGB agent-runner. He had left the embassy, crossed the Bayswater Road and gone into a nearby flat. To whom did it belong? Joe Kagan.

A full-scale investigation was mounted into the links between the KGB man, Boris Titov, and the Lithuanian emigré who had so long been sus-pected of being a spy. Kagan's flat was thoroughly wired for sound by 'A' branch (MI5 officers from 'K' branch are the source for this). All the rooms were bugged.

To the excitement of the 'watchers' it was rapidly discovered that Kagan was still in occasional contact with Marcia Williams, Lady Falkender. This was scarcely surprising. When Kagan rang his friend Harold Wilson he would find himself speaking to his political secretary. He knew her – though less well than other Labour politicians he had cultivated, such as Lord Houghton in his own constituency. At one point, the 'watchers' even taped a conversation in which Kagan was raising the topic of whether and when Harold Wilson should resign. This too, was scarcely surprising – Wilson had been promising his wife he would retire for years.

But the most thrilling discovery the watchers made was that, on one occasion, Titov, Kagan and Marcia Williams were all apparently linked at the same time. The Russian was in one of the bedrooms while Kagan was in another room, apparently in conversation with Marcia on the phone. This had the flavour of possible indiscretion, if scarcely of espionage. Kagan snorts at the fruits of such eavesdropping: 'Arthur Parker was my London agent for textiles and he was the one who was using the London flat at the same time. He was probably having Titov measured for a suit! Lots of the Russians from the embassy went to him to get suits.'

243

In an effort to get confirmation that it had been Titov who was visiting the flat, 'K5' guardedly put the suggestion to one of their most sensitive sources – a Russian from the 'Soviet Colony' whom they had recruited. His code-name was HEAVY BREATHER, and he was being 'run' by a young MI6 officer, Peter Troughton. Troughton, who had connections both with the W. H. Smith bookselling firm and with the British Royal Family, was only twenty-seven. He had been in MI6 for five years and had just returned from a two-year tour in Indonesia, under diplomatic cover.

HEAVY BREATHER gave some confirmation. The development was the talk of the 'Wilson coterie'. In the hands of Peter Wright and his friends, these discoveries were later the sole basis for the claims, emanating from both MI5 and MI6, that Wilson's establishment had been 'bugged' and that Marcia Williams had been leaking secrets to the Soviet Union.

It was all nonsense, of course. Eventually James Speirs decided the whole thing must be another Soviet 'provocation', and took matters into his own hands. He went to a Soviet embassy function, where he sought out and had a meaningful conversation with the Russian diplomat, Titov. He introduced himself as 'Colonel Packer'. This was all that was needed to convey to the Russian that MI5 were aware of his activities. For 'Colonel Packer' was a 'house name', adopted as cover for years by a variety of MI5 and MI6 officers. It was so thoroughly 'blown' by then that the KGB would instantly deduce that their opponents were onto them. 'We wanted to warn the Russians off,' says one 'K' branch officer.

Brooks, for whom Kagan had become something of a preoccupation, remained suspicious. He told one of his agents at Kagan's premises: 'I'm sure the Prime Minister has the interests of the country at heart.' But he was not so sure about his friends. When Wilson made Kagan a peer in 1976, Brooks must have felt that much of his recent investigation had been a waste of time. But he stayed in MI5 long enough to get some satisfaction. Customs officials, alerted to the activities of Kagan and Douglas Morrell, pursued the new member of the House of Lords tenaciously. They raided him, extradited him when he fled abroad, and put him in jail for fiscal offences connected with the Panama company scheme. It was oddly similar to the fate of Stonehouse.

Peter Wright was not level-headed about the Kagan affair at all. He tried to persuade the cautious 'Jumbo' Hanley to authorise a full-scale investigation into Wilson himself. He failed. But, by his own account, he did manage to take a quick look at the contents of the MI6 dossier on Wilson, kept apart from the main 'Worthington file' in the Director-General's safe. He claims he saw copies of agents' reports on Wilson's days of Russian jaunting, in which there were 'missing weeks' when Wilson's whereabouts were unknown.

There were meetings between Wright and some of his colleagues, in his

244

laboratory or office – less often at the bar of the Eye Club. In his memoirs, Wright claims that they tried to persuade him to engage in a 'plot' against Wilson, in which they would steal and leak MI5 files. This is completely untrue.

What happened was that Wright tried to talk his colleagues into 'doing something' about the Prime Minister. He approached a number of officers in 'K' branch, who had, of course, been directly involved in the Kagan investigation. He also sounded out some of his old contacts in MI6 and elsewhere. Wright had no doubt persuaded himself that what he and they separately knew added up to a damning case against Harold Wilson. He tried to interest them in a proposition which, while irregular, was not strictly treasonable. The idea of wholesale leaking of the files as a last resort was something he kept at the back of his own mind – he was determined not to be cheated out of 'the biggest thing in my career'.

What Wright suggested was that, in the national interest, it was their duty, knowing what they did about Wilson's 'treachery', to confront the Prime Minister privately. First they would amass documentary material. He, Wright, in his capacity as consultant to the DG, would pull the MI6 file from the DG's safe. This, he assured them, showed conclusive evidence of Wilson's treason.

There were never more than half a dozen trusted colleagues to whom Wright put this proposition, but he was correct that between twenty and thirty officers in all heard something was in the wind. It was a junior officer on the fringes of 'K' who supplied accurate descriptions of the attitude of some of the participants to the author, unaware that they coincided with Wright's own eventual admissions. From his position, it was clear that a large group of 'K' Branch officers shared his knowledge.

Nobody in 'K' wanted to know. Brooks said the proposition was not only improper but 'a waste of time'. Doyne-Ditmass said that the right way to proceed in such circumstances was surely to approach the Cabinet Secretary, Sir John Hunt. Wright now confesses that he then announced he would do the deed alone, if need be. This important confession was first made in an interview filmed by BBC TV in Tasmania in 1988:

I believed that we could do this as a secret operation, that we could create a situation which would frighten Wilson into going . . . to make it clear to him that he was heavily compromised. I was intending to pinch the records from the DG's safe about Wilson's journeys behind the Iron Curtain . . . show it to him. Me, show it . . . I had no difficulty in seeing Wilson whenever I wanted to . . . I thought of starting off in [these] terms: 'There were a number of us who didn't trust him and the reasons for it were as follows . . .' and I would have produced the documentary evidence. Eight or nine of my colleagues knew I said I was going to do this.

245

I honestly think Wilson would have folded up – he wasn't a very gutsy man, you know. Everybody was on my side but most people faded out of it. It needed a leader to do it . . . I only knew what some of the evidence was from verbal briefings, because I'd never actually read all the documents – but I was convinced it would never reach the public domain. Wilson would just go.

Wright was living in a fantasy world. But some people's actions were innocently helping his fantasies along. Another of the younger officers in 'K5' was Jeremy Wetherell, who had been transferred over from 'F' branch. One of the 'K' branch officers recalls:

Wetherell was Harry Wharton's blue-eyed boy. It was Wetherell who first told him that MI6 had just released to the K6 registry in MI5 a copy of an old photograph of Harold Wilson in Moscow in the company of a young woman. Wetherell was friendly with some of the women in K6 – there are a lot of women in the office. MI6 said the picture had just 'become available' for circulation because their source was no longer vulnerable. This picture didn't seem to be damning in itself, but it definitely showed Wilson with a moustache, when he was Overseas Trade Secretary. The point seemed to be that it must have been taken with a KGB approach in mind. But Wilson never reported any such approach.

Anthony Cavendish, the former MI6 officer and confidant of Maurice Oldfield, later told the same story. His version was that Oldfield had circulated the evidence that 'came into his hands' more widely than merely to MI5. Privately he says, 'Maurice told me about it.' Publicly, in his memoirs, he is almost as assertive: 'It was always very clear to me from things he said that Maurice was somehow involved in the sudden departure of Harold Wilson from the premiership.'[20]

The other boost to the circulation of Peter Wright's fanatasies was provided by *Private Eye* and the newspapers. One of the *Private Eye* staff was Patrick Marnham, a Catholic public schoolboy of a rather secretive disposition. He says that in 1974, a package of information about Wilson was sent to a friend of his, a reporter on *The Times*. Because it was too hot to handle, the anonymous reporter passed it over to Marnham. Marnham implies that other such dossiers were passed direct to the *Eye*. He says, in a rather cavalier manner, that they all came from MI5.

Marnham's value as a witness is limited by his refusal to name the *Times* reporter, his inability to produce the full dossier from which he quotes, and his failure to substantiate the MI5 claim. But his dossier certainly contained remarkable material. The general line was that Harold Wilson was a Soviet-Zionist agent. There was a full, if misleading account of Wilson's long-forgotten role in the sale of jet-engines to Russia:

In 1947, the year in which Wilson became responsible for all overseas trade, the Rolls-Royce jet engines were the best in the world ... Surprising then that not just one but two RR engines were able to be exported to Russia in 1947 to be copied ... the Russians paid for only one example of each engine ... RR themselves objected, the Asst. Chief of Air Staff (Intelligence) objected, other Service ministries objected – but all were overruled ... It would be interesting to see the Board of Trade, Foreign Office and Treasury papers relating to this particular incident ... what and how many other arrangements were arrived at over the years between the Board of Trade, the Russian Trade delegation and British traders such as, for example, timber importers? ... the Russian trade delegation and its proliferating agents flourished and expanded ... the principal cover for Soviet intelligence agents ... In London, protests to the Foreign Office from the Service ministries were of no avail and they had to see their own information-gathering more and more severely curtailed whilst those of the USSR were proliferating, and all went hand in hand with the Burgess-Maclean-Philby-Blake and no doubt other members of the subverted native pro-Russian spy ring.[21]

The attacks on Wilson focused on his links with Montague Meyer, Rudy Sternberg and Joe Kagan. Meyer's links with the groundnuts scheme connected him to Plummer and hence to Sternberg in a paranoid series of accusations which certainly bear the hallmarks of the Peter Wright school of counter-intelligence. Marnham appeared to take this farrago seriously.

Auberon Waugh also kept up the attack in *Private Eye*, fortified by Massie's MI5 gossip and Marnham's 'dossiers', as well as by the leaks from Candler of the old No. 10 staff. A Christmas card Mikoyan had sent Wilson in 1961 was filched from No. 10 and given to the *Eye*; papers burgled from Wilson's store at Buckingham Gate were also offered to the magazine, with the selling-line that they showed Wilson had been secreting 'government documents'.

During this period, Waugh continued to write a series of attacks on Kagan and Sternberg, coupled with assertions that Wilson was a Soviet agent. After the Stonehouse allegation surfaced he wrote sarcastically:

There is not a shred of evidence that Stonehouse was a Czech spy, apart from the first-hand evidence of his Czech spymaster. No wonder Wilson decided to let him stay in the government ... I have never attempted to hide my belief that Wilson is a Russian agent ... I think I would be prepared to back my intuition with a small wager. Perhaps I will place it with my old friend Ian Mikardo, the House of Commons book-maker ...[22]

Mikardo was a left-wing Labour MP and 'East-West trader'. Waugh wrote facetiously about Wilson a few days later, speculating that, 'He will spend the autumn of his days in the miserable loneliness of an official flat in Pushkin Sq, Moscow ...'[23] The following month he recalled that Sternberg (to whom Wilson had now defiantly given a peerage) had accompanied Wilson to Moscow in 1971: 'How strange that Sternberg, the man at the centre of the government Leipzig trade fair uproar in 1962, should have got a peerage in a list which included this name: KCMG Maurice Oldfield.'[24] In the autumn of 1975, mentioning a frivolous suggestion that Henry Kissinger was a Soviet agent, Waugh added: 'I have never attempted to disguise my belief that Wilson is one, recruited in Moscow and London in 1956–58.'[25] The following year he denounced him strongly over Angola:

> Wilson's efforts to secure a Soviet victory in Angola would be shocking if they were not so foolish. Nobody can seriously suppose that after seven years of Wilson ... the English have any fight left in them. If Wilson really wants to help the Russian effort, he should arrange for as many mercenaries as possible to join the FNLA ...[26]

Just a few days before Wilson was to announce his resignation, Waugh recorded: 'Today is Wilson's 60th birthday ... the old crook hasn't done too badly ... I still think Wilson is probably a Soviet agent, but I am sure he is an unwilling one, and in any case, I've decided not to expose him for the present.' After Wilson's departure, Waugh amused himself with a long fantasy in *The Spectator* implying that Wilson was photographed in Moscow in the summer of 1959 by the KGB, and blackmailed. In succeeding years he went on to repeat whenever the subject of Wilson and MI5 came up, that Wilson had been a Soviet agent. In 1977, for example, he observed: 'Maurice [Oldfield] is a gentle retiring man. To look at him you would never guess that it was his threat of resignation which precipitated Wilson's retirement in 1976.'[27] He continued to hint that Wilson had managed a 'cover-up' over Stonehouse and also over 'The political news story of the century, which concerns political control over security and the steps taken in this country to prevent a scandal even greater than the discovery of an Iron Curtain spy in Willi Brandt's private office.'[28]

Private Eye was very much the focus of anti-Wilson campaigners. Hartley Shawcross wrote a letter to *The Times* in 1974, about the corruption he had discovered at the Board of Trade at the end of the 1940s. This was widely taken to be a reference to Wilson: Shawcross became an unlikely guest at *Private Eye*'s weekly lunch at a pub in Greek Street, where he guardedly talked about Wilson's social connections in the old days at Montague Meyer. It all became grist to the mill.

Meanwhile, what had happened to Peter Wright's plot to make Wilson resign? He claims that he fully intended to go ahead with it alone, but

Victor Rothschild and Maurice Oldfield talked him out of doing so. He says Oldfield refused to back his plan and instead forced him to go and confess to Hanley what had been going on, at which Hanley went 'as white as a sheet.'

It was scarcely surprising. Even the normally placid Wilson, confronted with such an accusation from MI5 officers, might have become very angry indeed. Sufficiently angry to sack Hanley and have MI5 purged from top to bottom. He had an instrument to hand already – thanks to complaints from the MI6 officer, Stephen de Mowbray, that he was convinced Sir Roger Hollis really had been a spy, the Cabinet Secretary had re-launched a secret review of the whole mole-hunt under Sir Burke Trend. Once Wilson was fully briefed on that mess, he could turn the Trend Report into an instrument to destroy MI5 and Sir Michael Hanley along with it. Yet he did not do so. This is the biggest mystery of all.

There is no doubt that Wilson got news, late in the day, of the tide of talk against him. Martin Gilbert, the historian, had already warned Wilson that at a 1974 lunch-party at the house of his relative Michael Sacher, of Marks & Spencer, Marcia Williams had been accused of leading a Communist cell in Downing St. The journalist Harry Pincher admits he was there and had talked loudly of, 'Problems with MI5 over the security clearance of Marcia Williams'. Pincher had been talking to Marjorie Halls, the widow of Wilson's Private Secretary and the acquaintance of various MI5 officers.

George Weidenfeld the publisher lunched with Wilson in early August 1975. He had much more grave news – the whole of London was now awash with talk about the 'Communist cell' in Downing Street. He confided in Wilson – according to Marcia Williams – that the Gilbert house-party had been a much more worrying affair than he might have imagined. He had heard reports of it via Minnie Churchill, who, like her husband, did not let politics interfere with personal honour and decency. There had been an MI5 officer there who had spoken very freely. Pincher, in his later memoirs, confirmed this in a veiled fashion. He said of the lunch, 'Wilson did have cause to suspect that his enemies in MI5 might be assisting.' At the lunch there had been 'several people there I knew well, including a former senior figure from the Defence Ministry.'[29] Pincher did not name this mysterious figure. He was clearly someone more senior than Peter Wright.

On hearing this intelligence, on August 7, 1975, Wilson was furious. He called in the head of the rival service, Maurice Oldfield of MI6, and asked him whether he knew of any 'plots' against him by members of MI5. Oldfield said, yes, he did. There was a section of MI5 which was 'unreliable'. Oldfield was referring to Peter Wright, and the scheme in which Wright had tried to enlist him. There is really little doubt that Oldfield had this conversation, although there is some uncertainty about the circumstances. Both Pincher and Anthony Cavendish have testified in print that they received a version of it from Oldfield. The journalist Barrie Penrose says that he heard a similar version from the other participant – Harold Wilson himself. This makes three good witnesses, even though Oldfield is dead now, and Wilson silent.

Wilson's next move is also well-documented. He angrily called in Sir Michael Hanley, and, putting the onus on Oldfield, said he had been informed by the head of the Secret Service that there was an 'unreliable' section in MI5. Wilson went on heatedly that these people had been plotting against him, accusing him and Marcia Williams of being 'Communists', and trying to bring him down.

The present British government has tried to pretend that this conversation never took place. But Penrose and Pincher, two journalists from different political sides, both testify that it did. Penrose tape-recorded Wilson saying that Hanley had confirmed there was a 'problem' with some officers, but that it had all been dealt with by him. Pincher testifies: 'Wilson ... told me personally ... that Hanley had replied that he believed this to be true, but that only a handful of officers were concerned.' This seems good enough testimony to conclude that the Prime Minister of Britain was not telling lies ...

The key point is that the head of MI5 admitted that some of his officers considered the Prime Minister himself to be a security risk. It is no accident that successive British governments have refused to confess that this conversation occurred – it is probably the most significant achievement of the publishers of *Spycatcher*, flawed as the book is, that their disclosures have made further cover-ups impossible.

It is no accident, of course, that successive British governments refuse to admit it. To confess that this one conversation took place is to admit the whole of the 'Wilson plot'. It is to admit that MI5 contained some destructive and stupid people, who thrived there. It is easy to confess this about any other second-rate British government department, but not about an arm of the British Secret Service. To do so would be to put MI5 in its proper place. And this is one retreat from fantasies of power which the governors of Britain do not yet seem able to make.

Hanley admitted that there was a group of 'young Turks' in the office (although most of them were pretty long in the tooth). He appears to have suggested that the preoccupation with Wilson was an outgrowth of the frustration of some of these men, over many years, because of their inability to resolve the 'mole-hunt' within MI5 itself.

According to Wilson, Hanley did not, even at this stage, confide in him the identity of Hollis, the chief MI5 internal 'suspect'. He merely said that 'one of his predecessors' had been suspected. This was what Wilson told Marcia Williams immediately afterwards, and he later said the same to

Pincher. In an interview with Barrie Penrose, Wilson later spoke in detail about his challenge to Hanley:

> He'd confronted Sir Michael Hanley about this whole thing . . . Hanley, he said, had been forced to confirm that this group of right-wing officers existed within the service, within MI5, and had been up to no good as far as Wilson was concerned . . . He'd also mentioned, oddly enough, another man, who hadn't been in MI5 but in MI6, who'd also been part of this dissident right-wing group . . . Hanley had said to him, 'It's unfortunately true,' but said he had cleared the position up and that was the end of it.[30]

The evidence suggests that, up to this point, Wilson had not even been properly briefed on the approach Stephen de Mowbray had already made to the Cabinet Office, urging a re-opening of the Hollis inquiry. De Mowbray had succeeded in reaching the Cabinet Secretary, Sir John Hunt, the previous year, but no decisive action had yet been taken. To the last, Wilson stayed in the dark.

What exactly Wilson did to commission full-scale inquiries into these partial revelations remains a mystery. All one can say with certainty is that there was no vengeful purge by the Prime Minister, and that Sir John Hunt, the Cabinet Secretary, eventually produced a report, or a series of reports, which were kept rigorously secret. Their conclusions emerged years later: they were firstly that Hollis was not proven guilty and that the matter was to be hushed up. Hunt's second conclusion was that recruitment into MI5 needed to be reformed, in an attempt to stop anti-Labour factions developing, but that this should also be kept secret. His third conclusion was that Sir Michael Hanley – the 'insider' in the top job who bore responsibility for the state of M15–should be replaced by a new broom from outside. This recommendation, like all the others, was intended to be concealed from the British public. Finally, Hunt proposed that a statement should be drawn up about Anthony Blunt, and – if the government's hand was ever forced, but not before – a public admission should be made of what their predecessors had done.

By the time these discreet reforms had been worked out, however, Wilson had gone. Immediately after his confrontation with Hanley, he decided to resign, and began to prepare the stage for his departure. During the rest of August, he went to the Scilly Isles for his annual private holiday with his wife. The couple then travelled to Scotland, where the Queen was in residence at Balmoral: such a Prime Ministerial visit was a fixture every autumn. Inveterate Royalist that Harold Wilson was, he gives a mawkish description in his memoirs of the moment of parting between himself and his sovereign:

> The Queen . . . had built another little chalet in the grounds, I think to mark her silver wedding anniversary, and this time she really did leave

the detectives behind and drove Mary and me a mile or so down to the chalet. The Queen filled up the kettle and Mary helped her to lay the table. After a most agreeable tea, the Queen passed an apron to Mary, put one on herself and they both proceeded to wash up the crockery. In that sort of atmosphere, it seemed to me that the time had come to inform the Queen of my resolve . . . I was left with the impression that she had enjoyed our two-way seminars over the years and that I might still have second thoughts on the matter . . .[31]

Whether Wilson's feelings of disgust and alarm about MI5 altered his timing or increased his determination to go is still an open question. As he hints, he had long promised his wife that he would retire and 'rebuild our home life'. In a patriotic way, he also kept quiet about the festering Blunt and Hollis scandals, which would have shaken national confidence in the Secret Services.

However, Wilson was not allowed to go quietly. The gossip continued unabated that MI5 knew something disgraceful about him. The parading of Frolik's testimony in Washington that November clearly made him feel that the CIA were still gunning for him. He grew afraid that the CIA, MI5 or the South Africans were bugging his premises and conducting burglaries of his own and his associates' houses, looking for 'dirt'. He allowed himself to be persuaded that a similar 'de-stabilising' exercise was being conducted against the Liberal leader, Jeremy Thorpe. (In fact, as Rhodesian Intelligence chief Ken Flower admitted before his death, there was a crude smear campaign by him against Wilson and Thorpe being organised in Britain and the US. But it was never at the heart of the real 'Wilson plot'.) Wilson sent a letter to new CIA chief George Bush, via George Weidenfeld and Senator Hubert Humphrey, demanding to know if the CIA was trying to infiltrate his office. Bush, appalled, flew to London to try to reassure him. And when, after his carefully contrived resignation announcement in March, there were unprecedented leaks about the Honours List in which he had given Joe Kagan a peerage, Wilson's resentment increased. The hints in Fleet Street that he had resigned for a secret reason, fostered as they were by MI6 and MI5 gossip, clearly infuriated him. They drove him to make complaints to journalists about his treatment by MI5.

The new Prime Minister, James Callaghan, was unhelpful. He told the Commons that he had confidence in MI5 (although being careful not to say whether there had been cause for lack of confidence before).[32]

No one knew of the extraordinary history of CIA and MI5 hostility towards Wilson, Wilson's friends and Wilson's ministers. No one knew of the witch-hunting and covering-up which had characterised MI5's activities for the previous twelve years. No one knew of the malign undercover activities of Peter Wright. And so Wilson's charges seemed bizarre and incomprehensible. The general public had no yardstick by which to evaluate the activities of MI5 and MI6: it was easier to think that Wilson himself had lost his senses.

So, ironically, Peter Wright won, in a way. The Prime Minister was finally discredited, in an unexpected fashion.

The few remaining Intelligence Officers who knew something of what Wright's 'Wilson plot' had consisted of, soon left the service. Tony Brooks opted for retirement in 1977 at the early age of fifty-five: perhaps he felt he had been in counter-espionage too long. He told the Parkers, his agents in the long and frustrating Kagan investigation, that he was thinking of setting up an employment agency in Morocco. But an Australian businessman, Morris Barr, met him at a party in 1977. Upon being told that Brooks was bi-lingual in French and 'looking for a job', Barr recalls, he offered him consultancy work in talks with a French building firm. Brooks took Barr to hear talks by industrialists at the Conservative Carlton Club, of which he was a member. Later Barr put him on the board of Associated Consultants (Construction) Ltd.[33] In 1982 Brooks became involved in another business venture called Heavy Goods Vehicle Parking Ltd. His fellow-directors were a Conservative MP, Anthony Baldry, a former Conservative MP, Roger White, and the publisher Alexander Macmillan, son of the Conservative minister and Intelligence operative, Maurice Macmillan, and grandson of Tory Prime Minister Harold Macmillan. Brooks continued to live in his small London mews house. After all, no 'outsider' knew how he had spent the preceding thirty-five years. Finally, Brooks finished up back in the world he knew best: a discreet brass name-plate in Knightsbridge advertised the services of Russell Brooks Associates, a firm of 'security consultants'. His partners were his close friend Barry Russell-Jones, now himself retired from MI5; the SAS officer Sir Julian Pagett; and Richard Stolz – the former London chief of station for the Central Intelligence Agency.[34]

Russell-Jones himself only cheered up with the return of a Conservative government in 1979: 'Thatcher is doing a remarkable job,' he wrote. Looking forward to a return of what he called 'economic sanity'[35], he clearly hoped the downtrodden right wing would renew their strength under the new regime.

Harry Wharton, the head of 'K5', was decorated in 1978, like Peter Wright, with the Order of Commander of the British Empire. He switched departments for his last couple of years and retired in 1980 to Wiltshire where he became a parish councillor.

Sir Michael Hanley did not last long in office after Wilson's retirement. He, too, retired in 1977, saying to his friends that he was frustrated about the problems of computerisation.[36] There was no chance, this time, that an 'insider' would inherit the job. Too many copybooks had been blotted. To the fury of the old guard, it went to Howard Smith, a Foreign Office man. John Jones, the trade union specialist, became No. Two, 'a disappointing deputy' as Russell-Jones observed to Peter Wright: 'It is not a happy ship.' The morale of the senior ranks in MI5 was low, he said.

But Wright, the veteran would-be spycatcher, had already left the scene. He retired in January 1976, before Wilson even announced his resignation, and went to Tasmania to open a stud-farm. Wright was no more successful at that than at catching spies. A decade later, he was continuing to make long-distance mischief: but it is thanks to him that the story of the Anglo-US 'Wilson plot' was finally unravelled.

Few political leaders can have been hounded with as much suspicion and ill-will as was Harold Wilson. So were his colleagues and friends. And yet, for all the repeated probes by MI5 and the CIA, nothing real was ever found. Sir Michael Hanley, the head of MI5, confided as much to associates after Wilson's resignation.

The one lingering speculation at Leconfield House was a thoroughly tortuous and unreasonable one – that Wilson confided in his political secretary, Marcia Williams, who in turn had dealings with Joe Kagan, who in turn was in contact with Russians from the KGB – and that this somehow made Wilson a 'security risk'. It is probably true that the KGB tried to exploit Kagan's links with the Soviet Union. Kagan himself suspected that there was a danger he would help people to get out of the Soviet Union into the West who were not all that they seemed. But Kagan was never a Communist sympathiser – far from it. Nor was he a spy. He was not perhaps the world's most honest person, nor the most likeable: but this is a far cry from demonstrating that he was a disloyal friend to Harold Wilson or a Soviet 'agent of influence'. Marcia Williams, Wilson's secretary, was never a Communist sympathiser either: one MI5 counter-intelligence officer claimed to the author that he had seen Marcia Williams' 'PF' in the MI5 Registry and that it showed she had once been a subscriber to the Communist *Morning Star*. Any such records were – like so many of MI5's files – simply wrong. She was not a 'security risk' at all. She was a loyal, tough-minded, sometimes unreasonable lady, whose political views moved appreciably to the right as she grew older.

And as for Harold Wilson himself, one would be hard put to see in this conventional Yorkshire Royalist any genuine touches of extremist political thought, or any private flamboyance that might lay him open to blackmail. He was 'security-minded' to the point of pomposity, but resented US dominance and had, over some issues, a genuine social conscience. Of the ministers he appointed, the two who were the most striking targets of MI5 – John Stonehouse and Niall MacDermot – were not even particular personal or political friends of Wilson. Against Stonehouse, in any event, nothing was proven: MacDermot and his wife were the victims of a most unpleasant miscarriage of justice. Trade Union leaders like Jack Jones and Hugh Scanlon had close links with Wilson's Labour Party, of course, but their only 'crime' was that they had a different view of the world from that of the Cold Warriors in MI5.

Does this mean then that counter-intelligence men like James Angleton and Peter Wright were monsters of conspiracy? The evidence certainly shows that the 'Wilson plot' was a reality. Wilson was indeed plotted against by members of the Intelligence services. But they were sincere enough in their suspicions. In the spectacle of Peter Wright, one sees a curiously sad story – a clever, self-taught 'outsider' in British society, who had a good mind and worked a lot of hours. In a secretive and ill-run Intelligence organisation which adapted far too slowly to the post-war world, he and others were driven to take up ever more extreme positions. Like Angleton in the CIA, the more he brooded on the 'Russian menace', the more unreasonable he became.

Perhaps the most constructive thing Peter Wright did in a long secret career was to make it finally possible to restore the reputation for loyalty of a long-suffering and much-maligned British Prime Minister. It was a reputation which Wright himself had helped to sully.

The last word on the unaccountable secret departments of the West in which Wright served ought not to go to a radical politician or an embittered victim of MI5's mistakes. Instead, perhaps one should listen to a distinguished soldier, an impeccable member of the British 'Establishment', with long experience as a secret customer of the Intelligence services. The one-time Chief of the British Staff, Field-Marshal Lord Carver, says of MI5:

The people concerned seem to live in a completely closed world, whereby what really went on, and what people actually thought and did, they just did not understand.[37]

This would make a good epitaph. But the secret police organisations to which Carver refers are still alive and flourishing, unaccountable, in Britain at least. Perhaps, therefore, one should take Carver's words as more in the nature of a warning.

255

REFERENCES

General note on sources. The material attributed to Peter Wright comes from several sources:

1) His correspondence with former colleagues, which he preserved in Australia.
2) A 30,000 word correspondence he held with the journalist Chapman Pincher in England, between 1980 and 1983, copies of which Wright also preserved.
3) Documents Wright prepared for Victor Rothschild in 1980, of which he kept copies.
4) The original and the published MSS of *Spycatcher* (the latter contained some deletions on libel grounds).

Where possible, I have preferred to use Wright's earlier, private material, rather than the ghost-written *Spycatcher* text.

Preface

1. Barbara Castle, *Diaries 1974–76*.
2. *Sunday Express*, May 19, 1976.
3. Personal interviews with William Massie.
4. Chapman Pincher, *Inside Story*, Sidgwick & Jackson.
5. Personal interview.
6. Personal interview.
7. Chapman Pincher, *Web of Deception*, Sidgwick & Jackson.
8. Chapman Pincher, *Inside Story*, Sidgwick & Jackson.
9. Anthony Cavendish, *Inside Intelligence*, privately published.
10. Unpublished Wright correspondence.
11. Information from an MI5 officer who does not wish to be named.
12. Wright correspondence.
13. Copy in Peter Wright's unpublished papers.
14. *Observer*, June 22, 1986.
15. Hansard, May 9, 1987.

Chapter One

1. Anthony Verrier, *Through the Looking-Glass*.
2. Jeffrey Richelson and Desmond Ball, *The Ties that Bind*.
3. Nicholas Bethell, *The Great Betrayal*.
4. Tony Benn, *Out of the Wilderness: Diaries 1963–67*.
5. Public Records Office, London. PRO file CO 537/5129.
6. *Ibid.*
7. George Kennedy Young, *Subversion and the British Riposte*.
8. *The Times*, June 1, 1977.
9. Anthony Verrier, *op. cit.*
10. Nicholas Bethell, *op cit.*
11. M. R. D. Foot, *SOE in France*.
12. Nicholas Bethell, *op. cit.*
13. George Young, *op. cit.*
14. Anthony Verrier, *op. cit.*
15. Wilbur Eveland, *Ropes of Sand*.

16. *The Times*, October 29, 1975.
17. Robin Winks, *Cloak and Gown: Scholars in America's Secret War*.
18. Anthony Cave Brown, *The Secret Servant*.
19. *Ibid.*
20. Archibald Roosevelt, *For Lust of Knowing*.
21. Anthony Verrier, *op. cit.*

Chapter Two

1. Christopher Andrew, *Secret Service*.
2. *Ibid.*
3. Chapman Pincher, *Too Secret Too Long*, Sidgwick & Jackson.
4. George Thomas, *Mr Speaker*.
5. Tony Bunyan, *The Political Police in Britain*.
6. Anthony Verrier, *Through the Looking-Glass*.
7. Alec MacDonald, head of MI5 counter-espionage. Private interview.
8. Sir Percy Sillitoe, *Cloak Without Dagger*.
9. *Ibid.*
10. Chapman Pincher, *op. cit.*
11. Peter Wright and Paul Greengrass, *Spycatcher*.
12. Philip Williams, *Hugh Gaitskell*.
13. Nigel West, *A Matter of Trust*.
14. Tony Benn, *Diaries*.
15. Christopher Andrew, *op. cit.*
16. Alec MacDonald, private interview.
17. *Ibid.*
18. Robin Winks, *Cloak and Gown*.
19. Anthony Masters, *The Man who was M.*
20. House of Lords, June 21, 1956.
21. Hansard, March 22, 1948.
22. *The Times*, April 2, 1981.
23. Chapman Pincher, *The Secret Offensive*, Sidgwick & Jackson.
24. Private interview.
25. Christopher Andrew, *op. cit.*
26. Thomas Powers, *The Man who Kept the Secrets*.
27. Private interview.
28. Stansfield Turner, *Secrecy and Democracy*; Leonard McCoy, unpublished analysis of *Spycatcher*.
29. Comte de Marenches and Christine Ockrent, *The Evil Empire*.
30. John Cloake, *Templer – Tiger of Malaya*.

Chapter Three

1. Anthony Verrier, *Through the Looking-Glass*.
2. Andrew Roth, *Harold Wilson – Yorkshire Walter Mitty*, and Simon Hoggart and David Leigh, *Michael Foot – A Portrait*.
3. Anthony Cave Brown, *The Secret Servant*.
4. Andrew Roth, *op. cit.*
5. Harold Wilson, *The Making of a Prime Minister*.
6. Public Records Office, Kew. All quotations in this chapter, unless otherwise specified, are from declassified government archives at the British Public Records Office, filed under BT 11/3742; BT 11/3417; BT 11/LOC; CAB 131/5; and FO 371/86790.
7. Harold Wilson, *op. cit.*
8. *Ibid.*
9. *Liverpool Daily Post*, May 6, 1948.
10. Harold Wilson, *op. cit.*
11. *Daily Telegraph*, August 28, 1950.

12. *Manchester Guardian*, January 5, 1950.
13. *The Times*, November 22, 1951.
14. Marcia Falkender, *Downing Street in Perspective*.
15. Christopher Andrew, *Secret Service*.
16. Harold Wilson, *op. cit.*
17. Andrew Roth, *op. cit.*
18. Harold Wilson, *op. cit.*
19. *Ibid.*
20. *Ibid.*
21. Tom Driberg, *Ruling Passion*.
22. Harold Wilson, *op. cit.*
23. *Ibid.*
24. *Ibid.*
25. Andrew Roth, *op. cit.*
26. *Ibid.*
27. Harold Wilson, *Ibid.*
28. *The Times*, May 2, 3, 1974.

Chapter Four

1. Anthony Sampson, *Anatomy of Britain*.
2. *Ibid.*
3. Archibald Roosevelt, *For Lust of Knowing*.
4. Harold Wilson, *The Making of a Prime Minister*.
5. Andrew Roth, *Harold Wilson – Yorkshire Walter Mitty*.
6. Harold Wilson, *op. cit.*
7. Hansard, July 23, 1963.
8. David Martin, *Wilderness of Mirrors*.
9. Montgomery Hyde, *George Blake*.
10. Philip Williams, *Hugh Gaitskell*.
11. Chapman Pincher, *The Secret Offensive*, Sidgwick & Jackson.
12. Harold Wilson, *op. cit.*
13. Andrew Roth, *op. cit.*
14. Interview, 1988.
15. Private interview.
16. Interview with Roger Courtiour and Barrie Penrose, 1977.
17. Private interview.
18. Andrew Roth, *op. cit.*
19. Private interview.
20. Chapman Pincher, *The Secret Offensive*, Sidgwick & Jackson.
21. Wright correspondence.
22. Chapman Pincher, *Secret Offensive*, Sidgwick & Jackson.
23. Chapman Pincher, *Inside Story*, Sidgwick & Jackson.
24. Harold Wilson, *The Labour Government 1964–70*.
25. Private interview, 1988.
26. Hansard, July 23, 1963.
27. Wright correspondence.
28. Peter Wright and Paul Greengrass, *Spycatcher*.
29. Archibald Roosevelt, *op. cit.*
30. Nigel West, *Molehunt*.
31. *Ibid.*
32. Wright and Greengrass, *op. cit.*
33. Private interview.
34. Wright correspondence.
35. Wright and Greengrass, *Ibid.*
36. Private interview.
37. Private interview.

38. Wright and Greengrass, *op. cit.*
39. Wright correspondence.
40. Wright and Greengrass, *op. cit.*
41. Private interview.
42. Private interview.
43. Wright correspondence.

Chapter Five

1. Wright and Greengrass, *Spycatcher.*
2. Private interview.
3. Harold Wilson, *The Labour Government 1964–70.*
4. Tony Benn, *op. cit.*
5. 'The Profession of Intelligence,' BBC Radio 4, February 10, 1982.
6. Chapman Pincher, *Inside Story*, Sidgwick & Jackson.
7. Barbara Castle, *Diaries*, July 6, 1967.
8. Private interview.
9. Tony Benn, *op. cit.*
10. *Ibid.*
11. Anthony Glees, *The Secrets of the Service.*
12. Magnus Linklater and David Leigh, *Not With Honour: The Westland Affair.*
13. Thomas Powers, *The Man who Kept the Secrets.*
14. Wright and Greengrass, *op. cit.*

Chapter Six

1. Interview with Roger Courtiour and Barrie Penrose, 1977.
2. Barbara Castle, *Diaries.*
3. Tony Benn, *Diaries.*
4. Harold Wilson, *The Labour Government 1964–70.*
5. Chapman Pincher, *Inside Story*, Sidgwick & Jackson.
6. Wright correspondence.
7. Barbara Castle, *op. cit.*, April 20, 1967.
8. *Ibid.*, February 7, 1967.
9. Tony Benn, *op. cit.*
10. Barbara Castle, *op. cit.*
11. *Ibid.*
12. Andrew Roth, *Harold Wilson – Yorkshire Walter Mitty.*

Chapter Seven

Note on sources: the material in this chapter, unless otherwise specified, is based on personal interviews with Alec MacDonald, Niall McDermot, Ludmila Benvenuto, Roderick Floud and Jean Floud.

1. Wright correspondence.
2. *The Spectator*, July 15, 1987.
3. Simon Hoggart and David Leigh, *Michael Foot – a Portrait.*
4. Unpublished letter to *The Times.*
5. Letter to Roderick Floud.
6. Andrew Boyle, *Climate of Treason.*
7. *The Times*, March 30, 1981.
8. Nigel West, *Molehunt.*
9. Wright and Greengrass, *Spycatcher.*

Chapter Eight

1. Philip Agee, *On the Run*.
2. Barbara Castle, *Ibid*.
3. Anthony Cave Brown, *The Secret Servant*.
4. Thomas Powers, *The Man who Kept the Secrets*.
5. Kim Philby, *My Silent War*.
6. Robin Winks, *Cloak and Gown*.
7. Harold Wilson, *The Labour Government 1964–70*.
8. Barbara Castle, *op. cit.*
9. Philip Ziegler, *Mountbatten*.
10. Barbara Castle, *op. cit.*
11. Wright and Greengrass, *Spycatcher*.
12. Wright correspondence.
13. Richard Crossman, *Diaries*.
14. Philip Ziegler, *op. cit.*
15. Barrie Penrose and Roger Courtiour, *The Pencourt File*.
16. Chapman Pincher, *Web of Deception*, Sidgwick & Jackson.
17. George Young, *Subversion*.
18. *Ibid*.
19. *Ibid*.
20. Penrose and Courtiour, *op. cit.*
21. *Daily Express*, June 28, 1968.
22. Wright correspondence.
23. Wright correspondence.
24. Peter Wright, untransmitted BBC TV interview. Wilbur Eveland, *Ropes of Sand*.
25. *Sunday Telegraph*, May 10, 1987.
26. Barbara Castle, *op. cit.*
27. Andrew Roth, *Harold Wilson – Yorkshire Walter Mitty*.
28. Harold Wilson, *op. cit.*
29. Barbara Castle, *op. cit.*
30. Josef Frolik, *The Frolik Defection*.
31. Frolik, unpublished chapter.
32. Frolik, *op. cit.*
33. Frolik, unpublished material.
34. Frolik *op. cit.*
35. Wright correspondence.
36. Chapman Pincher, *Inside Story*, Sidgwick & Jackson.
37. John Stonehouse, *Death of an Idealist*.
38. Frolik correspondence with Leo Cooper.
39. Frolik correspondence.
40. Hansard, December 17, 1974.
41. Frolik, unpublished material.
42. Wright correspondence.
43. Chapman Pincher, *op. cit.*
44. Wright correspondence.
45. Wright correspondence.

Chapter Nine

1. Andrew Roth, *Harold Wilson – Yorkshire Walter Mitty*.
2. *Daily Express*, August 8, 1970.
3. *Sunday Times*, July 19, 1981.
4. *The Times*, December 19, 1980.
5. *Observer*, August 9, 1970.
6. Private interview.
7. Wright correspondence.
8. Private interview.

9. Marcia Falkender, *Downing Street in Perspective.*
10. Pseudonym.

Chapter Ten

Note on sources: the bulk of the material on Frolik in this chapter is documented in the files of his publisher, Leo Cooper.

1. Hansard, January 15, 1988.
2. *Ibid.*
3. Quoted in Jack Jones, *Union Man.*
4. Jack Jones, *op. cit.*
5. Barbara Castle, *Diaries.*
6. Tony Benn, *Diaries.*
7. Chapman Pincher, *Inside Story*, Sidgwick & Jackson.
8. Wright correspondence.
9. Correspondence with Leo Cooper.

Chapter Eleven

1. Wright correspondence.
2. Penrose and Courtiour, *The Pencourt File.*
3. Col. Robert Butler, unpublished paper.
4. *The Times*, July 29, 1974.
5. *Daily Telegraph*, September 5, 1974.
6. George Young, *Subversion.*
7. *Sunday Times*, March 22, 1987.
8. Wright correspondence.
9. John Ranelagh, *The Agency.*
10. Richelson and Ball, *The Ties that Bind.*
11. Philip Agee, *On the Run.*
12. Barbara Castle, *Diaries.*
13. House of Lords, March 16, 1988.
14. Barbara Castle, *op. cit.*
15. *Ibid.*
16. Penrose and Courtiour, *op. cit.*; Barbara Castle, *op. cit.*
17. *Private Eye*, September 20, 1974.
18. Hansard, December 17, 1974.
19. Chapman Pincher, *Inside Story*, Sidgwick & Jackson.
20. Anthony Cavendish, *Inside Intelligence* (privately published).
21. Patrick Marnham, *Trail of Havoc.*
22. *Private Eye*, No. 340.
23. *Private Eye*, January 10, 1975.
24. *Private Eye*, February 21, 1975.
25. *Private Eye*, September 19, 1975.
26. *Private Eye*, March 19, 1976.
27. *Private Eye*, November 11, 1977.
28. *Private Eye*, December 23, 1977.
29. Chapman Pincher, *op. cit.*
30. Interview with Barrie Penrose.
31. Harold Wilson, *The Making of a Prime Minister.*
32. Hansard, August 23, 1977 and December 8, 1977.
33. Personal interviews.
34. British Company Records, Company House, London.
35. Wright correspondence.
36. CIA source.
37. House of Lords, March 16, 1988.

BIBLIOGRAPHY

Agee, Philip, *Inside the Company*, London, 1975.

Agee, Philip, *On the Run*, London, 1987.

Andrew, Christopher, *Secret Service*, London, 1985.

Benn, Tony, *Out of the Wilderness: Diaries 1963–67*, London, 1987.

Bethell, Nicholas, *The Great Betrayal – The Untold Story of Kim Philby's Biggest Coup*, London, 1984.

Bloch, Jonathan and Fitzgerald, Patrick, *British Intelligence and Covert Action*, Dublin, 1983.

Blum, William, *The CIA – A Forgotten History*, London, 1986.

Boyle, Andrew, *The Climate of Treason*, London, 1979.

Bunyan, Tony, *The History and Practice of the Political Police in Britain*, London, 1977.

Castle, Barbara, *The Castle Diaries 1974–76*, London, 1980

Castle, Barbara, *The Castle Diaries 1964–70*, London, 1984

Cave Brown, Anthony, *Bodyguard of Lies*, London, 1976.

Cave Brown, Anthony, *Secret Servant: The Life of Sir Stewart Menzies*, London, 1988.

Cloake, John, *Templer – Tiger of Malaya*, London, 1985.

Crossman, Richard, *The Diaries of a Cabinet Minister*, Three vols, London, 1975, 1976, 1977.

Deacon, Richard [Donald McCormick], *C – A Biography of Sir Maurice Oldfield*, London, 1984.

Dodds Parker, Douglas, *Setting Europe Ablaze*, London, 1984.

Driberg, Tom, *Ruling Passions*, London, 1978.

Eveland, Wilbur C., *Ropes of Sand*, London, 1980.

Falkender, Marcia, *Downing Street in Perspective*, London, 1983.

Foot, M. R. D., *SOE in France*, London, 1966.

Frolik, Josef, *The Frolik Defection*, London, 1975.

Glees, Anthony, *The Secrets of the Service – British Intelligence and Communist Subversion 1939–51*, London, 1987.

Grant Duff, Shiela, *The Parting of Ways*, London, 1982.

Haines, Joe, *The Politics of Power*, London, 1977.

Hoggart, Simon and Leigh, David, *Michael Foot – A Portrait*, London, 1981.

Hyde, H. Montgomery, *George Blake Superspy*, London, 1987.

Jones, Elwyn, Lord, *In My Time*, London 1983.

Jones, Jack, *Union Man*, London, 1986.

Leigh, David, *The Frontiers of Secrecy – Closed Government in Britain*, London, 1980.

Linklater, Magnus and Leigh, David, *Not With Honour*, London, 1986.

Marenches, Comte de and Ockrent, Christine, *The Evil Empire*, London, 1988.

Marnham, Patrick, *Trail of Havoc*, London, 1987.

Martin, David C. *Wilderness of Mirrors*, New York, 1980.

Masters, Anthony, *The Man who was M*, London, 1984.

Masterman, John, *The Double-Cross System*, New Haven, 1972.

McWhirter, Norris, *Ross*, London, 1976.

Montgomery Hyde H., *George Blake Superspy*, London, 1987.

Page, Bruce *et al.*, *Philby – the Spy who Betrayed a Generation*, London, 1968.

Penrose, Barrie and Courtiour, Roger, *The Pencourt File*, London, 1978.

Philby, Kim, *My Silent War*, London, 1968.

Pincher, Chapman, *Inside Story*, London, 1978.

Pincher, Chapman, *Their Trade is Treachery*, London, 1981.

Pincher, Chapman, *Too Secret Too Long*, London, 1984.
Pincher, Chapman, *The Secret Offensive*, London, 1985.
Pincher, Chapman, *Traitors*, London, 1987.
Pincher, Chapman, *A Web of Deception*, London, 1987.
Powers, Thomas, *The Man who Kept the Secrets – Richard Helms and the CIA*, New York, 1979.
Ranelagh, John, *The Agency: The Rise and Decline of the CIA*, New York, 1986.
Richelson, Jeffrey and Ball, Desmond, *The Ties that Bind – Intelligence Co-operation Between the UKUSA Countries*, Sydney, 1985.
Roosevelt, Archibald, *For Lust of Knowing*, London, 1988.
Roth, Andrew, *Harold Wilson – Yorkshire Walter Mitty*, London, 1977.
Sampson, Anthony, *Anatomy of Britain*, London, 1962.
Stonehouse, John, *Death of an Idealist*, London, 1975.
Stockwell, John, *In Search of Enemies – A CIA Story*, London, 1978.
Summers, Anthony and Dorril Stephen, *Honeytrap – The Secret Worlds of Stephen Ward*, London, 1987.
Thomas, George, *Mr Speaker*, London, 1985.
Turner, Stansfield, *Secrecy and Democracy*, New York, 1985.
Verrier, Anthony, *Through the Looking-Glass – British Foreign Policy in the Age of Illusions*, London, 1983.
West, Nigel, [Rupert Allason], *MI5 1909–45*, London, 1981.
West, Nigel, *MI5 1945–72*, London, 1982.
West, Nigel, *MI6 1909–45*, London, 1983.
West, Nigel, *Molehunt*, London, 1987.
West, Nigel, *The Friends*, London, 1988.
Williams, Marcia, *Inside No. 10*, London, 1972.
Williams, Marcia [as Falkender, Marcia], *Downing Street in Perspective*, London, 1983.
Williams, Philip, *Hugh Gaitskell*, London, 1979.
Wilson, Harold, *Final Term, The Labour Government 1974–76*, London, 1979.
Wilson Harold, *The Making of a Prime Minister 1916–1964*, London, 1986.
Wilson, Harold, *The Labour Government 1964–70 – A Personal Record*, London, 1971.
Winks, Robin, *Cloak and Gown: Scholars in America's Secret War*, London, 1987.
Wright, Peter with Greengrass, Paul, *Spycatcher* New York, Dublin, Sydney, 1987.
Young, George Kennedy, *Subversion and the British Riposte*, Glasgow, 1984.

INDEX

Main references are in **bold** print

Bruce, David, 63
Brundrett, Sir Frederick, 30, 31, 32, 33
BRUSA agreement (*1943*), 5
Brzezinski, Zbigniew, 103
bugging, 32–4
Bulgaria, 12–13
Bum, Elana, 181
Bum, Yasha/Irina, 181, 191
Bundy, McGeorge, 103
Bunyan, Tony, 21
Burgess, Guy, 2, 6, 30, 60, 74; IRD, 8; Liddell, 23; memoirs, 24, 177; Sillitoe, 26
Burn, Michael, 224
Bush, George, 226, 233, 252
Butler, Col. Robert, 218–22
Buzwk, Antonin, 72, 205
Byelorussia, 14

Cairncross, John, 125
Callaghan, James, Prime Minister (*1976–9*), 149, 162, 226, 229, 252
'Cambridge Communists', 2–3, 101, 124
Cameron, Clyde, 232–3
Cameron, Ian, 209
Camorra (Frolik), 211–13
Campaign for Nuclear Disarmament *see* CND
Canada, 34, 104; ABCA agreement, 4; chemical warfare, 5; UKUSA treaty 6
Candler, David, 196–7, 247
Cannon, Elise, 61, 66
Carr, Robert, MP, 191
Carter, Gen. Pat, 122
Carver, Field-Marshal Lord, 222, 255
Casey, William, 218
Castle, Barbara, MP, 52; Canada with Wilson, 53–4; Hart, 229–30; Jack Jones, 205; 'Keep Left' group, 60; Kosygin, 120; security, 106; Swingler, 161–2; trade unions, 162–3; untrue sexual rumours, 68, 116,178; US, 121, 122, 154–5; Wigg, 105, 108
Castro, Pres. Fidel, 87
Caunt, George, 72, 113, 194
Cavendish, Anthony, 13–14, 214, 221
Cavendish, Arthur, 246
CAZAB, 104, 152, 228, 232, 235
CCCC(Centralised Comint Communications Centre), 6–7
Central Intelligence Agency *see* CIA
Central Policy Review Staff (think-tank), 203
Chalfont, Lord (Alan Gwynne-Jones, MP), 95, 107, 220
chemical warfare, 5
Chile, 228–30, 232
Chorley, Lord, 28
Churchill, Minnie, 249
Churchill, Sir Winston Leonard Spencer, Prime Minister (*1940–45;1951–55*), 36, 39, 66
Churchill, Winston, MP, (*the younger*), 237–8
CIA, The – A Forgotten History (Blum), 232
CIA (Central Intelligence Agency, US): 16–19; *and* BBC, 7; assassinations, 86–7; Australia, 232–3; *Encounter*, 63; founded, 10; investigated, 201; Iran, 15; Labour Minister agent, 96; MI5 investigation, **102–4**; Pike/Church Committees, 227; propaganda, 8; Syria, 15; trade unions, 212; UK infiltration, 213; Wilson rumours, 69
CIG (Central Intelligence Group, US), 17
Citrine, Walter, 29
Clark, Brig. Terence, MP, 111
Clayden, Harry, 170
Climate of Treason, The (Boyle), 2
Cloake, John, 183–4
Cloak Without Dagger (Sillitoe), 26–7
CND (Campaign for Nuclear Disarmament), 63, 69–70, 161
code-breaking *see* communications Intelligence
Cohen, Sir Andrew, 127

Colby, William, 201, 233
Committee for a Free Europe (US), 8, 13
communications Intelligence, 5–7, 226
Communist Party: blacklisting, 27–30; MI5 investigation, 21; records copied, 71–2; telephone-tapping, 229; trade unions, 24, 29–30
Cook, Tom, MP, 49
Cooper, Chester, 16, 63, 120
Cooper, Leo, 211–13, 235–6
Cort, Joe, 93
Courtiour, Roger, 229
Courtney, Commander Anthony, MP, 13–14
Cousins, Frank, 105
Cowles, Fleur, 63
Coyne, Patrick, 103
Crabb, Cmdr 'Buster', 65, 98
Craig, Ailsa *see* Floud, Ailsa
Craig, Priscilla *see* Allan, Priscilla
Cram, Cleveland, 16, 84, 85, 103
Credock, Jack, 209
Cripps, Sir (Richard) Stafford, Pres. Bd of Trade (*1945–7*); Chancellor (*1947–50*), 36, 38–49, 52
'Crocodile' (Czech agent), 177
Crosland, Anthony, MP, 63
Crossman, Richard, MP, 25, 90, 97, 137, 161–2; PWE, 7; Wigg, 106
Cuba, missile crisis, 63
Cuckney, John, 99
Cudlipp, Hugh, 114, 157–8
Cudlipp, Percy, 114
Cumming, Col. Malcolm, 30, 33, 34, 101, 207; CIA investigation, 103–4
Cyprus, 121, 220
Czechoslovakia, 163–80, 212, 235–6; Buzwk, 72; Driberg, 24; Heath, 97; Wilson, 192–3, 197

Daily Express, 71
Daily Mail, 20, 238
Daily Mirror, 236
Daily Telegraph, 196
Dalton, Hugh, MP, 23, 37
Dansey, Col. Claude, 53
Davidson, J. C. C., 20–21
Davies, Harold, MP, 161
Day, J. Wentworth, 51
Deedes, William, 161
defectors, **77–84**, **163–5**, **199–201**, **211–13**
Defence, Ministry of, 107–8
Delmer, Sefton, 7
De Mowbray, Stephen, 75, 80, 116, 211, 249, 251
Denning, Lord, 87, 89, 99
DGSE (Portugese security police), 228
Diamond, John (Jack, later Lord), MP, 91, 159
Diem, Pres. Ngo Dinh, 87
disinformation, 240
D-Notice system, 26, 108, 212–13
Dodds-Parker, Col. Douglas, 68
Domville, Adml. Sir Barry, 31
Double-Cross System, The (Masterman), 27
'Double-Cross' (XX) system, 22, 27, 114, 138
Douglas-Home, Sir Alec, Prime Minister (*1963–4*), 116
Doyne-Ditmass, Hal, 101, 242, 243, 245
Drayson, Burnaby, MP, 111
Drew, John, 107
Driberg, Tom, MP, 24–5, 70, 92, 129, 177; Frolik, 164–5, **177–8**; 'Keep Left' group, 60; MI5 agent, 90, 177; Plummer, 57
DRUG (VENONA) code-system, 6–7
Dubcek, Alexander, 164
Duff, Shiela Grant *see* Grant, Shiela Sokolov

Earle, Peter, 193
Economist (journal), Philby, 15–16
Ede, Chuter, MP, 22, 29, 43

Eden, Sir (Robert) Anthony, Prime Minister (*1955–7*), 15, 86, 98, 220
Eden, Walter, 85–6, 89
Egypt, Suez intervention, 15
Eisenhower, Pres. Dwight David, 103
Elizabeth II, Queen, 251–2
'Elli' (Soviet agent), 78
Elwell, Charles, 80, 100, **166–72**, 209, 242
Encounter (journal), 63, 213
England, Whose England? (film), 214
Evans, Harold, 152
Eveland, Wilbur, 15, 86

Falkender, Lady *see* Williams, Marcia
FANY (First Aid Nursing Yeomanry), 217
FAO (Food and Agriculture Organisation), 54
Farnhill, Admiral, 212–13
Farran, Capt. Roy, 9–10, 218
Farrar-Hockley, General, 222
FBI (Federal Bureau of Investigation) (US), 69, 74
Field, Tony, 69, 191, 194, 234
Finland, 50–51
Fisher, Lord, 192
Fischer-Williams, Jenifer *see* Hart, Jenifer
Fleay, Martin, 242
Fletcher, Rex, MP (*later* Lord Winster), 25–6, 60
Floud (*nee* Craig), Ailsa, 129, 131–2, 134
Floud, Bernard, MP, 3, 29, 75, 92, **127–36**, 160
Floud, Sir Francis, 128
Floud, Jean, 129, 131, 132, 136
Floud, Peter, 127, 129, 131
Floud, Prof. Roderick, 129, 131, 132–3, 134, 135
Flower, Ken, 106
FLUENCY committee, 123
Foot, Michael, MP, 36, 52, 60, 128, 129
Foote, Alexander, 211
Foreign Affairs Research Institute, 239
Forum World Features, 213
France, 35, 200
Franks, Arthur, 14
Franks (Sir Oliver) Committee, 198
Freeman, John, MP, 59–60
Frolik, Josef, 163–80, 193, 203, 204, 213, 252; memoirs, 210, 234ff
Fuchs, Klaus, 6, 30, 43, 60, 101

Gaitskell, Arthur, 85
Gaitskell, Hugh Todd Naylor, Labour Party leader (*1955–63*), 3, 7, 59, **62–9**, 128; Chancellor (*1950–51*), 59; CND, 70; death, 59, 62, 69, **80–87**, 117, 193–4, 216; dossiers on left wing, 70–71; Minister of Fuel and Power, 23–4
Gallacher, Willie, MP, 28
Gallone, Madame, 141, 148
Gardiner, Gerald (Lord), 94–5
Gardner, Meredith, 6
Gaulle, Gen. Charles de, 200
'GB 75' organisation, 222
GCHQ (Government Communications Headquarters), 6–7, 108, **121–2**, 168, 226, 228
Germany, West/Berlin, 13, 14, 64, 230–32
Gibson, Col. Harold, 14
Gilbert, Martin, 249
Goddard, Miss E. M., 45, 47
Godson, Joseph, 63
Goldsmith, Sir James, 224–5
Golitsin, Anatoli, 76–7, **79–85**, 123, 166, 200–201; CAZAB, 152; McCoy, 216; memoirs, 211; Rothschilds, 154
Goloniewski, Michael ('Sniper'), 78–9
Goodman, Arnold (*later* Lord), 117
Gordon-Walker, Patrick, MP, 63, 70–71, 95
Gorshkov, Nikolai, 17, 140, 141, 144, 145–9
Gouzenko, Igor, 4, 23, 27, 42, 77, **78**; Hollis/Mitchell investigations, 123
Grant, Micheal Sokolov, 166–7

Grant (Grant Duff), Shiela Sokolov, 3, 166–7
Grant, Ted, 209
Gray, Gov. Gordon, 103
'Gray-Coyne Report', 103–4
Greece, 12, 21, 121, 151
Greene, Benjamin, 28
Greengrass, Paul, 133, 185, 210
Greenwood, Anthony, MP, 132
Gresha (film director), 181
Grivas, Gen. George, 220
Groser, John, 115
GRU (Soviet military Intelligence wing), 77, 87
Guardian, 16
Guillaume, Gunter, 230–31
'Gustav' (Czech agent), 176
Gwynne-Jones, Alun *see* Chalfont, Lord

Hailsham, Lord (Quintin Hogg), 116
Haines, Joe, 194
Hall, Adml. 'Blinker', 20
Halls, Marjorie, 196–7, 249
Halls, Michael, 170, 196–7
Hamdi, Mohammed, 176
Hammerling, Mrs, 204, 205
Hammond, Val, 100
Hampshire, Sir Stuart, 3, 122, 226
'Hampstead Set', 63
Hanley, Sir Michael, 78, 166, 202, 253; Hart, 229; investigated, 123; MI5 head, **208–9**; Stonehouse, 237; Wilson, 109, 234, 249, **250–51**, 254; Wright, 210, 224, 232
Hare, Alan, 8
Harold Wilson, Yorkshire Walter Mitty (Roth), 55
Harriman, Averell, 83-4
Harrison, Francis, 208
Hart, Herbert, 127, 153
Hart, Jenifer, 3, **127–8**, 133, 134, 136, 153
Hart, Judith, MP, 91, **228–30**
Harvey, William, 86
Hastings, Stephen, MP, 220, 238–9
Hathaway, Reverend, 193
Healey, Denis, MP, 128, 151
Healey, Gerry, 209
Healey, Tony, 35
Heath, Edward, Prime Minister (*1970–74*), 97, 106, 176, **202–14**; Spanish Civil War, 205, 220; Stonehouse 173; think-tank, 195, 203
'Heavy Breather' (MI6 agent), 244
Heenan, Bishop John, 64
Helms, Richard, 104, 163
Helsinki agreement, 230
Henry, John, 30
Herbert, Auberon, 114, 196
Herbert, Christopher, 185–6
Hill, Ted, 179
Himmler, Heinrich, 138
Hiss, Alger, 6
Hobsbawm, Eric, 130
Hobson, Sir John, 91
Holden, Robert, 242
Holdsworth, Gerald, 217
Hollis, Sir Roger, 23, 29, **48–9**, 71, **97–8**, 100; Blunt, 74–5; budgets, 34; bugging, 33–4; CIA investigation, 103–4; Double-Cross, 27; Gaitskell death, 81, 84, 85; investigated, 75, 78, 102, 110, 123, 209, 235, **249–52**; Labour Party purges, 72; Martin, 101–2; Mayhew, 7, 70, 71; Mitchell investigation, 75; Profumo, 76, 87; Wilson *as* PM **89–91**
Home, Sir Alec *see* Douglas-Home
Hooper, Sir Leonard, 122
Hoover, J. Edgar, 26, 69, 92, 102
Hope, Mr Justice, 232–3
Horner, Arthur, 24
Houghton, Douglas, MP (*later* Lord), 238, 243

267

270

ABOUT THE AUTHOR

David Leigh has been a reporter for the London *Guardian*, the London *Times*, and the Washington *Post*, and has won numerous journalism awards including Special Press Award and Reporter of the Year. He is currently the leading exposé writer for the London *Observer*.